The Film Crew
of Hollywood

The Film Crew of Hollywood

*Profiles of Grips,
Cinematographers, Designers,
a Gaffer, a Stuntman
and a Makeup Artist*

JAMES C. UDEL

McFarland & Company, Inc., Publishers
Jefferson, North Carolina, and London

LIBRARY OF CONGRESS CATALOGUING-IN-PUBLICATION DATA

Udel, James C., 1959–
The film crew of Hollywood : profiles of grips, cinematographers, designers, a gaffer, a stuntman and a makeup artist / James C. Udel.
    p.   cm.
Includes bibliographical references and index.

ISBN 978-0-7864-6484-5
softcover : acid free paper ∞

1. Motion pictures—Production and direction.
2. Motion picture producers and directors—United States—Interviews. I. Title.
PN1995.9.P7.U34 2014   791.4302'33'092273—dc23   2013035497

BRITISH LIBRARY CATALOGUING DATA ARE AVAILABLE

© 2014 James C. Udel. All rights reserved

No part of this book may be reproduced or transmitted in any form or by any means, electronic or mechanical, including photocopying or recording, or by any information storage and retrieval system, without permission in writing from the publisher.

On the cover: Gaffer Earl Gilbert (frame right, pointing) instructs the placement of his favorite Kansas arc lights for a scene in George Stevens' *The Greatest Story Ever Told* (Earl Gilbert Collection)

Manufactured in the United States of America

McFarland & Company, Inc., Publishers
Box 611, Jefferson, North Carolina 28640
www.mcfarlandpub.com

Table of Contents

Preface 1
Introduction 3

1. Dan Striepeke, Makeup Artist 5
2. Carl Manoogian, Key Grip 22
3. Gene LeBell, Stuntman 42
4. William Fraker, Cinematographer 69
5. Earl Gilbert, Gaffer 83
6. Tommy May, Key Grip 118
7. George Barris, Motion Picture Automotive Designer ... 135
8. Albert Brenner, Production Designer 152
9. Richard Kline, Cinematographer 168
10. Gaylin Schultz, Key Grip 193

Glossary 225
Index 233

Preface

This book is intended for everyone who loves classic films and television. While most movie buffs are aware of their favorite actor, director, and even some writers, the missing piece of filmdom's puzzle has been the crew. An in-depth look at ten individual career paths encompassing the end of the studio system through the independent age of Hollywood, this book focuses on the work of Dan Striepeke, Carl Manoogian, Gene LeBell, Bill Fraker, Earl Gilbert, Tommy May, George Barris, Albert Brenner, Richard Kline, and Gaylin Schultz. Covering fifty years of Hollywood production from the perspective of cinematographers, grips, production designers, a makeup artist, an automotive designer, a stuntman, and a gaffer, this compilation of interviews includes rare, behind-the-scenes photos and the facts behind them. The book reveals production facts from the famous films *The Greatest Story Ever Told*, *Rosemary's Baby* and *Catch 22*, naming just a fraction of the hundreds covered in the process. The crew interviews include humorous on-set anecdotes and never-published accounts of everything from camera placement and film emulsion to proprietary gadgets created to solve production problems.

Giving these largely unsung individuals a moment in the spotlight, to share recollections of their triumphs, films, and friendships, the book also serves to enhance the appreciation of these crews and the great shows to which they contributed.

During the course of over thirty years in the motion picture industry, working on everything from professional wrestling to *Pee-wee's Playhouse* and from *Miami Vice* to *The Rockford Files,* I have come to know some fascinating individuals within the various crafts. I was forced to quit due to a severe back injury incurred while on the neo-classic *Being John Malkovich*, but still had a desire to participate in the field I loved, and did so by telling the histories of those I met along the way. Beginning with interviews at the Motion Picture Home, I was soon contributing to a Hollywood trade magazine that published shorter versions of the stories drawn from the retired locals, who were experienced in every walk of production life. Receiving a first-rate education in film history during the course of the conversations, I shot them in the hopes of making a documentary. After the movie concept proved too expensive without corporate funding, I decided to turn them into a book project.

The Film Crew of Hollywood is important because it captures and preserves these histories before they are lost to the world — the personal triumphs and tragedies of the aging crews who plied their skills for so long without recognition. These chapters illustrate the methods devised for motion picture-making during a time where arc lights ruled the night, and shiny boards filled the shadows.

Research for this book was exhaustingly inclusive. Each person's entire career was catalogued and turned into a time line to aid in the interview process. The end result allowed for a flow to the Q & A that often produced more information than bargained for, yet proved to be priceless in shaping the big picture. In addition to sources such as IMDb, Wikipedia, Google, and the Ephraim Katz Film Encyclopedia, certain movies were also viewed in order to be able to discuss the craft within specific scenes. This structured method of questioning prompted additional recollections from the subjects and the substance of the project grew.

There are few published works that strictly focus on individual crew member accomplishments; among them are Barbara Baker's *Let the Credits Roll* and Roy P. Webber's *Dinosaur Films of Ray Harryhausen*. This book fills the void between just knowing movies and learning the intricate details of their creation from those who lived it. Gaining personal perspective beyond the average writer in the field because of my own below-the-line grip experience, I was able to ask the proper technical questions for an open dialogue between writer and subject.

Finally, *The Film Crew of Hollywood* is different because it focuses on the production of specific movies and on the people who made them, as told in their own language.

With current consumer demand dictating content through digital downloads on everything from smart phones to laptop theaters, connection to the hard-lit heyday of the past is like appreciation of any fine art made generations before: It requires time and study to get it. In listening to this last generation of greats tell their stories of artistic providence, well-planned mechanics, and paying dues, one can only hope that the next wave of filmfolk who read *Profiles* will be as enlightened as I have been by the extraordinary experiences of these men.

Introduction

Growing up in Baltimore during the '50s post-war boom, I was hardly groomed for literary success. While the town had its share of local culture including the Walters Art Gallery, Center Stage, and Sabatinos restaurant, the bulk of my artistic awakening came from my father, through the films he took me to see. Although I was born to the burgh of Barry Levinson and John Waters, my heroes were Brooks Robinson and Johnny U; but then Dad's influence as the city's finest portrait photographer set me on a path to life in the film business. Drafted as his assistant at ten, I started humping gear to help, since a war injury had left him minus a leg. Taken to movies on afternoons off, I was exposed to everything from Buster Keaton and the Marx Brothers to the modern movies *Lawrence of Arabia, Cat Ballou,* and *The Guns of Navarone.* Dad pointed out strong composition within the pictures, and answered endless questions pertaining to the how and why of their photography. After the father-son phase of blind allegiance bowed to making it on my own, I left the family studio to work for others. Starting with local production gigs at Lee Bonner Films with Mark Birnbaum (where my sole qualification for employment was as kid brother to the director's girlfriend), I began in the biz like many greats — through nepotistic cunning!

Ultimately moving to New York City at age 17, I did everything from rental house work to production assistant chores in pursuit of the gold-plated dance ticket known as a union card. Unable to break into the I.A. after years of effort (despite charm and attempted bribery) I was compelled to seek my fortune elsewhere. Packing all that I was into a thirty-foot truck (including a wife and fourteen-month-old son) we "hauled house" across the country and moved to Tinseltown on a hunch.

Chasing the dream by working my way up the food chain, I built sets, assisted art director Sidney J. Bartholomew and did a stint with Roger Corman until I was able to get my card within our first year out west. Working for the next twenty years in Los Angeles as a production grip and occasional still photographer, I came to understand the difficulty of producing great motion pictures like those from my childhood, and I began to have a curiosity about the guys who made them, and where they ended up. I started with visits to the Motion Picture Retirement Home armed with a list of my favorite flicks and room numbers of folks living there who worked on them; before long I found faces to fit the credits and subjects willing to share their stories. While their recollections grew richer as my visits became more frequent, the idea of a "golden age" project became my passion. I submitted requests to do a documentary (tentatively titled *Tales from the Home*); a corporate refusal dashed that plan to the rocks. Yet all was not lost. A Hollywood trade magazine ran my biopic articles in a shortened form called *Footnotes*; from these, *Profiles of Hollywood* was born. With its focus on the careers of ten extraordinary subjects — (each with sixty years in the industry), the book allows for a comprehensive look at motion picture production as done by some of the finest craftsmen Hollywood has ever seen.

While researching and writing this book, I received inspiration from a lot of folks and would like to thank them for their support. First, Mom and Dad for raising me to pursue my dreams, even if it meant moving to the West Coast with their only grandchild in pursuit of a film career. Thanks to the Crest Theatre for its wonderful Saturday double matinees, and industrial-size boxes of Jujubes. A serious nod should go to Mr. Peiffer, my seventh grade English teacher from McDonough, who said that despite any shortcomings in grammar, he liked my writing. Speaking of teachers, I must also give thanks (posthumously) to character actor Bob Cornthwaite for instruction in proper bedside manner while interviewing.

I wish to thank my union, IATSE's Local 80, for its years of belief in me not only as a grip and call steward, but as their archivist as well. From head honcho Russ Nordstedt to International V.P.s Mike Miller and Thom Davis, support of my writing has never been lacking. Above all, I must honor my subjects: the late Gaylin Schultz, Dan Striepeke, the late Bill Fraker, Earl Gilbert, Carl Manoogian, Gene LeBell, Albert Brenner, Dick Kline, George Barris, and Tommy May; all are owed my sincere thanks for taking the time to help me get it right. My only hope is that I've done half the job telling these amazing stories as the guys did living them. Putting up with thousands of questions, repeated phone calls, and Sunday morning visits where I occasionally pushed for answers, these humorous craftspeople were most generous with their time; I am grateful to call many "my friend" now that the writing is done. Like a dozen more fathers at the movies, these dads not only told me how the shots were done, but when and by whom.

Lastly, but of paramount importance, is thanks to my wife and best friend Maryann, our brilliant son Douglas Sean and Dino the black Burmese. From her hours of tireless typing to the woman's brilliant edits of my work, Maryann was pure *foxhole* when it came to phrasing, research, and grammar. And then there is Doug. Like my father before me, I too have shown my kid composition when watching features at the theater. As savvy as a film critic yet knowledgeable in the grip process, he is more inclined to write a screenplay if involved in motion pictures, than to haul gear like his dad. As to my everpresent muse, Dino (whose pawing of the keyboard forced me to take breaks from my writing), thanks for letting me know when I worked too long. His feline intelligence provided my fingers with a break from typing to scratch his head instead. I have to also thank my head shrinker, Dr. Robert Schallenkamp, for aiding my understanding of the kid I once was. In writing this book, I celebrate the movies I grew up with. Does anyone have any Jujubes?

1
Dan Striepeke, Makeup Artist

Among the myriad of crafts that converge to bring a motion picture to the screen, few are more demanding of an individual's artistic talent than the profession of makeup. Its focus is on skills of the hand and judgment of the eye; the abilities of the face-fixer require a rare mix of colorist, painter, sculptor and psychologist, all in the same day's work. One such master of maquillage know-how is Dan Striepeke. Born and raised on the West Coast, Striepeke (pronounced stree-peck) began doing makeup for plays during high school in Santa Rosa, California. Seeking his destiny upon graduation, he and a pal embarked on a soul-searching trip throughout southern and central Mexico, driving a 1937 Plymouth Coupe. Returning to the States at ride's (and money's) end, the 19-year-old had the idea of using his high school experience to land a job as a "powder man" in Hollywood. As they cruised La Cienega Boulevard in the Plymouth one afternoon (with 20 bucks left), opportunity presented itself when young Striepeke spotted the Civic Playhouse advertising a play he manned in high school, *The Fabulous Invalid*. With no connections or clue of how to land a gig, Dan confidently strode into the theatre and convinced the play's director, John Claar (who later founded KTTV in LA), that he could handle the job by turning one of the young actors into the Louis Wolheim character from *All Quiet on the Western Front*. Nailing the makeup test, the kid not only did the play, but ultimately was hired by Claar to do non-union television work on early KTTV stuff such as *McMann's Minstrels*, *The Jack Rourke Show* and live local newscasts. After ten and a half months with the station, however, Striepeke's career was temporarily sidelined in 1950 by the start of the Korean War. Due to the likelihood of being drafted, the youngster opted to enlist in the Air Force, where he served until 1954 as an electronics-navigation tech on the B-47 bomber program.

Returning from military service, Dan approached KTTV (which had gone union during the War) to ask for his old position back. Due to Hollywood's practice of "closed shop" unions at that time, he was refused membership. Following six futile attempts to meet with Fred Phillips (the business agent for Local 706), Striepeke appealed to a higher power, the National Labor Relations Board. After a ruling in his favor, Dan was reinstated as a "permit worker," and then allowed to obtain his "30 days" on various shows to qualify for the union.

Initiated into the Makeup Local in March of 1955, Striepeke toiled on biggies such as *Kismet*, *Around the World in 80 Days*, and *Giant*. Working on extras and bit players on those colossal pictures, the rookie learned his craft one look at a time. Regarding Cecil B. DeMille's *The Ten Commandments*, he recalled the first day of filming the brick pit scenes with its 400

During the summer of 1946 in Santa Rosa, at just 16 years of age Striepeke was drafted for one of his first professional makeup gigs. He was hired by San Francisco costume impresario Louie Goldstein for a production of *The 49ers*. Used as a background actor, he was charged with fixing his own face as well. Striepeke first aged his young mug with the application of a cheek scar by use of stretched rubber appliances and a covering makeup. He also grayed his hair and brows to match while wearing dental pieces to pucker his lips. A full moustache and scraggly set of chin whiskers rounded out his look; the results were startling, especially considering he was self-taught. The makeup fooled all who saw him, even though Striepeke (still a minor) was driven to the location by his mother (courtesy Dan Striepeke).

slave extras requiring blood and body dirt makeup as well as wigs and scraggly beards. "DeMille saw the extras wearing hook-on whiskers," Dan said, "and, dissatisfied with their cheap appearance, shut down the movie for two days while real hair beards could be procured." This turned out fine for young Striepeke as he could lay-in facial fur as fast as they could bring in the actors. In the bullpen (the rows of makeup artists attending to large numbers of extras), the makeup artists who did the best stuff had the longest lines in front of their work stations. Watching over the seventy daily hires of the department, makeup head Wally Westmore would lay off those practitioners whose craft was not up to par, as evidenced by the shortest lines. Amazingly, between the venues of Warner Bros, Paramount Pictures, 20th Century–Fox and MGM, all four of Striepeke's early gigs were done at about the same time. With the studios collective emphasis on large casts in period looks, the makeup end of the biz was in full bloom that year. In actuality, the reason for the need for fresh folks was the advanced age of most of the members of Local 706. During the mid–1950s, half of the 164 available journeymen makeup artists in Hollywood were at least sixty years old.

Among the first features that Striepeke did in '55, none was more exciting than *Around the World in 80 Days*. "Double dipping" (doing start-up makeup on the hundreds of extras employed during the movie's Chinese laborer sequences), Striepeke would leave 20th Century–Fox after his morning shift, then go to NBC in the afternoons for work on local news and live television shows. Just 25 years old, he received some kind mentoring from the taskmaster of Fox's makeup department, Terry Miles. Issued a bald cap to fit on one of the laborers, Dan thought it would be easier to install if placed over a lamp on his makeup table, to warm the material. However, the bare bulb burned through the latex, ruining the piece. After he sheepishly explained his need for another appliance to his boss, the understanding Miles said in his gravelly voice, "Here's another one kid. But remember ... it's a rubber skull cap, not a football helmet. Don't let it happen again!"

After working the quartet of "studio tent poles" in 1955, Striepeke was next hired by the head of Warner Bros "face-fixing" department, Gordon Bau, for the television pilot of *Maverick*, along with Eddie Butterworth and journeyman Newt Jones. Allowed only to crew the pilot, "the kid" was laid off once principal photography wrapped as union seniority hiring rules came into effect.

Continuing to earn a living by grabbing "hall calls" on NBC shows through mid–1957, Striepeke picked up invaluable experience on *Playhouse 90*, *The Tennessee Ernie Ford Show*, and *Pinky Lee*, on which he met a makeup ally for life, John Chambers.

Eventually obtaining his journeyman's card in late 1957 on venues such as *The Lux Video Theater*, *Red Skelton*, and *The Jack Benny Show*, Dan returned to Warners under Bau (toiling on *Maverick*, the series) as well as other television fare like *Sugarfoot* and *77 Sunset Strip*.

One gig in the fall of 1959 presented Striepeke a front seat to Cold War history: *Can-Can* at 20th Century–Fox. Starring Frank Sinatra with Shirley MacLaine, the Walter Lang–directed film featured multiple scenes of the infamous high-kicking line of leg-baring ladies. Around the same time, Mr. and Mrs. Nikita Khrushchev were visiting the US on a détente-building trip. A tour of Hollywood was arranged by the Eisenhower administration (at the request of the famous Soviet couple), to see an American movie being made. Approached by State Department types that morning, Dan (like the rest of the *Can-Can* cast and crew) was instructed not to talk to Khrushchev or otherwise embarrass the administration. Then the visitors saw the long-legged showgirls doing their provocative kicks into space. Enraged at the "filth of American entertainment" (as Khrushchev put it), the dignitary from Moscow grabbed his wife by the arm and commanded the Spendatz Team (sweating in their Russian wool suits) to remove them from all that debauchery.

After *Can-Can* finished kicking, Striepeke was a 29-year-old journeyman whose only direction was up. And "up" was Universal Pictures. Approached at the end of '59 by makeup demi-god Bud Westmore, Dan was offered the chance of a lifetime: to run the studio's lab. He would be responsible for everything, including the process and formulas for creating various makeup materials from blood to prosthetics, and bald caps to molds (including rubber, foam arts, dental sciences and hair); to head a Westmore lab, one had to be skilled. Honing the craft of effects makeup (prior to landing the position), there was very little that Dan could not do in a facility as complete as Universal's. Working with any of the Westmores in Hollywood was the makeup gold standard of its day. However, Striepeke was still under the employment of department head Gordon Bau at Warners. Seeking his mentor's blessing, he told of the opportunity at Universal. Bau kindly replied, "Listen, son, don't be a damn fool. Take the job. If you get into trouble, I'm only a phone call away."

Soon after Dan settled in as lab head at Universal, Stanley Kubrick's *Spartacus* began production at the studio. Tasked with manufacturing the prosthetics on the feature (including Laurence Olivier's regal nose for the Crassus character), Dan also did work on the front lines of the film, rendering body makeup including sweat, blood and dirt (as well as facial hair and beards) during the large second unit battle scenes, directed by stunt coordinator Yakima Canutt. In addition to doing the severed head prosthetics in the gladiator training sequences (shot at the ten-acre camp amid its 187 stunt fighters), Striepeke further labored with the patch fixing of body makeup on the sweat- and dirt-covered actors. "With the gladiators fighting so hard," he said, "we had to constantly refurbish the treatments as the combat and perspiration would produce bare spots in the body makeup that made it unphotographable." Continuing on the picture after principal photography had ceased, Dan did amputation gags and "crushing" makeup on the rolling log sequences. George Bau was the sibling of Dan's Warner Bros. mentor Gordon; Dan engaged him to assist with the special foam body parts used in the movie. Specially trained at the Goodyear plant in Akron, Ohio, regarding the chemical process and manufacturing of foam and various rubber compounds, George taught Striepeke much of what he knew and was actually the craftsman responsible for the eventual widespread industry use of latex for effects makeup.

One of the most dramatic scenes in the picture (of gladiator Woody Strode dead and displayed hanging upside down for Kirk Douglas to see) is owed to Striepeke's prowess with a brush. Carefully painting the body makeup on Strode's ripped physique, he used shading and slight color to accentuate the actor's perfect muscle tone. The result produced a profoundly sad image that is still memorable to audiences today.

Following *Spartacus*, Dan was chosen by makeup man Emile LaVigne to go on location to Mexico for *The Magnificent Seven*. Picked for his hustle on *Spartacus*, he went from earning $276 per week running the lab at Universal to $640 a week as on-set face fixer for the feature. Attending to a stock company of twelve stuntmen portraying cowboys and Mexican bandits requiring dark makeup, mustaches and beards, Dan also did Steve McQueen, Charles Bronson, Robert Vaughn, Eli Wallach and Brad Dexter. The only actors not in Striepeke's chair were Yul Brynner and Horst Buchholtz, who had long standing ties to LaVigne. Directed by John Sturges, *The Magnificent Seven* was a breakout movie for the Mirisch brothers as producers, as well as McQueen and Bronson as bankable actors. Remembering a bit of acting competition between McQueen and Brynner, Striepeke laughed as he told of the up-and-coming McQueen playing with his hat or sitting on his horse in odd positions to gain attention while the more famous box office draw of the two (Brynner) said his lines.

Returning to Westmore's Universal labs after *Magnificent Seven*, Dan landed on the new Tony Curtis picture *The Outsider* (1961). Hired by production manager Marshall Green (from *Spartacus*), he was put under the gun to replace a makeup artist who was too slow on the dark skin and false nose work required for the transformation of Curtis into the Ira Hayes character. "The first time I did the Pima Indian makeup and affixed the nose," Striepeke recalled, "I nailed it in one-third the time of the other guy. Curtis, admiring himself in the mirror, said to me, 'Where the hell have you been all my life?'"

Pictures like Basil Rathbone's *The Magic Sword* and Elvis Presley's *Follow That Dream* were given to the up-and-coming makeup man by mentor, Emile LaVigne. "Elvis was charming," Dan said, "He was a dedicated actor with a solid work ethic. Plus, he knew his lines!"

Dan was invited by Tony Curtis to be 'his guy' on the motion picture *Taras Bulba* (1962), made in Argentina. During an evening of bar-hopping with key grip "Big John" Livesley and second assistant director Terry Morse Jr., Striepeke and pals were accosted by military police with machine guns as they walked down the street to their hotel. Mistaken for criminals lurking about after curfew, the drunken trio was taken by gunpoint to the local police station. Producer Harold Hecht got them freed after establishing their identities, paying a sizable cash bail in the process.

Back to back with *Taras Bulba*, Dan's next Tony Curtis picture was Universal's *40 Pounds of Trouble*. After breaking the lock of studio control regarding makeup assignments with specific stars, he was free to pick his own projects, even sleepers like the underappreciated *40 Pounds*.

By 1963, Striepeke's reputation as a solid practitioner of men's looks was on the rise. Hired by "bail pal" producer Harold Hecht for his next project *Flight from Ashiya*, Dan was busy doing Richard Widmark on the action movie (as well as George Chakiris and Suzy Parker). Emile LaVigne attended to Yul Brynner. A close friend of the famous actor from *The King and I* (where they began working), Emile would continue powdering Brynner's bald pate and exotic good looks until his retirement from the makeup biz a few years later.

Returning to his favorite genre, the western, Striepeke next worked with LaVigne on the Yul Brynner morality play *Invitation to a Gunfighter* (1964), costarring George Segal, Brad Dexter and Janice Rule. Dan made up all in the cast but Brynner (including cowboy extras, shopkeepers and saloon patrons). Dan remembered the relationship between him and Yul as good: Even while Emile was Brynner's man, Striepeke was often invited to breakfast with the star and his wife. By the time the picture 20th Century–Fox *Morituri* was shot a year later, after LaVigne's retirement, Dan was Yul Brynner's new makeup man.

Another motion picture credit for Striepeke in 1964 was director Robert Wise's *The Sound of Music*. Tasked with doing makeup for Christopher Plummer and Eleanor Parker, Dan's focus on Angela Cartwright, Debbie Turner, Heather Menzies, Kym Karath, Duane Chase, Nicholas Hammond and Charmian Carr kept him busy as the kids were in nearly every scene. In order for Hammond to have the prototypical Hitler youth look (with its blond hair and blue eyes), the young actor had to endure multiple dyeings at Striepeke's hands. More problem-solving by the makeup department occurred when Charmian Carr (during the song "16 Going On 17") cut her ankle and calf on a pane of glass on the gazebo set. The injury was tended by Dan (who stopped the bleeding, then bound the wound in a flesh-colored sheer bandage), who then used his makeup skills to render the cut invisible. Over the course of filming, Debbie Turner lost her baby teeth; this was easily remedied by Striepeke, who fitted the gap-toothed child with dentures.

In the spring of 1965, Striepeke was signed by Yul Brynner to do his makeup on *Morituri*. Having known the star for years, it was a natural progression for Dan to take over the reins from his now retired mentor LaVigne. He also made-up co-stars Marlon Brando and Trevor Howard. He recalled Brando's playful energy in the makeup chair and his willingness to try anything that the below-the-line ranks asked of him; versus his distrust of directors and producers to whom he gave very little cooperation.

One television series Dan did in the mid-sixties became part of Hollywood history: *Mission: Impossible*. Filmed at the Desilu Studios (formerly RKO), the cutting-edge spy series was the best of its type, continuing its franchise prowess into the current day with a string of big-budget feature films. With other shows such as *The Man from U.N.C.L.E.* and *I Spy* hitting the airwaves then, *Mission: Impossible* was the grown-up's version of the Bond era coming to TV. Dan partnered with effects makeup genius John Chambers to produce the famous "peel-off-face" gag that was the signature effect on the show. First utilized by Chambers when working for the VA after World War II, the latex molded face masks were implemented as an aesthetic aid for soldiers with disfiguring facial wounds. Adapting those proprietary techniques to the medium of television and film, Chambers and Striepeke changed forever the way makeup affected the industry. Somewhat a product of good editing and effects, the often used double-whammy reveal was a live action occurrence, incorporating careful cutaway shots to avoid small glitches in the process. Regardless, the gag worked well enough that government agents (after Hollywood training) used the "new face" technology to move subjects in and out of European embassies during the Cold War.

The process devised for the face-change was as simple as it was brilliant. By casting a plaster mold of the actor's head, a perfect sculpture of the face was created. Next, a negative mold is made from the sculpture. That way, the makeup artist could paint the liquid latex into the hollow mold by hand, gradually building up layers. After the final coat of material is applied, a drying process of three to four hours was required for the rubber to set up. The final step involved gently peeling the mask from the mold. Then the coloring of the piece began and necessary hair could be added.

Finishing two straight seasons of 17-hour work days on *Mission: Impossible* (he was responsible for effects makeup as well as the show's stars Martin Landau, Steven Hill and Greg Morris), Striepeke was looking for a break. However, a call from retiring Ben Nye at 20th Century–Fox offering Dan "the department" was too much for him to refuse.

Dan took over the Fox lab at the end of 1967; his first movie as department head was *Planet of the Apes*. Beginning with tests to figure out the makeup technology, Striepeke (with partner Chambers again) needed to solve two issues that would allow for the picture's apes to speak like humans. First, engineering the lower jaw and dental physiology to work like a human's and, second, for the masks to be made of several inter-working sections, providing facial articulation for the actor beneath. To accomplish the lower jaw correction, Chambers (who had a background in dentistry) was able to provide the solution during the sculpture process. As for the interlocking concept, Striepeke sculpted individual chin pieces which married perfectly to the face components, resulting in a fit that allowed articulated speech. The process of applying the foam rubber prosthetics required an early call (as it took four hours to do the work). However, it proved to be time well spent as Chambers was rewarded with an Academy Award in the new category of special effects makeup for his efforts.

Another of Striepeke's challenges as department head on the film was the daily hire of 80 makeup technicians to work the three-week-long corn field sequences. The scenes required 36 fully made-up gorillas and sixty near-naked humans; just getting everyone fed at lunch was a major undertaking. Once the "ape actors" were made up, they had to stay that way all day. With the construction of the latex appliances limiting what could be chewed, the menu consisted of finely cut salads, milkshakes, ice cream, Jell-O, mashed potatoes and Chinese food. One ape extra thought he could eat split pea soup for lunch without anyone noticing. Spied by Striepeke with the lower flap of his jaw hanging down (covered in green peas), the young man blushed when told not to do it again as Dan mended the soupy prosthetic.

Engaged by old friend Tony Curtis, Dan crewed *The Boston Strangler* in late 1967. Running the department simultaneously, he would do Curtis' main makeup in the mornings and allow others to touch him up throughout the day. With his attention divided between so many features at 20th Century–Fox that year (including *Patton*, with *M.A.S.H.* just around the corner), Striepeke focused on the finer makeup needs of the Strangler, such as imbuing the character with a dark eye design and a cruel broad nose to enhance his menacing appearance.

On the heels of *The Boston Strangler*, 20th Century–Fox began testing for *Butch Cassidy and the Sundance Kid*. Dan ran the mustache tests on Robert Redford to determine the perfect style for the part. Ultimately agreed upon was the modified Fu Manchu that made the film; the process of choosing the proper "lip bristle" was labor intensive as Striepeke made and applied various false mustaches on the actor, from bushy and larger to shorter with the ends clipped off, until a choice was made. The final style was actually grown by Redford himself. Within six weeks of *Butch Cassidy and the Sundance Kid* coming out, Dan saw scores of guys wearing the Redford mustache he had designed. "I realized then," he mused, "the power in movies."

Shooting simultaneously with *Butch Cassidy* in 1969 was the Gene Kelly–directed musical *Hello Dolly*. Continuing as makeup department head (responsible for hiring and firing as well as the design on the feature), his artistic impact on the movie was all-encompassing, from the beginning screen tests on. Convincing director Kelly and DP Harry Stradling Jr. that the entire look of the picture should mirror a John Singer Sargent painting, Striepeke believed that the muted colors along with their pastoral sanded-down hues created an "old feel" look that fit the period perfectly. Incorporating everyone in the creative process (from the lab's color saturation rendering muted flesh tones) to Stradling using colored gels over diffused lighting, and makeup applying a subdued tonal range of warm shades, the entire look of *Hello Dolly* was affected by Striepeke's vision of it.

By 1970, Striepeke was considered one of the most talented makeup guys in Tinseltown. Bringing two very different war stories to the screen that same year, Fox enlisted his laboratory prowess for the blood and guts of *Patton* and the comedy *MASH*. On *MASH*, Dan was charged with the problem of coming up with the right type of prop blood so prominently displayed in the movie. With Robert Altman under the misimpression that pig blood be used for the "first of its kind" operating room scenes, Dan had to show the director 16 actual samples of coagulated, wet, dripped, dried or otherwise real blood (including an attention-getting stab of his own finger), to sell his lab mix of slow congealing artificial plasma, made from an old-school syrup, dye and coloring based formula.

Patton was about the makeup design for the actors. Given the duty of transforming George C. Scott's gnarled nose into the aquiline slim snout which graced Patton's face, Dan incorporated a specially crafted nose support that literally pulled Scott's sniffer straight. He utilized a fine lace of muslin-deswa with its edges pinked; the material was then affixed from the bridge of the schnozz to its tip where it would then pull the nose into a straight line. Covered and blended with a skin makeup to hide any seams in the prosthesis, the treatment was further embellished with the use of yellowing false teeth, sideburns, and white bushy eyebrows with a subtle white wig attached to Scott's shaved head. Dan hired journeyman makeup artist Del Acevedo to go on location in Spain as George's primary powder man on the picture. Remembering the day when the makeup came together for the fabled actor,

Dan said, "George was really getting into the Patton character as we perfected his look. [He was] originally uptight with the idea of playing an actual person for the first time in his career. Once we had the nose right, as well as the white sideburns, eyebrows, hair and facial mole glued down, he became Patton and began to effect the eccentric general's character around set." He won an Oscar for Best Actor with the role. One could make the argument that the supportive collaboration of the crew (be it makeup or otherwise) was an invaluable tool to Scott's effort of bringing Patton to life.

Striepeke's next Fox project was Ted Post's *Beneath the Planet of the Apes*. Due to budget cuts, everything — from head molds to hair pieces — was reused this time around. In a bit of forward green-thinking, Dan came up with a preservation method for the time-consuming ape facial prosthetics. It involved carefully sweating off the devices at shooting's end, then sanitizing and drying the pieces to be reused the following day.

Later in 1970, Striepeke toiled on two X rated flicks, Russ Meyer's *Beyond the Valley of the Dolls* and *Myra Breckinridge*. He hired old friend John Chambers for the effects makeup on the Ebert-scribed ripoff of the Jacqueline Susann sexcapade *Valley of the Dolls*; the only makeup worth recalling on *Beyond* was a pot belly stuck on John Huston and false breasts that Striepeke and Chambers had made so well, they joked of putting them on the market for cross dressers. Talking about Gore Vidal's *Myra Breckinridge*, Dan became animated when describing working with Mae West, who at 77 found joy in teasing Striepeke by revealing her still ample breasts and saying in her lilting fashion, "Not bad for a broad my age, huh, Dan?"

Also on the flick, Striepeke had brought in an old mentor from MGM, William Tuttle, to help bend a brush. Tuttle, who had done masterful work on *Cat on a Hot Tin Roof*, *North by Northwest*, and *7 Faces of Dr. Lao*, was at the twilight of his career when picking up days from his previous student.

In 1970, Dan worked solely as an administrative department head, designing the makeup and then staffing the films with competent people who could fulfill his vision. He made an exception for Shelley Winters on *The Poseidon Adventure* the following year; he surfaced on the waterlogged epic after she came to him with a multitude of issues that only he could solve. Striepeke's experience and psychological "chair-side" manner enabled the age-conscious star to put in a performance that would get her Oscar nominated for Best Supporting Actress.

Whether it was boredom with difficult actors or just a desire to take a shot at total filmmaking, Striepeke left Fox in 1971 to pursue a script he had written and would produce, *Ssssss*. Partnering with his old pals from *Mission: Impossible*, director Bernie Kowalski and producer Bruce Geller, Dan put together the picture which was released in 1973. With an ingenious snake metamorphosis taking place "on camera" (and real king cobras on the set), the movie eventually gained an effects cult status with a fairly large fan base. With offices on the Universal lot, Striepeke continued to pursue producing, pitching stories with partners at the company. After two years with no breakthrough projects, however, Dan needed to earn a living and returned to 20th Century–Fox.

Coming back just in time for the TV series *Planet of the Apes*, the old monkey mender was in familiar territory. Already a master of the proprietary techniques for the ape gimmicks, Dan's focus as department head was simply the hiring of good makeup mechanics to apply the latex and fur looks. As if the *Apes* series wasn't enough to keep him busy, Fox also launched the television show *M*A*S*H* in 1974. It was much like the original film for him (replicating his blood formula); as department head, once again his primary duty was hiring people to do the makeup.

Running out of gas on the show-boss routine (laboring two years without a break on the various Fox series), Striepeke decided to go freelance. His first gig as an independent was on the sci-fi crossover *Embryo* in 1976. He teamed up again with effects maestro John Chambers on the Fred Koenekamp–lensed flick; the duo had one major makeup effect to solve that took them to the pathology labs at UCLA for a solution. During the scenes where an advanced growth rate is depicted in a human embryo, the four weeks to full-term fetus models used were molded and sculpted from actual infant bodies. They were accessed via Dan's brother who was an OB-GYN at the University. The unprecedented use of the actual unborn cadavers allowed for an amazing believability in "the look" of the transformation. To give the embryonic models that membrane appearance, they were covered in a silicone-elastic mix (scilli-static); the end result was the most memorable images in the motion picture.

Following the trend of special effects makeup films (all the rage in Movieland), Striepeke's next noteworthy assignment was *The Island of Dr. Moreau* in 1977. Lensed on location in St. Croix, Virgin Islands, the Don Taylor–helmed horror film starred Burt Lancaster, Barbara Carrera and Michael York. Convincing the director "less is more" when it came to the animal makeup design, Dan and John Chambers engineered a series of latex and fur head masks that sold the crossover creatures as frighteningly real. Inspired by drawings in old zoological textbooks, the makeup required a 3:00 A.M. talent call, as the process utilized not only foam pieces and latex layering, but full body makeup as well. Dan's favorite creations on the motion picture were the Bull-man and Tiger-guy. The distant location required him to do double duty, applying makeup to Lancaster and Michael York as well.

Continuing to stay booked as a freelance journeyman, Striepeke's next engagement was on the '50s period throwback *Grease*. Applying the makeup to John Travolta as well as supporting players Jeff Conaway, Frankie Avalon and Sid Caesar, Dan employed the minimum amounts of powder that he could, preferring to utilize blushes and sheers (reduced to almost nothing) to give a more translucent, scrubbed look.

Striepeke was nosing about for a gig when called by UPM Elliot Shick to take over a movie in Thailand called *The Deer Hunter*. Things were going badly for effects makeup guru Dick Smith (due to constant clashes with helmer Michael Cimino over set etiquette and safety of the difficult effects); Dan and makeup artist Del Acevedo were faced with the same issues from the impatient director when doing the film. One iconic scene is the Russian roulette action played out while Robert DeNiro and Christopher Walken are held captive in the jungle shack. The resulting "head shot" gag was the movie's most difficult makeup for Striepeke to pull off. The action called for an entrance shot to the forehead and an exit wound blowing out the back of the skull; the rigging of the effects makeup was crucial to the safety and success of the shot. Starting with the exit mechanics, Striepeke attached a malleable lead shield tight against the rear of the actor's head, securing it with special rubber bands and bobby pins. Next, the explosive squibs and blood pack were glued down to the shield, upon which bits of white rubber duplicating shattered bone were laid under an application of mortician's wax, covering the edges of the metal and hiding the detonation wires beneath. He sealed everything with a viscous latex skin material. The chore was completed by affixing a hair piece to hide all from camera.

For the entry wound, the process was far more challenging as the camera was seeing the entire effect. A lead shield was placed against the occipital lobe; a smaller squib was used to duplicate a bullet opening, appearing in the forehead as though shot. Finished off with a concealing layer of makeup, the side view looked like a Klingon; however, when framed from the front (square on) and flat lit, the result was dazzling. This effect had an element of danger (for the actor and makeup man alike). During the 16 ensuing takes, not everything went smoothly. On one occasion, Cimino was holding the live remote detonator in his hand, impatiently waiting for Striepeke to finish his final touches, when he mistakenly set off the charge. Dan's thumbnail was blown off; the injured makeup man had to be restrained by crew mates to keep him from grabbing the director. Another instance of forced error came about when Cimino was rushing makeup to reset the exit wound apparatus. A small gap was mistakenly left between the lead plate and the back of the skull; the Thai actor used in the role was knocked unconscious, suffering a concussion. Because of this incident (and others) of perceived disrespect toward locals working on the movie, the infamous director required multiple bodyguards during filming to ensure his safety.

Once recovered from near exhaustion after *Deer Hunter*, Striepeke chose to do Richard Gere's makeup on the Paul Shrader-penned and -directed *American Gigolo*. Shrader called for Gere's look to be that of a fresh-faced angel with a devil underneath; Dan's makeup choice was a special sheer Max Factor powder that came in a Grecian urn. Having a translucent quality, the fine composition of the stuff allowed a visibility of the skin beneath, yet looked as though the actor wore nothing at all.

Striepeke's face-fixing faculty was also put to the test on Richard Fleischer's *The Jazz Singer*, starring Laurence Olivier and Neil Diamond. Aside from producing the obligatory "false smeller" for Sir Laurence, he was also called upon to put an Afro black makeup on Neil Diamond for the "You, Baby, You" number. Utilizing a technique of layering a dark base makeup, then applying a sheer cover on top, Striepeke produced a depth to the skin tone that looked completely natural.

Dan's next important motion picture assignment, *Continental Divide* (1981), starred the bigger-than-life John Belushi. Striepeke told of the actor sitting in his makeup chair, refusing to lower a newspaper shoved up against his face. The director, Michael Apted, burst into the trailer, giving his star twenty minutes to be on the set or else! "After that," Danny said, "John was as good as gold." Sticking to his word to stay straight (with help from the two studio cops put on him to keep him out of trouble and get him in shape), Belushi worked out hard and was really taking the Ernie Souchak role seriously. "By the end of the picture," the makeup man recalled, "John had not only lost 50 pounds, but was enjoying his newfound health while doing it." Belushi would make only one more film (*Neighbors* with pal Dan Aykroyd) before dying of a drug overdose the following year.

In the fall of 1981, Striepeke powdered the cheeks of Bernadette Peters on the Herbert Ross remake of *Pennies from Heaven*. Starring Steve Martin and Christopher Walken, the richly photographed drama (shot by Gordon Willis) had a subdued color palette. In order to fine-tune his makeup under those shooting conditions, Dan had lights with the various colors of gels rigged in his trailer during the two-month rehearsal for Walken's "Born to Be Bad" dance routine. Striepeke had a process of previewing his looks before they went to set; not only did this save production a lot of time, but allowed makeup supervisor Frank Griffith a chance to see his own concepts ahead of shooting them and making changes if he chose to do so.

After an unexciting second outing with Peters on John Huston's *Annie*, Dan took a project (and a client) who was a little closer to his heart. The client was Peter O'Toole and the film was *My Favorite Year*, a comeback vehicle for the great actor. Striepeke's makeup design was as big as the star himself. Pulling back O'Toole's cheeks (with a sort of temporary facelift technique) as well as tightening the flesh behind the ears, he was proud of the results and glad to see O'Toole in such good cheer while being transformed. In addition to attending to O'Toole early in the mornings, Dan also worked on co-stars Mark Lynn-Baker, Jessica Harper, Joseph Bologna, and Bill May (as long as O'Toole came first).

Ultimately Svengalied by the colorful actor, Striepeke accompanied him to New York for the film's PR launch, providing O'Toole the same youthful look on the talk show visits which he so appreciated during the making of the picture. "I would have gone anywhere with that guy," Dan said with a grin of infatuation on his face.

The next few flicks for Striepeke, *Doctor Detroit* (1983) and *Footloose* (1984), were both simple, production-friendly fare. On *Doctor Detroit*, Dan got along well with Dan Aykroyd (having known his best friend John Belushi) and, as far as concept went, kept the makeup direct. On *Footloose*, however, he was not only busy making up Kevin Bacon, but supporting actors John Lithgow, Chris Penn, and Lori Singer as well. Dan relied upon a thin emollient-based formula for the 24-year-old Bacon (it acted like a translucent cover, allowing the skin underneath to shine through); Striepeke recalls little else done to Bacon's face. To prepare for the role, Bacon had the idea of attending Payton High School in Utah as a transfer student from Los Angeles, to help him "get inside" the character. He was so badly treated by his classmates (due to being from LA) that after the first day of posing, he abandoned the gag completely.

Between November of 1984 and March of '85, Striepeke was part of the crew on one of the best modern westerns ever made: Lawrence Kasdan's *Silverado*. He was engaged to provide principal makeup for the entire troupe, including Kevin Klein, Scott Glenn, Brian Dennehy, Danny Glover, Jeff Goldblum, Linda Hunt, John Cleese and Kevin Costner. Kasdan's desire was to see no makeup show; easier said than done. Striepeke used a thin base makeup to keep the shine down, then added contouring and shading with a brush, to accomplish the low-key natural look that the director was after. Dan laughed when recalling Costner begging for eyeliner one day, then fooling him into believing he was applying it by painting imaginary lines under the actor's eyes with a brush dipped only in water.

Dan Aykroyd hired Striepeke again in 1987 to do makeup on his pet project *Dragnet*, a feature blown up from the original Jack Webb TV series (one of Aykroyd's favorites). Dan's co-star was a young up-and-coming actor from a television series called *Bosom Buddies*, Tom Hanks. Having already done several movies after the popular show, such as *Big*, *The Man with One Red Shoe*, *Splash* and *The Money Pit*, the actor had now been around long enough to know what he liked in a makeup man. A near-instant bond developed between Striepeke and Hanks, based (according to Dan) on mutual love of motion pictures, dedication to one's craft, and a personal kinship of both coming from broken homes.

Just before reaching an exclusivity arrangement with Hanks, however, he took a quick assignment in January of 1988 (from Robert DeNiro, whom he knew from *The Deer Hunter*) to do *Midnight Run*. Dan's biggest chore (after powdering co-star Charles Grodin) was the maintenance of DeNiro's facial stubble, adding or subtracting beard for continuity purposes.

Always preferring the understated, Striepeke's choices for Grodin's look kept it simple, with a minimum of shadow and color but enough dishevelment to sell the look.

A few months after the wrap of the DeNiro job, Dan got a call from Hanks to do another film with him, *The 'Burbs* (1989). Shaking hands over the arrangement, the makeup man recalled it was at this point that Hanks said, "We're a team, Dan — you and I." Covering the entire cast on the Universal offering, Striepeke not only made-up his new teammate Tom, but also the rest of the cast including Bruce Dern, Carrie Fisher, and Rance Howard.

Continuing with Hanks on *Turner and Hooch* later that year, Striepeke began to realize the "Jimmy Stewart qualities" of his new partner. Watching him work opposite the scene-stealing Dogue de Bordeaux co-star, he saw in Hanks a depth of humility and a focus of craft like no other that he had experienced in the industry. "What you see with Tom is real," Dan said with a smile. "Like Jimmy Stewart, he cares about folks and that quality projects in his acting."

The fourth outing for the pair was *Joe Versus the Volcano* (1990). Although directed by famous playwright John Patrick Shanley, the lensed-in-Hawaii dramedy failed to ring the bell with theatergoers. However, as a test run in dealing with sunburn, long hours and keeping makeup looking good when challenged by saltwater (all problems ten years later on *Cast Away*), the experience was worth its weight in gold for Striepeke and Hanks.

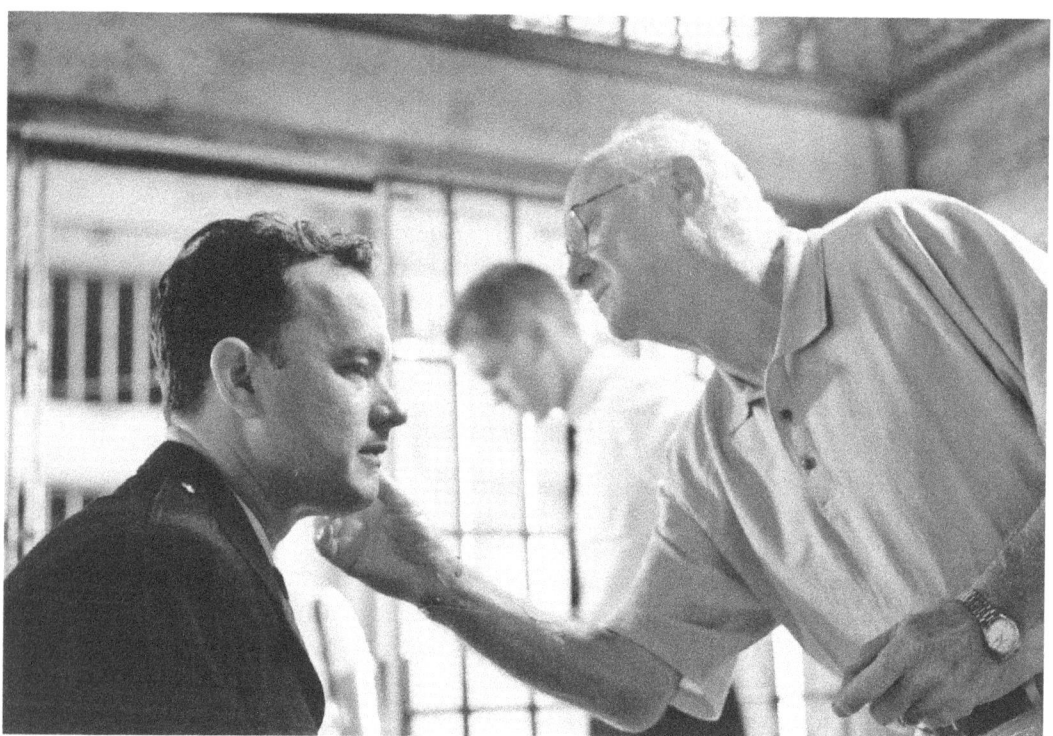

Makeup artist Dan Striepeke carefully applies a touchup to Tom Hanks during the filming of Frank Darabont's *The Green Mile* (1999). Striepeke was employed by the actor as his sole "powder and paint" man; the two worked together on *The 'Burbs* (1989) and continued through *The DaVinci Code* (2006). Striepeke retired after that film; the two made 16 features together and remain close friends (courtesy Dan Striepeke).

After manning *My Blue Heaven* (while on studio-politics–induced hiatus), Dan returned with Hanks for Brian De Palma's *The Bonfire of the Vanities* in the summer of 1990. Strictly responsible for Tom, Striepeke executed a makeup which allowed for the build-up of stress to show on the character's face. Incorporating a series of dark shadows under the eyes that ultimately form puffy bags (as the situation for Sherman McCoy worsens), Striepeke also implemented a deteriorating dental effect that was subtle, yet convincing in selling the undone look of the beaten man.

After "rent projects" such as *Lost in Yonkers* and *Made in America*, Striepeke returned to Tom Hanks' side for the megahit *Forrest Gump* in 1994. In a smooth synergy of style and technique, Dan's abilities were showcased while progressing Forrest from his young days through Vietnam to those of the running sequences, where Hanks is wearing a full beard. That "chin warmer" was hand-laid one hair at a time by Striepeke (during a one-hour process at 5 A.M.) which became a daily non speaking ritual between the friends. Also doing aging makeup on Sally Field, Gary Sinise, and Hanks, Dan was so busy throughout the feature that he labored 27 days in a row (at one point) without a day off. He was Oscar-nominated for his makeup artistry on the picture. Striepeke also played a part as Bear Bryant's assistant football coach, saying his often repeated line "Look at that son of a bitch run!" upon seeing Gump first fly across the practice field.

One compelling bit of makeup on the feature was the fatal wounding of Gump's best friend Bubba, played by Mykelti Williamson. He combined fresh coffee grounds with acetone (then set it on fire to produce an ultra-realistic melted skin and burnt flesh visual); the end product was drip-applied to the actor as it cooled, forming a dark, blistered-looking injury.

For Gump's character, Striepeke used the span of time to show real differences in the man while getting his hair cut by the barber. Whether it was Forrest the wide-eyed college kid or Forrest looking like a tough Marine, those shots were points of growing up for Gump. Dan added, "As such, things like hair line, sideburns, and aging around eyes and the mouth were used to show life experience over time on the man. Considering Gump didn't really mentally age, the haircuts and makeup became vital to show the character's span of time."

Now into his seventh feature film with Hanks, Striepeke face-fixed his pal on Ron Howard's *Apollo 13*. "Some pictures with us [he and Hanks] are about makeup; others acting. On *Apollo 13*, it was more about showing the passing of time with beard stubble." As such, he utilized only sheer covers minimally applied to achieve the real look required by director Ron Howard.

Again filling his plate between available Hanks projects, Dan was contracted to do Universal's *The American President* in the fall of 1994. He applied his brush and sponge skills to Martin Sheen, Michael J. Fox and old alum Richard Dreyfuss; the job, like many of his later non–Hanks gigs, was pretty much a walk in the park.

United with Hanks on Fox's *That Thing You Do*, Striepeke once again demonstrated his acumen with understatement while transforming his boss into the Mr. White character. He relied upon an age modification of Hanks' hairline, as well as period sideburns and haircut. Personal tragedy struck midway through the film: The death of Dan's wife forced him to leave the picture prematurely.

Coming back a year later for *Wag the Dog*, Striepeke transformed Dustin Hoffman into a Robert Evans type. A special deep bronzing makeup gave the character an over-the-top, tanned look. He also attended to co-stars Dennis Leary, William H. Macy, and Woody Harrelson. Striepeke used the picture to get back into the swing of things, recalling Hoffman and crew as being very kind in his time of transition.

The next motion picture that Striepeke undertook was one of the most exciting filmmaking experiences of his life; the makeup for Hanks on Steven Spielberg's *Saving Private Ryan*. Once again called upon for his mastery of the realist look, he used slight makeup and sheers mixed with natural dirt shadows and Hanks' own beard stubble, to sell the character of Captain John Miller. At one point Striepeke had to say no to Spielberg regarding his desire to have Hanks' eyes rimmed in the red of battle exhaustion. Stating that Janusz Kaminski's cinematography was exposed on the warm side and the magenta concept wouldn't read on film, Dan said it was he alone who decided upon the makeup for the character. "Tom is the kind of person who entrusts you with a responsibility to do your job. His thing (according to him) is to stand in front of the camera and say the lines they give him."

Sticking with Hanks, Striepeke manned *The Green Mile* in 1998. Again attending only to Tom, he was in the enviable position of being able to lavish focus on his favorite star. With the freedom to create, earn top money, and the respect of his peers (not to mention his terrific partner Hanks), Striepeke was now in the prime of a long and prosperous career. However, his challenges of craft were far from over. In early 2000, Dan got the nod from Tom Hanks to shoot *Cast Away*. Aside from the obvious problems of keeping makeup on an actor who's exposed to tropical sun and surf all day, Dan was charged with engineering a mechanical leg-bleeding gag (the footage never made it into the picture). In the shot, Hanks is badly injured on the coral reef (cutting his leg deeply) after the crash. Striepeke manufactured a full prosthesis involving a blood bladder and waterproof pump that would shoot the plasma out of Hanks' leg as though he had severed his femoral artery. "It worked great. We did it with four cameras on the reefs in Fiji," Dan said.

Dan constantly hustled to keep the proper makeup on Hanks while working through SP 75 sunscreen all day. Needing to reapply after every three takes amid the surf and sand shots, Striepeke and a team of four would gently swab off the makeup and goo underneath as many as eight time s a day. "We had one gal just for his feet," Dan laughed. Hanks' beard grew rather quickly, so Striepeke only needed to maintain its length to stay true to continuity rather than apply false whiskers every morning.

Road to Perdition (2002) was the next Striepeke-Hanks collaboration. No longer interested hustling fill-in gigs between assignments, Dan was now well rested and only served one piper, Tom Hanks. Charged with the makeup for Paul Newman and Jude Law as well, Striepeke's prowess was called to action on the Sam Mendez–skippered crime drama. While Striepeke was fitting Newman with a prosthetic "mean nose" and mustache for the role, the star of *Butch Cassidy and the Sundance Kid* (who knew Striepeke since that movie) said jokingly, "Are you sure you know what you're doing, kid?" Dan also did a nose for Hanks that was especially gnarled and scary. Along with the makeup design of darkening Hanks' cheeks to give a more angular look, he also opted for a down-turned mustache in a 1930s Chicago gangster style. "My goal," said Striepeke regarding the character of Michael Sullivan, "was to portray him as a hard, tough man. With Tom Hanks being the guy everyone loves, I had to rough his look up a little to make the Sullivan hit man persona feasible. It's one of the best transformations I have ever done."

Costume designer Albert Wolsky was afraid the look wouldn't work; he was silenced

1. Dan Striepeke, Makeup Artist 19

While filming *Cast Away* (2000) on the Fiji Island location of Monuriki in the Mamanuca Archipelago, Striepeke (holding a beach umbrella) does all he can to give actor Tom Hanks a break from the brutal tropical sun (courtesy Dan Striepeke).

upon seeing the entirely made-up Hanks (including prosthetic nose, a bang-on 1930s haircut and a small Clark Gable moustache) walk into the room, clad in fedora and great overcoat. Stunned with the impression Hanks made just standing there glaring at him as Michael Sullivan, Wolsky said, "Jesus Christ, Dan — it works!"

A last-minute challenge for Striepeke was director Mendez's desire to do a head shot gag like the one from *The Deer Hunter*. Dan obliged with the same type of lead plate technology used on the previous movie. Despite objections from DP Conrad Hall about the obvious bulge down its center, the experienced makeup man was vindicated as the dailies looked perfect.

Later in 2002, Dan jumped on another Hanks feature, Steven Spielberg's *Catch Me If You Can*, about an adolescent thief (aptly played by Leonardo DiCaprio) and Hanks, the square investigator after him. The Striepeke makeup was again "less is more." Responsible for both actors (on his fourth collaboration with Spielberg), Dan utilized luminescent sheers on Leonardo's character of the fresh-faced kid. In contrast, the Hanks persona was a pasty office guy who didn't get out much, complete with cop sideburns and a mid-life receding hairline. The approach was one of schoolboy versus the principal when it came to the two looks.

Following a year's break, Dan was engaged on Hanks' next motion picture, *The Lady Killers* (2004). Although marveling at the Coen brothers as directors, the end product of the film didn't do much for him. Other than a basic powdering of Hanks in the morning, Dan intimated that he could have phoned in the rest of the gig. "Tom even picked the Colonel Sanders mustache," he said with a hint of disapproval on his face.

Adjusting to the new era of CGI digital capture taking Hollywood by storm in 2004, Striepeke labored on the granddaddy of all live-action animated flicks, *The Polar Express*. Directed by Dan's favorite Robert Zemeckis (and lensed by Don Burgess), the production used a process dubbed "image motion" which scanned live actors, then digitally placed them into sets and applications on screen. Striepeke is proud of his rendition of a Finnish Santa Claus. Inspired by popular illustrations from his grandfather's era in Norway, he designed a look for Hanks that evoked a paternal St. Nick with the feel of a living Norman Rockwell painting.

To achieve the amazing results, the makeup process began with the affixing of prosthetic foam pieces under cheeks and eyes, as well as the attachment of a Nordic nose. After blending the schnozz lines with latex filler, Striepeke layered a foundation of a mixed cream base makeup over all, giving the skin an opalescent depth of rich blush color. He finished with an oversized, hand-laid beard (with matching white sideburns and bushy eyebrows). The appearance of the actor was so extraordinary that when he led Hanks to the stage, the entire crew gave them a standing ovation. "At that moment," Dan revealed with a tear of pride in his eyes, "I knew what I had created was truly a work of art and appreciated by my peers." Literally adapting his old-school know-how to the new technology of motion capture and digital placement, Striepeke proved that aged dogs can create new tricks.

For the next Spielberg-Hanks offering *The Terminal*, Dan gave Hanks a receding hairline as well as the pale complexion of someone residing at the airport; the "living" study was another example of Dan's "less is more" mantra.

Striepeke's final motion picture was Ron Howard's *The Da Vinci Code* in 2006. Still enjoying Hanks personally (but starting to grow weary of traveling the world to earn his living), Dan began to consider retirement. Realizing that *The Da Vinci Code* would probably be his swan song, he cherished the opportunity of spending time with his pal amid such amazing locations as the Ritz Hotel and the Louvre in Paris. Striepeke fondly recalled Hanks' presentation of a huge cake on set, when his birthday occurred during the last few days of shooting.

Ultimately a nasty chest infection (caught while wrapping the film in London) forced Striepeke's decision to hang up his brushes. Talking with Hanks two weeks later on the phone while convalescing in LA, Dan came to an epiphany which he voiced to his buddy: "I love ya, man, but I can't live out of a suitcase any more."

Friends to this day, Hanks and Striepeke speak on a regular basis about life, the Cleveland Indians, and the future of the motion picture business. Enjoying retirement, Striepeke's biggest worry lately is getting a good tee time at Sherwood Golf Course.

In addition to receiving his "gold card" from Local 705 with fifty years of service to his credit, Dan stays connected to the craft by regularly attending union meetings and making time for writers like me to get the inside story for books about the biz. Having begun his career during the age of powders and sponges, Dan Striepeke saw Hollywood (and the craft of motion picture production) evolve from a small, interconnected town of artisans into the era of multi-million dollar, effects-laden films. Through it all (from hand-laid beards to latex face peels to motion capture), Striepeke stayed true to his craft and created a lifetime of memorable characters.

When pressed for words of advice for the next generation of makeup artisans, Dan smiled and said quietly, "Read all you can. Go to seminars. Stay current. And above all, immerse yourself in the trade by being a student of the craft."

2

Carl Manoogian, Key Grip

When a studio mechanic logs 98,000 hours of work (spanning 75 features over 50 years), chances are he's enjoyed an interesting career. In the case of retired key grip Carl Manoogian, "interesting" is an understatement.

Carl's story began with tugboat service in the Navy during World War II, hauling disabled ships back to port. Taught marine skills such as salvage rigging, welding, torch cutting and hydraulics, his quick grasp of mechanics and strong work ethic served him well in wartime, as well as in his future craft of gripping. After the war, Carl attended Occidental College, playing three championship seasons with the baseball team. He parlayed that exposure into a tryout with the California Angels in 1952 (along with fellow vet and actor-to-be Chuck Connors); Manoogian missed making the Big Leagues whereupon he married the daughter of a crane and dolly impresario (Ralph Chapman) a year later. Accepting advice from his father-in-law to give the film business a try, he went to the grip local office and was approved as a permit on the spot, and then assigned construction work at Paramount Pictures under department head Fred Johnson.

Beginning with gang calls in early 1954 (pulling hangers for "pusher" Earl Miller), Manoogian did high-work on iconic pictures including Hitchcock's *Rear Window*. After 14 grueling months on the gang, the 29-year-old rookie was called down from the perms and given extra hammer gigs on Paramount's *The Naked Jungle* and *The Far Horizons* in 1955. Continuing to labor at Paramount on such epic flicks as *The Ten Commandments* the following year, Manoogian was finally admitted to Local 80 for a #3 card (after nearly three years as a permit in town). Furthering his production grip efforts through dolly and crane, Carl began learning the skills required to work the specialized equipment by hanging around the Chapman warehouse on off days, practicing moves with the wheeled camera platforms until he could do it with his eyes closed.

A production, crane and dolly man throughout the late fifties, Manoogian worked on *Gunfight at the OK Corral* and *The Devil's Hairpin*, to name just two of the 17 pictures on which he day-played in 1957 alone! The next couple of years, Manoogian continued to hone his craft by doing. Working mostly as an extra hammer on movies such as *Some Like It Hot, I Married a Monster from Outer Space, Teacher's Pet, Tarzan's Greatest Adventure* and *Lil Abner* in 1959, he was taking the first step towards becoming a key grip by meeting DPs who would want to hire him.

In 1960, Tinseltown went "TV crazy" looking for shows to fill the airwaves, and westerns like *Bonanza* became network gold. Catching work on the series that year, Carl labored for two fine cinematographers who would later engage him as their key grip: Lucien Ballard and Bob Surtees.

Manoogian landed grip work on some first rate features like Frank Capra's *Pocketful of Miracles* in 1961. That same year he worked a week in the desert around Misfit's Flats (in Stagecoach, Nevada) on John Huston's *The Misfits*. Remembering the dangerous and thirsty work of filming the mustang roping scenes, Carl said, "When shooting Clark Gable being dragged behind the truck [the 59-year-old actor did his own stunts in the picture], small details became critical." Rigging the drag-line to the tail of the pickup (as per second unit director Tom Shaw and DP Russell Metty), Manoogian was figuring out the length of the rope when Gable walked up to him. Worried about the actor, he told him the desert ground was too rough for the gag. "Thanks, Carl," Gable said, "but you only live once, old friend, so I'm playing it full out!" Following the last day of shooting *The Misfits*, Gable suffered a severe coronary thrombosis, resulting in his death from a heart attack only ten days later. Some attributed the stunt to killing him. Others said it was working with Marilyn Monroe.

Later in 1961, a stroke of good luck would connect Carl with the first big-time professional relationship of his career. Working on Jerry Lewis' *The Ladies Man*, DP Wallace Kelley was having problems with the operator assigned to him for "old #2," the Chapman crane on the film. Hearing of the issue, grip department head Fred Johnson brought Carl down from the perms (he was already rigging on the picture) and had him take over on the

Jerry Lewis and Carl Manoogian playfully wrestle while the rest of the *Cinderfella* (1960) grip crew lays down 2" × 12" lumber for a moving crane shot. Note the stage crane (right) positioned to be placed on its boards, as a company grip bends to fit the "drive-on" wedges required for the weighted Titan's ascent to its platform truck (courtesy Carl Manoogian).

crane. Carl was an expert with the Chapman gear (having been tutored by factory techs at his father-in-law's plant), *so* good that Lewis asked him to stay for the entire show. One particular challenge recalled by Manoogian was the three-story doll house set. With the standard Chapman studio crane of that day only allowing 12 feet of vertical height to the platform, he attached an eight-foot extension on the arm in order to achieve the desired coverage. Carl rigged and operated old #2 like a violin for his new director, who even rode the platform on some shots. When asked his favorite gag in the picture, Manoogian laughed as he described Lewis driving a convertible through a Hollywood carwash with the top down. "We only did it once," he said, "as the Dodge had a foot of water inside it, and turned out to belong to one of the transpo guys who hadn't read the script before allowing the use of his car."

After *The Ladies Man*, Manoogian was on everything that Jerry Lewis did at Paramount Pictures. The next feature *The Errand Boy* (just a few weeks later) saw Carl handling all of the dolly and crane responsibilities. He saved his new boss a ton of money and time (thanks to his efficient use of the Chapman equipment); he and Lewis were rapidly bonding.

Early in 1962, Carl (then known in town as the hot new crane guy) was hired by John Ford's people to operate a Titan crane on *The Man Who Shot Liberty Valance*. Impressed with his touch on the arm, Ford offered Carl steady work, which he declined because he was already slated for Lewis' upcoming flick *It's Only Money*.

Along with a raise, Manoogian was now working on the picture with one of the world's most respected comedic directors, Frank Tashlin. "Jerry Lewis and Frank Tashlin learned from each other," Carl said. "Jerry knew physical," he added, "while Tashlin was a first-rate guy with camera and dialogue." The next Lewis movie, *The Nutty Professor*, was perhaps the actor's most successful at the box

Manoogian (left) mugs a play fight with writer-producer-star Jerry Lewis, on location in Hollywood (off La Brea Avenue) while shooting *The Nutty Professor* (1963), the breakout comedy success of that summer (courtesy Carl Manoogian).

In the middle of a parking lot at the University of Arizona–Tempe while filming *The Nutty Professor*, Manoogian (white shirt facing camera) watches as pal Jerry Lewis does trick shots for a small crowd, including a campus cop. Pool tables, basketball hoops, ping pong tables — wherever Lewis was working, modes of relaxation were close by (courtesy Carl Manoogian).

office. It was shot mostly on campus at Arizona State University. Manoogian told of a comment made before shooting one day that caused Lewis to double over with laughter. As Jerry prepared to enter the Purple Pit for the first time as Buddy Love (dressed in a blue sharkskin tux made by his personal tailor, Sy Devore), Carl said, "Who let Liberace on set?" Unbeknownst to Manoogian, wardrobe goddess Edith Head (the picture's costume designer) was standing behind him with a look of scorn on her face. As it turns out, she didn't like the comment or the tux very much, for that matter.

By the summer of 1963, Manoogian was "keying" on Jerry Lewis' *Who's Minding the Store?* Now pals with the boss, Carl spoke of pulling practical jokes on the comedic actor while working (for example, waiting for Lewis to take a drink of hot coffee, then dropping a heavy crane weight just behind him, causing him to spill his cup). Lewis reciprocated with neverending taunts regarding Manoogian's good looks and muscular build. Carl said, "Jerry had a saying: 'Film is for fun.'" On the first day of shooting, Manoogian and a grip buddy dressed as female mannequins on display in the window of the department store set. Looking through the finder while checking the shot, Lewis said nothing for about 30 sec-

Top: Although constantly playing gags on his friends, Jerry Lewis as a director was quite the student of motion picture production and technology. In this shot, Lewis is on a Chapman studio crane in between set-ups on Paramount's *Who's Minding the Store?* (1963); Manoogian (left) teaches his pal the finer points of backing up on a straight line (courtesy Carl Manoogian). *Bottom:* On location at the Greystone Mansion shooting *The Disorderly Orderly* (1964), Jerry Lewis holds court among the crew as cops and bystanders crack up. Hanging on his boss' every word, Manoogian (in white t-shirt) waits for the punch line. Note the circa 1960 ten-ton movie equipment truck with its button-up canvas sides. Today's location vehicles, in excess of 40 feet and complete with offices, refrigerators and satellite television, make the old stuff seem primitive in comparison (courtesy Carl Manoogian).

onds, then barked to the DP, "Looks great, Wally, except for the two knock-kneed gorillas in the back. Can somebody stick a lampshade over Manoogian's head, please?"

Ensuing pictures such as *The Patsy* and *The Disorderly Orderly* further cemented the friendship between Lewis and Manoogian. No longer just director and the grip, they now shared "off time" on set as well. Often gambling (one of Lewis's favorite time-killers in those days), they would bet on everything from ping pong to pinochle. The twist was, Jerry always contributed any cash he won to the Muscular Dystrophy box he had on set at all of his movies. On one occasion, Manoogian had been on a hot streak with basketball and whipped Jerry five times in horse. Undaunted, Lewis asked for a double or nothing shot on the 500 dollars he already owed. Agreeing, Manoogian won again and was up a grand. Lewis handed Carl a $1000 check to cover his loss; Manoogian tore it up, stating, "Remember, Jerry, I'm with you because I love *you*, not your money."

Now that he was in demand, other Paramount assignments came Manoogian's way in the spring of 1965 when he did Howard Hawks' *Red Line 7000*. The melodrama, starring

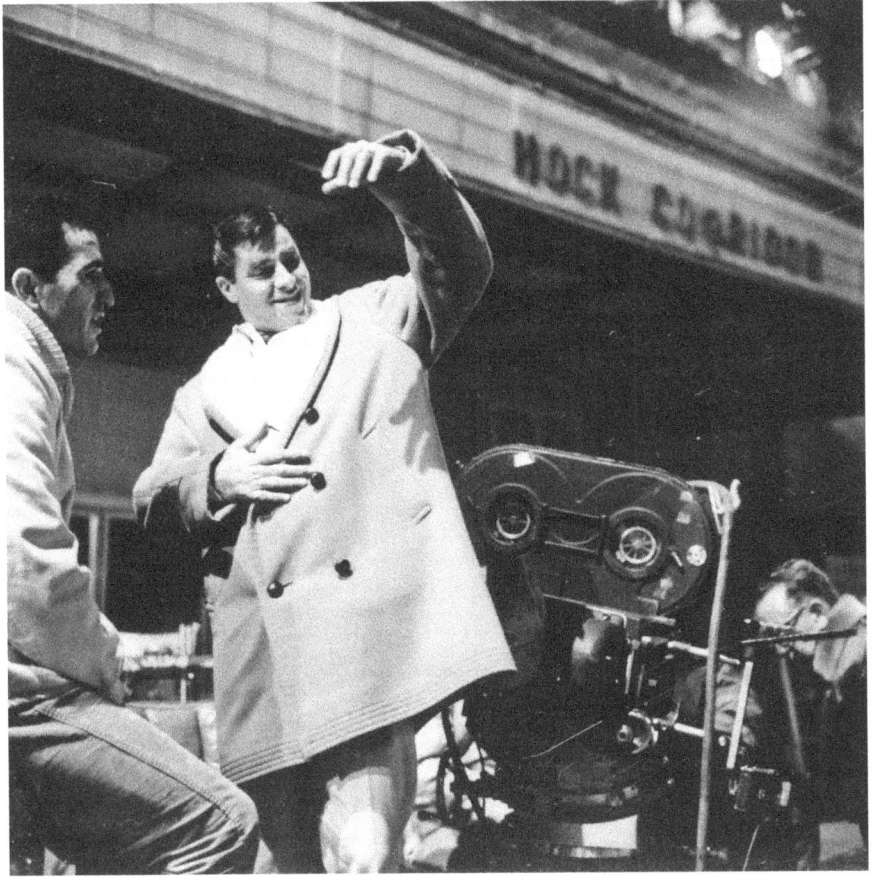

Hanging out after hours on the Paramount backlot with Lewis while shooting *The Disorderly Orderly* (1964), Manoogian listens to the boss's stories of his early days in show biz. Always an impeccable dresser, Lewis sports a Sy Devore shearling lined camel hair coat which he would only wear for one season before giving it away (courtesy Carl Manoogian).

James Caan, was shot at major US speedways such as Daytona, Charlotte Motor, Riverside and Ascot. Picking up the skills to rig car mounts on the film (with all the racing sequences), Manoogian enjoyed the challenge of automotive camera platforms so much that it ultimately became a specialty. Using the metallurgy skills acquired during his Navy days, he began machining his own custom and hostess hood mounts in his shop, which came to be known as the best in the industry.

Returning to the Lewis group for *Three on a Couch*, his close relationship with Jerry continued. Pushing dolly and operating crane on the picture, Carl was such a beloved character on set that for his birthday director Lewis had a cake served with a candle and kiss from co-star Janet Leigh.

In the mid–60s, Lewis' star waned and the studio held off on funding his projects. Still in demand, however, Manoogian was able to go back to the Paramount grip department and get assigned by Fred Johnson to work on the new Henry Hathaway western *Nevada Smith*. With Steve McQueen in the title role and heavies played by Karl Malden, Martin Landau and Arthur Kennedy. The action was capably lensed by old school master Lucien

Regaled with a rousing version of "Happy Birthday" on the set of Columbia Pictures' *Three on a Couch* in October 1965, Manoogian smiles broadly as Janet Leigh (center) and pal Jerry Lewis ham it up with a cake included. It was the eighth of a dozen pictures they did together. By this point the guys were so close that Lewis was giving Manoogian all his second-hand Sy Devore wardrobe, generally after wearing it only once (courtesy Carl Manoogian).

On location in Lone Pine's Alabama Hills region to film *Nevada Smith* (1966), key grip Carl Manoogian (standing on platform to the right of camera) poses for a quick snapshot as he shows the picture's star, Steve McQueen (seated on top of ladder), the framing for the action to come. Standing behind McQueen (wearing a white cowboy hat) is director of photography Lucien Ballard. Steadying the ladder behind McQueen is company grip Howard Hagadorn. Note the "cutting-edge" camera tripod, known affectionately as a "stomp-up" due to the need to use a pneumatic foot pump to fill the movable column with air (courtesy Carl Manoogian).

Ballard of *True Grit*, *The Wild Bunch* and *The Getaway* fame. Another of Manoogian's supporters, he would come to be one of his favorites. Pushing dolly on the feature, Carl remembers the evening of the knife fight in the corral scene, where Max Sands (McQueen) sticks it to Jesse Cole (Landau). It was staged above long horn steers in a pen. Manoogian watched in horror as some of the cattle hooked a post from the corral, causing a momentary surge of animals towards McQueen and the camera. Luckily the steers turned back when faced

Working as a small splinter unit on the edge of Convict Lake in Inyo National Forest in Bishop, California, during filming of *Nevada Smith* (1966), Manoogian (standing behind camera in a white sport shirt) listens to the staging ideas of director Henry Hathaway (center with cigar in hand) as he imparts them to his actors. Kneeling in the water (left) is Steve McQueen while Brian Keith (squatting next to him) delivers his lines. Standing extreme right in a cowboy hat is cinematographer Lucien Ballard, whose efforts to make the picture look natural are evident from his choice of locations and the simplicity of the shiny board set-up lighting it (courtesy Carl Manoogian).

with the lights and equipment in their way. "McQueen moved fast," Carl said, "He was five feet away when the steer hit the rail!"

The next couple of years seemed like one long western for Manoogian, often shooting at difficult locations such as Vasquez Rocks or the various ranches. His ability to operate cranes on bad roads and trails enabled pictures like *Hostile Guns* (starring George Montgomery and Tab Hunter) as well as *Fort Utah* (with Virginia Mayo) to become money in the bank for the Paramount crane man. Continuing western work in 1968, Manoogian did the Charlton Heston film *Will Penny*, then found himself back on familiar turf at Vasquez Rocks for *Buckskin* that fall. Kidding about the often utilized location, he joked, "I was considering building a nice motel across the road for film crews that year."

In 1969, Manoogian was happily key gripping on DP Wallace Kelley's *The Comic*. Well versed in all aspects of cameras, cranes, dollies and construction, he took to the leadership position with a well-grounded appreciation of the work to be done. Manoogian next did another 1960s assignment which was one of the most challenging of his career: *Hud*, starring Paul

Newman and Patricia Neal. Regarding the issues of working with the cinematographer James Wong Howe, who photographed such iconic films as *Sweet Smell of Success* and *The Old Man and the Sea*, Carl told of a dolly move covering Paul Newman as he walked up the sidewalk leading to the door of a house. Howe wanted the dolly's timing one way, whereas the director Martin Ritt instructed him to do the opposite. The outcome was a bad take which resulted in a five-minute private conversation between Ritt and Howe. Returning to the set, the DP said to Carl in front of the crew, "That's one argument we don't need to have again, right, Mr. Manoogian?" Buying Carl dinner later that night, the DP explained that there was nothing wrong with his dolly moves; he just needed to get things straight with director Ritt so he could stay on the picture and shoot things his way.

The second important relationship that Manoogian forged (after Jerry Lewis) was with

Thigh deep in rushing water while shooting the climax of *Nevada Smith*, Manoogian (in white t-shirt) helps to steady the camera aimed at Karl Malden as cinematographer Lucien Ballard (standing on platform in a cowboy hat) and director Henry Hathaway (megaphone in hand) watch the scene play out. The sequence was shot in the Hot Creek area of Mammoth Lakes, California, in August 1965 (courtesy Carl Manoogian).

BBS Productions, the brainchild of producers Burt and Bob Schneider and Bob Rafelson. The first flick Manoogian key gripped for them was *Getting Straight* in 1970. Paired with cinematic royalty Laszlo Kovacs, the feature was one of many that the group would do together.

After pushing dolly for cinematographer Wallace Kelley on the second BBS outing, Godfrey Cambridge's *Watermelon Man* (1970), Manoogian was off to Hawaii for the epic *The Hawaiians*. Working again for Lucien Ballard as crane man and all-around problem solver, he was put to the test when told to construct a 24-foot platform off a cliff's edge, 600 feet above the ground. He engineered a cantilevered diving board rig from 2" × 12"

Pictured left holding a hammer is key grip Carl Manoogian on the Jerry Lewis–helmed *Which Way to the Front* (1970). Close friends with Lewis throughout their many features together, Manoogian attributed their great rapport to a combination of trust, humor, and mutual respect for each other's craft. In the background (between Manoogian and Lewis) is ex–Dodger great Willie Davis and Borscht Belt funnyman Jan Murray. As a gag to break his boss' concentration during rehearsals, Manoogian would noisily drop a hammer or some other tool. In retaliation Lewis put up a $100 bounty for anyone who could seize Manoogian's hammer. With no bona fide takers on the crew, Manoogian had the best boy try to claim the prize. It didn't work—Lewis got wise and refused to pay (courtesy Carl Manoogian).

Manoogian (right) shares a light moment on the set of *Which Way to the Front* (1970) with producer-director-actor Jerry Lewis. Note the warm inscription by Lewis (courtesy Carl Manoogian).

lumber and plywood arching out into space. The platform allowed for the downward coverage of a sacrificial ceremony to be shot, substituting a dummy for the human to be thrown off the cliff. Ballard had confidence in "his man": He was the first to walk out on the new rig after Manoogian declared it safe.

As cutting-edge mechanics interested Carl, new technology and gear were one of his loves. Manoogian was proud of his contribution to the creation of the Chapman Pee Wee dolly. The Pee Wee (at half the weight and size of other machines of its day) still allowed for maximum camera boom heights of 59½ inches as well as precise operator-ridden performance, on or off portable track. Manoogian's Pee Wee epiphany came as a result of the back pain experienced from carrying a heavy dolly (on end) up a narrow staircase while shooting *Prisoner of 2nd Avenue*. Beginning with his father-in-law's company (Chapman),

Carl assisted in the design and manufacture of the first prototype of his idea. Unfortunately, Ralph Chapman never gave Carl any credit (or money) for his concept. In return, Manoogian stayed away from the old man for good. Ironically, the Pee Wee is still widely used today as an in-between dolly, where larger units are not feasible.

Back with boss Jerry Lewis on *Which Way to the Front* in late 1970, Manoogian served as key grip and playmate to the comedic impresario. Consumed with his directing and acting on the film, Lewis often sought momentary diversions such as playing "hot-pepper" baseball catch with Carl, where the two really let the leather fly! One day after throwing it around at lunch, a new assistant director came over to the former pro and told him to stop playing catch with Lewis as it was costing production time and money. After lunch, Jerry asked his old friend what the AD wanted. "He says for me not to play catch with you between set-ups any more," Manoogian sighed, "'cause it's costing the production too much time." Infuriated, Lewis strode over to the young AD and said, "Listen, pal, so long as I'm signing the checks on this picture [which he was, as producer and director], I'll play catch with my friend Carl whenever I like. Do you understand?"

Picking up more films through BBS in 1971, Manoogian was paired with DP Bill Butler on Jack Nicholson's directorial debut, *Drive, He Said*. Another BBS production that year, *The Last Picture Show*, was a surprise success: Helmed by Peter Bogdanovich, it received multiple Oscar nominations including Best Picture, Cinematography, Writing and Directing, and won Oscars for Best Supporting Actor and Actress. Contributing to the real-life look of the feature was Carl's method of placing the camera at eye level, whether on dolly, sticks or crane. To ensure the perfect height of the various actors' points of view, Manoogian devised a measuring stick method to match each established line of sight quickly. This simpler approach would be Manoogian's trademark throughout his career. Joking that no one working on the film thought it was going to be very good, Carl said that with funds short for crew salaries, he and Bob Surtees were each given one percent of the gross deal to make up for the difference in pay. "As the movie was a hit," he added, "that one percent came out to over 10 grand."

Carl key gripped for old friend Laszlo Kovacs on *The King of Marvin Gardens* in 1972. The BBS projects finished with a low-budget whimper: the Jane Fonda-Donald Sutherland snoozer *Steelyard Blues* in 1973, followed by *The Terminal Man* late in the year.

With the end of one connection for the now in-demand key grip, another opportunity presented itself with the third important career marriage for Carl Manoogian: his work with cinematographer Philip Lathrop. They did 17 pictures over ten years; the two made not only films but a friendship that lasted long after the lights went out. The relationship began early in '74 when Manoogian was assigned to key some makeup tests being shot at Warner Bros for the movie *Mame*. Since Warners was not Carl's home lot, they wanted to have their own key grip do the movie. Impressed with Manoogian's hustle and imaginative problem-solving from the tests, however, cinematographer Lathrop went over some heads and insisted that Carl get the feature.

Speaking of imaginative problem-solving, the latter half of 1974 was filled with big-budget catastrophe for Manoogian as he did *Earthquake* and *Airport '75* that year. Regarding *Earthquake*, he told of his amusement at using a rippling mirror technique to duplicate a building tremor for the initial action sequences. Utilizing Universal's Black Tower (where all the studio big shots work) in the scene, Carl laughed at the insider's joke of that structure being destroyed. "When it was shown in dailies," he said, "everyone applauded when it crumbled." After *Earthquake*, Manoogian and crew were immediately drafted to begin work on *Airport '75* in the fall of '74. Moving quickly to seize the momentum of *Earthquake*'s box office, Universal spared no expense at bringing the Jack Smight-directed feature to screen. Manoogian was required to construct a hidden safety handle for the dangerous airplane-to-airplane transfer that star Charlton Heston's stunt double Joe Canutt performed in the picture. Without the invisible grab-bar, the stunt man could have easily been swept off the top of the jet due to air speed. (Joe's dad Yakima Canutt was Heston's stunt double in the chariot race from *Ben-Hur*.)

Forever hustling, Carl Manoogian grabbed his next assignment between Lathrop flicks keying for old pal Bob Surtees on the pilot and first season of *Starsky and Hutch* in 1975. Happy as a kid in a candy store with the numerous car rigs needed on the action-oriented series, Carl said, "That Gran Torino was built like a tank, which made it fun to rig every show."

Back with Lathrop in '75, Manoogian keyed two movies that were almost complete opposites: *The Black Bird* with George Segal and Neil Simon's *Prisoner of 2nd Avenue*, starring Jack Lemmon and Anne Bancroft. However, it was Walter Hill's breakout hit in 1975, *Hard Times*, which would test Carl's abilities to their max. Aside from the tight 38-day shooting schedule and Lathrop photographing the fight scenes with up to five cameras (as well as Charles Bronson doing his own stunts), the key grip was challenged to engineer a 14-foot-high platform to capture direct overhead shots of the fighters. Required to "bridge down" from the original roof timbers of a 100-year-old New Orleans warehouse (to allow the lens an unobstructed image), the perch was constructed on site from available 2" × 12" lumber and nails. The resulting shots (including the final fight, which took all night to photograph) earned Carl a round of applause from the crew and Bronson alike at evening's end.

While still recovering from the physical strain of making *Hard Times*, Carl was called back to work his fifth feature with Lathrop: Sam Peckinpah's *Killer Elite*. Carl recalled a humorous goof on the movie: The opening sequence of blowing up a building didn't go quite the way Peckinpah had envisioned it. Rigged with explosives designed to flatten the structure, the steel-reinforced former fire station withstood the blast, and when the smoke cleared, to the amazement of the crew, it was still half standing. Peckinpah, never at a loss for words, declared angrily, "I guess we should have used more explosives!" He was unable to do it again; the shot with the frame of the building still showing was the one used in the picture.

With his next assignment staged at sea, Manoogian was challenged by Lathrop to do some of the most dangerous camera rigging of his career. *Swashbuckler* (1976) with Robert Shaw, James Earl Jones and Peter Boyle, was filmed aboard a tall ship in the waters of Puerto Vallarta, Mexico, and Singapore Lake on Universal's backlot. To illustrate the difficulty of rigging the cameras high in the mast heads, Manoogian told of situating a young operator 80 feet above the deck for a shot; the inexperienced cameraman froze due to temporary acrophobia. Using a calm voice, Carl tied the man to himself and brought the nearly catatonic assistant down.

Motion pictures were getting bigger in Hollywood by the late '70s while Manoogian was mellowing, working only three large projects in 1977: *Oh God*, *Airport '77*, and a TV

Walter Hill's *Hard Times* (1974) was among the best work Manoogian did with director of photography Phil Lathrop. It was lensed around old New Orleans docks and warehouses; the 38-day shooting schedule allotted by Columbia Pictures left little time for fun. In this photograph, though, Manoogian is sharing a joke with jail guard Lee Cosgrove, a part-time actor and full-time grip (courtesy Carl Manoogian).

version of *Captains Courageous*. Subbing for Victor Kemper's key grip on *Oh God*, Carl loved the stories George Burns told in between set-ups and was sorry to see the film end.

The flooding aircraft scenes in *Airport '77* nearly washed Carl out of the business. While shooting on a 747 mockup, 500-gallon forced fluid dump tanks were released without warning, as Manoogian was tying down his camera. Staying underwater to avoid being slammed into the cockpit walls or being struck by the toppling loose gear, he was able to

Crane operator Carl Manoogian and director Jerry Lewis play blind man's bluff aboard the camera platform known as "Old #2." *The Errand Boy* was shot in the summer of 1961 with Paramount Pictures' administrative building doubling as "Paramutual Studios." After replacing the first operator who had trouble with the crane's size, Lewis immediately procured Manoogian from the grip department for the remainder of the feature after hearing of his skill. Manoogian showed a deft touch on the camera platform (seen beneath Lewis as well as in the top left corner of the frame), which was employed for coverage on the massive doll house sets. It required the addition of a 19-foot extension to clear the three-story structures; Manoogian was the only operator capable of controlling the 32-foot-long arm on all the moves (courtesy Carl Manoogian).

surface after the wave subsided and call out to effects to stop the test. Undaunted, Carl continued the mechanics to secure his camera rig until lunch was called and he was able to dry out and change clothes. Once again his Navy salvage days were paying off.

Finally in 1977, *Captains Courageous* proved to be just the vacation Carl needed after surviving the "disaster era" films. Revived by the beautiful scenery of late autumn Maine, he returned to Hollywood ready to work and didn't have long to wait. The new project was Walter Hill's dynamic chase film *The Driver* (1978) starring Ryan O'Neal. Back in familiar territory, Carl was doing the car mounts for the feature. One crash taught him an interesting lesson. Rigging three cameras along the side of a Mercedes Sedan (using one of Manoogian's proprietary mounts), he was inside the vehicle when the Mercedes hit a dip at high speed. Loaded with cameras, the sedan went into a spin and hit a cement column. Shaken but not seriously injured, Carl vowed from then on to let others do the stunt gags.

Manoogian's success continued as he keyed *Moment by Moment* for Phil Lathrop. Next Carl and his DP were presented with another effects-laden film, *Airport '79*. By this time, mechanical gimbals and blue screen were just starting to get really big, so it was only natural that Universal and director David Lowell Rich would incorporate these techniques in this cutting edge cinema. They utilized the outside blue sky wall at Universal; Manoogian

Sailing off the coast of Puerto Vallarta, Mexico, for the Robert Shaw pirate movie *Swashbuckler* (1976), cast and crew merged into one during the 46-day shooting schedule aboard the *Golden Hind* replica tall ship. Barking orders from the bridge, director James Goldstone (center, with his right hand up) checks the port bow light while key grip Carl Manoogian (to the left of ladder, perched on a railing) laughs at his sudden pirate-like snarl. *Swashbuckler* was a difficult undertaking due to the cramped space on the ship as well as the blazing sun. It was an underappreciated gem, with fine acting by Shaw and first-rate lens work by Phil Lathrop (sitting at the bottom of the stairs in a white hat and shirt). Very much in the swim of things, helmer Goldstone fully embraced the idea of working at sea by taking ocean dips each morning — despite warnings of sharks in the area (courtesy Carl Manoogian).

On *Swashbuckler* (1976), Manoogian (shirtless in long pants) sets a high hat mount for the camera. Required to do everything from rig cameras in the crow's nest to acting as substitute ship's carpenter (fixing leaks in the bow), Manoogian had only two grips to help him cover the entire boat. Squatting in the craft's center, wearing a white jacket and holding a pole, helmer James Goldstone focuses on the task at hand despite bouts of seasickness he experienced in the small vessel (courtesy Carl Manoogian).

remembered the rigs being 20 feet high to allow for all the up-angle photography. "These things were huge," he said, recalling the gimbals and Concord set pieces built into and around them. "Hardly mock-ups, they were full-scale and heavier than the real Concord because of the weight of the Fiberglas."

The next decade for Manoogian proceeded at a pace where he could relax and enjoy. No longer grabbing anything that paid his freight, he was now more interested in fare closer to home and more inviting to his heart. Or those that paid the mortgage, as he says.

The first flick Carl keyed in 1980 was his fourteenth with Lathrop. By this time, the two men had formed a working relationship that seldom required more than a look and a few words between them to discuss an entire set-up. On the Jack Smight–directed *Loving Couples*, starring Shirley MacLaine and James Coburn, even words were often not necessary. "We had Shirley MacLaine going," Manoogian says. "She thought me and Phil were clairvoyant with how he asked for stuff, as it came without any conversation. Actually, in a way we kinda were, having been on all those shows together."

Universal Pictures' *All Night Long* came next in 1980 for Manoogian. The location-heavy story starring Gene Hackman and Barbra Streisand was lensed by Lathrop so shooting it was pretty much a snap. Already acclimated to lighting female lead Streisand, Manoogian's rapport and flag-setting skill on the sometimes persnickety star had her happy throughout the movie, as well as beautifully lit.

Lathrop took 1980 off while Carl was hired by DP Dennis Dalzell for Richard Pryor's soapy kid-fest *Bustin' Loose* in 1981. Never losing his touch with rigging vehicles (even buses), Manoogian created lamp mounts that bolted under the bus frame to allow the placement of lights below the windows. The rig worked so well that once installed, it lasted the entire picture without any failures. And as a good one-third of the film takes place on the bus, it was a vital piece of engineering that helped keep an otherwise troubled production on schedule.

After finishing *Bustin' Loose*, Carl returned to his old standby Phil Lathrop on director Wim Wenders' *Hammett* (1982). Produced by Francis Ford Coppola, the Zoetrope offering was a throwback piece of *almost* film noir that Carl thoroughly enjoyed making. The final Lathrop project key-gripped by Manoogian was back at Paramount Pictures in mid–1982, *Jekyll and Hyde Together Again*. The Mark Blankfield farce of the Robert Louis Stevenson classic was not much of a capper to the great cinematographer's career, which had finally come to its end. Although panned by critics due to Blankfield's mugging for the camera, the photography of the Jekyll-to-Hyde transformation was first rate.

Approaching 60 years of age by the time Manoogian did his final large features *Johnny Dangerously* (1983) and Michael Crichton's *Runaway* (1984), the path of his 30 years of filmmaking would next branch off into the realm of episodic television and movie-of-the-week projects. Much like a baseball player whose career begins as a starting pitcher throwing fast balls, then becomes a reliever with a good curve as the years diminish his physical skills, so too is the fate of motion picture mechanics over the course of time. After three decades of gripping 14-hour shifts, six days a week — eventually the machine wears down. The answer for Carl would be keying pilots and television shows until his retirement some 20 years later.

Whether key-gripping diverse network offerings like *Scarecrow and Mrs. King* or the NBC mini-series *The Atlanta Child Murders* (1984), Manoogian gave back to the industry that he loved by teaching the next generation of grips the tricks of the trade. Further NBC minis and episodic programs would keep Carl busy throughout the mid–80s. Titles such as *Love on the Run* and *Promises to Keep* would pay the bills; yet it was on Angela Lansbury's *Murder She Wrote* that Manoogian would feel personal fulfillment. Passing the torch of leadership to his dolly-pushing protégé Russ Nordsteadt on the series, Carl would ultimately see his mentoring result in Nordsteadt's rise to the president of Local 80, which is a position he still holds today.

With the ever-expanding universe of television content encompassing cable venues, by the late 1980s, Manoogian was busier than ever. Hired by past DP Dennis Dalzell to key grip *The Betty Ford Story* in 1986 (then *Mike Hammer* and *Hotel* throughout the next year), Carl became the episodic–mini-series master of Hollywood; providing producers with a million dollar motion picture mind, at the cut rate price of television. Often called upon to put out production fires, Carl's wealth of knowledge regarding cranes, dollies and lighting meant that the shows he did usually came in on time and under budget.

The final decade of Manoogian's craft was an extraordinary study of a man who loved what he did. Still much in demand, at 65 years old he often worked two shows at a time as a dolly and crane specialist. Getting pilots like 1988's *Sisterhood* off the ground (again with Dalzell), as well as *Perfect Strangers* that year, Manoogian lived for the challenge of the dolly shot or crane move and how to teach others how to get it.

The final three series that would carry Carl Manoogian to retirement were *Family Matters*, *The Love Boat* and *Step by Step* which he did on and off for seven years, making it the most prolific program of his career. "*Love Boat* was great," Manoogian said when queried about the guest stars used on the show. "We had everybody from Milton Berle to Van Johnson on the boat and as old school Hollywood, they were fun to work around."

When asked for words of advice to the next generation of grips, Carl replied empathetically, "Learn the profession. Study lighting. Be prepared so that if you get a shot, you know what to do." Certainly, Carl Manoogian has always known what to do. Among his crowning achievements during the long service to Tinseltown was the issuance of his gold card, signifying 50 years with IATSE's Local 80. Always true to his grip craft and respected by his crews, Manoogian loved what he did and it still shows.

Back in his packed machine shop (amid camera risers, hostess trays, special car mounts and crates of expensive-looking hardware), the eighty-six-year-old grip excitedly demonstrated his newest hood mount. A beautiful one touch ball leveler rig made from polished billet aluminum stock, it looked like a piece belonging in the Museum of Modern Art. "If you know anybody who could use these things," Carl called to me as I began down his driveway at interview's end, "they're here for the asking."

Like the man who mastered all from lathes to dollies at his father-in-law's crane factory, to the guy who permitted my four-hour interview sessions for this book, Carl Manoogian is one of those rare folks of motion picture below-the-line lore, who meet up to the reputation of their work in the business. His love of the job is only equaled by his love of people who did the work. And like the innovator that Carl was in his own times, he still believes in the strength of the individual to make a difference in Hollywood today.

3

Gene LeBell, Stuntman

Of the many departments that comprise a film crew, one below-the-line faction stands apart from the rest: stunts. Aside from the various physical characteristics these bold folks possess (such as athleticism, balance, tumbling ability, and a general disregard for the laws of physics), they are also infused with a good dose of ego, guts, brains, and brawn. While this odd mixture of performance and painful make-believe has been part of the motion picture business since Vasquez Rocks saw its first western, one such storied practitioner of the art of filmed self-abuse is legendary stuntman Judo Gene LeBell, "the toughest man alive."

Born in Los Angeles the second week of October 1932, Gene's early days were one of privilege and love. His father Maurice was a well respected Hollywood surgeon whose young son was the apple of his eye. Gene was also doted on by his mother Eileen. LeBell's childhood took a tragic turn when his dad was mortally injured at the beach while body surfing with his children. The sole support of the family after her husband's demise, Eileen quickly found employment as the personal secretary to Frank Garbutt, owner of the Olympic Auditorium. Unable to look after a small boy while working full time, she enrolled six-year-old Gene into the prestigious California Military Academy. Initially having difficulty adjusting to life in uniform (not to mention feeling the crushing loss of his beloved father), the young cadet was frequently punished for attention-seeking outbursts which landed him countless demerits and the nickname "Mr. Looking for Trouble." One infraction (which would later become LeBell's trademark in the wrestling ring) was choking out a bully who had pestered him during parade formation. Hiding in the school's stables to avoid being paddled for his transgression, Gene was discovered by an old Cossack who worked there. Becoming the lonely kid's first mentor, he taught him all about horses, from psychology and grooming to English saddle and trick riding. "Years later," LeBell said, "his instruction was responsible for me landing horse-work in westerns as an Indian, because I could ride bareback."

When Gene was ten in 1942, his mother married a major fight promoter who did a lot of bookings at the Olympic, Cal Eaton, a well respected businessman and top-notch boxing guy. The marriage would eventually lead to Eileen becoming a promotions icon in her own right, alongside her husband.

By the age of 13 (following more years in military school while wrestling in the summers), Gene began to take odd jobs at the Olympic for his mother. They seemed to provide training for his stunt career to come. Tasked with changing the spent par-lamps mounted fifty feet above the arena floor, he had to transverse nine-inch catwalks covered in pigeon waste, while risking electric shock or falling to his death while screwing in the replacement globes. "I liked the adventure of being up so high," LeBell said, "the danger made me feel grown up."

At fifteen, LeBell was hanging out with all types of fighters that he met at gyms and various venues like the Olympic while working for his mother, then manager of the auditorium. An interesting footnote from this time was Gene's friendship with gangster Mickey Cohen. A regular at the fights, Cohen was well acquainted with Eileen (as he also backed boxers) and used to dote on "the kid," buying him handfuls of candy and hot dogs whenever he saw him. "As my mom ran the concessions," LeBell said with a boyish grin, "I didn't pay for anything. But the fact that it was Mickey handing me those foil-wrapped torpedoes (with two dogs in each bun!) — that I found so cool at 15." When the gangster was shot and landed at Cedars Hospital, Gene (who was there due to a bout with anemia) wandered up to his pal's police-guarded room for a visit. Startled by the sudden sight of a teenager in nothing but skivvies, the cop on duty demanded in a loud tone to know what he wanted. Before he could answer, a huge bodyguard stepped from the room and vouched for Gene, inviting him in. "There was Mickey Cohen," LeBell recalled, "buck-shot wounds red with blood through his bandages, and he says, 'I hear you don't feel so well, kid. Anything I can do?'"

Coming off his brief illness, Gene sought to work out as hard as ever, and went to Van Rose's fitness supply in Burbank to purchase additional barbells. Talked into Judo lessons by Rose as the quickest way to build bulk up, he was soon studying with a Master of the Osaka system from Oakland, Larry Coughran. Embracing his first Sensei's teachings like the Holy Grail, LeBell instantly gravitated towards the art, and became a self-proclaimed Judo nut. A Hollywood bit player and fellow Judo enthusiast, John Halloran once took him to work out with a friend — who turned out to be movie star James Cagney. Halloran had trained Cagney for a terrific Judo fight (and played his opponent, the evil Japanese Captain Oshima) in Frank Lloyd's *Blood on the Sun* in 1945); therefore, Halloran knew the famous actor was wild about the sport and thought he would enjoy sparring with 16-year-old prodigy LeBell. Taking the impressionable young man off to the side, Halloran gave him his first solid bit of mentoring when it came to working with stars in Tinseltown: "Don't go too hard," he warned, "and don't try any throws. Just be defensive and make *him* look great in the process." Taking the advice to heart, Gene allowed Cagney to totally dominate him, flying through the air and bouncing off the ground as though he was fighting an unbeatable Master each throw. At workout's end, unaware that LeBell had held back, Cagney (in a moment of feeling all-powerful), said to him, "You're incredible, kid, terrific. Keep up the practicing and you'll be beating me in no time!" and then strolled away to take a shower. Turning to Halloran, LeBell muttered, "But John ... I barely did anything. It was *all* him." Years later, Halloran said it was part of LeBell's martial arts and acting education, to know when to go full-out, and when *not* to.

Gene continued to gain skill while studying with increasingly better Judo instructors, such as the L.A.P.D.'s Jack Sergil. By the time he was 17, he was attending some of the toughest dojos in Los Angeles. Just six months later, Larry Coughran sent him to study at a strict Japanese school called Hollywood Dojo. It was run by old-school Nipponese Judo Masters Tadasu Iida and Tasuke Hagio; the rules of study were pure to the art's form including the speaking of Japanese at all times as well as physically brutal sparring which often left participants bruised and bloody. Rising to the dojo's challenges over a two-year period, Gene ultimately became one of the Master's prize pupils.

Although immersed in all things Judo, the 17-year-old was still answerable to his mother, and soon found himself enrolled at Pierce College studying Animal Husbandry. Less than a year later, the Korean War began and Gene opted to enlist in the U.S. Coast Guard Reserves, rather than be drafted when turning 18 that fall. Continuing to pursue Judo in the Reserves, he was able to persuade Coast Guard brass that he should represent the Service in the 1954 A.A.U. Judo Nationals, held at Cesar Pavilion in San Francisco. Ultimately winning the heavyweight title by defeating Kenji Yamada (a seasoned Japanese veteran of the sport), then repeating with a victory as National Champion in 1955, Gene's accomplishments began to gain worldwide notoriety. The only Caucasian to compete and place first from a Judo event *in* post-war Japan, Gene won 18 matches in two days, and did so with all standing throws — never leaving his feet to grapple on the mat with his opponent.

As much as LeBell enjoyed Judo, he soon realized its amateur status would prohibit him from ever making money competing in the sport. Opting for his first love of grappling instead, Judo Gene was soon booked in pro wrestling bouts at his family's Olympic Auditorium. Performing under the ring name "The Hangman" (a masked heavy of the nastiest kind, who carried a prop noose), LeBell's exposure on the live-televised wrestling matches soon had Hollywood knocking on his door to do gags for TV shows. After being bad-guy bait for the likes of Bo-Bo Brazil and Superstar Billy Graham, Gene would next be dominated by a different sort of adversary — the movie star.

This desire to make believe and have fun while doing it drew LeBell to his next passion — stunts. In 1955 he was hired to do a fight gag for *The Adventures of Ozzie and Harriet*. Brought in by old wrestling pal Jack Alaina (who had transitioned to stunt coordinator), Gene was tasked with playing a heavy who gets out of line with Ricky Nelson at a dance. He was to be thrown into a real brick wall in the sequence. Director Ozzie Nelson asked him if he wanted a pad attached to the surface before being flipped into it. Responding in his best bandito accent while channeling *The Treasure of the Sierra Madre*, the twenty-something tough-guy said, "Pads ... I don't need no stinking pads!" Earning a much coveted SAG card during the series (allowing him to work on union projects in Hollywood), LeBell said, "Ozzie was such a considerate person. In addition to caring physically, he also taught me about contracts and residuals. That education made me a lot of money in the long run."

Continuing to seek the limelight in all its forms, Judo Gene added another training regimen (in addition to martial arts, grappling, and boxing disciplines) when wrestling a Canadian black bear owned by friend Tuffy Truesdale, a well respected purveyor of various animals for motion picture and television. The bear, Victor, was an excellent means of workout (and PR) for the up-and-coming stuntman. "Victor was a sweetheart," Gene said. "Wrestling him at supermarket openings then later for movie stunts was great for my Judo. If you can get used to being grabbed by a 700-pound bear, then a human isn't much of a challenge."

Gene was tipped-off by promoter Jules Strongbow at L.A.'s Olympic auditorium, about an open call for a villain needed on a live action Superman road-show. Casting for Mr. Kryptonite drew fighters, ham actors, and washed-up athletic types from all over Los Angeles; LeBell who showed-up wearing a white martial arts Gi and proceeded to exaggerate a series of falls at the hands of George Reeves during his audition. Upon seeing Gene hit the mat, and then flip over into a tumble-sault while bouncing back to his feet, Superman said to the audition manager, "That's it. He's our guy. Tell everyone else to go home." Traveling on the road in a caravan of three autos, Reeves, Noel Neill (the original Lois Lane), Gene

LeBell, and a band would make live appearances at movie theatres and television stations to put on the Superman skits. During one appearance at a Culver City theater opening, a seven-year-old boy holding his father's pistol squeezed off a shot at Superman, to see if bullets really bounced off. Luckily for Reeves, the kid's aim was poor, and the Man of Steel was spared the accidental lead injection.

Befriended and ultimately mentored by the down-to-earth star, Gene often worked out with Reeves (whom he viewed as a father figure), doing everything from wrestling and Judo to weight-lifting together. Not without its danger, the sparring was rather spirited between the two men. While practicing a submission move with Gene, the actor's larynx and fine baritone voice were damaged when too much force was accidentally applied to a choke hold. Unable to continue singing for the live radio broadcast parts of the show, Reeves bore no grudge, instead playing classical guitar accompanying the band.

Gene told of being conned into coming over to Reeves' house (allegedly for a routine workout), then being served a full steak dinner, with waiter, delivered from the Brown Derby. "There were two beautiful filet mignons," LeBell said like he could still taste them,

Gene LeBell (left) celebrated his 25th birthday at the Benedict Canyon home of George Reeves (right) in October 1958. LeBell's arm around Noel Neill hints at slightly more than a casual relationship. A dozen years his senior, the vivacious former pin-up girl helped LeBell with his fledgling acting skills while he tutored her in stunt work (courtesy Gene LeBell).

"and after I devoured the first one (including a big salad and baked potato), George told me he was really not hungry and that the food had been for me all along. I ate that one too. He was the kindest man I ever knew."

While theories regarding Reeves' untimely demise continue to sell books, it's Gene's belief that the shot which killed his friend was fired by the actor's girlfriend and not by his own hand. According to official studio sources (and LeBell), Reeves had been offered a lucrative lead in the upcoming western TV series *Wagon Train*, and was looking forward to *not* wearing "the monkey suit" (as he jokingly called his Superman costume) in the future. Reflecting on his friend's fate, Gene said Reeves told him he would only do *Wagon Train* if he (Gene) accepted the Gabby Hayes sidekick role in the series.

By 1960 Gene was starting to get regular stunt work in town. Continuing to build his name recognition while still wrestling, he picked up a tailor-suited fighting gig on *The Jack Benny Show*. Contacted by producers (as the comedian was a big wrestling fan), Gene was brought in for a charity event featured on the live program. Recalling his first meeting with the sarcastic comic, he said that Benny came over and introduced himself by saying, "I've seen you wrestle on TV, and I'm not impressed with you one bit." Turning to the grappler standing by LeBell (6' 2" Billy "The Count" Vargas), Benny added, "And I'm not impressed with you big guys. You're a couple of Jabones. If you two smart off to me, I'll annihilate you, I'll mutilate you, I'll sue you!" The skit had Benny getting tangled in the wrestling ring ropes upon his entrance, then getting into it with pro grapplers Vargas and Gene "The Hangman" LeBell. When Benny was thrown from the ring at fight's end, he was doubled by stunt man Ronnie Rondell, Jr. The next scene takes place in a hospital room where all the wrestlers are shown lying in beds, sporting casts with traction; the comedian is standing by the door looking refreshed. Speaking into camera, Benny said in a tough voice, "Don't mess with me boy, or you'll regret it!"

"I liked him right away," LeBell said, "Guys like Jack Benny were human beings who brought a sense of humor to the job with them. And the viewing public could tell."

Gene continued to make Hollywood contacts, especially while teaching at his newly formed dojo around the corner from Paramount Studios. He met a young actor named Michael Landon from a new western called *Bonanza*. After signing-up for Judo lessons, Landon soon drafted Gene to be shot off horses and beaten up in bar fights as the show needed him. Recalling a day's work on *Bonanza* where he went from being the back end of a mule suit to having his lights punched out by the 6' 4", 300-pound Dan Blocker, LeBell mused, "I always got beat up on that show, but never killed. And as hard as Blocker could punch, even pulling it, death was an option." Ultimately forming a long-lasting friendship with Landon, Gene did many episodes of his later show *Little House on the Prairie*, including one episode where he played a sizable speaking role opposite Merlin Olsen. Told by Landon that his character would wrestle Olsen, and needed to have a thick German accent, Gene went off to study with a dialect coach to ready himself for his big part. Reading during a rehearsal, LeBell's German was so awful that all Landon could do was laugh. "I was a little hurt at first," he admitted, "But then I realized, I can do a hundred things better as a stuntman, than *any* actor can. Maybe I'll improve."

Becoming known for an ever-increasing repertoire of stunt abilities in Hollywood, (especially martial arts and odd animal calls), Gene was once tasked with doing a bear attack for *Lassie*. Hired because of his reputation of training with bears during his earlier Judo

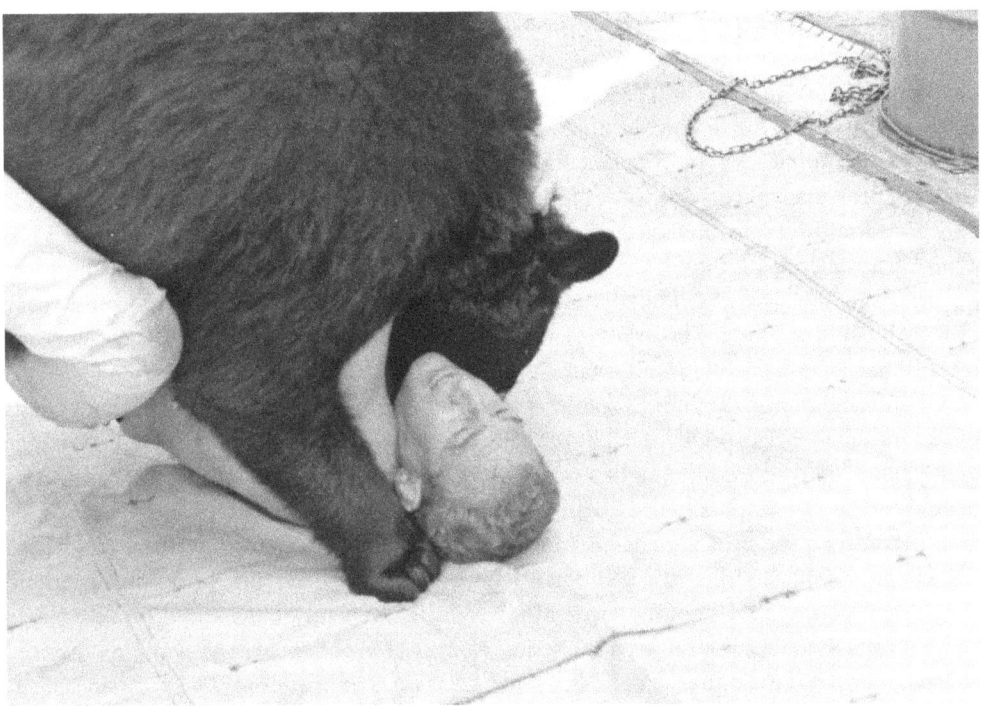

"Judo Gene" LeBell is pinned beneath 700 pounds of Canadian black bear named Victor. Trained by well-respected animal whisperer Tuffy Truesdale (and raised in his home like an overgrown child), Victor worked with LeBell on everything from supermarket openings to movie stunts (courtesy Gene LeBell).

days, Gene doubled the show's bad guy in a sequence that included being molested by the enraged animal, then knocked into an eight-foot-deep trench. An ice cream cone suspended from a fishing rod (dangling just out of frame) was used to attract Victor the bear. Unfortunately, it was 102 degrees that day and the director, William Beaudine, was pushing for every shot. With the ice cream melting on Gene's arm, Victor became confused by Beaudine's loud commands of "Bite! Bite! Bite!" and accidentally chomped into LeBell's forearm, while snapping for the dripping treat. Due to the animal's extraordinary muzzle strength, his arm was punctured clean through in four spots, and began to immediately spurt blood. "Cut!" Beaudine yelled. "What are you doing? This is a Disney show. We can't have blood!" Returning to his trailer to regroup with the aid of stuntwoman Lorainne Chargon (whom LeBell knew from her days at the Olympic working as a cut-man on fights), he was soon mended with a combination of butterfly bandages, dog bite salve, and gaffer's tape. Returning to the set for more, LeBell withstood eight additional bear attacks before his day's work was completed. "After the final take," he said, "Victor came over and started nuzzling my injured arm through the costume. It was his way of saying, 'The bite was an accident.'"

One of LeBell's early stunt mentors was movie tough guy, Mike Mazurki. Knowing Gene from the wrestling world, Mazurki was fight coordinating the Bob Aldrich film *4 for Texas*. Starring Frank Sinatra, Dean Martin, and Ursula Undress (with appearances by everyone from Charles Bronson to the 3 Stooges), the western had a big bar fight sequence that required a shot of a man being body slammed to the ground. Gene was chosen because of his well known Judo falls. After the first take where Mazurki picked Gene up over his head and slammed him to the saloon floor, the first A.D. scurried over to ask him what fee to pay LeBell. "Give the kid 300," Mazurki answered. Unsure of protocol, Gene silently marveled at getting so much for one throw. When Mazurki informed the first A.D. that he wasn't happy and needed another take, the inexperienced LeBell asked the stunt coordinator what the problem was with his work. Telling him to shut-up and do it again, they completed another take with Gene hitting the floor like a sack of rocks. Receiving an additional $300 adjustment for each attempt, he soon realized the game and did as he was told. Nine hundred dollars richer at day's end, LeBell approached his mentor and asked how he could repay him. "Ah, shut up, kid," Mazurki said in his signature gravelly voice. "You're choking me up. Just get me a box of Havana cigars."

Not long after *4 for Texas*, Gene was involved in one of the most talked-about fights of its time when facing professional boxer Milo Savage in December of 1963. Despite Savage being a high-ranked middleweight since 1945 (and greased for the bout from head to toe, making a firm grip impossible), LeBell "put him to sleep" in the fourth round of the scheduled five, after a series of violent hip-throws, sending the fighter to the canvas head-first. Collecting $1,000 as well as the priceless P.R., Gene was back to stunt work soon after and even began getting small acting parts. Stunt coordinator Paul Stader hired him to play a bad guy on a Russian submarine on the series, *Voyage to the Bottom of the Sea* in 1964. Excited to finally have real dialogue, after he delivered a few lines of his improvised Russian accent, producer Irwin Allen said, "If I were you, big fella, I would stick to the action stuff and leave the acting to professionals."

Doing high falls and more, Gene was beginning to snag a lot of freelance gigs in Hollywood. Landing regular assignments on *The Man from U.N.C.L.E.*, he stayed busy as either an East German or Russian guard, getting knocked on the head, poisoned, or run over at a roadblock in nearly every episode. "The rest of the time," LeBell added, "I was one of the uniformed goons to some South American dictator ... who got killed."

By 1965 Lebell was doing everything on TV from *The Big Valley* (being beaten over the head with a barstool) to *The Munsters*, where he was hired by the producers to stunt-coordinate the "Herman the Great" episode. Playing Tarzan McGirk, he had a funny wrestling sequence where Herman (Fred Gwynne) is dominating him, then feels sorry for McGirk after being conned by a sob story of hungry kids to feed, thus losing the match. Spreading the wealth while doing the show, Gene was able to employ members of his old wrestling clique such as Vic Christie, Billy Varga, Jay York, and K.O. Murphy to play the other heavies. Becoming production-savvy, he was cautious not to damage the extensive Frankenstein makeup that Perc Westmore had applied to the Herman Munster character. Even amid numerous takes of a close-quarters flip-over gag, not once did Gwynne's prosthetics become mussed. "Fred was wonderful," LeBell said, "and even wearing four-inch platform boots wrestled very gracefully."

Gene also did stunt work on *I Spy*. Starring Robert Culp and Bill Cosby, the Sheldon Leonard production was the most hip series in town. Initially brought in to Judo train the actors by line producer Morton Fine, he was soon utilized for mainstream gags such as high falls, car crashes, and fights. Joking about his daily work on the series, Gene said he was knocked out so many times by karate chops from Cosby and Culp while playing a bad guy that his wardrobe had permanent creases from being hit.

More Judo-based assignments came LeBell's way such as teaching *Honey West* star Anne Francis the basic holds and throws for character use on the series. Hired by line producer Don Ingalls for this Aaron Spelling offering, he taught Francis so well that she once thwarted an attempted mugging in a Macy's parking lot by simply standing in her combat-ready Judo stance, then issuing a series of low growls in preparation to fighting the perp.

Seemingly everywhere at once in '65, LeBell's next challenge came with his work on *The F.B.I.* Hired by coordinator Loren Janes to perform a thirty-foot high-fall, Gene's game plan included the use of a new type of fall safety apparatus, the air bag. The large inflated air-bladder (twenty feet square and eight feet deep) was a vast improvement over what came previously (piles of hay, stacks of cardboard boxes, old mattresses). However, it was not enough to keep the 200-pound stunt man from bottoming-out upon impact, fracturing his ribs in the process. Preparing himself for following takes with foam padding on his elbows, knees, and lower back, LeBell completed the remaining shots with little difficulty, having also reduced the crucial venting on the air bag's sides to firm up his landing. Later versions of the pads would be larger, with multiple inflated compartments allowing for even higher falls without serious injury. Once he was given the nickname Michelin Man due to his padded costume's resemblance to the tire icon, the moniker would stay with him for years to come. Appearing regularly on *The F.B.I.* for Loren Janes (always the heavy), by series wrap in 1974, LeBell had done over 30 episodes.

Gene's last project of 1965 was director John Ford's final feature, *7 Women*. Teamed again with mentor Mike Mazurki, he was brought in as an expert in Mongolian wrestling for a big fight scene between Mazurki and Woody Strode. Demanding an authentic trainer, Ford was assured by Mazurki that there was only one real Mongolian wrestler in the United States, "and that's Gene LeBell!" He was hired for $1,000 a week to teach Strode and Mazurki the brutal intricacies of the ancient style. A rehearsal ring was assembled on an empty stage, and a first run-through was called for the following morning. Arriving in an elaborate wrestling robe the next day with a box full of cigars under his arm, Mazurki proceeded to lie in the ring with his feet propped up on a stool in the corner, reading magazines as he puffed on one stogie after the other. Watching his boss smoke Havanas until lunch time, Gene finally asked when the workout would begin. Scolding him in response, Mazurki said, "Don't bother me, kid, I'm in mental training!" There was a week of Mazurki doing nothing while Strode religiously trained his chiseled body with a strict regimen of weightlifting, push-ups and jumping rope. An hour before the sequence was to be filmed, Mazurki took both aside and worked out the choreography for the six-minute fight. It went off without a hitch. The director was congratulating Mazurki on bringing reality to the film, and appreciated all the extra training done to accomplish that feat. "We owe it all to LeBell," Mazurki said without a trace of malice in his voice. "Give him another 500 bucks!" Shocked and pleased, Gene took his mentor aside and asked how he could thank him. Holding up one of his big illegal cigars, Mazurki said, "I'll take a crate of Havanas."

In 1966 Gene was cast as a martial arts instructor in the Jerry Lewis–Mary Ann Mobley comedy *Three on a Couch*. Gene had taught Mobley Judo, and she was responsible for him being on the picture. One gag that Gene had with Lewis involved holding boards for the comedian to break; Lewis would go through a series of exaggerated katas, only to hurt his hand when finally making contact. Lewis was so funny, that Gene had to look away to keep from ruining the scene. Recalling an on-set television that Lewis was using for what he called video play-back, LeBell said, "The guy was a perfectionist who could be tough if you messed up. He had a creative mind second to none and the monitor saved him tons of time and money in getting his comedy to screen. Now, everybody uses one!"

LeBell's next big assignment came by way of referral from a pal, fellow martial artist Ed Parker. He was hired to work on *Paradise Hawaiian Style*, starring Elvis Presley, with whom he had worked on *Blue Hawaii* (1961). Gene was to get thrown over the King's shoulder in a barroom brawl sequence and land with his patented high bounce off the ground, take after take. Impressed with his skill (and sense of humor while doing it), Elvis tipped the stunt player a $100 bill for his morning's work. LeBell said he went out that night and consumed the biggest steak he could eat, saving the remaining $92 for the month's rent he owed.

In 1966, stunt coordinator Victor Paul (a sword master from the old days) got Gene to work on a new comic book–based series called *Batman*. Playing supporting henchmen roles for the likes of Burgess Meredith as the Penguin and Cesar Romero as the Joker, LeBell was being kicked, swung into, and otherwise knocked silly by Batman and Robin on a regular basis. Gene said that whenever he saw words like BAM, ZING and WHAM in the script, he was happy because that meant he was making money for extra gags.

Becoming one of the "go-to" players for stage combat in the latter half of 1966, LeBell

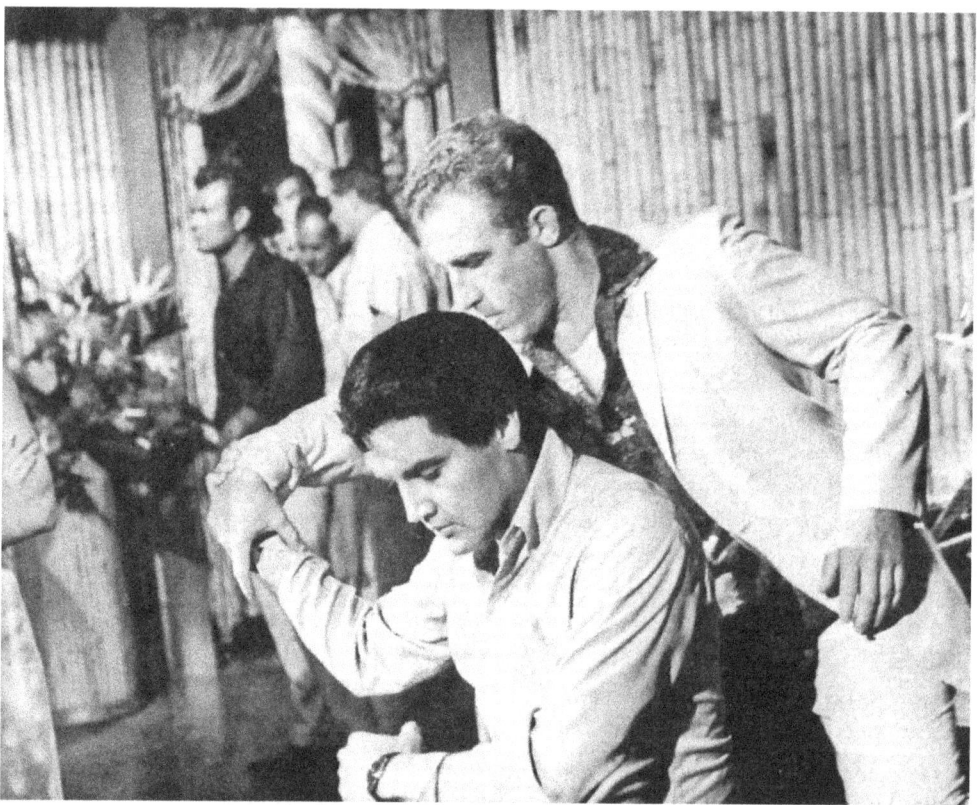

A stuntman on *Blue Hawaii* (1961), Gene LeBell treated Elvis Presley as an equal when teaching him. To simulate a jujitsu throw, LeBell reached over Presley and then, once grabbed, flung himself to the floor (courtesy Gene LeBell).

was called by stunt coordinator Benny Dobbins for the new crimefighter series *The Green Hornet* starring Hollywood newcomer Bruce Lee (who had done some martial arts work in Hong Kong prior to moving to Los Angeles). Dobbins told LeBell that Lee was so fast, the other stunt fighters' reactions seemed out of sync and silly. Gene recalled the first time he met Lee on set: He was prompted by Dobbins to place him in a head-lock as a joke. Approaching the 140-pound dynamo, LeBell was suddenly subject to a series of Lee's famous fighting growls. Snatching Bruce to his shoulders in a sudden fireman's carry, the 240-pound Judo champ began running around the stage with the smaller man like a bag of potatoes. Amused more than angry, Lee demanded, "Let me go, you big gorilla, or I'll have to kill you!" Laughing about one fight sequence in the "Hunter and Hunted" episode of the series, LeBell recalled being stunned by the power of Lee's famous running side kick, which sent him flying backwards six feet on impact. "Bruce was a tremendous athlete with a kick like a mule," he said seriously. "It's a good thing he only weighed 140 pounds and had a size six foot, otherwise the man was nearly unstoppable!" LeBell and Lee studied each another while sparring: LeBell focused on Lee's lightning-fast combinations, while Bruce was busy absorbing Gene's mastery on the ground. When he was shooting *Enter the Dragon* a few years later, Bruce paid homage to his pal by incorporating LeBell's patented "arm-bar" lock, subduing Sammo Hung in the film's opening fight. Gene was offered a gig on *Enter* but turned it down due to the difference between Hong Kong and Hollywood's pay scale: Overseas it was $200 a week versus four grand a month stateside.

Following *Green Hornet*, Gene did stunt work on *The Wild Wild West*. Brought in by prolific director Virgil Vogel, he was cast as a villain in "The Night of the Sedgewick Curse." Gene began poring through a script in search of his lines. In the last act, he finally found his character, but all that was written lay in the margin as stage direction for a big fight with Robert Conrad, culminating in Gene getting thrown down a flight of stairs. Frustrated, he asked Vogel about the lack of dialogue. "In case you haven't figured it out, LeBell," the director scolded him, "you're playing a deaf mute. And they don't talk!" Settling for the bonus pay given for being tossed down the stairs (300 bucks), Gene reported to the set and took his position for the big fight scene. Suddenly a pair of Standards and Practices agents strode across the stage, demanding to see Vogel. It turns out there was a law against a character with a disability, being harmed on television, and the Standards folks were not about to let it happen on their watch. LeBell came up with a solution that he excitedly began to demonstrate: Affecting the speaking tone of a deaf person, he haltingly said to cast and crew, "But, but, but ... I'm learning to talk." Unimpressed, Standards had the scene squashed, costing Judo Gene the gag's pay.

LeBell's next noteworthy gig was on Franklin Schaffner's *Planet of the Apes*. Hired by coordinator Joe Canutt (son of stunt icon Yakima Canutt), LeBell was cast as a gorilla soldier on horseback for the frenzied human-hunting scenes. Covered in an ape fur suit and head prosthetic (as well as heavy leather body armor during the sweltering days of shooting in Calabasas), he was also required to endure three and one half hour makeup sessions starting before dawn, just to "go to work."

Talking about the enormous difficulty of being knocked backwards off a moving horse while wearing a bulky costume and layers of facial latex, the stunt pro said the combination of blinding sweat, weight, and physical restriction made the otherwise simple reverse saddle fall a huge effort. Struggling to keep hydrated, as well as cool, Gene resorted to squirting water down his costume when not drinking it, as the temperatures on some days soared to over 110 degrees.

By the summer of '69, LeBell was one of the busiest stuntmen in Hollywood. Now part of a core group of journeymen including Terry Leonard, Charlie Picerni, Loren Janes, Chuck Hicks, and Royden Clark, his phone seldom stopped ringing. With his cross-over skills including fighting, high falls, motorcycles, animal work and automotive gags, it was no wonder Gene was constantly on film; he did so many jobs that his résumé contains well over 1,000 titles.

Gene also did numerous episodes of *Mission: Impossible.* Playing gangsters, guards, and other bad guys opposed to the I.M. force, he was hit by gun butts, karate-chopped, gassed, and occasionally shot by everyone from Peter Lupus as Willy to Martin Landau's Rollin Hand. In one episode, Pete Dial (doubling Peter Graves) and Gene fell down stairs while fighting. "The idea," he said, "is for both guys to tumble rapidly, barely grazing the steps in the process. That way you lessen the impact of the stair edges, which can break your neck if you land wrong on them."

LeBell also did a fight scene on the Sam Arkoff camp classic *Blacula*, having been hired by stunt coordinator George Wilber. The sequence didn't go quite as planned when Gene struck the title character (played by William Marshall) over the head with a breakaway plate. Marshall recoiled from the blow, crumpling to the ground, dazed, and complained of blurred vision and a headache after being revived by smelling salts. Director William Cain had to shut down production for a week while Marshall mended. Kidded by fellow stunt players Charlie Picerni and Jesse Wayne for having laid-up the picture's star by hitting him too hard, Gene was also celebrated by his pals for getting them a week's pay while the movie was down.

One show custom-suited to LeBell's stunt fighting mastery was *Kung Fu*. Created by Ed Speilman for Warner Brothers just as the martial arts craze hit American theaters, the series gave viewers a taste of the Orient at home. *Kung Fu* was a commercial success which spurred more martial arts–based action fare in the years to come. Pictures such as Charles Bronson's *Hard Times, The Karate Kid, Blood Sport, The Octagon,* and Jackie Chan's first US hit *Rumble in the Bronx* would ultimately lead to an explosion of fist flicks today, as evidenced by the creation of the Ultimate Fighter franchise. Remembering work on *Kung Fu*'s "Barbry House" episode (featuring actor-stuntman Orwin Harvey and Gene as the Macavee brothers in a fight versus Carradine), LeBell laughed when describing a double knee-roll attack from Kwai Ghang Cain — supposedly knocking both men out. Gene was lying on the ground "unconscious" at take's end when director Alex Beaton suddenly dowsed him with a bucket of ice water, saying, "You looked a little warm, old boy, I thought you might like a cooling-off." It was over 100 degrees while shooting the segment so the joke was well received. An extraordinary casting opportunity, *Kung Fu* used great supporting actors such as John Doucette, Will Geer, Jack Elam, and Slim Pickens to help sell the largely predictable scripts. "Being around all those great actors," LeBell admitted, "made me want to be better. Even if it was only while falling off a horse or taking a punch."

In the fall of 1972, Gene was engaged by stunt coordinator Carey Loftin to do *Walking Tall*, starring little-known actor Joe Don Baker, the true life story of Sheriff Buford T. Pusser (who had a penchant for using an ax handle to subdue violent rednecks). LeBell was tasked with training Baker for five weeks to use "the stick" on film. Playing an angry bouncer in one of the many fight sequences, LeBell was rammed by a rubber ax handle and knocked to his knees with the follow-up blow across his back. Attesting to the humorous disposition of many stunt types, Gene recalled boss Loftin giving an electrical shock to Royden Clark while shooting a motorcycle sequence. Loftin rigged the bike's seat to its battery with a hidden hot-lead; the end result made it into the film as the stunt player's eyes bulged wide open after jumping on.

For the American International picture *Slaughter's Big Ripoff* (1973), Gene was hired by stunt coordinator Tony Brubaker for a "to the death" fight scene with Jim Brown. Having worked together on *The Split* some five years previously, LeBell felt comfortable enough to pull a trick on the actor. Following their heated, "anything goes" fight sequence, Gene is finally subdued by a neck-breaking move. Lying on the ground after the take with a totally limp body, he fooled everyone into thinking that he was seriously injured; Brown called for a doctor. Springing to his feet seconds later with a smile on his face, Gene said, "Thanks, Jim, my neck feels much better!"

Another payday for LeBell in the blaxploitation genre was the Fred Williamson action vehicle *Hell Up in Harlem*. Released in December of 1973, the "B" movie from schlockmaster Samuel Arkoff's American International Pictures was lensed in Manhattan and Coney Island. Playing a Mafia solider who kidnaps the hero's wife, LeBell gets shot to death in the end by Williamson (doubled by Bob Minor), who unleashes a full clip into Gene with his M-16 rifle. Recalling the multiple squib-hits used to sell the violence, LeBell said that after the day's shooting, he had a series of bruises across his chest, arms, and stomach that made him look like a leopard. "When the explosive contacts go off," he explained, "It feels like being slapped with an open hand. It won't kill you, but depending upon who's loading the powder, it sure can smart."

Around the time LeBell's work on the hero pictures ended, a new elite group of stunt professionals and coordinators surfaced in Hollywood; they came to be known as Stunts Unlimited. Comprised from the "best of the industry" who had earned at least $100,000 in one year, founding members included Hal Needham, Ronnie Rondell Jr., Glen Wilder, LeBell, and many others. Masters at a wide range of stunt skills including horse work, high falls, cars, and stage combat, Unlimited's idea was to do it all, while being paid a premium for better work. Still the preeminent action group in filmdom today, their folks have been responsible for some of the biggest gags in Hollywood history.

Content to fill his days cast as a heavy, LeBell's next interesting stunt role came on James Tobak's darkly written *The Gambler* (1974) starring James Caan in the title role with supporting actors Paul Sorvino as "Lips" the bookie and Burt Young playing a mob enforcer. Gene was tapped to play the hapless victim of loan-sharking after some bad bets. Stunt coordinated by Jim Nickerson, the film's physical violence was infused with a realism that cinematographer Victor Kemper brought to the screen with frightening candor. Using close-ups on LeBell as he is punched and kicked to the sidewalk, one could feel the heavy blows impacting his body. One of the secrets to realistic stunt violence (according to Gene) is always matching the intensity of the blows to the character being hurt. "That way," he said, "there is an emotional connection to the victim."

With the return of the full-blown Hollywood mega-picture in the mid–70s came films like *Earthquake* and *The Towering Inferno*. Over 100 stunt players worked on each; LeBell worked on both projects. On director Mark Robson's *Earthquake*, Gene did a combination flame and falling segment, plummeting through a burned-out roof as a firefighter. Wearing

30 pounds of costume (including canvas turn-out coat, fire helmet, and heavy boots), he navigated the blinding flame; and smoke-filled set and safely hit his air bag. "There was so much smoke," he said, "that you couldn't see the stage floor below. Visualizing my landing point was the only way to insure I hit the bag dead center. And with the flame effects licking through the roof as I dropped, my margin for error was very narrow."

On *The Towering Inferno*, LeBell was again surrounded by a who's who of the stunt industry: Steve Burnett, Royden Clark, Bennie Dobbins, Bud Eakins, Mickey Gilbert, Larry Holt, Loren Janes, John Moio, Dar Robinson, Terry Leonard, Bob Yerkes, Joe Canutt, and 80 other paid risk-takers were all on hand for the action caper. Gene recalled the process of doing a crowded stair-fall as the most challenging of the picture. With so many stunt players entangled in the stairway (and infamous pyro-technician A.D. Flowers setting off cork bombs just feet from the actors), he said the chance of being trampled was very real: "After falling, I was lying on the landing, underfoot of about 50 background stunt-extras. I got stepped on so much, there were footprints across my back resembling a dance chart." *Inferno*'s A-list cast included everyone from Paul Newman and Steve McQueen to the likes of William Holden and Faye Dunaway to sell the flaming flick. Further one upsmanship occurred when stars Newman and McQueen did their own stunts whenever possible. One potentially deadly sequence with McQueen occurred during the flooding set-ups, with a 7,000–gallon forced dump tank used to duplicate the tidal wave–like run-off from the above floors. Gene said the physically tough cinema icon did so well that even during the multiple takes required to film the deluge, he was able to stay on his feet despite the tremendous force of the oncoming water.

Back in mainstream television in late 1974, LeBell took driving work with stunt buddy Royden Clark (James Garner's double) on *The Rockford Files*. Having already done numerous episodes of the series playing bit parts with a physical twist, Gene was hired for a difficult car chase around an outdoor parking lot full of crew automobiles. After the first wild take, there was a rush of concerned grips wishing to move their cars before damage occurred. In reality, not a single auto was scratched during the day of filming.

LeBell's next noteworthy television series, *Kolchak, the Night Stalker*, was television fare perfectly suited for stunt-play. Starring Darren McGavin as a relentless reporter in search of the supernatural, the series went from one dynamic ghoul to another; all were capable of throwing Kolchak around like a rag-doll. One episode, "The Spirits of the Night," cast Gene as officer Tim Olsen; he was manhandled by stunt coordinator Paul Baxley as a ghoul, and hurled himself violently into a brick wall. One of LeBell's specialties, the gag looked so good that it was repeated in a "Legacy of Terror." Ultimately Gene did several stunt appearances for the series (doubling McGavin occasionally as well). He recalled, "It was a good show for me as the bad guys were heavily made-up fiends or vampires with superhuman strength. Playing friend or fiend, there were lots of stunts!"

Another of the major shows for LeBell in the late seventies was *Starsky and Hutch*. Hired by coordinator Charlie Picerni, Gene did tackles and tickles, as he put it. Tackles means fights or physical prats; and tickles include everything else, like driving, high falls, water work, and plate-glass window stuff. Having appeared in over 20 episodes as everything from a Police Academy Judo instructor to a bad guy on a motorcycle, LeBell was awarded a special producer's plaque of appreciation which hangs in his office to this day. Working on the big-budget feature remake of *Starsky and Hutch* in 2004, he and stunt coordinator

Gary Davis brought a taste of the original series to the present project. Commenting on why the show's old formula still works today, Gene replied, "Anything around long enough in Hollywood always becomes new again."

Getting back to the sort of film for which he was born, in the summer of 1975 Gene labored on Sam Peckinpah's *The Killer Elite*. Brought in by stunt coordinator Whitey Hughes to wrangle the platoon of martial artists thrown together for the fight-driven flick, LeBell had his hands full. Saddled with soothing the egos of skilled practitioners like James Caan's fight double Jimmy Nickerson, Take Kubota, George Cheng, and Koop Lien Ying and others, Gene's method of allowing a say in the combat staging of their various disciplines, insured swift cooperation as the fighters had control of how their style was depicted on screen. While shooting the fight finale aboard the Navy's mothballed fleet in Suisun Bay, LeBell was used as a bad guy in a machine-gun wound sequence that was more than he bargained for. Attaching multiple squibs across Gene's chest and stomach to portray rapid bullet hits striking his torso, effects legend Sass Bedig used too hot a charge for the gag. After being sprayed by automatic fire, then lying against a bulkhead playing dead during the remainder of the long take, LeBell began to smell something burning. While the action continued around him, he cautiously opened one eye and saw puffs of smoke and small licks of flame issuing from the squib holes in his pea jacket. Realizing he was on fire, Gene

Another part of LeBell's fame came from professional boxing and wrestling. Refereeing a "mixed bout" between Muhammad Ali (right) and Antonio Inoki, Gene protects the Japanese wrestler, who spent most of the fight lying on his back trying to kick Ali. LeBell took countless refereeing gigs for actual sporting events (courtesy Gene LeBell).

did a slow death-clutch to the affected location, and then groaned as he rolled over to extinguish the fire in his coat — without ruining the take.

Yet another project came LeBell's way in the fall of 1975 on the Robert Blake TV detective drama *Baretta*. Starring the tough actor as a vice cop, the series often called for LeBell to play thugs on the receiving end of violence. Cast as a "john" in an episode where he's caught in a motel room with an underage hooker, the ensuing action resulted in Gene being knocked out from a series of punches from Blake. Joking with the actor about the over-the-top ferocity of his attack in the scene, he said, "Sorry, Bobby, I didn't know she was your sister."

Returning to John Guillerman's direction in 1976 (post–*Towering Inferno*), Gene was brought in by coordinator Bill Couch to work on *King Kong*. He was tasked with doing live-action train stunts as the big ape rips a subway car full of screaming people from its tracks. The hydraulic gimbal used to create the sensation was so powerful that it had to be slowed down, for fear of seriously injuring the enclosed stunt players. "With elbows flailing and heads banging due to Kong's violent shaking," Gene explained, "we were all crashing into each other — which is an easy way to get hurt. Using restraint but still selling the gag is the mark of professionals who can 'make it look real,' without losing control of the physical contact." While working with Guillerman, he reminded the director of their work on *Towering Inferno* a few years previously. Without missing a beat, the humorous helmer offered to have LeBell set on fire during the train wreck gag, for old time's sake. He declined the offer.

Every so often in movieland, a bunch of talented stuntmen get together and decide to make a film of their own. Joe Tornatore's *Zebra Force* was just such a flick. Featuring a VIP list of stunt performers including Charlie Picerni, Jimmy Nickerson, Henry Kingi, Tommy Huff, Gary Epper, and Eddie Donno as coordinator, the picture was written, directed, and financed by big-time stunt folk. The story of the mob versus a band of ex–Vietnam vets fighting for their neighborhood, the movie had everything from explosions and car crashes to high falls, machine-gun killings and knife fights. Recalling his part of the stunt orgy, LeBell said he did an exploding door gag in the film's opening with an air-ram that was so powerful it threw him into the ceiling pieces over the set instead of through the door. Other set-ups included a high fall where Gene is machine-gunned through a second story window and lands in a swimming pool 20 feet below. Despite the stunt expertise, the feature was less than a stellar success with rumors that even the lab technicians refused to watch it while it was being printed. Perhaps the film's best use would be as a demonstration for its action-craft, and appreciated for that.

One final film that Gene worked in 1976 was John Avildsen's *Rocky*. Appearing as little more than a ringside judge, LeBell's true input began when unknown producer Sylvester Stallone was scouting the Olympic Auditorium for possible locations. The movie was written just after the Ali–Chuck Webner fight of 1975; Stallone picked Gene's brains regarding the staging of the boxing action. As for his early advice on the picture, he laughed at having told Stallone he saw *Rocky* as a corny western, with the underdog getting the girl in the end. "It will never sell." LeBell warned him. "After all, there hasn't been a heavyweight champ from Philly since Smokin' Joe Frazier."

In 1979, LeBell was drafted by stunt coordinator Everett Creach for Paramount's *Black Sunday*. Directed by John Frankenheimer, the feature revolved around a Vietnam vet who masterminds a terrorist attack during the Super Bowl. Utilized in the picture's large crowd sequences (when a Goodyear blimp crashes into the stadium, causing mass panic), Gene was tasked with doing running shots where he falls to the ground and is trampled to death. To ensure his safety (after rehearsals left him bruised and bloodied), the stunt player upped his protective package to not only include knee, elbow, and shin pads, but also catcher's chest-rig and cup hidden beneath his oversized wardrobe, in hopes of being spared serious injury from the masses running over him. Recalling one take where hope was not enough, he said that as stunt buddies Larry Holt, Paul Stader, Richard Washington, and Dean Smith trod upon him, one of the bunch accidentally kicked him in the mouth. Kidding about it later, Holt said, "Hell, Gene, that's not the first time you've been caught with a foot in your mouth."

Rising from freelance stunt mercenary to part of an actor's troupe, LeBell began a relationship with director Clint Eastwood in September of 1978 that would span multiple features. Gene was hired by stunt gaffer Buddy Van Horn to do motorcycle stuff on *Every Which Way But Loose*; Clint took one look at him and decided to feature him as a bad guy. Playing a member of the "Black Widows" motorcycle gang, he was on the receiving end of a hit-and-fall gag where Eastwood punches him in the face, smashing his glasses while knocking him off his chopper. "Clint is great to work with," LeBell said. "He's trained for years in boxing and is very good with his hands. Because of that, I never had to worry about him doing something unpredictable, that could get us both hurt. Plus, Eastwood has the best catering in Hollywood." LeBell's biker stuff provided a lot of the film's comic relief. "That's why it was so important that everyone cast could be funny while still doing a gag."

The Dukes of Hazzard was a never-ending payday for stunt players of all types. From fighting to explosions and car jumps to crashes, coordinator Paul Baxley liked to use Gene whenever he could. Gene said that Baxley was the first stuntpusher in Hollywood history to get his people more money for dangerous or additional takes. "Before that," LeBell offered, "you would have to repeat the same risky or painful move take after take for your paycheck. Under Baxley's leadership, we were paid *each* time we did a gag. The end result was stunt guys making a decent living." During one episode, he did a sequence riding in the rear of a sedan, firing a gun out the back window at the pursuing Dukes. As a special effect was scripted for the glass to be shot out while driving, LeBell watched with keen interest while an inexperienced pyro-technician set the window charges with reckless abandon. Knowing from experience that a poorly placed charge can result in auto glass fragmenting dangerously, Gene thought it prudent to slip on a pair of safety shades, in case things went badly. When the effect blew glass shards all over his face, he was calm despite cheek lacerations and his powder-burned black forehead. Turning to the technician (frozen in horror at Gene's approach), he pointed to his face and said with a forgiving tone, "Well, at least I won't have to shave tomorrow!"

Cautious about the stunt's next phase (jumping the vehicle into a large ditch during the pursuit's finale), LeBell was concerned that all the residual window glass could be hazardous during the impact. Seeking help from the assistant director proved futile, as he was coldly informed that the glass had been *established* in the previous shot, and that the company was losing the light (which is movie code for "Hurry up and do what you're told"). Reluctantly Gene did the stunt. The resulting collision with the embankment caused his face and neck to be impacted with flying debris, slicing open his head from eyebrow to jaw in an instant. Multiple stitches would be required to close the wound (which couldn't be accomplished until his last shot was finished); LeBell turned his horror movie face away from camera while doing final driving P.O.V.s. He went to Henry Mayo Hospital three hours later, with a blood-drenched towel stanching the wounds. Healing up over a two-week period, the toughest man alive lived up to his name and continued to perform driving stunts on *Dukes* with Frankenstein-like stitches, claiming it was just another day at the office. LeBell was awarded a plaque from the show's producers for his dedication and prolific work on the series. He is as proud of this citation as if it was an Academy Award.

Throughout the end of the decade LeBell showed no signs of his stunt work slowing down. Two pictures done in 1979 which illustrate that non-stop ethic were *The Jerk* and *Goldie and the Boxer*. Gene was brought to *The Jerk* by stunt coordinator Conrad Palmisano (Steve Martin's double) for a kung fu tussle; the sequence ended with a kick that sent Gene airborne into a pool. Done for the day later than expected, he raced from the location (still wearing wet wardrobe) to a previously set casting audition for a two-week acting job on a major feature. Running into the production offices out of breath (due to the sprint from the parking structure), he arrived just in time and was ushered by a receptionist to a rehearsal room where the director was already waiting. Looking up from his clipboard, the man did a double take as he focused on the soggy stuntman waiting eagerly to read his copy. Bumming a quick ride to the audition with the show's animal trainer in his cramped van full of German Shepherds, Gene had unknowingly tracked blackish footprints and dog hair all over the shag carpet and white furnishings of the plush office. Standing there with his uncombed red mane, streaked makeup, and soiled outfit, LeBell was asked to leave the office immediately.

LeBell's other noteworthy foray for 1979 was the television picture *Goldie and the Boxer*. Hired by Glen Wilder as fight choreographer, he was asked to fill in for pugilist turned actor Gerry Quarry, who opted out of a big boxing sequence opposite O.J. Simpson. (Quarry, a serious heavyweight contender who had fought Muhammad Ali, Joe Frazier, and actually beaten Floyd Patterson, refused to take a fall to ex-footballer Simpson.) Doubling Quarry with LeBell, the U.P.M. approached Gene, asking how much he wanted for doing the boxing gag himself. Realizing he was already on payroll for a tidy sum, he sarcastically requested whatever Quarry was getting. The production manager approved Gene's new deal with a sour look on his face. Gene was confused until he saw his paycheck in the amount of $2,300. "The lesson learned," said LeBell, "is to keep your mouth shut and wait and see. Sometimes, things can work out."

The '80s ushered fresh challenges for LeBell on features like *Airplane!*, *The Big Brawl*, and Martin Scorsese's *Raging Bull*. Although only performing minor stuff on *Airplane!* (as per coordinator Conrad Palmisano), Gene was truly put to the test on the latter two pictures. For *Big Brawl*, starring Jackie Chan in his American film debut, LeBell was used by coordinator Pat Johnson for a featured fight with Ox Baker. Baker, a 1960s pro wrestling bad guy famous for his massive body, bald head, handlebar mustache, and heart punch (which allegedly could stop a man in his tracks), got the best of Gene as scripted—knocking him out with a final series of blows. Opening his eyes after hearing "Cut" called, Gene was stunned when he was suddenly kissed by the 300 pound grappler, who said, "Time to wake up, Cinderfella, your Prince Charming is here!"

Unfortunately, the picture was not all laughs for LeBell. Injured when thrown through a barroom window by H.B. Haggerty (and hitting cement instead of the pad rigged to protect him), he fractured his shoulder and required over six weeks to heal. Estimating his freelance time at $5,000 a week, Gene lost thirty grand from the poorly aimed toss.

Getting to work with Scorsese on *Raging Bull* in 1980 was a career high which LeBell will never forget. Meeting the famous New York helmer on the first day of filming the Jake LaMotta-Billy Fox riot sequences at the Olympic Auditorium, Gene jokingly informed the director that his choice of shooting the movie in black and white was a huge mistake, as the kids today are hungry for color. Taken aback for a moment until told by stunt coordinator Jimmy Nickerson of LeBell's odd sense of humor, Scorsese ultimately laughed, promising to have Gene taken care of later. Inflicting vengeance in his own fashion, Marty cast him as the referee for the alleged fixed fight where he's struck with a chair thrown into the ring from the audience. A bit of cinematic magic was created by Thelma Schoonmaker's clever editing, which made Gene the first man in the history of motion pictures to ever throw, and then get hit by the same prop. He received two checks for the same day's work (as both referee and disgruntled fan). Gene was made-up with a funny hat and glasses so he would look like another guy tossing the furniture.

LeBell's third feature with the Eastwood group was the Buddy Van Horn–directed *Any Which Way You Can*, a simple rehashing of the Philo Beddoe character (returning this time for a big-money fight versus baddy William Smith). One iconic moment occurred when Gene was socked in the face at a stop light by Beddoe's orangutan sidekick Clyde. Doubling the dangerously strong primate in a fur body suit, stuntman Bobby Porter actually threw the punch, as it was far too risky to have Mannis (Clyde's real name) hit LeBell himself.

Continuing his quest throughout 1980 for serious acting assignments, Gene landed an audition to play an ex–Vietnam vet in the Richard Donner drama *Inside Moves*. Arriving for his appointment early and excited, he was met by a young assistant from Fenton and Feinberg, who was handling the picture's casting. After asking Gene for his résumé and being informed he never had one, she angrily replied, "Well...what have you done?" Sarcastically, Gene answered *Birth of a Nation*. Not realizing she was being put on, the woman asked him what part he played. He said, "I was the guy in a white hood on horseback with a torch in my hand." Thinking she was dealing with a flake, the casting assistant sadly looked at LeBell and said, "I don't think we have anything for you this time, but we'll keep you on file for the next one!"

If ever there was a series designed to keep stuntmen working (or in the hospital), Glen Larson's *The Fall Guy* certainly fit the bill. The Lee Majors series employed twenty or so of the finest stuntmen in Hollywood (all with multiple and/or specific specialties). LeBell and friends pulled off every gag in the book, and made a fortune while doing it. Paid a minimum of $5,000 a week, performers such as stunt coordinator Mickey Gilbert, Dar Robinson, Terry Leonard, Loren Janes, Larry Holt, Nick Dimitri, Chuck Hicks, Whitey Hughes, John Moio, and the Gill brothers (Jack and Andy) were tasked with topping what had come the week before. With each script revolving around a specific series of stunts, the Black and Blue crew (as they were called) did everything from plate glass window gags, car chases, fights, and high falls to the more challenging stuff such as leaping from one moving vehicle to another, stair falls, motorcycle jumps, air rams and fire effects, to name just a few.

Recalling a dangerous building-to-building jump (from a six-story roof onto a roof two stories below), Gene clarified the formula of travel as every foot of distance covered forward, you simultaneously fall two feet downward in open space. While Mickey Gilbert provided his scout information (facts like the distance between buildings and the condition of the roofs involved, as well as wind and other specifics), Gene practiced his running broad jump to span the twelve feet between structures. Atop the building the morning of the stunt, however, LeBell realized that there was no room for a running leap, as the roof had an air-conditioning duct blocking his way. Frantically working his stationary broad jump, he was only able to muster ten feet no matter what he tried. Fearing he might come up short (or slip on launch), he enlisted his son David to invisibly safety him from the edge of the other building. Just before the camera rolled, Gene was moved to hear his son's voice crackle over the radio, wishing him luck. He responded with "Thanks, kid." Then he was shocked when his boy came back with a request for his favorite motorcycle if "Dad" didn't make it! Making the leap with just six inches to spare on landing, LeBell watched his pursuer (Mickey Gilbert) sail four feet past him, while coming down on his feet in a full run. With no room for air bags or nets possible at the location, both leaps were done on a life-and-death basis.

LeBell's next stunt duty worth recording came in 1982 on MGM's *The Beastmaster*. Starring Marc Singer as the title character, the Don Cascarilla–directed sword-and-loincloth fantasy classic had everything from damsels in distress to tigers. In fact, Gene did so much sword work and falling from horseback, he said he was bowlegged for months after the picture. He was tasked one chilly morning with doing a canoe-sinking gag where he and fellow stunt journeyman Chuck Hicks had to abandon an overturned craft and swim 200 yards in Lake Pyramid, a bit of underestimation almost cost the pair their lives. Working in bulky costumes including heavy torso armor and nine-pound broadswords, the duo nearly drowned as the water was not only extremely cold, but the lake's current had taken them farther from shore than anticipated. "We lost the swords right away," LeBell said. "But they got the shot!" Swimming together during the ordeal, the two spoke of signaling for help and thus ruining the take, but decided second unit director Charles Bail would figure they were hamming it up and probably continue filming anyway.

Another long-running series which LeBell worked was *Knots Landing*, beginning in 1983. The episode "Nowhere to Run" saw Gene doubling actor Ken Swofford, who was to be mauled by a Bengal tiger. On the advice of coordinator Larry Holt and the animal trainer, Gene bonded with the 600-pound cat and played with it in its holding pen. When they were ready to shoot the attack insert, LeBell stood on his mark by a streambed waiting for the call of action with the trained tiger just twenty feet away. After director Nick Sparrow quietly gave the order, the Bengal was released and immediately leapt the distance to Gene in three strides, knocking him over in an instant. During the following 30 seconds of footage, however, the big cat proceeded to lick and gently paw at his new friend, anxious to see if he was okay. Apparently LeBell and the tiger had become a little too friendly, causing the animal to forget its training and only care about playing.

By 1985, Gene had come to a point in his profession where he could work with anyone in the biz he wanted. Following some fast money automotive work on Chevy Chase's comedic P.I. picture *Fletch* (in which Gene performed a high-speed car rollover stunt staged on a closed freeway off-ramp), he did a made-for-television project called *Dalton — Code of Vengeance*. He was brought in by stunt coordinator Chuck Walters for a segment involving a huge Brahma bull charging directly at some cowboys. Steer wrangler Fred Leonard instructed him not to move as the bull was trained to stop before impact with humans.

After six blown takes with the professional cowboys running away, Gene did exactly as he was told, standing his ground before the 1500-pound animal, only to be suddenly gored, then flung over a six foot fence with a single jerk of the beast's massive neck. Landing safely in a mound of steer manure, he unknowingly sliced open his leg when he hit the top of the corral. By the time he returned to the set the following day for a stair-fall payday, LeBell's leg had become so swollen that he could barely walk, much less do stunt work. Attributing his high level of pain and temperature to the shot from the bull, he had no idea how serious his condition was becoming. Seeing his personal sawbones later that night due to excruciating pain, Gene was treated at the home of Oakland Raiders surgeon Dr. Nicola in the physician's own kitchen. Draining the pus-infected leg with the aid of his-seven-year-old son, the doctor informed him that the problem had been cow dung infection in the wound; without treatment within 24 hours, the limb would have been lost to gangrene.

One under-appreciated stunt masterpiece that LeBell did in mid–1985 was Guy Hamilton's *Remo Williams*. Utilized as a heavy who chases martial arts master Chun (played by Joel Grey) across wet cement in a construction area while the actor performs a walking-on-water gag, LeBell sank straight to the bottom in an attempt to follow. Accomplishing the effect by laying planks just beneath the surface of the wet concrete mixture, LeBell simply stepped between the boards to sink into the eight-foot-deep tank used to stage the shot. There were multiple attempts to achieve a fully submersed look (sold by air bubbles rising to the surface of the quagmire). Due to 11 degree temperatures at the Statue of Liberty location in New York harbor, the stunt man had to be warmed up after each take to avoid catching pneumonia. Gene recalled being pulled out of the frigid sludge, then led to a filthy room of lockers with a shower where he could wash off the mixture of dyed corn flakes and Elmer's glue which gave the cottage cheese–like liquid the look and feel of concrete. Tasting like sawdust-flavored oatmeal, the heavy liquid wheat paste also had a grit-like adhesive quality, making LeBell's shower a painful task: "Basically the goop acted like a wax job after it set up, tearing out clumps of body hair wherever I scrubbed it under the shower."

By 1985 Gene and hundreds of other stunt players in Tinseltown saw the explosion of the cable networks and other independent sources. While creating lots more content for public consumption (and jobs in Hollywood), the quality of some of the films and television series made under those circumstances possessed a somewhat diminished luster, compared to the work of the '60s and '70s. Subsequently, folks like Gene became nomad stunt specialists, going from one job to the next, doing anything that paid a dollar, instead of working for a single show or boss. By the time he coordinated *Runaway Train* at the close of '85, LeBell was playing by the rule of self-preservation — as the wide variety of films during his lifetime will testify.

Working next for longtime pal Blake Edwards on *A Fine Mess* in 1986, Gene was hired by the director to coordinate a slew of old slapstick gags including pratfalls from ladders, bumping into doors, and outlandish car chases. Truly in his element (having loved the early comedic stunt legends such as Buster Keaton, Charles Chaplin, and Harold Lloyd), LeBell brought some of that style to Edwards' film. "Blake always wanted to hear your ideas," Gene recalled, "and if he started laughing before you got to the punchline, you could bet it would be in the movie!"

Million Dollar Mystery started off like 100 other flicks that LeBell had done before; only on this film, he would see a good friend perish needlessly. Working out the angles for a motorcycle sequence while on location in Page, Arizona, he and world-renowned stunt player Dar Robinson saw no danger during the rehearsal. With the action requiring Robinson to jump on his motorcycle and race around a corner till out of frame (some twenty yards up on a rise), the shot seemed relatively simple for second unit DP John Cardiff and his small crew. Determining the proper camera placement (as well as speed and maneuver techniques during practice runs), Dar was convinced that going at top speed towards the embankment, then transitioning with a slide turn past the lens to be the most compelling shot. On the final test run, Gene recalled his friend racing past him, (with two bad guys on bikes just behind) traveling at 70 to 80 miles an hour into the gradual curve. Instead of a controlled slide followed by a rapid acceleration into a straight line as worked previously, this time Robinson careened off the road and over the embankment, landing 40 feet below in a field of boulders and jagged rock formations. LeBell was the first to Dar's side, where he assessed his friend's injuries and the proper course of rescue. Seeing a fractured femur, as well as broken ribs and a serious chest injury, Gene knew time was of the essence. Speaking to him in a labored, wheezy voice, Dar said, "I think I bought it, Gene." Assuring Robinson that he would be fine, but knowing that he was in shock and getting worse, LeBell carried the 190-pound man back up the steep embankment. Placing him in a pickup truck bed, he yelled for someone to get an ambulance. With no emergency personnel on hand, it took over two hours for the hurt stuntman to receive medical help. The end result was the death of Dar Robinson. Plagued to this day wondering if the fatality was avoidable, Gene felt there was strong evidence that hospital treatment could have saved his pal's life. "After all," he said, "Dar was young and in perfect condition."

LeBell's next film of importance was Paul Verhoeven's *RoboCop*. Lensed in downtown Dallas' commercial underbelly in sweltering 110 degree temperatures, the movie possessed a cartoon-like quality to its violence that would become one of the quirky Dutch director's trademarks. Cast by Texas stunt coordinator Gary Combs as part of Bodekker's gang, Gene performed a second story balcony fall into an air bag, while being riddled by Robo's automatic machine pistol. Selling the gun's high rate of fire, effects technician Don Waller wired him with over a dozen squibs fixed to his chest, stomach, arms, and legs. So many bullet hits were employed in close proximity that by day's end Gene had quarter-sized bruises covering his body, resembling a connect-the-dots puzzle.

Drafted for more futuristic violence on *Running Man* by longtime employer Bennie Dobbins, Gene's expertise on a motorcycle was tapped for a cutting edge pursuit sequence. Surrounded by stunt-wrestling big names like Jesse Ventura and Professor Toru Tanaka, LeBell put in a memorable performance when set on fire in the sequence. Crawling over 30 feet before director Paul Michael Glaser called "cut," Gene said he felt like a grilled hot dog by scene's end.

Never one to turn down a featured gag in a film, LeBell leapt at the chance to do a plate-glass window stunt on *The Presidio*. Knocked through a store-front when struck by a car during the movie's Chinatown chase scene, he also did ATV camera moves on the reverse of the same sequence. "That was the first time," Gene said jokingly, "I was filming my own gag while in it!"

Another wrestling picture which received the LeBell touch was Hulk Hogan's *No Holds Barred*, released in mid–1989. Hired by longtime Hogan stunt double and fight coordinator Buck Dancer for a big wrestling sequence against buddy Terry Bole (Hulk's real name),

Gene decided to play a "swerve" on his old friend who was now a big star. Showing up for his pre-call the morning of filming at 7 A.M., he began saying nasty things to the makeup folks about Hogan. Continuing the onslaught to bystanders in the breakfast line as well as in wardrobe right after, Gene spread the bad word around camp to anyone he saw regarding his intentions for the actor. Just before lunch, when the big sequence was to be rehearsed, Hogan was leaving his trailer cautiously (having heard the rumors of a crazy man on set swearing to get him). Walking through the sound doors, Hulk heard a voice whisper from behind, "I'm gonna get you Bole." Hogan let out a huge belly laugh when he recognized Gene as his stalker. "We had a great time on set," he recalled of the Hulk Hogan life story, "plus Terry paid everyone over-scale and fed us like kings."

Perhaps one of LeBell's more challenging flicks in this period was the Sylvester Stallone jail film *Lock Up*, lensed on location at East New Jersey State Prison during the fall of '89. Charged with executing a featured open field tackle on Stallone, he was told by coordinator Frank Orasatti (who hired LeBell) not to hurt him. After finishing over a dozen tackle-takes in the semi-frozen mud of the prison yard, Gene jokingly asked DP Donald Thorin, "What's the matter with a nice state pen in Florida to shoot this, instead of freezing in this muck in New Jersey?" Responding in kind, Thorin answered, "Because you're wanted for bad acting there, LeBell, and I don't think we can afford the bail!"

For *Tango and Cash*, another Stallone picture, he was tapped by second unit director James Arnett to perform a dangerous high fall from a rocky cliff 35 feet above camera. Taking multiple gun shots via squibs attached to his chest and arms on the way down, LeBell had to thread his air bag landing between multiple sharp granite formations, jutting two stories into space. Landing unscathed thanks to careful planning and execution, he grabbed a radio after the take, asking the 2nd A.D. if it was good for camera. He was told they needed another take, but the joke was on him as he saw the camera being broken down and the grips removing their overheads. Watching the company leave while he was still deflating his air bag, LeBell knew Stallone had set him up for a lonely van ride back to base camp despite being the hero of the morning's shots.

In 1990 LeBell experienced two monumental firsts in his career. One was earning in excess of $300,000 for the year. Laboring on more than a dozen films in less than six months, his annual total topped twenty-five pictures. He appeared in several sequels such as *Die Hard 2, Another 48 Hours,* and *Problem Child*. LeBell's other first came when he crewed on the Steven Seagal beat-'em-up *Hard to Kill*, released in February of that year. Tasked by stunt coordinator Buddy Van Horn to bring a realistic depth to the show's fisticuffs, Gene accomplished that and more while going one on one with the picture's lead, Seagal. When queried as to the storied star's work ethic, he answered in a monotone, "Steven Seagal is a great actor and wonderful martial artist." Sensing more, I got the full story: Seagal's manager said that no one person could take his client. Knowing better, LeBell said nothing until the actor himself offered $500 if anyone could "put him down." Within 20 seconds of engaging, Seagal was trapped by one of Judo Gene's patented submission holds, choking him out. Revived, the embarrassed action star claimed luck on LeBell's part and re-issued his challenge. Allowing the actor another chance, Gene absorbed a series of punches, then swept Seagal into a fight-finishing sleeper hold, leaving him unconscious and drooling. Unfortunately for all, the entire thing was blown out of proportion as it was little more than a disagreement between two superbly skilled fighters. With the reputation of being a tough guy,

Continuing to work the rough-and-tumble trade while approaching 60 years of age, LeBell was employed on John Flynn's *Lock Up* (1989), delivering a tackle to star Sylvester Stallone (right). LeBell said between the frozen ground of Rahway State Prison and the real inmates used in the picture, it was one of the most dangerous days work he ever did (courtesy Gene LeBell).

however, the 6'4", 300-pound Seagal found out first hand just how hard to beat Gene LeBell really is.

Another LeBell stop on the cash-machine year of 1990 was on Warren Beatty's *Dick Tracy*. Brought in by Billy Burton to take a slap in the face while falling backward in a chair, LeBell earned $1,500 for that stunt alone. He said the smack he received from Academy Award–winning actor Al Pacino was as painful as it appeared. "He really let me have it," LeBell revealed. "After flipping back in the chair, I nailed the ground skull first, which gave me a pretty good headache."

LeBell's final opus in 1990 was on the Sam Raimi film *Darkman*, another comic book transference to the big screen. He was hired by coordinator Chris Doyle to be tossed off a three-story roof. The gag was shot at night and it was difficult to see the air bag below because of the blinding movie lights. Another complication: He was being thrown by another person (versus jumping himself), which meant that if Doyle's aim was off, then Gene could miss the bag completely. Never one to ignore an opportunity for a swerve, he doused himself with the most repulsive aftershave he could find moments before reporting to the roof. Lifting Gene into position on his broad shoulders for the toss, Doyle (while gagging on the putrid odor) groaned under his breath that he would get even. Looking down at his partner just before being launched three stories into the cool night air, LeBell said, "But not tonight, right?"

Following his work on the big studio film *Patriot Games* in 1992 (in the motorboat chase sequences), Gene was tasked with *Article 99*, shot in Kansas City, Missouri. He was drafted by stunt coordinator Rick Avery to do a dog-attack sequence in the picture. Reporting to the stage for his morning's work, he was instructed by director Howard Deutch to familiarize himself with the 125-lb. Doberman Pinscher Rex who was to be his co-star. Finding the massive dog backstage in a cage, Gene bonded with the animal for 15 minutes, including wrestling and face-to-face play with a pull toy. Called to set to shoot the scene, LeBell suddenly noticed another dog in a cage by the opposite wall; it looked exactly like the one he just met. He was informed by Deutch that the Doberman he had been petting was the vicious one (only to be used with caution for snarling inserts), and that *the other* dog was tame and intended for the fight; Gene almost fainted when informed he had mixed the animals up. "Luckily," he said, "I get along with animals fine. So Rex didn't eat me!"

The "world's toughest guy" poses in Klingon makeup and costume on the set of Paramount's *Deep Space Nine* in 1993. LeBell was hired to do a "fight and fall" off a second-story gantry, but he also ended with a small speaking role during the gig. "Aside from the fur jacket being hot as hell," he recalled, "the reinforced leather shoulder pads and tunic weighed thirty pounds. Combined with three hours of makeup and my Frank Zappa wig, I was in a perfect mood to do the crusty part, with made-up, gurgling dialogue as my big acting chance! It's no wonder that I didn't get many speaking roles from it" (courtesy Gene LeBell).

By 1994, Gene had become one of the crown princes of Movieland stunts. No longer compelled to take everything offered (having well over 600 features to his credit), he was finally able to pick and choose projects as he saw fit. With his newfound concept of quality over quantity, he made choices like Stephen Hopkins's *Blown Away* and Tim Burton's *Ed Wood* as his next assignments. Hired by stunt boss Vince Deadrick Jr. for air ramp work and automobile collisions leading up to *Blown Away*'s climactic pier explosion (which was powerful enough to shatter 8,000 windows in the East Boston area); LeBell also worked with stunt-mates Lloyd Catlett and Cliff Happy, doubling Jeff Bridges and Tommy Lee Jones respectively. Recalling his days while on *Ed Wood* (cast as a ring announcer for the Jesse Hernandez-Tor Johnson wrestling match filmed at Long Beach Auditorium), Gene said he enjoyed watching Martin Landau work, especially when teasing the Academy Award-winning actor about their shared past on *Mission: Impossible*. Unable to place LeBell while in the midst of his Bela Lugosi role on the biopic of the B-movie boss, Landau later laughed when informed that he had bludgeoned, gassed, and knocked out the stuntman so often while on the spy series that he helped put his son David through private school.

LeBell's next film role came on Kathryn Bigelow's "end of the world primer," *Strange Days* (1995), filmed on location amid the alleys of downtown Los Angeles. Gene and Larry Holt were engaged by stunt boss Doug Coleman for the limousine chase sequences shot off of Figueroa Street in the wee hours of the morning. Much of the on-camera damage was done real speed while Gene drove in excess of 50 miles an hour. A pit crew of quick-fix mechanics, equipped with a paint compressor, spare body panels, and enough Bondo to stop a tank followed the action, keeping LeBell's limo on the road — often with the paint still wet.

Following more "tackles and tickles" on *Money Train* the same year (Gene did a bit getting run over by Wesley Snipes on an escalator), his next big studio feature was *Independence Day*. Again part of a stunt performer's dream team assembled by coordinator Dan Bradley, LeBell recalled the Roland Emmerich feature as a blast, literally. Utilized for the alien attack sequences as part of a throng of pro–U.F.O. enthusiasts zapped while atop the Bonaventure Hotel roof, Gene was ram-jetted over camera for his day's pay.

Finishing 1996 on a comedic note, LeBell was hired by stunt coordinator Joel Kramer for Arnold Schwarzenegger's Christmas offering *Jingle All the Way*. Instructed to attend a costume fitting based on the promise of a speaking role, the wannabe thespian was impressed upon seeing a rack of Santa suits until realizing he was only one of 20 other actors playing the part. Kramer's true purpose for hiring Judo Gene was for a sock-in-the-face stunt, as one of three Santas simultaneously knocked out by a single Arnold punch.

LeBell's next choice assignment came via coordinator Glen Wilder as he doubled comedian Rodney Dangerfield on *Meet Wally Sparks* in 1997. The resemblance between the two was such that when Dangerfield saw Gene in full makeup as his character, he said, "I guess George Clooney was busy." Filling in for Rodney on everything from banister slides and sword fights to being flung off a drunken horse through a window, LeBell spared the frail comedian the bumps and bruises of slapstick film making.

Challenged by coordinator Jeff Imelda to take some lumps on *L.A. Confidential* in the summer of '97, Gene was used as a cop during the jail riot scenes. Attesting to the inherent danger of stunt work, he was accidentally punched in the forehead (rather than the jaw as planned), driving his costume's metal hat pin straight into his skull on impact. Noticing that LeBell was bleeding profusely, director Curtis Hanson mistook it for a special effect and gave makeup man Tommy Cole a big thumbs-up for the added realism.

Joel Schumacher's *Batman and Robin*, released in the summer of 1997, was the sort of film stunt guys dream of working. It contained every imaginable trick from high falls and fights to fireworks, acrobatics, car chases, diving, and air-rams; an army of over 100 stunt players were drafted by coordinator Ronnie Rondell Jr. to be part of the action. Cast as one of the henchmen of Mr. Freeze (aptly acted by Arnold Schwarzenegger), Gene did a featured bit where he's pulled through a wall by the 22-inch arms of stuntman Jeep Swenson. Using special plaster board sets, the resulting impacts during the four takes required to get the shot caused LeBell to see stars, but put cash in his wallet as well. Paid for each take (unlike actors with a set fee), he made over $2000 for the day.

At the same time Gene was doing nights on the film's second unit, he was also engaged by day working on Jackie Chan's *Rush Hour*. Hired by longtime friend Terry Leonard for some stunt driving, he furthered his fun into a speaking role as a crazy cabbie. LeBell did a series of aggressive corner-slides and skidding moves that culminated into a final 360 degree spin, pulling into a stop. Holding the cab's two occupants at bay via a big pistol (he suspects they are robbers), the cabbie is questioned by Jackie Chan about the gun, which was supposed to end the scene. Once again deciding to be an actor, Gene improvised in a gruff voice, "'cause you guys owe me ten bucks cab fare!" Convinced he had added to the picture by the crew's laughter around him, LeBell was let down after director Brett Ratner approached him and said, "Nice try, pal, but only leading men get final lines like that one, not stunt guys!"

After the chore of rendering Greg Kinnear's believable beating sequence in the James Brooks feature *As Good as It Gets*, Gene went on to *US Marshals*. Continuing the trend of Hollywood mega-films during the '90s that produced bigger-than-life stunt crews, he was one of 80 performers cast by coordinator Gary Davis for the crash sequences of the prison transport plane. Describing the full-sized jet mock-up with its massive gimbal apparatus which rotated upside down before being flooded, LeBell said that between being violently thrown around then inverted with water slamming you in the face, you run the risk of real danger while smashing into other stunt guys. "The trick," Gene added, "is it to keep your motions as controlled and to the point as possible so when it's cut together it looks real and flows."

Perhaps the closest Gene would ever come to being a real actor was when cast as Rod Steiger's double in Peter Hyams' *End of Days*. The millennial downer was a dark portrayal of good versus the devil with Steiger's character Father Kovak meeting his doom in the end to help save mankind. Drafted by stunt boss Steve Davidson because of his close resemblance to the Oscar-winning actor, Gene further filled in for Steiger accidentally while grabbing a snack from the craft service truck. He was clad in perfect makeup applied by Louis Lazzara, including dentals and a priest costume; the sandwich guy mistook LeBell for the star and asked for his autograph. Always willing to oblige fans, he signed Steiger's name to a paper plate, thrilling the man to no end. *End of Days* was a lucrative undertaking: His pay-day as Steiger's double was near $3,000 per day.

Finally slowing down his frenetic pace of filmmaking after 40 non-stop years, LeBell's choices of employment post-millennium were mostly lucrative assignments where the danger factor was somewhat reduced. Remembering a gathering of older stunt performers cast in

Jim Carrey's feature *Bruce Almighty* in 2003, Gene revealed that he and the guys were hired by coordinator Mickey Gilbert due to their superior driving skills and calm demeanor after years behind the wheel. In one scene, Bruce is stuck in traffic while driving a pricey Mustang Saleen sports car; the payoff came as Carrey (given God's powers) forces the other motorist to the curb, affecting a Red Sea–like parting of the traffic before him. It required the seamless timing of 22 stunt drivers to pull it off; LeBell credited the group's longtime experience for the day's success.

At over 80 years of age, Gene continues to do stunt work in Hollywood. From television assignments on series like *Malcolm in the Middle* (where he played a clown in a batting cage brawl staged at Sherman Oaks Castle Park), to a Velveeta commercial where he's jerked through a wall after tasting the product, the guy just never stops. With no plans for retirement, he continues to hope that one day he'll be taken for the serious actor he's always wished to be. Until that time, however, Judo Gene is one of the instructors at a Dojo in North Hollywood, along with greats like Benny "The Jet" Urquidez, training the next generation of stunt folks and fighters on the finer points of stage combat and grappling.

One can rest assured that in the future, stunt actors will be just as in demand as they were in Gene's day. Regardless of CGI or digital morphing, there will always be a need for brave fellows and gals to do the physical work of stunts. One can only hope that the next generation of people doing it, are all at least half as talented as Gene LeBell. Having given his entire adult life to the pursuit of the grappling arts, as well as Judo, jiu jitsu, boxing, and the stunt crafts, the man is a walking encyclopedia of film world knowledge.

Constantly giving back to the communities which provided him so much, "the toughest man alive" continues to mentor young fighters and teach the fundamentals of stunt work to those who wish to make the transition as he did a half century ago. He is currently coaching MMA ladies contender Ronda Rousey (herself a judo champ) Although no longer wrestling bears, Gene LeBell is still making a contribution to Hollywood today.

4
William Fraker, Cinematographer

In 1950s Hollywood, the expansion of the independent studios produced a talented young crop of cinematographers. Armed with faster film stocks and more capable lenses, this new breed of shooters would ultimately change not only the way motion pictures were photographed, but the very stories that would come to the silver screen. One such visionary-to-be (who at 86 years of age continued to shoot and teach) was "style chameleon" and storyteller extraordinaire William Fraker (1923–2010).

Billy (to his pals) began his ascent to rank among Tinseltown's elite lensmen by way of near manifest destiny. He was raised by a doting grandmother, Alva (who made it to the States in 1910 on mule back from Mazatlan, Mexico); it's no small wonder that Fraker wound up in the biz, as he was often told by her as a child that motion pictures were his future. Possessing her own photographic talents, within a few years of becoming an Angelino, Alva landed a gig as a still photographer at the Monroe Studios in downtown Los Angeles. It was through the photographic labors of his father, William Fraker, Jr., and his uncle, Charlie Fraker, that young Billy began on his path to becoming one of the preeminent shooters of his generation. He was aware of the work of his uncle (a still man at Paramount) and that of his dad, who shot glamorous production photographs at Warner Bros. and First National Pictures as well as Columbia (where he was head of the still department). It was in the early 1940s that Fraker's own interest in making films was sparked.

"As a kid I saw the pictures *Gilda* and *Here Comes Mr. Jordan*," Billy recalled when asked about the movies that influenced his earliest desire to be a DP. "Watching the great action photography of cinematographer Joe Walker blew my mind," Fraker said with a look of admiration on his handsome face. "And of course, to anyone who served during World War II, Rita Hayworth was, well ... Rita Hayworth!"

The Walker-lensed *Here Comes Mr. Jordan* was remade in 1978 as *Heaven Can Wait*, starring Warren Beatty as Joe Pendelton (here a pro quarterback instead of a boxer like in the 1941 Robert Montgomery original). Fraker was the DP, and the feature was Oscar-nominated for Best Photography. The film's shooting required Fraker to handle everything from long-lens (1,000mm) football action photography to special effects camera movement and more. When asked about the toughest shot to pull off, Billy smiled and told a story of director-star Beatty coming up to him the first morning of principal photography. Telling Fraker how he wanted co-star Julie Christie photographed, Beatty said with a deadpan expression, "Now listen, Billy. I want you to make Julie every bit as beautiful as she is ... just not more beautiful than I am!"

To tell William Fraker's story completely, one must go back to September of 1945. During his Coast Guard service aboard the attack transport *Arthur A. Middleton*, he saw action in support of the 2nd and 4th Marines towards the end of the Pacific campaign of World War II. Honorably discharged with the rank of 2nd class signalman, Fraker utilized the G.I. Bill to attend the freshly formed U.S.C. film school in 1949. Along with fellow student Conrad Hall (another industry giant-to-be), they pursued the newly offered major of Motion Picture Cinematography. Studying under extraordinary teachers like montage master Slavko Vorkapich (of *The Good Earth* and *Meet John Doe* fame), Billy fondly recalled his favorite instructor's encouragement to "tell stories with the moving images, not just filming fancy set-ups of the actors saying their lines." Echoing the mantra of his college mentor Vorkapich, Fraker offered these guidelines to be a good filmmaker today: "Always move the camera as it pertains to telling the story — not just as an exercise in ego or senseless coverage."

Fraker graduated from U.S.C. in 1950. The closed labor ranks in Hollywood (and membership into the camera guild in particular) were stumbling blocks for the young shooter. Interestingly, in those days a film education had little to do with getting work. In fact, the oldtimers may have resented the college boys. Around the same time that Fraker earned his tasseled cap and gown, the new medium of television was breaking onto the horizon. With TV in direct competition to the studio fare (or so the bosses thought at the time), the job market was evolving, but it was still "every man for himself" to find work.

To survive financially, as well as to continue to develop his craft as a camera operator, Fraker hustled grab-shot assignments at 25 bucks a reel, for the likes of Lockheed Aviation and Kaiser Steel. "I would get a call from Movietone or some other producer looking for footage of workers arriving for the split shift at Lockheed," Fraker recalled of his early paying jobs, "and I would show up and film sequences of workers funneling into the front gates. It was a marvelous education. It was my camera and film perched atop that old Model A Ford, and my shot, composed on the spot. If the images were no good, I didn't make any money!"

Finally, after several long years of bouncing around town photographing anything that would pay, on July 1, 1954, Fraker's destiny moved one giant step towards fulfillment. "The phone rang that morning," Fraker said, "and it was the head of the camera guild, Herb Aller, inviting me to join the local. He told me to come down to the union office the following day and to bring 300 bucks to pay for my initiation fees. After hanging up the telephone, heart pounding, I immediately borrowed the cash from a friend and, disregarding Aller's suggestion of waiting until the next day to see him, I flew down to the Camera Local's office and was sworn in within 15 minutes of handing over the cash."

The relationship between the two men flourished over time. In fact, Aller ultimately liked Fraker's lens work so much that, within five years of seeing him get into the Guild, he was personally repping the young shooter on commercial assignments.

Among his early union gigs, Fraker toiled as a film loader at General Service Studios. Eventually the well-trained rookie rose to assistant camera while crewing over 100 half-hour episodes of the *Lone Ranger* television series. After the Lone Ranger rode into the sunset, Fraker wound up on other early TV offerings such as *Here Come the Nelsons* (later morphed into *The Adventures of Ozzie and Harriet*).

In a twist of fate, Fraker bumped into Conrad Hall while working on a car commercial and happily reunited with his old college chum. In 1962, in the process of operating camera on a new television series for DP Ted McCord, called *Stoney Burke*, Hall hired Fraker for the first time on his regular crew.

Fraker progressed through a multi-year transition from loader to assistant camera, eventually making the grade as operator, alongside pal Hall. As friendship between the two gifted lensmen grew, so did the myriad of projects they shot together. From an unknown television movie in 1964 aptly titled *Unknown*, to the Marlon Brando World War II thriller, *Morituri* the following year, their shared work was special. "Connie was more like the brother I never had," Fraker said quietly with a bit of emotion in his voice.

As Fraker's skill set continued to grow with experience, great opportunities began to surface for the up-and-coming cameraman. In the fall of '64, he was hired to operate camera for the legendary director of photography Charles Lang on the hilarious Cary Grant vehicle *Father Goose*. When queried about what he picked up from the master of lighting responsible for shooting such iconic flicks as *The Big Heat*, *Some Like It Hot*, and *The Magnificent Seven* (among others during his four-decade career), Fraker remembered Lang for his simple, strategic use of light. "Lang was a great teacher," he said, "very patient, and as he lit so simply, was always willing to explain his methods when asked."

Fraker pointed to other cinematic legends as having influenced his broad palette of camera craft. After mentioning shooters such as Leon Shamroy (who lensed *Twelve O'Clock High* and *Cleopatra*) and Bob Surtees (of *Ben-Hur* and *The Graduate* fame), Fraker recalled teacher and boss Ted McCord as having taught him the most about how to be a complete cinematographer. McCord, whose major works include *The Treasure of the Sierra Madre*, *East of Eden*, and *The Sound of Music*, demonstrated the concept of laying in photographic textures to Fraker, who would later be known for that very technique himself. Textures, whether manifested by lens selection, diffused lighting, atmospheric smoke, camera movement, or film emulsion, are among the magical elements of a DP's style; and as such were the keys to an original photographic approach for cinematographers like McCord and later Fraker.

Soon after his success with McCord, Fraker was hired by Hall (then a DP in his own right) to be his camera operator over the next ten years on projects like *The Outer Limits*, *The Wild Seed*, scores of car commercials and more. Upon completion of his metamorphosis through the ranks (and paying more than his share of the "waiting dues"—considering his education and skill set), Fraker was now finally on the path to the grand seat of his chosen craft: director of photography. When asked what he learned from Hall along the way, the suddenly animated DP responded, "I really loved Connie. His tremendous abilities allowed him to break traditional rules of cinematography for that time, and showed me that trusting one's instincts was the surest way to original, better shots."

The notion of "following one's instincts" was first put to the test when Fraker was hired by Hall to operate camera on the 1966 classic adventure western *The Professionals*, helmed by a gritty workhorse of a director, Richard Brooks. When asked about the picture, Billy smiled broadly while remembering his first (and nearly his last) conversation with the old-school director. About a week into the shooting schedule, a large complicated scene took place involving an Army train with dozens of troop extras and horsemen positioned around the tracks and platform cars. While shooting the intricate sequence with its secondary focus of a woman riding on horseback through frame, Fraker became fixated with a lucky accident. Upon holding a pan shot on actress Claudia Cardinale (instead of cutting away after a three-second beat as Brooks had instructed him to do), he was questioned by the livid director at scene's end. "What the hell did you do that for?" Brooks roared into Fraker's serene face. "Because it was so damn beautiful," Billy replied candidly. "It better be," the director said, turning and walking away. Fraker was certain that he was going to be fired (and feared for his situation with Hall), but on the following day he was surprised to be invited into the screening room, as Brooks' habit was to share dailies with as few folks as possible. When the take in question was shown during dailies (with its hold on Cardinale and the horse, neck high flowing through the frame), Brooks had the projectionist in the back of his hotel room stop the machine. "Fraker," he began sternly, "you were right to stay on her. Your shot was better. Would you like to see dailies with us from now on?"

As a result of this type of "better shooting," Fraker's rapid move up to DP was a sure bet. That break came by way of a referral from unit production manager James Pratt to lens *Games*, a suspense thriller starring James Caan, Simone Signoret, and Katharine Ross. The *Diabolique*-like *Games* was the perfect exercise to show the studio heads that Fraker could handle his own films. He finished under budget and on time; other projects rapidly followed, such as Mark Rydell's *The Fox* as well as the James Coburn spy spoof *The President's Analyst*, written and directed by Theodore Flicker. "Coburn was terrific," Fraker revealed, "totally focused, he was so precise with physical direction that he barely needed marks!" One sequence where stage marks would be the least of the talent's problems was the outdoor assassination scene, where Coburn was unknowingly surrounded while picnicking in an open field and must survive the deadly onslaught of a platoon of enemy agents. It was photographed mostly from an overhead point of view (utilizing a three-story grip parallel as well as a low mode dolly or hand-held for the ground shots); the choreography of violence revolved around a circular plan of assault, the dead and dying surrounding their intended prey with patterns of matted grass showing the crawl trails of the newly deceased. Fraker admitted, "We must have staged and restaged those positions ten times until it all fit together like some sort of live action Rube Goldberg gag."

Reflecting a nation in change, Hollywood films (by 1968) also marched to the beat of a different drummer. From the war in Vietnam to the civil unrest at home, times and the pictures made in Tinseltown were in a state of transformation. Motion pictures suddenly became about real life. Whether it was a horror flick, love story, or cop movie being produced into the late '60s, reality was the formula of this latest generation of filmmakers. For Fraker, that reality push produced two of his most extraordinary films, one after the other, *Rosemary's Baby* and *Bullitt*.

Rosemary's Baby was essentially a stage piece, utilizing its apartment interiors as supporting characters in a play. The Ira Levin novel was brilliantly brought to the screen by writer Roman Polanski, who also directed the horror classic. It was photographed by Fraker using only 18mm and 24mm lenses (as he graciously subscribed to Polanski's insistence); this allowed for a natural look to the dimly lit interiors as well as providing a fuller frame for facial close-ups. Utilization of those particular prime lenses also permitted an increased depth of field as well as broad latitude in apertures, allowing the backgrounds to literally wrap around the actors. Adding to the surreal look of the picture, Fraker chose to use Kodak 5254 film stock (rating it at 50 ASA) which delivered an extreme range of exposure while still rendering natural-looking skin tones and blacks as dark as duvetyne. The feature was shot in 98 days, two weeks on location in New York City and the remaining twelve weeks on stages at Paramount Pictures in Hollywood.

One scene that Fraker spoke passionately about was a two-minute continuous take of Mia Farrow standing in a phone booth. The shot involved Rosemary telling her husband (John Cassavetes) that she wanted to change doctors. Fraker remembered that during this time in Mia's life, she was married to Frank Sinatra and he wanted her to quit the picture so that she could co-star in the new film he was starting, *The Detective*. When she refused, Sinatra threatened to divorce her and ultimately cast Jacqueline Bisset in the supporting role of Norma MacIver. However, Farrow was determined to act in *Rosemary's Baby* as she thought the world of Roman Polanski and his script. "The next day," Fraker continued, "on the morning of the phone booth scene, a lawyer showed up on set and served Mia Farrow with divorce papers. Stunned and in tears, she went to director Polanski and told him of the situation. Compassionately, he [offered to shoot] around her for the day. Farrow refused and did that extraordinary scene in one take, which was used, uncut, in the picture."

Director Polanski also had knowledge of camera placement. While Fraker was lining up a shot of Ruth Gordon sitting on a bed, Roman purposely had him move the camera halfway out of frame instead of shooting her straight through the open door. Fraker questioned the move's purpose and was told to wait until dailies. Once he saw everyone in the dark screening room bend to their left when the shot came up, Fraker knew his friend's

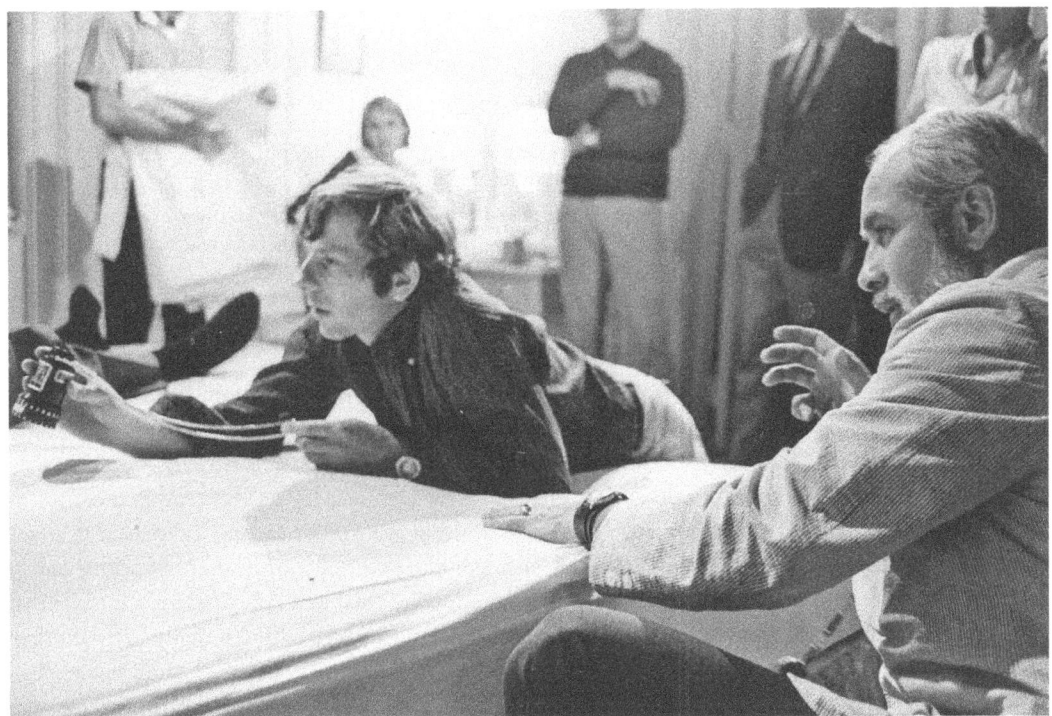

Lining up a bedroom scene for *Rosemary's Baby* (1968) on the stage at Paramount, director Roman Polanski (with finder) and director of photography William ("Bill") Fraker (right) converse over camera position. Polanski often chose the less expected shooting angles; the feature was filled with photographic tricks to build suspense (courtesy William Fraker).

Sitting in the now-famous green 1968 Ford Mustang Fastback (390 GT 2+2), Steve McQueen enjoys a morning cup of coffee as DP Fraker (white hair and beard) leans in through the open passenger window to adjust placement of the inside-the-car cameras used for the driving sequences in *Bullitt* (1968). Behind McQueen, camera operator David Walsh is doing a final lock-down on his second camera position. The employment of individual inside-the-car cameras was a first for the industry and was largely the result of the specialized use of aluminum tube and steel plate hardware mounted into the chassis or frame of the car. These technologies, brought into practical use by Detroit "car guys" shooting commercials in Hollywood in the late 1960s, enabled filmmakers for the first time to put the smaller Arriflex cameras anywhere they wanted (courtesy Bill Fraker Collection).

trick of forced framing to be a cinematic gag to throw folks off, while building suspense in the process. At *Rosemary's Baby*'s premiere, the DP laughed out loud when the audience of 300 all did the same sideward move, while struggling to see what she was doing on the phone.

Asked what makes Polanski such a great director (Fraker admits Roman his favorite), the maestro of light meters replied, "Roman is a visual storyteller second to none. He is a man of stunningly unique vision who can take the most complex of human emotions and lay them bare on the screen." Chuckling, Fraker added, "Plus, he's really funny. One of his ongoing jokes around the set was that Rosemary's newborn devil-child actually grew up to be producer Robert Evans!"

As Polanski's *Rosemary's Baby* was the perfect intellectual "demonic-horror" flick of that year (1968), director Peter Yates' *Bullitt* set a new cinematic standard for cop-action dramas. Starring the king of cool, Steve McQueen (partnered with an equally macho Mustang Fastback), the picture's gut-wrenching car chase scene through the hilly streets of San Francisco is still considered to be the finest in all of motion picture history. (No disrespect intended to Owen Roizman's Pontiac-punishing train chase (and near-miss baby carriage gag) in *The French Connection*; each was extraordinary in its own way.)

The cat-and-mouse beginning of the picture's iconic chase scene (shot at 24 frames per second, actual speed, with Arriflex cameras utilizing 200-foot magazines) was staged over an eight square block route which was first scouted, then walked by Fraker and Yates. Looking to work out camera shots as well as the stunt choreography, safety margins, and driving techniques required to accentuate the steep terrain, they were also in search of the type of "turn after fast turn" chase scene that would wow audiences with McQueen's driving. Ford's Mustang sold thousands of units after its featured role in this film.

The unsung hero of the chase sequence, however, is not just a car or a great driver. It was actually the special camera mounts. Rubber isolation gaskets combined with triangulated speed rail fittings were bolted straight into the car's frame; the concept freed-up camera mountings on vehicles completely. Designed and built by key grip and car rigging genius Gaylin Schultz, this "first of its kind on a feature" engineering allowed for filming at tremendous speeds without the appearance of the previously suffered camera vibration, experienced under early, lesser systems. Additionally, the use of the smaller Arriflex cameras, when combined with the tinker-toy concept of aluminum tubing, or speed rail (and custom-made cast mounting hardware), allowed Fraker to safely place cameras inside an occupied stunt vehicle for the first time in motion picture history. The danger of this application of the new camera rigs was amplified because the hero of the picture (McQueen) was doing much of his own stunt driving, when legendary stunt man Bud Ekins was not doubling him.

Fraker was confident about the movie star's wheelwork; his concept from inception was to have the audience's point of view of the chase be that of the driver. This was unlike previous hood and hostess mounts on car-rigs (which allowed the camera to either "look" into the vehicle through the windshield or open front windows). By placing the lens literally at eye height inside the automobile, Fraker created a new visual reference for action car sequences, which produced a real-life fast-driving experience, previously unseen by the public. The result of this inspired idea became a more realistic viewing experience for moviegoers. In some cases it even caused motion sickness to those watching the stomach-churning action in theaters.

Solar Productions (McQueen's company) hired well-known stunt driver and race car fabricator Pat Hustous to design, build and drive a special, low-slung open cockpit camera car on the film. Equipped with camera positions in the front and rear, the vehicle was constructed using the suspension and guts of an A.C. Cobra (all bolted to a custom Formula One–type chassis and covered in a light weight aluminum skin). The picture car was rocket-sled quick with a top speed in excess of 150 miles an hour. Fraker, recalling his first day of shooting with the radical new wheeled camera platform, began to question stunt driver Hustous about their breakneck speed, as the low whine from the tires became a wailing shriek as they crossed the Oakland Bay Bridge in excess of 120 miles per hour. Fearing for his life, Fraker shouted over the tremendous roar of the engine, demanding that the veteran driver slow down. Suddenly pulling over and power-skidding the vehicle to a tire-punishing halt, Hustous said sternly, "I've mortgaged my house for the bread to build this buggy, and I will be damned before I crash it. This is my money we're driving, Billy!" "At the fastest run we shot," Fraker said, "we did 125 miles per hour along the edge of Vermont through Russian Hill. If you tried to film it like that these days, you would wind up in jail."

Seeing the finished picture for the first time along with an audience in a theater, Fraker was astounded when movie patrons broke into sudden thunderous applause at the finale of the chase scene between the Mustang and the black Dodge Charger. "It was a moment of satisfaction," he said tearfully, "that I shall never forget."

Upon the box office success of *Rosemary's Baby* and *Bullitt*, Fraker became a DP in demand. A few months following his breakout in the biz, he took on the western *Paint Your Wagon* late in 1969. "Somebody at Paramount thought it a great idea to put Lee Marvin and Clint Eastwood in a musical western together," Fraker mused. "Both guys were great but *Paint Your Wagon* sort of petered out at the theaters."

Now an A-list cinematographer, Fraker was tapped to direct his first feature in 1970, *Monte Walsh*. (Most of his subsequent director gigs were for television series such as *Wiseguy*, *J.J. Starbuck*, and *Walker Texas Ranger*.) On the "throwback western" *Monte Walsh*, Fraker enjoyed his most complete artistic control. Combining his visual prowess for the composition along with a fine bedside manner when dealing with actors, Fraker found the captain's hat fit him well. However, known in Hollywood as a great shooter, he was ultimately more comfortable as a busy DP than a one-project-a-year director.

Mike Nichols' *Day of the Dolphin* (1971) came to Fraker next, when Roman Polanski

Shooting the fishing trip sequence for *One Flew Over the Cuckoo's Nest* (1974), Fraker (back to the camera on the dock, wearing a parka) was one of the few people on the boat not seasick from his time on Oregon's Depoe Bay Harbor. On the boat's bow are Danny DeVito, Vincent Schiavelli, and Ken Kenny while Sydney Lassick, Jack Nicholson, Mews Small, and Brad Dourif man the flying bridge. In the stern are William Redfield (in the hat) and Christopher Lloyd (photograph by Peter Sorel, courtesy Bill Fraker Collection).

4. William Fraker, Cinematographer 77

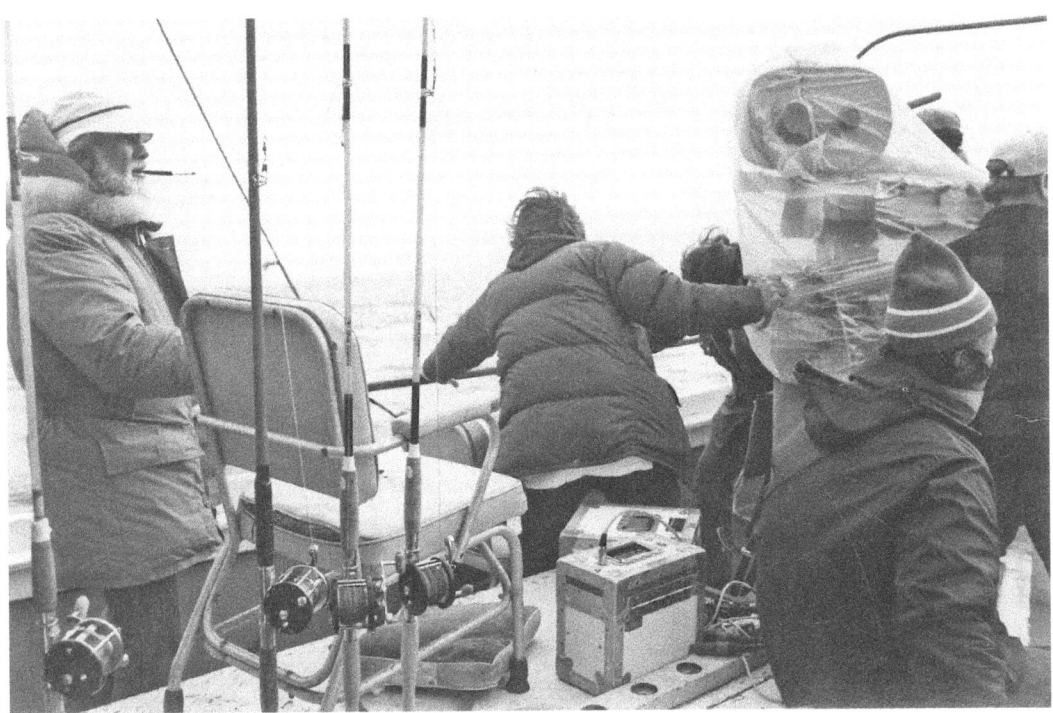

Having had disagreements with DPs Haskell Wexler and Bill Butler throughout the shooting of *One Flew Over the Cuckoo's Nest* (1974), helmer Milos Forman insisted that Fraker be brought in for the final two weeks of location shooting aboard the *Hyak* as it steamed back and forth across Depoe Bay, the smallest harbor in the world. Looking very Hollywood chic with his cigarette holder clenched between his teeth, cinematographer Fraker is pictured here during a particularly rough ocean day — a day that sent most to the ship's gunwales for relief. Between the intermittent rain (note that the camera is covered in plastic) and choppy seas, the day's work failed to match much from before. Operator Bob Thomas (center) "white knuckles" the camera to keep it from being thrown about (photograph by Peter Sorel, courtesy Bill Fraker Collection).

was still attached. Wishing to work with his old confidant once more, he signed on, and then stayed for the feature, even after Polanski pulled out. At the top of his game as a DP, Fraker surprised all on his next project when he took a camera operating gig for a director whose work he greatly admired. The picture was Milos Forman's *One Flew Over the Cuckoo's Nest* (1975). It won five Oscars, including Forman's Best Director and Cinematography for Haskell Wexler and Bill Butler. The camera crew was an A-list team. "It was a talented bunch of shooters," Fraker recalled. "As I was there kind of to 'play centerfield' shooting second camera, I had a ball!"

Ultimately repped by the exclusive Gersh Agency, Fraker was earning as much as a doctor or upper-crust lawyer for his lens-work by this time. Truly this was the "brass ring of success" that all artists in Hollywood hope for: cash *and* being in demand, which allows choice picks from the best projects in town.

Aside from the financial rewards of his work, Fraker was also thoroughly enjoying the artistic freedom given to those in Tinseltown whose films made money. No longer forced to take whatever pictures that came along, Fraker chose projects that suited him as an artist. In photographing *Rancho Deluxe* (1975) with his favorite film stock (Kodak 5254), his idea

78   The Film Crew of Hollywood

Opposite top: Caught in a pensive moment on the downtown Los Angeles set of *Looking for Mr. Goodbar* (1977) are director Richard Brooks (back to lens) and Bill Fraker. The film depicts Diane Keaton's character's search for sexual freedom and is based on the novel by Judith Rossner (which was inspired by the murder of New York City schoolteacher Roseann Quinn); the picture's look was dark and forbidding, reflecting the action in the film. Receiving an Oscar nomination for best photography, Fraker considered it a huge honor (courtesy William Fraker). *Opposite bottom:* Fraker confers with star-director Warren Beatty in 1978's *Heaven Can Wait* at Filoli Estate in Woodside, California. According to the cinematographer, Beatty asked him to make sure that his (Beatty's) then-girlfriend Julie Christie was as beautiful on-screen as possible. The actor followed up with, "Just don't make her prettier than me!" (courtesy William Fraker). *Above:* Shooting exteriors around the Filoli Estate, director Warren Beatty (left) and Fraker (white beard) talk about set-ups to come with co-helmer Buck Henry (to the right of Fraker). Beatty primarily employed his comedic genius pal just to direct his scenes, but Henry's input equaled Beatty's by the end. Note the large diffusion panels being employed behind camera, manned by a grip clasping the stand in the background (photograph by Peter Sorel, courtesy Bill Fraker Collection).

The war farce *1941* (1979) was another of Fraker's slapstick comedies that benefitted from his sense of humor. He is pictured here sitting behind camera while filming the surfacing of the Japanese sub (on Stage 16 in the Warner Bros. tank); director Steven Spielberg is in the plaid shirt. Fraker's early use of the Louma Crane for its unique ability to telescope while moving the arm (pictured in the background) led to the "French born" boom's employment as a shortcut to other coverage. Able to mimic a dolly without the time and space restrictions for track set-up and camera change-outs, it was ultimately used for more than half of the picture (courtesy Bill Fraker Collection).

was to focus on the surrounding beauty of Livingston, Montana, in contrast to the two, unkempt, inept rustlers of the story, so perfectly played by Jeff Bridges and Sam Waterston. "I wanted to frame these two social outcasts," Fraker revealed, "with the most beautiful, unspoiled geography that we could find. Livingston was perfect." That dichotomy between character and setting certainly worked as the dark comedy became a must-see for Frank Perry fans and in film schools the world over.

The famed director of photography takes great pride in the wide spectrum of the ever-evolving style of his lens work. From his Oscar-nominated efforts on motion pictures such as *Looking for Mr. Goodbar*, *Heaven Can Wait*, and *Murphy's Romance*, to the eclectic portfolio of some of his other films like Burt Reynolds' *Gator* and *Sharkey's Machine* as well as *1941* and *Best Little Whorehouse in Texas*, he is one DP who always did it "his way."

And whether lensing intricate fog effects on Spielberg's *Close Encounters of the Third Kind* or shooting a sequel to a hit like *The Exorcist*, Fraker has shown Tinseltown that he can shoot it all and do it well. In fact, it was on *Exorcist II: The Heretic* where Fraker (three years before *The Shining*) implemented a new type of camera platform, Garrett Brown's Steadicam. Able to take the camera anywhere that a specially trained operator can physically move (without tracks, wires or tripod), the gyro-stabilized counter-weighted arm and harness system would ultimately revolutionize free-form hand-held camera shots (which is standard in the industry today).

Slick spoofs like *The Freshman* (with Marlon Brando doing a parody of Don Corleone) and *Honeymoon in Vegas* show Fraker's photographic comedic timing as being spot on.

Fraker gives camera placement instructions while directing ***The Legend of the Lone Ranger*** (1981) in Moab, Utah. One of the famous DP's few outings as helmer, the picture was shot by old friend Laszlo Kovacs and starred Klinton Spilsbury as the masked man (courtesy Bill Fraker Collection).

Always with his eye on the details, Fraker was confronted with a problem when photographing the "Flying-Elvis" airborne finale for *Honeymoon*; he could not see the descending skydivers against the darkness of night. His solution was ingenious: He had wardrobe sew strip lights into the stunt actors' costumes, creating a comedic "human Christmas tree" effect, which went over big with audiences and critics alike.

One of Fraker's most photographically stunning features came late in his career: *Tombstone*. It was lensed in the summer of '93 in Arizona's Old Tucson for the "in town" stuff (versus the natural beauty of the Babocomari Ranch locations). His heavy use of existing light combined with prime lenses gave the picture a look of authenticity seldom seen in westerns, before or since. The moviemakers employed such period touches as wool costumes and firearms handling true to the day; personal comfort was left behind in pursuit of reality. With temperatures on set nearing 120 degrees on some afternoons, Val Kilmer (who played Doc Holliday) jokingly accused Fraker of recreating the uncomfortable working conditions just to mirror his character's true dislike of the Arizona climate. "Holliday was slowly dying of tuberculosis," Fraker explained, "and as such, the dry heat was his only relief, yet his taste for Eastern fashion caused him great discomfort. Some say that his desire to die in action was really about ending his suffering. By picture's end, with all the heat, we all felt like shooting someone."

Given such great "western faces" as Kilmer, Sam Elliott, Thomas Hayden Church, and Charlton Heston, Fraker was like a kid in a candy store while creating incredible portraits of his actors. When asked how he resisted the urge to indulge every shot as a close-up, the maestro of camera craft responded, "I'm there to tell a complete story photographically. Tight shots of faces are fun — but they alone can hardly cover the visual that a motion picture needs to be successful."

At conversation's end, when asked what has kept him going all these years, Fraker responded with the zeal of a missionary that teaching young film students at U.S.C. feels marvelous, as continuing to be part of the process is something he truly loves. In contrast to what he feels about the Hollywood of the past, he finds much of the film business today boorish, repetitive and poorly managed. Fraker's involvement with Tinseltown in his later years has been strictly on his own terms.

In parting, Fraker offered some words of advice to the next generation of filmmakers: "Dedication to one's craft is key," he preached. "Never stop learning or you're lost. Remember, think visually. Motion pictures are just that, pictures in motion that tell a story."

5
Earl Gilbert, Gaffer

When you talk about the collaborative effort of making motion pictures in Hollywood, one irreplaceable craft is that of lighting. From Eastman's days of glass-walled studios with 5 ASA film to the time of arc lights, and the modern world of HMIs, the practitioners of illumination are a largely unsung bunch. One man who transcended from old-school to the modern age of the independents (using lights as an artist his brushes) was gaffer Earl Gilbert.

Born in Bakersfield, California, in 1926 to parents Velma and Ray, his dad was a rigging electrician at the studios while Earl attended school locally until the family relocated to Culver City, closer to movie work. Leaving Hamilton High after his junior year to enlist in the Navy, the kid served aboard a destroyer (the *Mitchell DE-43*) as a quartermaster in the Pacific before discharge in 1945, after witnessing the Armistice signing in Tokyo harbor. Finally home in '46, Gilbert sought employment at 20th Century–Fox through the "Sons of Members" provision, which allowed returning veterans permit work because of their father or service record. Only granting "true" union membership to applicants who aced a difficult entrance exam (administered by the older card holders of 728 known as Blue Dogs), they ran the testing board with an iron hand, seeing the young guys as a threat to job security. There were tough written questions and a grueling four-hour gambit of standing 60 feet off the ground pulling pound-a-foot cable up to the perms. The physical and mental beating was not enough to deter Earl. While most failed (or were simply told they did), he passed due to his personal toughness and electrical knowledge gained through his dad.

Admitted into the union in November of 1946, the rookie caught on quickly at Fox with his new brothers from Local 728. Moving his way up while rigging, he wound up pushing the iron gang, as electrical construction was known, in record time. With the basic rule being a minimum of three years experience before getting regular show assignments, Earl progressed in half that when attached to his first feature, *Forever Amber*, in 1947. While more iron work followed on films such as *Gentleman's Agreement* and *Daisy Kenyon* throughout the year (rigging power and setting lamps in the perms), he was also learning how to play the studio game with full-time employment as his goal.

By late '47, a major Hollywood slowdown (due to television's growth) cut studio projects by 50 percent and stopped Earl's career advancement cold in its path. Laid off with hundreds of other new hires, he took a job in California's commercial fishing industry, the world's largest at the time. He worked non-stop for a year until Russian trawlers laid claim to West Coast waters; the gig came to an end when the locals went bust for lack of mackerel to make mortgage payments.

Once the fish work went belly-up, Earl returned to Fox under the preferred hire list, which reinstated laid-off vets before considering others. Within a year he was practically running the electrical rigging department garnered by his work on features such as *The Frogmen, David and Bathsheba,* and *The Day the Earth Stood Still,* among others. Aside from laying thousands of feet of 4 AWG cable for the heavy lighting effects on *The Day the Earth Stood Still,* Earl was responsible for lamp operation and underwater rigging on Elia Kazan's *Viva Zapata* that utilized innovative electrical safety techniques such as liquid proofing lights with a special sealant that (once applied to the brass connectors) allowed for totally submerged use without danger of electrocution or blown fuses. Employing frame assembles that held 12 globes each for a combined light of 12,000 watts, the end result was a perfectly illuminated sequence of a horse and rider galloping into the river, with camera coverage dropping below the water-level to see the bandito who had been shot-off, sink slowly to the bottom. Wearing nothing but shorts, a mask, and a homemade weight-belt to remain submerged, Earl operated the light-unit during the scene by panning with the horse as it entered the river, then held the six-foot rig beneath the surface for fill-light of the dying man.

Continuing to pick up work through the assignment board at Fox, Gilbert was given iron chores and, lamp operator duties on *Gentlemen Prefer Blondes.* Recalling the presence of both Jane Russell and Marilyn Monroe in the court sequences of the Howard Hawks–directed picture, Earl said that although Marilyn was sweet, she couldn't hit a lighting mark to save her life, while Russell (the more established star of the time) was not only charming, but occasionally liked to chat with the crew guys. "When she would walk on set and call out, 'Howdy Earl,' you felt like a million bucks."

Following *Gentlemen Prefer Blondes*, Gilbert was a "preferred hire" on Fox's *The Robe.* As Darryl F. Zanuck was behind the studio's big push with CinemaScope in an effort to outdo TV, this was the last all–hard light picture done in Tinseltown, and incorporated spectacular costumes and sets to show off the wide format's Technicolor hues. *The Robe* was touted as the "Modern Entertainment Miracle you can see without the Glasses"; the ad wording was a competitive dig by Zanuck regarding 3-D hitting the screen at the same time. First brought in to power the multiple stages at Fox, and the huge marketplace sets built at the Iverson Ranch in Chatsworth, Earl also lamp-operated on scenes including the rampages of Caligula (played by Jay Robinson) and the confrontation of Demetrius (Victor Mature) as he enters Jerusalem on Palm Sunday as a believer.

Returning to the iron gang at Fox, Gilbert took busy work dismantling scores of model 170 Kansas Arc lights, being modified for use as incandescent 10ks. As far as Hollywood was concerned, the age of the arc light was finished. In its stead, a myriad of other instruments replaced it, creating the need for electricians (like Earl) to handle all the new stuff. Continuing as a rigging wiz and lamp operator at Fox through 1954, he did a second religious blockbuster, *The Egyptian,* also starring Victor Mature. Blown-up by Zanuck as another biggie, this *Robe* wannabe was directed by Michael Curtiz and shot by Leon Shamroy. Despite its high production values and extensive locations in Red Rock Canyon State Park and Death Valley using hundreds of extras fighting epic battles (which Earl covered as arc operator), the film was a wash for the studio. To Gilbert, however, the picture was a plus for the tricks he picked up watching the DP and his longtime gaffer, Freddie Hall. Learning such nearly forgotten crafts as cloud mats, he was a quick study. Incorporated for plain

5. Earl Gilbert, Gaffer

20th Century–Fox's *The Robe* (1953) was perhaps the last "hard light" film Hollywood ever produced. The wide shots required more lights and operators to run them, as seen in this behind-the-scenes shot. Perched atop a ladder with his hand on the yoke of an arc lamp (right), Earl Gilbert takes in the scene (courtesy Earl Gilbert).

exteriors on sunny days, the addition of cumulus formations to the sky was all about texture and composition in the frame. It was achieved by first setting a 100-foot-long section of white muslin in front of a line of open face arcs; Earl watched as Shamroy manipulated a storefront-size piece of plate glass with a frosty mixture of Bon-Ami soap flakes stuck to it. It was sculpted into formations with raw lamps illuminating it; the set-up produced beautiful clouds on a screen, which could then be optically printed to the negative.

Gilbert's next tote-board gig from Fox was the color film noir offering by director-writer Nunnally Johnson, *Black Widow*. First tasked with rigging the picture, then staying on as lamp operator, he was having a blast aiming lights at movie stars Ginger Rogers and Gene Tierney. With his rigging skills getting noticed by the bosses in the office, Earl's career started to sprout wings when offered a job on director Jean Negulesco's big effects flick of 1955, *The Rains of Ranchipur*, starring Lana Turner, Richard Burton, and Fred MacMurray. In addition to electrical staging (he built water-proof troughs for all the power cables) Earl was assigned to a miniature crew for the village destruction finale that created a small monsoon right in the studio. They employed multiple Ritter fans and water from high pressure hoses; the combination of forces created 60 MPH wet gusts that impacted set walls with enough force to remove the paint; yet Gilbert's water-sealing held tight. Learning a valuable lighting gag from DP Milton Krasner on the palace destruction scene, he was shown a bounce lighting technique with a painted fabric ceiling piece, blended to the background with a softly lit gray sky on an overcast day. He used the method a quarter century later while gaffing *The Final Countdown*; it was still effective in blending textures despite the use of higher grain films.

Doing Fox's 1956 drama *The Bottom of the Bottle* (directed by Henry Hathaway and featuring Van Johnson and Joseph Cotten), Earl was beginning to become a sought-after key rigger. Proving his ability to get the job done while earning the respect of men twice his age, he was happy in his much-needed role and making plenty of cash while doing it. He was bringing home a thousand bucks a month at only 29 years old.

In the final days of 1955, Gilbert was hired to do one of the largest pre-rigs that 20th Century–Fox had ever undertaken for *The King and I*. Directed by Walter Lang and shot by semi-mentor Leon Shamroy, the picture required over three acres of backlot with 25 sets comprising an entire kingdom including stables, store fronts, markets and palatial rooms. A Westinghouse generator specially ordered 12 months before production met the movie's massive power needs. The plant had 6000 amps of capacity servicing five dimmers stacked on top of each other. Pulling thousands of feet of wire to power the multiple sets, Earl wisely incorporated Fox's underground tunnels (known as "the catacombs") to rig underneath the studio back to the main power house.

Recalling the challenges of powering such a large flick (as well as operating on the massive set-up where Anna [Deborah Kerr] is guided through the city streets on an elephant), Earl said using so many lights on the stage caused temperatures in the perms to sail past 130 degrees. With its coverage of the joined stages including Kerr's endless entourage, there was a danger of the emergency sprinklers going off and ruining the sets. Also, a spontaneous fire could break out due to the excessive heat caused by the forest of lamps. Studio chief Zanuck had two fire companies standing by with orders to first disable the sprinkler mains (saving water damage should they go off), then to extinguish the flames, while taking care not to wreck the sets. Laboring up in the perms as a follow spot man (exposed to the scorching conditions for hours on end), Earl said that in the process of keeping his light on the actor he watched Yul Brynner reach the point of near exhaustion. Yul would collapse in front of a large fan between takes to cool down; by film's end the already trim star had lost 20 pounds. Remembering the waltz numbers as exciting to do but a bit nerve-wracking because his follow spot provided Brynner's primary fill, Gilbert commented that despite rehearsals, the couple never hit the same mark twice and that it required anticipatory focus to keep them in the pool of light without error.

Taking whatever Fox had in store, Earl was next used on a small motion picture called *Bus Stop* (1956), directed by Josh Logan and starring Marilyn Monroe. Brought in to rig, Earl also picked up local lamp operator work on the picture. For the bedroom scene with Monroe and Don Murray, Logan requested that only essential crew members remain on set. Gilbert recalled her walking on stage dressed in a bathrobe, after refusing to come out of her dressing room for over an hour. As to rumors that Marilyn was nude beneath the covers, Earl said that if she wasn't bare, the only thing she could have had on was slippers, as his 10K was bright enough to read the thread count on the sheets, not to mention the naked outline of the actress underneath.

Although not overly impressed with DP Milton Krasner's stiff personality, Gilbert still gave him credit for having him make facial diffusion for Monroe's somewhat ruddy complexion. A tool was crafted by forming eye-slits and a cut-out for the mouth with a burning cigarette in a silk flag. The result was reduced unflattering lines on the face while giving the skin a smooth look without troweling on the makeup. Originally developed for actresses like Mae West, Greer Garson, and Merle Oberon to reduce the lenses' harsh glare of reality on otherwise less than perfect skin, the practice continues today.

An Affair to Remember (1957) was another picture on which Earl did grunt work before transitioning to lamp operator during the show. He was working a follow-spot for a scene between Deborah Kerr and Cary Grant where they improvised not only dance steps, but dialogue as well. Reacting to the series of unpredictable moves with a smooth pan or tilt of the light as needed, he kept the couple lit without missing a beat. "Anticipating Grant's movements by watching the direction of his feet," Gilbert explained, "I was able to stay one step ahead of the action since he was leading."

Just before Christmas of 1956, Gilbert traveled overseas for the first time in his career on the Jean Negulesco feature *Boy on a Dolphin*, starring Alan Ladd and Sophia Loren. A lamp operator under cinematographer Milton Krasner, he was promptly drafted as ship's electrician and underwater gaffer upon discovering the amount of diving work required. Handling the rigging of a submersible lighting grid, he built one 12-foot-square unit with a dozen 600 watt par lamps for illumination. It was designed for underwater fill of the initial diving sequences where Phaedra finds the statue (then swims to the surface, pulling herself aboard the boat); the transition was beautifully lit as Sophia's clinging blouse and scrubbed face had audiences falling for her the world over. Operating the semi-buoyant light in his hands (while below the boat with only a lead belt and mask), Earl followed her rise to the surface where she was blasted with a combination of bright sun and 5K fill producing the see-through effect that accented her body, while providing a sparkling catch-light in her eyes.

He also covered scenes with Ladd and Loren walking along the beach. Gilbert recalled that in addition to using low stands to light Ladd, production made sure no background extras were taller than Ladd, who at five and a half feet was three inches shy of his co-star. For the love sequences between the two, a ramp system of heavy planks was incorporated, giving the couple equal eye height when they kissed so she wouldn't have to awkwardly bend over. Taken with Loren's charm and natural beauty from her first morning's work on the boat in the Saronic Islands, Earl recalled her blazing eyes and acting ability to be enough for the entire crew to adore her.

Gilbert then settled back into the routine of running the Fox iron gang. Soon assigned as the head rigging juicer on *South Pacific*, he chose to do only the stateside work. Although offered a world-spanning jaunt to Ibiza, Spain, Hawaii, and the Timonian Islands of Malaysia, he declined because he was already employed full-time at Fox, making so much overtime dough that he didn't care to lose his spot. Skippered by Josh Logan and lensed by Leon Shamroy, its highly touted musical numbers were poorly interpreted by the director.

Continuing as gang boss, Gilbert was rigging key on Edward Dmytryk's poignant war piece *The Young Lions* starring Marlon Brando, Dean Martin, Montgomery Clift and Maximilian Schell. Though extremely well acted and staged, the production was not without its challenges for Earl and the crew. While they were laboring amid 130-degree temperatures in California's Sonoran flats area above the Salton Sea, dark clouds stalled shooting one afternoon as they suddenly rolled in, blocking off much of the daylight. A local extra approached Earl with a warning that a big storm was fast approaching the gorge they were in, and that the exposed electrical gear would create a dangerous situation. With high winds and flash-flooding a certainty he advised shutting down the production at once. UPM Bill Edwards pointed to an all-band radio on the front seat of his Jeep and said, "'If any storms were on the horizon, this baby would pick it up.' Almost on cue," Earl recalled, "the radio began beeping an emergency warning tone right in the middle of the first set-up with Brando and Maximilian Schell trading lines, as the background bushes began undulating all around them as though pelted by a million pebbles." Edwards was comically running for cover within seconds, after realizing he was caught in the middle of a downpour, with live cable on the ground around him. Still not comprehending the danger, the UPM ordered the production temporarily shut down until the storm passed. They covered everything with tarps; within two minutes the deluge was so severe that visibility was reduced to mere feet and the sound of the rain was like a bombardment in progress. "All of a sudden," Earl said, "a rumble could be felt, like an approaching freight train. It got louder by the second as the storm raged, while we huddled in our makeshift shelter of plastic sheeting." Glancing up to the surrounding hillsides, he watched in disbelief as a waist-high torrent of water came down the embankment at the company. Bracing himself against the location truck, Gilbert recalled the wave's force like that of a fire hose. The flash flood left all soaked, but none the worse for wear. In Brando's final scene, he gets shot and falls into a stream; Earl said the actor pretended to really be dead while lying face down in the water at take's end. "It was a tragic moment in the story when he dies, so when he cut up, everybody had a good laugh from it."

Among Earl's fond memories was of pushing the Fox gang on Vincent Price's *The Fly*. Shot between March and April 1958, the production incorporated lots of electrical effects from early Frankenstein flicks (Tesla coils, a Jacob's ladder, etc.) which Gilbert carefully rigged for use on the set.

Gilbert was next shipped out to lamp-operate in Utah for another Edward Dmytryk movie, *Warlock*, in December of '58. Starring Richard Widmark, Henry Fonda, and Anthony Quinn, the feature was another of the CinemaScope–Deluxe Color offerings so prevalent in Hollywood at that time. Finding himself crewed under gaffer Les Everson and shooter Joe McDonald in Moab's Dead Horse State Park, Earl was lamp-operating on the gun-shooting lesson between Widmark and Tom Drake (as Abe McQuown) when sent to adjust their light from atop a 14-step ladder positioned on a cliff ledge with a 1500-foot drop beneath it.

In the spring of 1959 Earl was assigned to work under new boss and future mentor Homer Planette (from *It's a Wonderful Life*). He was dispatched through Fox as rigging gaffer on George Stevens' *Diary of Anne Frank* (lensed by William Mellor); the job was a move up, owing to the helmer's top ranking in Tinseltown. Constantly adapting lighting ideas from the real world to studio use, when challenged to reflect the story's somber mood, Earl modified a series of low wattage fluorescent display lights to lend the place a gloomy look. Providing just enough illumination to highlight the room's unkempt conditions, the small fixtures could be attached to anything and hidden while deployed. Having made a good impression on the somewhat cantankerous Planette, it wouldn't be long before Earl hooked up with him again.

Consistently turning out good work on big pictures, Earl was now considered one of the best rigging gaffers in Los Angeles and was hired for the extremely challenging film *Journey to the Center of the Earth*. He was drafted as both electrical layout key and lamp operator for the locations in Carlsbad Caverns, New Mexico, as well as the underground sea-caves at Leo Cabrillo State Park; laying cable in the caverns was murder for Earl and his guys as the pound-a-foot rubber-coated wire had to be physically dressed over the craggly ground (versus the normal practice of pulling it) due to the caves' forest of stalagmites and snaking passageways. They shot at night and the electrical rigging had to be removed each morning to make the caverns presentable for the tourists, then re-installed in the evening before starting the night's work. Earl was also on the miniatures unit with effects gurus the Hammer Brothers who were busy gluing tiny sails on the backs of Rhino Iguanas, passing them off as Dimetrodons for the dinosaur battles. Operating several small instruments at once, Earl had to be careful while focusing his lamps and avoid melting the wax holding the fake wings to the lizards.

Riding the wave of rigging jobs that Fox provided throughout the decade, Earl was assigned to another studio blockbuster, Walter Lang's *Can-Can*, in September of 1959. Shot by DP William Daniels in 70mm Todd-AO format, the show required huge lighting set-ups with a stage full of instruments in the perms providing 800 foot-candles of illumination for the massive nightclub sets being shot on the 25 ASA film. Charged with running a dimmer board (after laying out the power specs for the stages), Earl was in the rare position to observe everything happening backstage thanks to his stationary position just off set. Privy to much of the usually unnoticed behavior of talent, he recalled Frank Sinatra being unfriendly to everyone including crew and co-stars alike (to the point of mocking Louis Jourdan's accent to his face), as well as never arriving on lot before 10 A.M., no matter the call time.

Encompassing hundreds of lamps, Earl's job was no walk in the park. With scores of dancing cues among the chorus line of high-kicking ladies (amid the theatrical lighting with its broad illumination levels and rapid changes), he had to stay extremely focused while the camera was rolling. Employing anticipatory trade-tricks like enlarged dialogue notes so he could follow the scenes' action, Gilbert also used grease pencil marks to indicate exact lighting levels for various sequences, with as many as 30 lamp cues on a single take. Recalling the September day in 1959 when Soviet premier Nikita Khrushchev and his wife visited the set, he said the Russian big shot's bodyguards were clearly taken with the long-legged dancers in the can-can procession. Then they were pulled aside by the group's ranking officer and given a verbal tongue-lashing that required no translation to understand that the guys were in deep trouble.

Gilbert was again matched with gaffer Homer Planette (whose reputation as "difficult" had made it hard to find folks to work with him) on the television series *Bus Stop* in 1960. He was slated as rigging head and lamp operator on this TV spinoff of the 1956 Marilyn Monroe film (only this time with Marilyn Maxwell in the lead). The studio sought a cheap lookalike of the movie, and hired cinematographer Bob Hauser to get it. Producing flat interiors with little contrast, Earl remembered filming the pilot with a bounced-fill instead of the beauty diffusion implemented on Monroe to get that creamy skin look. Although directed by Robert Altman and created by Roy Huggins, the series was ultimately cancelled because of a disturbing episode titled "A Lion Walks Among Us," with Fabian as a young psychopath. Planette once again offered Earl a full time best-boy position; he turned down the crabby gaffer due to his habit of yelling, and the regular money he was earning via his number one man status with department heads Ray Jones and Dave Anderson.

Still pushing Fox's iron gang, Gilbert was assigned as underwater gaffer on Irwin Allen's *Voyage to the Bottom of the Sea* in early 1961. Hired based on previous wet-work for *Boy on a Dolphin*, Earl and his operators were constantly pushing racks of sealed par lamps across the water tank floor while lighting the scale *Seaview* submarine in action. In addition to the miniatures and effects work (with second unit DP John Lamb), he also lit the full-scale mock-up sub, complete with its observation deck and distinctive array of windows.

In the spring of '61, Gilbert's next assignment would prove to be his final iron gang job at Fox: a difficult last-minute lighting rig for the picture *Battle at Bloody Beach*. Responsible for power set-up and illumination of a naval supply dock being used for a nighttime action sequence in San Pedro (despite having already worked a ten-hour shift on lot), Earl and his crew got the job done quickly, which allowed production to get their shot without costly delays. Taking a cab back to the studio at night's end, the group was later denied reimbursement by department head Dave Anderson, based on not having the U.P.M.'s prior approval. Standing on the principle of the 14 dollars (as well as a lack of appreciation for his rapid overtime rigging), Gilbert quit his in-house position with Fox in protest. Suddenly without a job (and with a growing family to support), he decided to take up Homer Planette on his standing offer. Despite the gaffer's reputation, Earl's excellent work ethic and Homer's early days at Fox with his dad spared him the usual sour attitude the other number two men received. He was quickly on good terms with the persnickety guy; a strong bond developed between the two, leading to a teacher-student relationship that served them both well. Beginning with *Mr. Hobbs Takes a Vacation* in early 1962, Earl was no longer under studio control but instead working with Planette as his sole boss. It was directed by Henry Koster and lensed with incidental light by William Mellor in CinemaScope and Deluxe color. From the start Earl learned that independent features are creatively run by the cinematographer, not studio brass. He rigged the interiors with enough juice to provide Planette 800 foot candles at f-4 with 25 ASA film. The results gave the picture its Norman Rockwell light including a vibrant tonal range that made Maureen O'Hara's red hair blaze. Now in charge of everything from manpower to equipment as best boy, Earl hired using the Fox roster (as the production was still staged at the studio), but did so without employing department misfits. He attracted only the best electricians; the crews he supplied Homer were first-class technicians paid the top rate and treated by producers accordingly. Even the gear was better. Earl was free to experiment with his personal equipment designs for everything from small clip-on lamps to huge underwater rigs. His supply of instruments was ever-expanding. He recalled the use of his biggest toy on the picture, a clickity-clack: He modified a military surplus transport to work as a mobile lighting platform. Since the tracked vehicle was capable of going anywhere, he utilized it as sun-fill on overcast mornings by attaching two 10Ks on a pair of 12-foot risers, while running power off a voltage converter on the engine. It was ahead of its time by two decades, eventually the industry would adopt such machines as location work increased along with faster film and lenses.

Given a second unit gaffing gig on the picture, Earl was challenged to match the same high-noon angle of the sun on stage, and recreate the colors of the sky and sea-line shot the previous day on the beach. Rigging an arc light with an amber gel at the same pitch and direction as the original sun, he incorporated a sky-blue overhead and painted-sea backing behind; secondary illumination blended the set together, including the sand-covered stage floor below. (He had learned the technique from Milton Krasner on *The Rains of Ranchipur* a few years earlier.) Earl was given "attaboys" by Planette and William Mellor after seeing how well his stuff matched the original. One day when Earl was manning a light on the Yacht Club sequences (where Jimmy Stewart dances with his daughter), he told a young trumpet player in the band that his sound was pretty good. Six months later Gilbert recognized the dynamic musician from a record poster and realized he had been talking to Herb Alpert, before his A&M break made him famous.

Taking his second independent project as Homer Planette's best boy on *State Fair* in '62, Earl pushed the iron gang for the interiors on lot, while also traveling to Dallas and Oklahoma with the shooting company for logistical duties. Charged with providing power at the antiquated Fair Park main hall in Dallas without a generator, he bravely used every available outlet while pulling so much house-juice to feed his high wattage lights that he was forced to run hundreds of feet in extension cords plugged into outlying buildings. Offsetting the drain on the old system to avoid blowing fuse panels, Gilbert joked that he knew his wattage levels were maxed out when adding one final Junior caused "Big Tex" to dim. Earl was beginning to develop a system of location lighting through "borrowed" sources; his imaginative solutions continued to build his repertoire of rigging skills which he would implement for the remainder of his career.

One morning while preparing to shoot a scene featuring a bull in a pasture, Earl was intrigued by a local rancher who drove up to the company in an Eldorado convertible dressed in bib overalls, boots, and a well-worn cowboy hat. Munching peanuts from a large cloth sack after exiting the vehicle, he then leaned against the dusty car watching the crew at work while spitting shells on the ground. Paying strict attention to the camera crane and an array of grips busily working to set up the shot, the redneck asked Earl in a thick draw, "What's all the fuss over one old bull?" He finally introduced himself as oil billionaire O.L. Hunt, and mentioned that he had a little spread in the area. When asked by helmer Jose Ferrer if his ranch had a name, he told the director with a straight face, "Yeah, it's 180 acres right up yonder....called Dallas."

Returning for another Homer Planette-William Mellor film, Gilbert signed for George Stevens' *The Greatest Story Ever Told* in the summer of 1962. Prepping multiple stages at Culver Studios beginning months before production was announced, Earl and his crews toiled tirelessly on the massive Biblical project, the biggest movie in town that year. Bob Surtees was originally slated to be the Cinematographer, based on Stevens' desire to match "the look" seen in the shooter's previous feature, *Ben-Hur*. It was purposely underexposed while lit with high contrast ratios for the "dark interiors"; the helmer was particularly taken with the scenes of the four white stallions in Sheik Ilderim's tent and wanted that dynamic applied to his film. Unfortunately, constant clashes with Stevens over taste issues caused him to quit, whereupon DP William Mellor came in as a replacement. Tragically, he died three weeks into production of a massive heart attack. Next to join the project was seasoned vet Loyal Griggs, who did *The Ten Commandments* and viewed Bible fare much like Stevens did. A team of cinematographers were drafted for the director's round-the-clock multiple units, learned from his military days when manpower was no object. Working with shooters like Charles Lang, Leo Tover, and George Folsey to get the miles of coverage needed, Planette assigned all second unit gaffing duties to Gilbert, as the older man could hardly work nights or be in two places at once. Standing in, Earl not only thrived under the added responsibility but learned the necessary people skills for handling a major shooting unit.

Aside from helping Earl to excel at best boy from experience gained through sizable features like George Stevens movies, the work also accelerated his rapid rise to gaffer because of the on-the-job mentoring Planette ultimately provided. Although the winter of '62 was a slow production season in Hollywood, Gilbert was able to give 105 lamp operators a better Christmas when hiring them for two weeks of arc light work on the Market Village night exteriors, shot at Selznick's 40 Acres Studios amid 50,000 feet of indoor sets. Learning that rank doesn't always dictate wisdom, he was ordered by Stevens to "get out the big ones" when lighting the front gates for the market sequence. Referring to a gigantic pair of Army surplus "Sun-arcs" to create a God light for the 30 × 30 foot entrance, he explained to the boss that the units were designed for nocturnal aircraft spotting out to 10,000 feet; the director insisted they be implemented nonetheless. He aimed them at the massive wooden gates from 40 feet away; the surfaces rapidly began to smoke under the unit's intense tem-

Lighting Jesus' last procession coming from the desert on George Stevens' *The Greatest Story Ever Told* in the summer of 1964, gaffer Gilbert (pointing) is supervising the placement of his favorite Kansas arc lights, while shirtless operators brave the midday heat of California's Death Valley. "The sun was so brutal out there," Earl recollected, "that we all wound up with tans so deep, people thought we were local Indians when we returned to the hotel" (courtesy Earl Gilbert).

perature, then smolder as the paint peeled before Stevens' eyes. Suddenly alarmed at the sight of his set getting cooked, he turned to Earl and demanded to know what could be done. "Try moving them back to Baldwin Hills," Gilbert responded jokingly. He replaced the search gear with a brand new concept made in his shop: a nine-light (as they were not yet manufactured) which he incorporated for the market stalls while aiming a series of arc lamps through a panel of white muslin; he lit the gates from a high scaffolding to obtain a Heavenward angle. Another of his "best boy fixes" came while lighting a quarter mile stretch of crosses for the crucifixion scene at picture's end. Once again utilizing muslin panels (40 feet by 400 feet long), Earl set-up 100 arc-lights, hitting them at four-foot intervals with each martyr cross-lit by an individual beam. Looking to intensify the illumination on Jesus above the others, he constructed a monster-arc with a focusable 60-inch diameter parabolic lens (generating 150 amps of power), which could be aimed with pinpoint accuracy. Earl's remark that he had to use caution or risk burning Max von Sydow right off the cross was no joke as wood actually burst into flames while positioned within 30 feet of the beam. Along with the ethereal light on Jesus, the scene's CinemaScope framing allowed eight additional lightning strikes to blend with the blue sky panels and painted backings throughout the set, issuing a believable transmission of supernatural atmospherics and weather that helped sell the otherworldly dimension of the action. He strategically placed the lightning by staging four machines behind the set with two in front and two more filling from the sides; the results provided a wrap-around depth to the mechanical effect that had never been realized before. Between his Lord-light and lightning bolts, the gaffer's electric-brush painted most of the image, with the exception of von Sydow's portrayal of Jesus. According to Earl, all on set showed the actor a level of kindness that was not only tied to the role he was playing but the fact that he was staying in character full time. Taking meals alone and strolling barefoot around locations with a calm reserve in his stride, Max ignored the heat of day and the surface walked on, further blurring the line of those observing his actions.

Speaking of Gilbert's engineering of nine-lights, focusable lightning machines, and gel innovations rapidly manufactured by start-up companies like Lee: He also had a hand in developing the first Big-Eye 10K light. Approached by cinematographer Charles Lang (who liked Gilbert's 60-inch Parabolic Arc), the best boy was challenged with creation of a large Fresnel lamp with a focusing element. He employed lighting manufacturers Grosso and Grosso to build a prototype, and the Big-Eye was born and immediately copied by various makers who ultimately wound up in a stalemate over proprietary ownership as no singular patent could be awarded.

By the summer of '64, Stevens was in the painful process of secretly dropping expensive miracle shots (like Jesus water-walking), on which he had already spent considerable money. Rearranging his shooting priorities, he occasionally made the crew's life tough, especially Earl Gilbert's. While filming the Sermon on the Mount sequences (shot on the Green River overlook in Moab Utah), the director wanted more color in the surrounding hills (they were brown after the summer season). To make it look like God's gardener had cleansed the earth, an army of scenic artists and greensmen armed with Hudson sprayers were brought in to work through the night. They applied 7500 gallons of paint while infusing blue, yellow, and red highlights to the scorched sod and dirt; the efforts were successful in obtaining a rich green hue to the ground that was just what Stevens wanted for the following morning's shots. Aside from being tasked with staying ten additional hours through the night to set up and run a dozen Arc lights (so the painters could see to work), Earl was busy into the morning, moving them around to dry up wet patches. Still on the clock when the shooting started, he had labored for nearly two consecutive days, non-stop.

In December of 1964 Earl was signed as Homer's best boy on *The Satan Bug*, directed by John Sturges and lensed by Bob Surtees. After introducing Earl to his DP, Planette bailed to work on *In Harm's Way*, as it was a huge film slated to run three times longer. He handed the job off to Gilbert (after getting Bob's okay). Within four years of mentoring, Homer's prodigy was fearlessly ready to light his own movies. He had already lit countless second unit set-ups as a stand-in gaffer (as well as excelling at rigging and lamp operation); there was little that Earl couldn't handle with the upward transition. "I had it all together," he recalled proudly, "so I was respected right away." Proving his lighting skill the first day of *The Satan Bug*, he came up with an open ceiling concept for the bio-weapons lab that produced a soft non-directional fill, which was perfect for the shot.

He employed lamps at angles up and over the walls into an opaque ceiling piece; its transverse pitch produced the impression from the ground-up of a solid roof for filming purposes. In addition to the overhead lighting, Earl constructed small incandescents with white diffusion built in. Putting out 30 foot-candles of detail illumination, the cup-lights could be recessed beneath counters or into walls providing fill for a prop or lab gizmo without separate instruments elsewhere.

Instantly trusted by Bob Surtees, Earl was treated with the respect of an equal when it came to setting up shots as well. Motioning where the lens was to be (sending the grips into a flurry of preparation), Surtees would let him know how many foot-candles he required and from which direction, whereupon the gaffer would call for the lights to be brought to set and placed. Surtees left many of the particulars to Earl as to which instruments went where; the guys' doubles match working style is one that only became better with time.

Continuing with Surtees (as Homer was still in Hawaii shooting *In Harm's Way*), Gilbert gaffed another John Sturges picture, *The Hallelujah Trail*, in the winter of 1965. Enjoying a shared view of motion pictures, he liked working with Sturges as the gutsy director approached getting his shots with common sense. Filmed on location in Gallup, New Mexico, and the Alabama Hills area of Lone Pine, California, the Western spoof was not without its lighting challenges. Equipped with a truck full of arcs for the daylight exteriors, Earl had to get creative with his "Kansas work horses" while shooting night-for-day sequences of Burt Lancaster and Jim Hutton on a porch. Incorporating yellow carbon rods in the lights, the resulting effect when mixed with the ambient darkness copied the warm color of the sunshine perfectly while providing natural flesh-tones when used without the standard 85A corrective filter. Most of the feature's interiors were done on stage at Goldwyn Studios including the painted backing inserts illuminated by 400 foot-candles of direct light on dimmers, giving a contrast to what was shot on location, so both would match. Knowing the Technicolor lab would automatically add night-time blue shading to the evening shots, Earl wisely under-lit the backgrounds by a half stop to compensate for the processing technique. Filmed in Panavision Ultra 70 format, the picture required a three-projector process to be seen on a Cinerama wide curved screen. Needing extremely sharp focus to provide adequate depth of field for proper function, the average F-stop on the film was eight or greater, which prompted Earl to provide lots of light.

Taking a sci-fi movie in the fall of '66 with cinematographer Alan Stevsvold, Earl gaffed a Griffith Park quickie titled *Cyborg 2087*. Directed by Franklin Adreon, the low-budget thriller starred Michael Rennie (from *The Day the Earth Stood Still*), cast as a robotic human crossover clad in a custom-fit silver spacesuit. Lighting the costume by applying a combination of white diffusion and hard-edged fill to sell the material's futuristic look, Gilbert also feathered Rennie's pale facial skin with nets and lavender scrims to give the actor an up-scale glow that the production quality lacked. Earl suffered when listening to Svevolds' ranting after being pressured by the ASC president to toe the line over job security. Calling for total control of lighting by cinematographers, the guild felt that gaffers were exerting too much artistic influence over their members. Earl was told by Stevsvold at breakfast that he was taking over the lighting; the DP ordered Gilbert and his guys to fetch the lamps and set them up at his direction. Following orders to a tee on the first sequence of the morning, Earl's electricians quickly configured every light from the truck, and then randomly aimed them around set while turning them all on. Having set a half dozen 5Ks, a couple of brutes and a forest of small instruments including a rack of Juniors and Babies, the gaffer then told his crew to take a 15-minute break. Turning to the cocky DP while walking off the stage, he said, "There you go, Alan, everything's hot, now just turn out the lights you don't need." Returning to find nothing touched, Earl said the cinematographer sheepishly apologized (producer Earle Lyon had threatened to file charges against him with the IA, for causing a problem over job classifications).

Back from scouting for *Doctor Dolittle*, Surtees immediately engaged Earl to gaff the picture as Homer Planette was experiencing medical issues that kept him away. Working locations from Marigot Bay in Saint Lucia, to Malibu Creek State Park and the 20th Century–Fox Ranch in Calabasas (plus three months in Castlecomb Village and Pinewood Studios, England), Gilbert was constantly challenged by the overseas crew's habit of doing things contrary to Hollywood practice. While inspecting the equipment on the first day in Castlecomb he was baffled by large wooden frames holding amber glass panels mounted to the face of each light. Told the 30-pound filters were made from quarter-inch thick pieces of color-corrected hardened gelatin and were fragile, he informed Pinewood gaffer Vic Smith that aside from the rigs being too bulky, in Tinseltown color like that was done from the camera (Earl showed him a yellow 1-y filter while it was being fitted to lens). Smith ordered his men to remove the boxes and stow them for the remainder of the picture.

Along with the English lighting issues, the show was sent a broken Chapman crane from Italy; Earl had to re-wire it for Surtees before it would operate smoothly. Then another procedural difference became obvious to the gaffer. Coming in to light the set-up, he was amazed to see English grips pouring rows of cement forms instead of the sleeper track usually employed for driving moves with a crane. It would require eight hours for the "channels" to cure. Director Richard Fleischer was outraged at having to scrap the day's shot when informed by Surtees that American track would have been fine.

Castlecomb locals took offense at a temporary dam built to produce a shootable lake for the feature; Earl recalled a former SAS solider from the village (Sgt. Ranulph Finnes) blowing up the structure to show his contempt for the Hollywood establishment. (The sequence was restaged later at Malibu Creek State Park.) Once everything was in sync, the picture settled into a daily challenge for Earl while lighting interiors. Dealing with a studio full of live animals during the talking patient scenes at Dr. Doolittle's house, he had to dodge pigs, sheep, ducks, goats, a monkey, two horses, some turtles, and a giant macaw, plus their collective droppings. The poor gaffer was getting pecked, crapped on, and otherwise abused by nearly every species on stage. Momentarily distracted while adjusting an arc lamp, Earl had something crash into him from behind that felt like a punch in the back. Turning around, he froze when suddenly face to snout with a 2000-pound rhino that had wandered away from his handler.

Checking his mail at the hotel the following morning, the gaffer received the script for *The Graduate*. With a few weeks still remaining on their current commitment, Surtees and Gilbert read the story. Penciling in lighting and camera notes on the backs of its pages, they worked out the picture's look even before producer Lawrence Turman asked them to do a weekend camera test for his project in a London studio. Employing 5:1 high contrast ratios (most pictures were lit 2:1), the guys sought to impress director Mike Nichols, who was known for his exotic production styles. Filming stand-ins for Anne Bancroft and Dustin Hoffman's bedroom scenes, they shot wide open on 50 ASA stock while using 200 foot candles on the bed with 1000 for the background to pump up the contrast. When Nichols saw the fantastic tonal range on the dailies (which fell somewhere between film noir and documentary), he immediately signed them up to make the picture.

While filming the initial seduction between Ben and Mrs. Robinson (with the camera shooting through Bancroft's bent leg lit at 200 foot candles and Hoffman framed in the background triangle at less than 50), Earl was maintaining Surtees' ratios with substitute cinematographer Joe Ruttenberg. Hired for three days of master shots due to Nichols' admiration for Elizabeth Taylor's look in *BUtterfield 8*, a special nuance was achieved through the old pro's set manner which enabled him to capture one of the picture's most iconic images. Staying in tune with Surtees' high contrast vision, Earl lit scenes such as the fish tank set-up (with Ben looking through the aquarium into the camera) by using a 1000-watt top lamp filling the water with a muted portrait light, then reducing the background values at 200 foot candles to make the actor's face in the foreground more prominent.

Other sequences containing Gilbert's signature touch: the room interiors filmed in LA's Ambassador Hotel, richly designed by Dick Sylbert as the high-priced hideaway for Mrs. Robinson's affair with Ben. Earl incorporated detail lights and practicals as well as soft bounces to show off the room's decor. Continuing to light in the same high contrast balances for the strip joint scenes with Hoffman and Katharine Ross, he employed a single overhead follow spot for the writhing topless dancer. With her forced perspective lensed vertically from below on a wide lens, the 4'10" actress appeared to be a giant from the pair's point of view as they walked through the club to a table. Lighting the kids seated with two separate single sources (then flagging off any stray light), Earl was able to produce a precise pool of illumination in the frame, which made the extreme depth of focus throughout the entire scene possible.

Revealing his psychology of building visual tension by allowing a subject to walk into dark patches of shadow, then back out through the light again, Gilbert said the practice freezes the image in the audience's head like a flashbulb going off. Utilized during Ben and Elaine's entrance (with Hoffman clad in black Ray-Ban sunglasses and she demurely walking two paces behind), the visual gaps of coverage when plunged in and out of the dark underlined a physical distance between the two that was more than just space in the frame.

Along with seeing the couple seated at the table, perched behind them in clear focus was a bulky extra eating a huge steak dinner. Drafted by Mike Nichols after seeing the jovial fellow selling Knapp work shoes at the studios, the director wanted his over-sized "Fred Flintstone head" to be voraciously inhaling food throughout the shot. Literally a metaphor for the carnal consumption of flesh known as a meat show, the salesman sat through dozens of takes while consuming six full T-bone dinners in the process, illuminated in a subdued pool of light all his own. Earl utilized a 3/4 overhead source that placed 50 foot candles on the Knapp eater while giving Ben and Elaine's table a contrasty 100 with flags separating the beams to give everything a cabaret effect.

Earl was always one to take advantage of what already works on a location: While shooting the underwater sequence with Ben in full scuba gear (sitting cross-legged on the bottom of the pool), Gilbert allowed natural light to envelope the actor while employing shiny boards across the top of the water to pop-up the sky above him, providing a higher contrast below. This gave the pool scenes a third dimension that Gilbert's wraparound light greatly aided.

Earl was present for the two nights of driving sequences shot on the just built 170 freeway, where he used small hidden lights in the Alfa Romeo Spider, including a face fill built into the rear view mirror, which was featured in several soul-searching glances while driving. He also incorporated reflective cards inside the doors and dashboard. The interior illumination on the day-to-night-to-morning run looked natural while providing just enough fill to gain a full stop in exposure.

While necessity (such as the driving gags) produced many of Gilbert's gadgets during his career, on *The Graduate* it was Beverly Hills city ordinance that compelled him to his biggest find. Denied use of generators for the show's night locations (because of past noise complaints), he built the first rentable "9-lites" in Hollywood. He approached Colortran's John Murray to manufacture six prototypes (made with individually articulated diachronic heads in a tic-tac-toe configuration); the sizable instrument utilized Fay bulbs for its lamp type. With a "beam throw" as broad as a Mack truck, the 9-lites were the answer to Earl's and Surtees' needs, as they could be tied into existing juice found along the streets, such as light poles and overhead power junctions feeding the block's private homes. Ultimately appraised on set by Mole Richardson powerhouse Larry Parker, the dynamic beasts are still in common use nearly fifty years later, with no real changes to the original concept.

Gilbert's next foray into network television pilots came when offered an easy gig (in the words of associate producer Robert Rosen), gaffing a cop show titled *Hawaii Five–0*, to be shot in the exotic island paradise. Starring Jack Lord in the McGarrett role and Tim O'Kelly as his #2, the shoestring production was based out of an old Quonset barracks in Pearl City called Mongoose Manor due to its leaking roof and local jungle rats gnawing on the power cables.

Earl was led to believe that much of the show's daylight exteriors were to be lit with shiny boards and available light. After seeing the reality of the harsh Hawaiian sun needing fill to balance, Earl wound up using a complement of scrounged-up gear he could repair. He was stuck with a cargo container of old equipment pawned off on the distant locale by CBS. The shipment had few working instruments other than a box full of shiny boards and a pair of ancient Arc lights with no filters. Earl was told it would take ten days for any replacements to arrive; his time ran out when suddenly tasked with shooting a 700-foot-long oil tanker for a major night sequence during his first week as gaffer. He had his people scour the Hawaiian Islands buying up all the photo flood lamps they could find. They constructed long rows of wired-together strip lights made from 1 × 3 batten stock with porcelain sockets every foot; the 20 × 50' banks were controlled by dimmers and used over 3000 bulbs combined to illuminate the massive ship. Once again employing practical solutions to produce big results on screen, Earl solved the equipment problem his way — with common sense and the mechanical know-how to make it all work.

Directed by Paul Wendkos and lensed by DP Richard Rawlings, the series may have been created by Leonard Freeman, but it was most certainly run by the ego of Jack Lord. Earl was asked to gaff *Five-0* when it was picked-up by CBS before the conclusion of its pilot production (based on test audience reactions); his homesickness and general disdain for the star's posturing (not to mention the continual sandbagging of inferior tack) caused him to turn the producers down, despite the show's tropical location and the promise to double his pay if he stayed.

Going from the humid hostility of Jack Lord's *Hawaii Five-0* to odd couple John Wayne and Kim Darby, Gilbert did Henry Hathaway's western classic-to-be *True Grit*. He was hired by producer Hal B. Wallis, who was looking for a gaffer to handle everything from lighting the picture's difficult exteriors in Durango, Mexico, to keeping senior shooter Lucien Ballard moving along. Earl's job was aided greatly by the director's work habits. Hathaway had a reputation as a stickler for keeping on schedule (including his routine of starting at 7 A.M. sharp with lunch at noon and wrapping by 4:30 P.M.), but he always gave Gilbert a head start when stowing his gear for the night: They were allowed to put everything back on the truck but the last lights still working, so that when the Martini was called, there was little left to do for the juicers but to go home. Ballard (originally a laborer who worked his way off Paramount's loading docks to become a DP) preferred single source high-key lighting with finite instruments and clearly cut contrast (like his new gaffer Earl Gilbert); the two agreed on how things should look from the start. "He was like Bob Surtees," Earl recalled, "in that he also liked simple, direct lighting. Once seeing that was my thing too, we didn't have any issues."

For the Rooster Cogburn trial sequence (shot in the original county courthouse in Ouray, Colorado, built in 1888), Earl incorporated daylight flooding the room through a large picture window with pairs of Juniors set in fill and key positions for individual faces, separated by flags on the other. Returning to stage two months later for additional coverage, he recreated the Colorado light by using an arc through a duplicate window as his key, and bounced a 5K into the ceiling piece for overhead fill; he finished with his Juniors split on the actors for facial close-ups. Viewing the dailies, Hathaway had to be told which was the location shot and which was done on stage, owing to Earl's superb match of color and contrast to the original courtroom.

Chen Lee's laundry was lit with an overhead midget through a muslin oval cut to mimic the shadow of a hanging lantern. It provided an eerie, dark-eyed view of the drunken Cogburn lying on his flophouse cot while being questioned by Mattie Ross (Darby). Earl's desire was to not only show what the dank storeroom would have historically looked like, but to also paint an accurate portrait of Cogburn's low station in life. Providing small top fills for Mattie's turn-around shots as well, he was careful to keep the light to less than 50 foot candles, or two-thirds of what was being realized by the lantern gag, to keep the imbalance realistic looking.

There was more clever lighting in the snake-hole scene, where Darby falls into the pit with only skylight illuminating her. A two-story cut-away set duplicating the original cave was created on stage for more camera and lighting access for the insert shots. "Filling" the mock-up with a 10K aimed into an 8 × 8 overhead bounce, Earl dialed-in her fill to 100 foot candles — muting it with double net scrims and a dimmer, while leaving the surrounding shadow of the cave at less than 50.

One of the picture's most iconic images was John Wayne on horseback, with the reins in his teeth and Winchester rifles blazing in each hand, charging Ned Pepper (Robert Duvall) and his boys at full gallop. It was shot from a fast-moving picture vehicle in which Earl had rigged two 5K's at converging angles for Cogburn's main; the existing daylight and incandescent fill (blown through a ½ blue frost) provided an organic look with perfect flesh tones and a facial catch light that made the Duke leap from the background like a poster.

Earl next embarked on another career landmark picture with *Catch 22*. One of his largest efforts (measured by lights and lamp operators), its immensity of scope was required to portray a working airbase of B-25 bombers during World War II's Italian campaign. It employed 17 flyable aircraft, with eight more Mitchells staged in front of the 7000 foot runway carved out of a flat stretch of San Carlos, Mexico. Earl was brought in by director Mike Nichols to light the airborne armada and "babysit" DP David Watkins, whose sole prior credit was the animated Beatles film *Yellow Submarine*. The movie required six months of location work to get all of the aerial coverage (including 1500 hours of flying time in B-25s). Watkins insisted upon only filming between three and five in the afternoon so he could capture the "golden light." Wishing to shoot the picture with an authentic look (but lacking the lighting knowledge to pull it off), he relied heavily upon Earl to provide gaffing solutions while Nichols filled in with the rest.

Coming to a forced-development process to get the white-hot look Watkins was after, Earl obtained it by placing the subjects' faces in the shade while fill-lighting to a high aperture such as f-11 or 16, then leaving the background light to be overexposed. The end result produced a bright and blown-out incidental illumination all around the subject. Printing only for flesh tones in facial close-ups, the remaining blue-white hues behind the actors gave a contrast to the images that produced a sharp separation in every frame.

Following a week of shooting in the process, Nichols asked to see the dailies. Watkins said that he not only didn't believe in them, but considered dailies an unnecessary crutch for a real filmmaker. Nichols soon discovered that the quirky cinematographer had been storing the exposed film in his hotel bathroom rather than shipping them off to Technicolor. He feared that the lab would mishandle the stock in response to the blown-out exposures. The DP was finally won over and began submitting his exposed work for all to see.

One of the film's most complex aerials was a sequence with Jon Voight and Martin Balsam walking in front of 16 aircraft as they taxi for take-off behind them. Transitioning through the interior of the hangar via a dolly move while continuing to show the B-25s reach altitude as they climb into formation, the six-minute gag had to be done four times before all the timing worked. Balancing the sand-blurred exterior of the tarmac to the incidental light in the flight offices, Earl incorporated a series of amber-gelled Juniors for facial fill to match the sepia-sunlight pouring in through the windows outside.

While the aerial combat contained beautiful lighting (whether enemy engagements or those subsidized by M and M Enterprises), one sequence in particular stands alone. It was staged in a B-25 when "the new guy," Snowden (played by Jon Korkes), is gut-wounded by flak and bleeding profusely as Yossarian tries to help; the entire interior of the plane is bathed in an ethereal light (blasting in and out of frame), as Arkin's character is driven to near hysteria, while helplessly watching Snowden die on the floor of the shuddering aircraft. In effect, Earl's lighting was a metaphor for the wounded man's journey into the white light of the unknown.

This was accomplished by a massive reflected lighting set-up comprised of 75 arcs focused through a bleached muslin panel 12 feet high and 80 feet long. The rig straddled a non-flying B-25 hanging from the high side of Stage 15 like some kid's model. It incorporated front-projected sky and clouds on both sides of the fuselage while filming on a long lens at over 100 feet away to effect linear compression. The claustrophobic feel of Yossarian's panic was magnified by Watkins and Gilbert's choice of shooting through the cockpit nose glass into the plane.

Gilbert and other crew members were constantly exposed to moving propellers, gaping bomb-bays, and missing windows and doors while utilizing the aged Mitchells as flying camera platforms. While shooting aircraft-to-aircraft footage with one B-25 just 100 feet behind the other, second unit director John Jordan plummeted 4000 feet to his death through an open tail gunner position because he neglected to wear his safety harness.

Another high fall in the feature, although scripted, was the startling scene where Charles Grodin (playing Captain Aardvark) tosses an Italian hooker out of a fourth-floor window. Lighting the reveal following Yossarian's burst into the room and look out the window to the dead woman below, Earl swapped out a 10K with a street lamp head to give the moment a stark focus that more lights may have detracted from. Encircling the victim in a pool of illumination resulted in a stage-like image which dramatically permeated one's memory while all else around was plunged into blackness.

Originally proposing a plan to light the entire bluff rising up to Garibaldi Street (the ancient hills above Rome where Nero fiddled), Earl was angrily turned down by cinematographer Watkins, accused of wasting time while playing director. Threatened with replacement, Earl instead pulled his crew off and went to the bar next door for a cappuccino, while the locals floundered minus his guidance. After 30 minutes of lighting without approaching a workable set-up, Watkins entered the bistro explaining to Gilbert that without him the Italians were lost; if he would return, all would be as he wished. Unable to ignore the plea, and rightly buzzed from two coffees while "on strike," Earl gathered his troops in triumph and returned to work. "After all," he said, "it wasn't like you could just hop in a car and drive home — we were in Italy!"

As the lighting concept of *Catch-22* was a realistic looking design, Watkins tasked Earl with producing hospital set lighting *on stage* that would have the same tropical cast as footage shot in Guyamas, Mexico. Solving the problem with his favorite solution — photo floods en masse — he made up a top light for the stage that used 2000 number 4s (at 1000 watts each) to mimic Mexico's midday sun. He brought Nichols in to see the massive rig the first day it was fired up for filming; the 110 degree temperatures on stage, combined with the 200,000 watts of light, literally brought the director to his knees, after standing beneath it for just 30 seconds. Covering his face to shield his eyes, Nichols yelled, "I love it, Earl, I love it. Now turn it off before you blind me!"

While the film was not always about big lighting coverage of airplanes or tarmacs for its gaffer, finite challenges were presented such as an insert shot of a urine bottle sitting below Yossarian's hospital bed. Watkins decided Arkin's specimen had to look like a high-end beer commercial shown during a ball game. After rigging a Baby 1K (pup) with a snout and calling the shot ready, Watkins took one glance at the set-up and ordered Earl to produce a more dramatic fill light while illuminating the beaker from below. Not happy to be rebuffed on such a silly shot (and offering a solution that was so complex, he was sure the impatient shooter would take his first idea instead), Gilbert was ordered to proceed no matter what the difficulty. Following orders, he had a hole cut in the stage floor of the three-story set, and then lit the bottle with a 10K fitted with a narrow snoot—shining up through the opening two stories above. Still not satisfied with the light's intensity, Watkins had him move up to an arc lamp, then a stadium-sized follow spot, to no avail. Tired of the game his DP was playing, while the company broke for lunch, he stayed behind and switched the rig, back down to his original pup—this time hidden under the bed. Returning to the set and seeing the bottle beautifully lit (without knowing its source), Watkins exclaimed, "That's it, Earl! Don't change a thing. How did you ever do it?"

One of the more tricky gaffing techniques in *Catch-22* was Earl's rim light and mirror rig incorporated for the exterior in which Hungry Joe (Seth Allen) gets sliced in half by a low flying airplane. It was shot in three parts with the first establishing shot of Joe on the wharf and the second a blood-spraying effects dummy being hit by a propeller; the final used a stuntman strategically illuminated with a combination of ambient and a water level light, aimed up to his waist. Catching sky and water with a contrast line beneath his torso, the downward camera angle shooting into a mirror created the illusion of being cut in two by the prop, with the help of his perfectly timed fall backwards. While the mirror and top half of Joe's body was rotoscoped out in post by matte artist Albert Whitlock, the wily gaffer's edge light on the legs provided just enough separation from the background to divert the eye, allowing a fast cut used by editor Sam O'Steen to make the sequence fluid and totally believable.

Earl was continuing to bring innovative approaches to lighting; *Catch-22* was a ripe proving ground for him. Having difficulty distinguishing allied aircraft from the enemy (during the nighttime strafing sequences orchestrated by Milo and carried out by the Germans), he created 200 aluminum cowbell instruments pop-riveted along the plane's tail section, fuselage and wings to effect dramatic rim lights while illuminating the two Air Forces' markings. Comprised of single 500-watt lamps run off the alternator, placement of the small units was figured out by a series of nighttime flight tests with Gilbert that were tricky all by themselves. In addition to first mounting the new lights, a system of ground-to-air warning signals had to be devised, as much of the aerial night sequences were slated to be shot over dangerous terrain including mountains and a dry lake bed. Earl engineered a series of flashing lights only visible to the pilots from the air; his concept kept aircraft from flying too low and hitting the ground during filming. They were constructed from car batteries and turn signal lights sealed into a black wooden box with a slot on top; the ground indicators also helped pilots stay geographically oriented while operating low over the set at night. Taking his warning lights expertise to the next level (after chase plane camera operator Alan McBride complained that the timing of the big strafing effects was out of sync with his air position to cover them), Earl devised a solution: a separate run of tiny red and green cuing lamps to coordinate all parties involved. Operating like a traffic signal (with green meaning all clear), the day- and night-visible device was appreciated by crew and director alike. Working dangerously close to munitions going off, as well as simulated machine-gun fire and low-flying aircraft, his cueing devices gave the stuntmen, effects technicians, and camera operators filming it all a perfectly timed flow of action that made the shots more precise as well as safer.

Taking the idea one step further for a night sequence of B-25s taking off, Earl incorporated a row of buried ground lights recessed into the runway providing under-wing separation between aircraft and dark sky. Also employing 30 Kansas Arcs with their light fields converging in long cones, he cued the operators when to fill each Mitchell (held in focus), lifting off.

With so much night work to cover and no large location power sources available in southern Mexico at the time, Earl requested that Paramount obtain one, no matter the cost. The studio's response was a World War II German submarine generator, still packed in its original crate with Kriegsmier stamps all over. It supplied 2000 amps of juice while springing to life with the roar of a Panzer (after Gilbert figured out the German dials and warning plaques). Watkins complained that there was a flicker in the lamps because of an improper control setting, as it seemed to undulate with the off kilter drone of the aged diesel engine. Ordered to overhaul the rig right away, Earl pretended to agree while informing the ignorant cinematographer that a camera shutter working at a 50th of a second would never see the slight variance the human eye does. Vindicated during dailies when all was constant, Earl enjoyed the last laugh, as he actually hadn't done a thing (other than let it warm up for an hour prior to shooting).

Charged with enhancing the look of the explosions used during the night-time bombing sequences of the American headquarters, Earl incorporated a dozen Kansas Arcs with red and orange gels to backlight the flames and make them appear more voluminous. Mounted on parallels and lit through a continuous 80-foot-long by 12-foot-high silk, the whole setup was seamlessly designed by key grip Bud Gaunt to help horizontally spread and magnify the initial blast. When Watkins insisted more 10Ks be added to highlight the fireball as well, his gaffer explained that the resulting illumination from the explosion would light up the sky all by itself, and that the lamps would never survive the blast. Earl reluctantly agreed to the extra lights while warning the cinematographer to be prepared to write a check to Paramount for the property damage. The resulting effects were so powerful that in addition to blowing out the arc lights from concussion, they totally cooked the 10Ks as well, rendering them into a melted blob of glass and smoldering metal.

Earl recalled some of the more subtle lighting techniques he employed in *Catch-22* such as Alan Arkin's scenes in the tent interior while talking to Bob Balaban about his plan to crashland off the Swedish coast. Using overhead silks with a single light source on each actor (providing a Rembrandt fill in the darkness), Captain Orr was foreground-lit with 50 foot candles while Yossarian was left in the shadows with barely 25. Adding a compelling contrast to the scene by having the character in the dark as the voice of everyone's hidden guilt and fears, while representing hope with the fellow in the light, Earl not only succeeded in telling the story, but did so with the intellectual vision of Mike Nichols firmly in place.

The ensemble cast included Richard Benjamin, Art Garfunkel, Buck Henry, Martin Sheen, and Jack Gilford as Doc Daneeka (keeper of the Catch 22 credo). The picture's previously mentioned actors (Grodin, Jon Voight, and Arkin) were upstaged by the presence of one man — Orson Welles. He originally had just two pages of dialogue as visiting Brigadier General Dreedle and he offered his expertise on everything from acting to camera placement and lighting. Before the end of his first day on set he had routinely staged himself in the foreground of what Nichols would later find to be largely un-cuttable sequences. Not only did Welles succeed in making a major impact on the film, but the scene of the soldiers falling over themselves to get Dreedle's WAC a chair (and the subsequent troop inspection during the medal ceremony with Yossarian nude) became movie stealers for the living legend.

In February of '72, Gilbert once again paired with cinematographer Lucien Ballard for Sam Peckinpah's *The Getaway*. Filmed primarily on location in the Texas towns of El Paso, San Antonio, Fabens and Huntsville, the opening sequences focus on the prison itself (it was shot in Huntsville Correctional). From its montage of iron-barred cells to well-worn locks and heavy doors, the viewer is walked through its corridors with Steve McQueen in frame, while on his way to be denied parole by crooked warden Jack Benyon (Ben Johnson). Earl used the penitentiary's existing fluorescent fixtures as his main illumination (after doubling their wattage from 50 to 100) as well as taking advantage of hanging incandescent practicals and banks of two- and four-foot fluorescents for key lights on facial close-ups while allowing the ambient bounce off the jail's white walls to work as fill. During McQueen's stoic stroll through the prison's elevated walkways, the only sounds are a cacophony of machine combines with their clacking and thudding gears too loud to even shout over. Using the wall of noise and close-ups of Doc McCoy's (McQueen) expressionless face to see it all from the hero's point of view, Sam Peckinpah was clearly letting the audience know this is not a nice place. Keeping the fill as natural as possible while still providing at least 50 foot candles on the actor at all times, Earl supported the director's vision by not lighting him into a corner with a 5K of story input all his own.

For the sex scene between Sally Struthers and Al Lettieri, Ballard requested 3000 foot candles for the sequence on the bed. Earl said, "The action in the scene is hot enough, Lucien. Why do you want to set Sally Struthers on fire? She didn't do anything to you." In excess of 2000 foot candles were used with an astronomically high f stop, but at the gaffer's prompting an ND filter was employed, bringing the aperture down to 11 for high key but flame-proof close-ups.

There were lots of driving sequences in the picture with McQueen behind the wheel. They rigged the star his own fill light for close-ups (to prove it was really him driving and no stuntman). A hood mount for the par lamps and camera were positioned straight through the windshield. The crew had to break down the entire set-up one day when Peckinpah thought he was seeing a light reflection in the glass; the resulting trouble was all for nothing after figuring out "the kick" was coming from a chrome seat belt latch catching the light. Powering the entire fill system with individual 24-volt camera batteries, the rig not only worked cordless to allow actual driving while shooting, but was easily charged and silent in comparison to a portable genny.

Another provocative scene, lit to look dark and dangerous, was the trash truck sequence with Doc and Carol McCoy (Ali MacGraw) trapped in the back. Doing the shot after already working a ten-hour shift (then breaking for a quick 30-minute meal), Gilbert was in no mood for elaborate night exteriors and as such, his quickie lighting set-up for the truck cabin interior was so dim (20 foot candles) that you can barely make out the driver as he pulls away. He was complimented by Peckinpah nonetheless; the director felt that by not seeing McQueen clearly, the truck itself remained the character, not the wheelman.

For the interior shots of the Dumpster with the stars hiding inside, Earl used a combination of overhead bounce lighting with a pair of small magnetic clip lights, supplying a 20 foot candle slash of light for each face. Allowing the background to fall to black, the two floating fills added a claustrophobic feel to the action that made the sequence more compelling and believable.

Providing a consistent light for the climactic hotel shootout (it starts in the second floor hallway, then proceeds down a stairway and into the lobby), Earl used the wall sconces and overhead practicals in the hall while bumping up the bulb wattage and utilizing an off-camera inky (500 watts) above the door frame for McQueen's facial fill as he first sneaks out the back door of his hotel room, while stalking Lettieri. Employing a line of midgets hidden by the banister and aimed down the stairwell out of frame, he also mixed reflected light coming into the hotel, with an amber-gelled Arc through the big lobby windows to match the golden afternoon light on the street. Lucien wanted the hallway and stairs lit much more classically (brighter), but Earl told the DP that they didn't need that much illumination as hotel hallways were dark. Unlike Ballard who came from the strict regimentation of big studio-controlled features (with intricate lighting and camera position for each set-up), Gilbert was more proactive, having done scores of smaller pictures, stressing speed and volume over quality or accuracy of lighting; Earl was more about winging it with materials, manpower and conditions on hand than creating a new universe. In the case of *The Getaway* (with its countless set-ups and detailed sequences of classic Peckinpah slow-motion violence), Earl recognized the picture's need for speed and simplicity of set-ups rather than complex solutions to problems that shouldn't exist.

Convincing the old school shooter that it was okay to cut corners once in a while, Gilbert lit the sequence of the sheriff's car being shotgunned by McQueen with a single 10K mounted waist-high to fill the dark grill area, instead of the elaborate lighting tent Lucien wanted to show off special effects like the hood and bubble lights being blown off the cruiser. Ballard finally agreed that sometimes less is more. Lending itself to a far quicker shooting style (including the morning's bus-stopping scene, and its six pages of dialogue), the two major locations shot were in the can by noon.

Challenged by Peckinpah for a natural-looking driving light for the picture's finale where Slim Pickens takes McQueen and Ali MacGraw across the border in his old pick-up truck), Earl set individual par lamps for each actor — cutting the spill light with flags between the three subjects. Along with the ambient fill outside the truck, he was able to give his cinematographer 400 foot candles for facial close-ups, which was then augmented by an ND 3 filter to control the bright El Paso afternoon sun.

Another of the run and gun features Gilbert did was Richard Fleischer's cop drama classic *The New Centurions* (1972) starring George C. Scott and Stacy Keach. The gaffer had his hands full with nearly eight weeks of night shoots revolving around the two officers' patrol experiences in the chaotic urban sprawl known as Los Angeles. Providing low-key interior lighting for the cop car (rather than the usual "lamp in the lap" deal), Earl used small dashboard instruments and a rear view mirror fill to add about 40 foot candles in the shadows of the front seats. Shooting with scant illumination to get a real-life look, cine-

Earl Gilbert gestures while positioning his lights for a climactic scene on Richard Fleischer's *The New Centurions* in the summer of 1972 (courtesy Earl Gilbert).

matographer Ralph Woolsey engineered a new type of focal device for camera called a Split-Diopter that was a game changer. Allowing for two separate planes (or objects) to be in sharp focus despite a distance between them (sort of like bifocal glasses), the Diopter gave Fleischer many two-shots of the officers at a depth not normally obtainable with such little light. It was able to hold focus while shooting three feet across the front seats (from a window-mounted hostess tray); both near and far faces were sharp, despite the motion of the moving vehicle. Required to create consistent fill for the daylight driving sequences as well, Earl set a Junior on each actor blasted through tracing paper to soften the look while gaining contrast.

The company filmed night exteriors all over Los Angeles, including locations in Watts and Boyle Heights. There was a happy accident while lighting the picture's violent climax, where Stacy Keach (Roy) gets shot and is lying on the ground in the hands of his new partner. Seeing a police helicopter shining his night-sun on nearby streets, Earl suddenly realized that the intensity and angle of the beam created a light from above that was a perfect metaphorical image of Roy's passage into the beyond when he dies. He convinced the director and Ralph Woolsey to shoot his ending; the final image was one of the most poignant of the feature.

By the spring of 1973, Earl was one of Tinseltown's go-to guys for lighting urban action flicks. He signed on for *Cleopatra Jones* featuring statuesque Tamara Dobson in the title role; the film was a street-hip "black man's James Bond" whose over-the-top heroine went from scene to scene decked out in outrageous costumes, while delivering karate kicks to drug dealers. Casting Shelley Winters as Mommy, the lesbian smack queen of LA, producer William Tennant had little cash left for necessities like a generator or location fees. Shooting off the cuff in South Central (without permits or cops to safeguard), Earl found the juice his lights needed by doing everything from power pole climbing to rooftop tie-ins while tapping the city's grid, risking death from 70,000 volts of electricity each time he did it.

For the interior lighting of a halfway house, director Jack Starrett charged Gilbert with making an already distressed room even worse. After increasing the wattage in the dilapidated overhead fixtures and wall sconces, he dirtied-down the light by spraying the bulbs with brown paint and affixing muslin strips inside the lampshades; giving the place an abused, smoke-stained look. When coupled with its shabby furnishings and broken fixtures, the set had a believable ghetto sadness that was depressing to cast and crew alike.

Since Jones was played by the six-foot-plus Dobson (often wearing costumes that included platform heels and hats with three-foot brims), Earl had to place his lamps at chest height just to keep the tall woman's face clear of shadows. He used a cosmetic beauty light with soft diffusion to smooth Dobson's prominent facial lines. The actress misunderstood Earl's motives when he asked her to sit down while lighting her so he could figure out her good side from bad. She refused to cooperate while telling him not to bother her with such trivial matters as she has a stand-in. The seasoned gaffer informed Dobson he could either make her look nice or like an Amazonian bulldog — it was up to her. Changing her attitude upon seeing the first dailies, Tamara accosted Gilbert in the screening room with a face-reddening smack on the lips, in thanks for making her look so beautiful. In fact, the actress was so taken with him by feature's conclusion that three weeks after wrap, she snuck up behind him in line in Goldblatt's Delicatessen and lifted him off the ground with her massive arms locked around his torso. Demanding to be put down while trying to regain his breath, he heard a familiar woman's voice roar, "What's the matter, Gilbert, don't you like getting picked up any more, sweetheart? It's me, Tamara."

Two of the movie's more difficult set-ups were the poppy field's destruction and the climax with Mommy and Cleopatra Jones fighting it out on top of a magnetic crane arm, with Winters ultimately being thrown to her death. Earl utilized arc lights on the ground with a hidden backlight rigged to the crane. The aerial fight had a serial quality to it that was far beyond the writer's description, as well as the budget. For the poppy burning, Earl and DP David Walsh manifested a quarter-acre version of *Gone with the Wind*'s torching of Atlanta when setting fire to a group of derelict Compton oil fields full of waist-high weeds sprayed with lacquer that made them highly combustible. He exposed for the six-foot flames while letting the background go black. The fields were side-lit with arcs blasted at a low angle through amber gel frames, wrapping the light up and over the fire, making it look much larger than reality.

Following five years of various cinematographers, Earl met the shooter who would be his partner for the next 30 pictures: Victor Kemper. They were introduced by the head of production at Paramount, Al McGuire. Kemper was looking for a gaffer for his next show, *Friends of Eddie Coyle*. While McGuire initially suggested Fouad Said's cinemobile package for use on the location-heavy picture, Earl interceded with first-hand knowledge of the gear's poor quality, and he promised a first-rate package in Boston as good as anything in Hollywood.

Shot in North Boston, *Friends of Eddie Coyle* was a Peter Yates film focusing on a group of middle-level Beantown wise guys (thieves and degenerate gamblers) who double-cross each other (and anyone else) as a way of life. Starring Robert Mitchum as Coyle with Richard Jordan, Peter Boyle, Alex Rocco and Joe Santos as heavy Artie Van, the picture had its share of violence. Once again on a feature with weeks of urban night work and no generator, Earl did his thing by tying-in any place he could (through bribe, bluff, or break-in). Continuing to risk electrocution while tapping into live power feeds, the bold gaffer would scale wooden poles with climbing spikes and be down again so quickly that he was routinely mistaken for a power company lineman whenever observed.

The movie featured a good amount of night driving sequences. Yates was able to shoot them live action by virtue of Earl's subtle interior lighting including one rig hidden on the front-seat floor with a bounce card, while the other was a rearview mirror gag illuminating the heavies in the back with barely 25 foot-candles of facial fill. Providing an ominous feel to the boys' night out, he also set small slash lamps to mimic car headlights randomly striking Coyle as he drove; they were operated by the actor himself with the flick of a switch, just below his steering wheel. Figuring out a way to duplicate the same lighting effect later (when Coyle is out cold in the back seat being driven to his execution), the seasoned gaffer stationed Par-lamp operators on roofs along the route to create the beams of oncoming automobile headlights, eerily flooding the car's interior, then diminishing to icy shadows when passed.

Shooting the Boston Garden footage during an actual hockey game, Yates challenged Gilbert to capture the morose ambience of the moment, including the character's flawed feeling of safety while in familiar territory. Running power from maintenance boxes at the end of each row, he used Baby 1Ks with snoots on low stands for his facial fill during the scenes. Reflected ambient light from the rink's white ice illuminated the surrounding crowds. Cast and crew worked in a low-key manner, with makeup and wardrobe issues conducted off-set; the Panavision camera and lights amongst the audience during filming were hardly noticed by those in the surrounding seats. Earl said, "We were looking for just enough foot-candles to add a little catch-light and slight fill to the faces, without overpowering the scene's subdued mood or blowingout the background."

For yet another nocturnal crime drama, Elaine May's *Mickey and Nicky*, Earl and Victor Kemper signed on for 83 consecutive nights in Philadelphia with only Sundays off to rest. It starred Peter Falk and John Cassavettes and was perhaps one of the most underrated experimental features that ever came from a Hollywood major. It was the director's desire to shoot the picture organically (including everything from actors ad libbing lines to continuous coverage without cutting camera); this caused the project to go wrong production-wise.

The bleak schedule, combined with May's odd ideas about coverage, created a revolving door of shooters on the feature, including Kemper, Gerald Fine, Jack Cooperman and Earl's occasional lens partner Lucien Ballard. Filming in a cramped hotel room for the story's opening, Earl watched Cassavettes and Falk quickly grow edgy during their exchanges, rarely reciting the proper dialogue or staying seated on the bed as scripted. This forcing the gaffer to light in zones with multiple instruments, practicals, and bumped-up hanging overheads to make it all work. The wall to window design was not exactly stadium lit but provided coverage anywhere in the room. At first Earl laughed when hearing talent complain to May that others on the small set (including lighting, grips and the camera itself) inhibited their performances. Instructing the cinematographer to operate camera by just turning it on and walking away, May was upset when informed that doing so would only capture out-of-focus footage. Frustrated by the director's lack of comprehension (after sarcastically offering to turn the lens toward a blank wall), Victor came up with the solution by allowing camera to run constantly while in a two-shot of the guys, without cuts. It was locked-off with no pans or tilts (on minimum close-focus requiring talent to stay precisely within their marks). The physical confinement of the scene didn't produce the desired results either. Relying solely upon her two actors for input on everything from meal breaks to dialogue timing, May burned through 30,000 feet of film the first night, before realizing the absurdity of her concept. They switched to a system of operators being the only crew in the room. Marathon takes included minutes of actors sitting without uttering a word and improvisational jags by Cassavettes which were totally unusable. Unable or unwilling to remain on the hot, cramped set during shooting, Earl said he found refuge in the hotel lobby between lighting changes. May burned through raw stock at a rate of 25,000 feet a night as production continued (which totaled 1.4 million feet by movie's end); the entire amount of celluloid used was more than triple that of *Gone with the Wind*.

Relying upon the street tactics of non-generator motion picture production, Earl continued to make do by tying-in through the rooftops of random buildings, bribing local business owners, or climbing light poles as a last resort to "borrow" power for the street location work. Illuminating eight square blocks for a continuous talking-while-driving sequence one night with Falk and Ned Beatty (searching for Cassavettes), Gilbert rigged lights from overpasses, store fronts, and the roof of a 24-hour massage parlor to get his street coverage, working at little more than 30 foot-candles in the car. Figuring his contrast from flesh tones produced by the combination of ambient night light and special automotive fills, he also let real illumination like traffic signals and lit-up business signage cause flare in the lens. The black-sky background kept all else in the car neutral while driving through traffic.

While lighting the forced-sex sequence between Nicky (Cassavettes) and Nellie (played by Carol Grace), Earl sought to convey the eyes-open vulgarity of the action performed within earshot of Peter Falk, who had nowhere else to go in the tiny apartment. Employing little more than "bumped-up" practicals for the three table lamps and a Junior bounced into a card at an unflattering angle, Gilbert was able to reflect the violent cheapness of the act through the use of his minimalist lighting, which was an appropriate metaphor of the dark activities depicted.

Covering a fight scene between the two Method actors (after the apartment tryst), Earl grabbed available juice from a light pole and lit the scuffle with a single open face 10K. The two fought so violently that Falk suffered a bloody lip while Cassavettes had a mouse over his right eye, clearly visible for the remainder of the picture. The gaffer's choice of employing the asphalt-blue light (in combination with their flushed faces) produced a surreal look that was visually interesting while helping to sell the frenetic energy of the moment. Earl felt that single source lighting was the most dramatically effective; when applied to the late-night street location, it allowed the actors to give it their all, without the psychological limitations of being in a studio.

Gilbert's next gig would be among the most celebrated of his career. The motion picture was Roman Polanski's *Chinatown*, shot in Los Angeles beginning in the winter of 1972. Roman originally drafted Bill Fraker to lens the flick, but producer Robert Evans feared the two buddies would take over the picture, as they did while shooting *Rosemary's Baby* years before. Earl arrived on the project by invitation from replacement cinematographer John Alonzo after legendary lensmen Stanley Cortez was fired due to creative differences with the director. The avant-garde shooter chose Earl for his mastery of arc lighting as well as his knack for thinking on his feet under pressure. Having worked together previously on high-end Lincoln commercials between features, the two were in logistical agreement from the start of the show. Supporting Gilbert's long-established preference for directional lighting to build drama, one of the movie's most memorable shots occurred when Jake Gittes (Nicholson) is caught around the city reservoir at night. He gets a nostril sliced open courtesy of a bad guy with a switchblade, Roman Polanski; the harshly lit encounter included the classic line hinting to the impending rhinoplasty, "You're a nosy fellow, kitty cat, huh?" Lighting the sequence with 1000 watt master lights, Earl perched one 22 feet up on a custom highstand along the chain link fence while setting the other low on the opposite side as a ¾ ground fill. Catching Nicholson in a cross-light to pick up his face and the knife-gag in Alonzo's medium close-up, Gilbert added a dramatic intensity to the image that made the scene momentarily freeze in time. He imposed a nightmarish sense of realism by keeping his lighting stark and without bleed-control. Everything from lens flares to lamp halos textured the violent moment, providing Polanski's picture with a signature.

In line with Earl's prolific use of direct fill, Alonzo's classic framing and lens choices gave *Chinatown* a period contrast and color that was as rich in its presentation as the time and place portrayed in the story. Achieving the tonal balance with straw and yellow #1 diffusion (while implementing wide apertures to blow-out the backgrounds with a saturation of warm hues), Earl perfectly complemented Polanski's vision of the film taking place during the hottest day of summer in Los Angeles. Tasked with day exteriors in the full sun of Evelyn Mulray (Faye Dunaway) on her veranda with Gittes, he again balanced the existing light of the Pasadena location with Arcs shooting through Amber diffusion to render a workable flesh-tone in the shadows of the harsh outdoor setting. Aside from accentuating the heat and deep colors of that time in the afternoon, the fill lights intensity broadcast every line in Dunaway's face, adding to her look of rigid discomfort during the questioning.

While many of the interiors were lit with single-source instruments, Earl also chose to increase the output of his hanging practicals, desk lamps, and wall sconces to provide contrasting chunks of shadow to offset all the direct light present. Helping to convey a casual Hollywood ambiance for the scenes in Katherine's Belinda Palmer house, Gilbert switched to reflected light with juniors bounced into white cards (softening hard edges), while applying his two-foot fluorescents evenly to slim the actress' face. Describing the difference between the two illumination styles used on the picture, he referred to incidental light as painting with the instruments versus bounce or reflective (which is a soft net cast, to cover a given scene). Complaining that reflective illumination lacks a definitive fall-off or sharp throw for actors to walk in and out of, Earl preferred direct light on *Chinatown* for its dynamic beam shapes and shadows—fitting the period's largeness of interior design and furnishings.

Sticking with Alonzo for his next project, Earl gaffed the film-noir remake *Farewell*

My Lovely (1974), starring Robert Mitchum in the Philip Marlowe role. Directed by Dick Richards and lensed all over old Los Angeles including downtown, San Pedro, and Long Beach's *Queen Mary*, *Farewell* demanded more creativity from its gaffer than a big studio offering like *Chinatown*, despite its period similarities. With its location schedule consisting of three to four company moves a day, and budget restraints limiting advance rigging crews, the movie was a throwback; creative energy ruled the production, not studio heads and their accountants. "The reason those independent films looked so good," Earl said, "was the crew's passion and execution while making them. On a smaller movie the art becomes critical, as you're working more for one another, than you do on a larger project, with lots of cooks in the kitchen."

Earl was tapped for his unique nautical abilities for the picture as well. When prepping the gambling sequences aboard the Catalina Freighter, the gaffer and his crew completely reworked the boat's auxiliary electrical system to power recessed practicals mounted throughout the ship's interiors; they provided invisible fill sources, where no rentable instrument could fit. Earl was constantly on the cutting edge with his modified lights and electrical gadgets. When one type of custom instrument proved effective for the inventive gaffer, it wound up in his toy box for use on a future project.

The shooting was not without its lighter side. As Robert Mitchum was being lit for the film's finale, the actor was standing before a blistering 10K awaiting camera direction. While fanning the air, he said, "That smell which you boys have no doubt caught a whiff of, is this farted-out suit I'm wearing from Victor Mature's gangster films, heating up under the lights."

Gilbert soon did another period picture, director Elia Kazan's *The Last Tycoon* (1976), with a star-studded cast including Robert DeNiro, Tony Curtis, Jack Nicholson, Robert Mitchum, and Angelica Huston. The F. Scott Fitzgerald book (chronicling the life of Movieland mogul Irving Thalberg) contained a richly descriptive narrative of Hollywood's studio system during its golden age. Enjoying the opportunity to light so many different leading men on the Sam Spiegel picture, Earl said the trick to making them all look great was simplicity in lighting. Again stressing a single broad source whenever possible for facial fill, he shaped the illumination by position and intensity of his lamps rather than number. He finished with flags, nets, and diffusion to sculpt the light to the individual. Gilbert repeated his favorite catch-phrase to describe a completed product: "If it looks good, it is good."

Recreating old Tinseltown, Earl helped production designer Gene Callahan get the early studio details correct and worked with John Alonzo using incidental light techniques for the style of cinematography prevalent in Hollywood at that time. He switched back to reflected lighting as the story progressed through Thalberg's later life; the latter illumination was a flatter, minimally contrasted look which came off as less staged.

As to Gilbert's "toys," his compact additions from *Farewell My Lovely* proved handy on *Last Tycoon* when lighting the dark interiors aboard Monroe Stahr's opulent yacht. As he did on the freighter, he hid small lamps in every overhead, passageway and recess, gelling the invisible units with Amber color to highlight the cabin's rich wood grains and to provide much-needed illumination to a set far too cramped for full-size instruments.

Earl signed on for the comedic quickie *Bad News Bears*, directed by Michael Ritchie in the latter part of 1976. Starring industry vet Walter Matthau in the coach Morris Buttermaker role, the picture was about as easy as they come for a gaffer, as it was nearly all daylight exteriors shot in a single location. He relied upon his master lights for fill on close-ups with bright sun overhead (like insert shots of slides at the plate or pitching); once the balance was dialed-in, all Earl had to do was point his finger and his guys would do the rest. Preferring to pull power the old-fashioned way, he again negated generator use by tying into electrical service boxes around the field, camouflaging his cable runs with sod to render them invisible to camera. "Even on a picture as simple as *Bad News Bears*," he recalled, "there were things like providing an even fill light for scenes inside the dug-out, that were extremely challenging." The gaffer employed fill cards lit by small instruments tucked into the ceiling (and a row of fluorescents placed on the floor), which provided facial contrast for the players, while balancing the abundance of ambient sunlight.

Continuing with Alonzo, Earl was the sole gaffer on Steven Spielberg's *Close Encounters of the Third Kind*. Charged with lighting six separate units run by the best cinematographers in Tinseltown including Vilmos Zsigmond, Bill Fraker, Laslo Kovacs, Michael Butler, David Davidau and Steve Postner, he kept everyone happy by giving each guy as much as he could material-wise without draining the resources of the entire budget just for the sake of unnecessary ego shots.

As Spielberg was the "hot kid" director (prone to impulsive photographic ideas that were gladly carried out by his gang of DPs), Earl had to be the gatekeeper of lighting concepts, since only he knew the logistical mechanics of making it all work. The only one not in competition with another shooter, he was the director's sole unbiased voice. On the verge of being replaced each time he said no to one of them, and yes to others, his honest manner and steadfast refusal to give in finally wore down his detractors and the movie got made.

Spielberg came up with the idea to have the mother ship be a series of lights (rather than the metallic disc concept of previous alien films) after seeing an oil refinery lit up at night in India. He enlisted Earl to come up with a more luminescent approach to the spacecraft that would suggest a superior technology as evidenced by a glowing energy source powering the vehicle. Giving the craft a blown-out, spectral look with blasts of intense beams emitting from above (via a helicopter's night sun rig), Gilbert provided a believable outline of a huge alien structure that was never really there! Using a combination of directional lighting, matte inserts, and the natural night sky, he created a "spaceship" that had a more tangible presence than any Dennis Muren or Doug Trumbull could have added in post-production.

While the alien ship frontage lamps were rigged individually with dimmers to allow Earl control of a given light's intensity (or an entire bank of 32 — amid the hundreds attached to the full scale prop suspended above the ground), those figures were dwarfed by the cavernous hangars at the Brookley Air Force Base in Mobile, Alabama, where it was shot. At 500 feet long and 100 wide, they became some of the biggest indoor stages ever used on a motion picture. A power sub-station was required to handle the banks of master lights disguised in milk glass as communication grids (which pulsed in conjunction with a mathematical language being exchanged between scientist and aliens). Gilbert engineered a high-speed cuing system for control of his instruments, so they could instantly transition from off to on to off again, without a voltage dip or blowing a fuse.

Vilmos Zsigmond often came up with last-minute additions to lighting that caused

Earl headaches, so he began calling him Zig-Zag on set, and attempted to deter the cocky cinematographer from dreaming up ideas that couldn't be fixed before the shoot day. While filming at the farmhouse location in Los Angeles, Vilmos decided he had to have a lightning effect added at the last moment. Unable to shut down the generator illuminating the rest of the set (or rebalance it for the voltage pull of the lightning machine, which would cause a noticeable drain on the lights anyway), Earl reverted to guerrilla filmmaking by climbing a nearby pole and tying into its live power with a 250 amp yoke, without disrupting service along the line.

Straying from the big pictures with Kemper and John Alonzo, Gilbert lit a funny little film with DP James Crabbe, Mae West's swan song *Sextette* (1978). Directed by Ken Hughes and co-starring Timothy Dalton, Tony Curtis, Ringo Starr and George Hamilton as her love interests, the picture also brought in George Raft (who was present during Mae West's debut on *Night After Night* in 1932) and Walter Pidgeon for their final feature roles. *Sextette* revolved around the bedroom appetites of character Marlo Manners (West)—and the 85-year-old actress was still totally serious when it came to her own sexuality and was not above propositioning members of the crew in jest, including Earl Gilbert. While lighting the ancient femme fatale for a close-up beauty shot (exposing her a ½ stop brighter than the background), Earl utilized the old cinematographer's trick of smoothing wrinkled skin by piercing a silk flag for eyes and mouth, then leaving the remainder of the material to cast a soft, beauty-enhancing fill light. Aware of this photographic procedure, West saw a grip atop a six-foot ladder setting the gag, smiled and said, "As always, Earl darling, I'm in debt to the hard work of a good man."

Continuing in the vein of Spartan productions, in February of '79 Earl and John Alonzo shot *Norma Rae* on location in Alabama. Approaching the labor bio with a lighting design matching its rural setting (simple and to the point), Gilbert used the existing fluorescent fixtures at the Opelika manufacturing company where the movie was filmed, while changing out the standard illumination with color-corrected Delux tubes. Also employing individual two- and four-foot units as fill and key light for faces on the factory floor, he wisely built them with 50-foot-long power cords so the noisy ballasts could be staged in another room, saving sound from their maddening buzz. Earl bumped up the hanging practicals and wall sconces to provide usable light without bringing in a generator. His lighting for the motel scenes (shot at the Golden Cherry in Auburn, Alabama), possessed the perfect broken-down look called for by the script. Using his master lights on stands and parallels for the motel exteriors, the gaffer was able to work effectively without breaking the producer's piggy bank for all kinds of special gear.

Still swinging between his two cinematographers, Earl's next motion picture done with Kemper was Norman Jewison's *And Justice for All* (1979) starring Al Pacino as a defense attorney in Baltimore's beleaguered criminal justice system. The 100-year-old city courthouse where it was shot had an antiquated electrical set-up and it was a challenge for Earl to find enough juice to make a movie. Using a pair of 2500 HMIs bounced into white cards for his basic interior fill, he also hid photofloods in every alcove, dome light, and architectural recess to boost another 100 foot-candles. Jumping the power boxes from 30 to 60 amps per outlet to keep from blowing fuses while filming with the juice-thirsty lights, Gilbert also made socket adapters which could turn any standard outlet into a compact lighting instrument with its own tungsten bulb, adjustable angle, and opaque lens cover. Staying with the concept of simplicity for all the picture's lighting, he rigged a couple of par lamps for the helicopter sequences with Jack Warden as the suicidal Judge Rayford flying inches above the frigid Chesapeake to see how far he can go on a tank of fuel. Earl attached the facial fill just above the chopper's door frame; the split-light gave both pilot and horrified passenger a sharp key which separated them from the background perfectly.

For the film's close with Pacino's "You're out of order" speech, Earl needed something with more contrast to help visually intensify the pivotal raw moment being played out. He employed his fluorescents; the result stood apart dramatically from the feature's previous look.

Negotiating the out-of-town rates for his department, Earl brokered a deal that included a ten-hour shift minimum guarantee for a seven-day week. Reasoning that his crew couldn't take any weekend work while away, he put in for compensation on the off days as well. Upon agreeing to the terms, producer Norman Jewison effectively made Earl's guys the next independent bunch from Hollywood to be paid the seven-day rate. When Gaylin Schultz found out that his pal had brokered a $200-a-week bump for his boys, he engaged the gaffer to negotiate all their deals in the future. Aside from later contractual issues like higher daily per diem, the resulting provisions carried the positive side effect of tending to attract and hold the best crews, who in turn became very loyal.

Continuing his "Victor Kemper phase," Earl gaffed Steve Martin's comedic warning tale of excess, *The Jerk,* directed by Carl Reiner in the summer of 1979. Lacking a definitive production style (as most of the locations were looks at various houses of social wealth along Navin Johnson's character arc), the majority of off-stage sets were lit naturally. From the sharecropper's shack and Navin's post-invention mansion in Beverly Hills, to the comedic gags staged at Hartoonians gas station in Pasadena, Earl's blending of ambient light coupled with a minimum fill was the perfect recipe to render the picture's look evenly, without succumbing to flat illumination for total coverage. He dialed in the shack interiors to a mere 60 foot-candles with bounce light and fluorescents to match its rundown façade. The old Sheik Al Fassi Mansion, in the other extreme, was lit with master lights raked at high angles along the endless white walls, showcasing the opulent wealth within.

A low-budget comedy, *The Jerk*'s popularity earned Universal a hefty gross of $73 million, while costing less than $10 million to make. In demand after the picture's success (along with partners Kemper and Gaylin Schultz), Earl and the guys were about to get very busy — for the next twenty years.

Don Taylor's *The Final Countdown* was the perfect venue for the dynamic threesome to strut their stuff. It was filmed aboard the USS *Nimitz* during ten weeks of night and day steaming throughout the Eastern Atlantic (as well as dock work in Norfolk, Virginia, and the Naval Air Station in Key West, Florida). The script required coverage of everything from jets flying off the flight deck to near–gale force weather that nearly shut down the production. Many of the set-ups required Earl to use existing practicals while increasing wattage of the overheads and improvising small fills all over the boat. A jet exhaust blew a Panavision camera into the drink due to operator error, after which Gilbert took it upon himself to handle the riskier tasks on board, such as mounting lights on the ship's radar mast, which emanated a signal of such strength that anyone close to the magnetic field would instantly have their brain fried. Earl was able to avoid injury by using extreme caution and being sure the power was off while setting his 10Ks.

Constantly pushing the electrical capacity of the *Nimitz*, Gilbert was assigned a liaison officer to replace fuses on the nuclear fighting craft, as his high-wattage movie lights routinely plunged the bridge into darkness. Well-informed as to the construction of military ships, he was able to parlay that knowledge when hiding photo-floods behind bulkheads or small 40-watt lamps over door hatches to provide authentic-looking interior fill for scenes in the ship's passageways where space for big lights was limited.

20th Century–Fox's *Chu Chu and the Philly Flash* was one of those non-offensive screwball comedies (shot in San Francisco's Potrero Hill area) that was being pumped out by Tinseltown in the 1980s. Continuing with his complement of master lights and fluorescents, the gaffer kept the lighting simple, like the minimalist story itself. Harking back to memories of transitional jobs with DP Lucien Ballard (who didn't like improvisational filmmaking), Gilbert knew that a B-picture's lighting depth was less critical, and that spending time on complicated set-ups was counterproductive. Much in demand due to their ability to work the way they did, Earl and the team bounced from gig to gig without a break.

Another of the all-night features that Gilbert gaffed in the early '80s was the Luis Valdez–helmed and –written *Zoot Suit*. Working the group effort with cinematographer David Myers (Victor bowed out due to last-minute health issues), Earl and key grip Gaylin Schultz called the shots on the film, covering a first time director with difficult subject matter. A big break for actor Eddie Olmos (who had originated the El Pachuco role on Broadway), the motion picture version was lensed on stage in the Wiltern Theatre, instead of on-lot at Universal, where lighting restraints would not have existed. Stuck with an Arbor system (used for theatrical rigging), Earl had to improvise everything from power patches (for the higher wattage movie globes) to employing reflected lighting on facial close-ups, in order to provide enough foot-candles for minimum exposure.

With the picture's back-story of Los Angeles amid the 1940s Mexican racial riots, Gilbert incorporated high contrast color to convey the feeling of anger and passion during that time, while showcasing the flamboyant dress that went with it. Getting the costumes to sizzle on the screen, he lit with broad sources bounced into white-cards, separating characters with flags and nets, while giving the multi-hued materials a full tonal range.

In 1983, *Mr. Mom* kept Gilbert's work plate filled and his bills paid. The movie included a strip-club sequence with Michael Keaton's character (Jack) surrounded by a bevy of partially naked dancers. As Earl was joking about lighting the girls from angles that would accentuate their assets, producer Bruce McNall warned him that the movie's silent partner (the Hunt family) would never go for nudity in their film. Telling the producer about knowing O.L. from *State Fair*, Gilbert said, "Judging from the old man's attitude back then, nothing naked on the screen (other than a Communist) was likely to get a rise out of that family."

In the spring of 1983, Gilbert and the guys signed on for *National Lampoon's Vacation*. A throwback road picture, it had the gaffer in some demanding locations during its three months out of town. They shot everywhere from Illinois and Missouri to the Grand Canyon and Lake Powell (as well as Six Flags Magic Mountain doubling for Wally World); the pace was getting tough for the 53-year-old, considering the 14-hour shifts of six-days-a-week filming. In a business where you're lucky if you work with the same folks twice, Earl said that the secret of his team's success was the fact that they were professionals and gentlemen who knew how to get the shot as a unit, by way of perfect communication with each other. "Once making the call for camera placement and lighting," he added, "the other set trades would follow suit and began doing their jobs seamlessly."

Working in harmony while shooting road sequences in the Ford LTD Country Squire station wagon where many of the movie's gags took place, Gilbert and the guys had to systematize the camera placement and lighting to work out a priority rule by which the lens frame and mounting could be accomplished first by Victor and Gaylin, then the lighting could be realized by Earl. Utilizing a series of hood, door, and roof mounts for camera position, the team also provided space for the gaffer to light in his own fashion. Relying upon smaller instruments such as babies and juniors separated by flags and diffusion to control the actor's light, Earl had fittings mated to Gaylin's mounting hardware that allowed him to easily clamp his light anywhere he wanted. They put the entire game plan to the test while doing the station wagon leap in Monument Valley. Gilbert said that between his lights and Gaylin's camera rigs, nothing moved an inch despite the tremendous impact from the airborne stunts.

Gilbert's ability to run lights with existing power on any location kept his gaffing skills in demand no matter the genre. Once again contracted for a Chevy Chase comedic vehicle, he lit Michael Ritchie's *Fletch* in 1985. Much of the picture revolved around Chase wearing wacky disguises with only two main sets to worry about lighting: the apartment on 4th Street in Santa Monica and Tim Matheson's mansion in Beverly Hills. Utilizing incidental light including small fluorescents hidden above the doorways (as well as juniors and babies cut with silks and flags blending into walls), Gilbert supported the rich Boris Leven design of the paneled library with the use of ambers and warm tone lighting, to bring out the room's fine finish. He was able to contribute his lighting finesse despite the picture's budget and endless daylight exteriors.

Tim Burton's *Pee-wee's Playhouse* was a departure material-wise for the gaffer. His lighting was consistently spot-on for the challenging flick, shot all over the Warner backlot as well as the L.A. Fairgrounds and Pasadena. One set-up in particular placed Gilbert on a pedestal for the impressionable Paul Reubens: At Culver City's old drive-in, while Earl was lighting the car's interior, Pee-wee saw him gingerly hide two midgets in the rear seat, while setting them as dual backlights for the driver and passenger. Reubens (who had previously done only television) was impressed by Earl's creative passion.

One challenge for Earl was Reubens' bicycle and the lighting rig for its many daylight exteriors. Not able to run power to the wheeled prop directly (batteries would show and power cables would be problematic), the wily gaffer engineered a follow-cart, invisibly rigged behind the rear tire, with a small Honda generator attached. Allowing for two babies to work (one on Pee-wee and the other raked along the bike), the fill lights gave it separation from the background including the dark road beneath its black tires.

Returning to Musketeers form late in the summer of '85, Gilbert and his guys did another Tinseltown tent pole on the whodunit *Clue*. Featuring Tim Curry, Eileen Brennan, Christopher Lloyd, and Lesley Ann Warren, the production was beautifully done, integrating colors like straws and oranges mixed with ND3s (to tonally blend everything together); the film possessed a European hue not normally produced in Hollywood. Lending an aged look of sepia in the whites (while rendering the flesh tones to a healthy pinkish beige), Gilbert's secret of getting the actors to pop from the background was a boxing of the lamps by grips (setting flags top and bottom while blocking in the sides to keep stray spill from leaking out).

Another job for Earl and Gaylin came on Columbia Pictures' *Violets Are Blue*, lensed by Ralph Bode in 1986. Bode was a poor substitute for Kemper. Gilbert incorporated a system of dual best boys which held his contact with the irritable cinematographer to a minimum. Assigning one to the pre-rigging end of the movie and the other on set to get the notes from the DP, he gave them both best boy credits as well as the higher rate.

Shot on location in Baltimore City and Rehoboth Beach, Delaware, the romantic drama was a far cry from Earl's days of climbing poles in the dark of night for power. By then it was standard practice on location to use a generator with its own operator. Earl's biggest worry on the picture was making sure his beat-up old best boy Cecil Lupton (who had once played catcher for the Cleveland Indians) had easy work as he needed the hours to see a heart specialist.

Gaylin and Earl worked for Bode again on Richard Pryor's jewel heist comedy *Critical Condition* in October of '86. Avoiding the genetic predictability of comedic lighting, the gaffer instead lit the picture like a straight drama. Employing as much available light as possible by changing out the overhead fluorescents in the hospital sets with brighter lamps and rigging dimmers for the entire set-up, Earl could dial in any lighting value he wanted at the touch of a knob. He also incorporated his favorite two- and four-foot fluorescent banks with Deluxe bulbs for facial fill and nook lighting. The feature had a production quality that far exceeded its shallow premise.

Still the master tinkerer, and wanting to use arc lights for the big night exteriors (without the hassle and expense of a generator), Earl built custom rectifiers to transform the household current on location. Allowing 220 power sources to sync with 110 current (without setting the building on fire), his devices were so stable that he even used them to run wind machines without blowing a single fuse. The rectifiers saved production manager Bob Larson so much money that he allowed Earl to keep his pal Cecil Lupton on payroll until the film's end. An ironic twist regarding Lupton was the picture's title, *Critical Condition,* which turned out to be his final credit; Lupton succumbed to his illness just three weeks after production wrapped.

The spring of 1988 saw the infield flowers blooming at Hollywood Park and Michael Dinner's "talking horse rules the stock market" flick *Hot to Trot* as the project beckoning "the boys" to shoot next. The movie required coverage from racing footage to stock market trading rooms, once again Earl employed existing illumination as much as possible. He also had HMIs for daylight fill combined with up graded practicals and 2 by 4 beauty lamps to obtain more stops as needed. Recalling the challenge of lighting the live-action racing sequences where he utilized HMIs on the horse and rider (while rigged to a picture car traveling at 35 miles an hour), the gaffer marveled at the sturdiness and quality of the light, lamenting that had these units been available 20 years earlier, he would have used them on *The Graduate*.

Earl was drafted for a second Michael Ritchie-Chevy Chase comedic vehicle, *Fletch Lives* (shot in late 1988), which was another makeup- and costume-heavy slapstick piece requiring a broad range of lighting solutions. It was filmed on location in the deep south (Burnside, Louisiana, including the Houmas House and Ashland-Belle Helene Plantations). Earl accentuated the region's color-tinted sunsets and antebellum architecture by incorporating lighting flourishes like large, cross aimed raking lights to highlight the tall columns on the houses and small ground units to outline their long driveways.

He employed bounced light for the interior fills from 5Ks blasted into cards. The soft illumination was augmented by two-foot fluorescent banks which were run on a custom dimmer with Deluxe lamps to give a sharp edge for contouring and shaping Chase's face in his many disguises. While makeup man Tom Miller did extensive facial gags with characters from Victor Hugo to Peggy Lee Zorba, Earl and Gaylin (at the prompting of cinematographer John McPherson) were giving the special effects their due with a careful lighting treatment employing ½ silks, nets and solids to control the cosmetic fill on Chase's various looks. Shooting the biker sequence at the Halfway House Café in Santa Clarita, Earl tapped every outlet, socket and exposed wire to light the wood-paneled bar. Utilizing the hanging pool table lamps and adding diffused fluorescents around the room, he gave the place a just killed look that was funny all by itself. He ran into a potentially dangerous fuse upgrade from 30 amps to 60 then to 100; by night's end he could smell the wiring bake within the walls of the aged wooden structure, while watching the power meter spin like a top from the non-stop juice consumption.

On the 1989 Paramount feature *Crazy People* (starring Dudley Moore as a successful account executive who winds up in a loony bin), Earl was again flanked by Kemper and Schultz. Using his overhead upgrades on the fluorescents and practicals for the mental hospital lighting, he continued to support the existing illumination with his two- and four-foot fluorescent banks, bulbed and placed on dimmers for facial fill and contrast. Recalling a humorous moment while lighting Dudley Moore for an in-studio sequence (filming a commercial with "the nuts" alongside his Entertainment Agency folks), Earl said the diminutive's star height was so far below Darryl Hannah's that when she walked into his established light, Moore's previous eye position barely came to her chest.

Gilbert's final opus was a Paramount romantic comedy about a clairvoyant woman (Demi Moore), *The Butcher's Wife*. It was directed by Hollywood vet Terry Hughes and lensed by Frank Tidy. Earl's last fling shone with the precision of a pearl's luster rather than the arc-lit billboards from his early days.

Still caring about catching the perfect light, the gaffer used the interior plate glass windows at the butcher shop location in Cape Lookout, North Carolina (in conjunction with HMIs shot through amber and frost diffusion), producing such natural illumination that it looked closer to an Edward Hopper painting than a motion picture. Like an aging slugger who smashes one last drive into the center field bleachers, Gilbert's efforts retired him on a positive note.

Without Victor Kemper as partner and minus good friend Gaylin Schultz, Earl was suddenly left to his own devices for finding a new cinematographer and key grip to ply his trade. Not interested in continuing with new guys he would have to break in, he decided to call it quits the way Gaylin did, hanging up his tool belt once and for all.

Pestered at interview's end for his fundamentals of lighting, the master gaffer said, "Keep it simple; single source whenever you can get away with it, but always have something bright in the background to offset the subject. And forget about trying to balance every frame you fill. In nature, nothing is perfectly balanced — nor should it be in movies.

"As I never used a light meter to figure my lighting, my theory has always been 'What looks good is good. And if it looks bad — fix it!' Just remember, sometimes the best solution to any shot can be the light left off or taken away."

6
Tommy May, Key Grip

Hollywood has always been a town of legends — some authentic, some not. One bona-fide character of "below-the-line stardom" is storied key grip Tommy May. Fondly known in the biz as "Chainsaw," the now soft-spoken retiree began work as a grip by way of his father's example: Cecil Thomas May, a member of Studio Mechanics Local 37 since 1936. Taking a cue from his dad, young Tommy began his career early. While Tommy was just a high school sophomore, his father took him to the grip union (which eventually became Local 80 by charter in 1939) and signed up the strapping lad for summer permit work. Physically capable of handling the back-breaking labor (thanks to his high school football days), one of May's earliest studio gigs was working as a permit on Cecil B. DeMille's *The Greatest Show on Earth* in 1952. Tommy's blooming interest in motion pictures (and the three bucks an hour it paid) led to more permit work at the studios, crewing 3:30 A.M. construction calls and learning the trade in the process. Upon completion of high school, the athletically gifted 17-year-old was recruited by his football coach for two life options. He chose both: college and the naval air reserve, where he ultimately served for twelve years as a crew chief, after playing linebacker at CSUN and LA State. Hanging up his football cleats for work boots following his senior year, Tommy made his move to the studios as a grip.

By 1953 the growing ranks of Tinseltown's production factory brought expansion to the union rosters. As the studios' demand for skilled labor created a need for new guys, May was sworn to the IA on February 2, 1955. Focusing on the physical aspect of gripping then, studio mechanics were responsible for everything from the position of the camera (whether it was on dolly, crane or lumber) to the making of shadows for all lighting, as well as moving walls. Factor in the construction element of the craft, working 60 feet up in the permanents (the stage ceiling super-structure built from 6" wide beams with 10-foot openings), and one understands gripping to be difficult and quite dangerous. No harness, just technique and guts kept these men safe. The sheer challenge of traversing "the perms" with a 20-foot-long plank underarm explains why the grip field employed many ex-athletes.

After making Local 80's roster in 1955, Tommy was qualified to work in Hollywood. Sent out by the Union Hall, one of his first calls was building shooting platforms on the Disney water fest *20,000 Leagues Under the Sea* with studio grip foreman Benny Moran. The wooden scaffolding was standard in the industry throughout the '50s until replaced by the erector set type of steel platforms a decade later.

Other jobs followed. Assigned work with studio key grip Dick Boreland, May fondly remembers his first off-lot call. Working as an extra hammer on the Civil War drama *Friendly*

Persuasion in 1956, he was amused by two things: Gary Cooper and the box lunches served on location. Another interesting call came in 1961 when Goldwyn Studios' grip department head Bill Thomas brought him in for 3:30 A.M. gang work on *West Side Story*. Describing the middle-of-the-night labor, he spoke of moving huge walls for the alley set used in the "Stay Cool" dance number: "The walls were 30 feet tall with storefront fascias built onto them, and weighed hundreds of pounds. Since the entire set was constructed on a six-foot riser (to allow low-angle camera shots), getting the things in place was a major hump."

Continuing to work for Goldwyn through 1962, Tommy was sent by Thomas to Utah for his first distant location on John Sturges' *Sergeants Three*. Again paired with studio key Dick Boreland, May was eager to work for the mentoring grip on the picture, handling everything from sleeper track to crane work and shiny boards amid the triple digit temperatures of Bryce Canyon National Park

May's next career builder was on the Robert Stack television series *The Untouchables*. He was introduced by production supervisor Argyle Nelson to the crime drama's key grip George Rader; under his tutelage Tommy learned such aspects of gripping as light control through the use of flags and scrims. This "setting of flags" (passed down from the days of the silent pictures) was an imperative hands-on part of the craft that all production grips had to master, and still do today.

During his years of learning the ropes under Rader on *The Untouchables*, Tommy began to get crewed on major features. As the level of his craft rose rapidly, DPs noticed that he was a talented young grip. It paid off when he took a hall call in 1964 for the series *Gunsmoke*, produced by TV giant Leonard Katzman (later of *Hawaii Five-0* and *The Wild Wild West*). May met the cinematographer with whom he would later spend half of his career, Harry Stradling Jr. When queried as to the spark that occurred between them on the iconic show, he referred to the camaraderie of doing the difficult location work at Simi Valley's Big Sky Ranch, with its hot and dusty days, filled with reflectors and laying of sleeper track for crane moves. "Harry and I got along great," Chainsaw recalled. "Plus, he was like one of the guys so you just wanted to do all you could for him."

In 1965 May gripped on George Stevens' last epic, *The Greatest Story Ever Told*, lensed by Loyal Griggs after William Mellor died of a heart attack on set. One of the jobs that stands out in Tommy's memory was the crucifixion, shot on stage at MGM Studios. John Wayne as the Centurion minding Jesus (Max von Sydow) was to say, "Truly this man was the Son of God." According to May, after a dozen takes, the director challenged Wayne to come up with a deeper reading. Rising to the task, he did another take, this time adding his own characteristic slant by saying, "Awww, truly ... this man was the Son of God." That take was the one used in the film.

The latter half of '65 became busy for May when he was sent out to New Mexico by his Goldwyn ally Bill Thomas as an extra hammer on John Sturges' *The Hallelujah Trail*. Assigned to grip and crane duties on the rugged western, he recalled a tragic accident that occurred when stuntman Bill Williams jumped a speeding wagon into a gorge. Shooting fifteen feet away while safety-ing cinematographer Bob Surtees, May watched in horror as the 1,000-pound buckboard (being pulled by a steel cable) hit a jarring bump upon reaching its point of launch. Williams was killed upon impact.

Tommy's next feature with Robert Surtees, *The Graduate* (1967), was a bit lighter fare than *The Hallelujah Trail* two years before. Engaged by key grip Bobby Rose to build the

Twenty-eight-year-old Tommy May was assigned an early out-of-town grip gig for Elvis Presley's *Follow That Dream* in the winter of 1961. He's seen here pulling on a rope along the sandy shore of Ocala, Florida's, Crystal River. The company shot for three weeks in the sub-tropical climate, with everyone becoming very tan in those pre-sunscreen days (courtesy Tommy May).

car mounts on the featured automobile in the picture (a red 1966 Alfa Romeo Spider 1600), May was joined by first-time cameraman Nelson Tyler of "Tyler-mount" fame. Aside from inserts done on the just built (but not yet open to the public) 170 freeway, a marathon run from Malibu to Oakland (driven by Dustin Hoffman) was completed by the small unit and included input from an innovative commercial car rigger, "Ratchet Head Frick." Starting with simplistic hostess and hood mounts, Frick utilized aluminum electrical conduit pipe (cut to size with its ends flattened) and then drilled out for bolt on application as reinforcement struts. The technique was not only innovative but rock-steady as his stuff allowed filming at speeds in excess of 120 MPH.

No longer limited by difficult-to-move and bulky car mounts (made from lumber and bolts attached to the vehicle), the new multi-strut technology enabled grips to rapidly configure the camera in any needed position. It was also used by other automotive-knowledgeable keys like Gaylin Schultz and Carl Manoogian until standardized camera mounts and pipe organ kits became commonplace in the 1980s. This strut-fit-to length method of specialized car rigging was the best available for its time.

Along with the scrum of feature films that May manned during the first decade of his career, a few iconic television shows were logged as well. *Get Smart* would epitomize the era through its brilliant writing by Buck Henry and Mel Brooks, with its tongue-in-cheek take on other popular spy shows of its day such as *The Man from U.N.C.L.E.*, *I Spy*, and *Mission: Impossible.* Tommy landed the job by mix of default and good reputation. DP Robert Wyckoff offered the show to experienced key grip Larry Milton; turning it down, he kindly referred it to the 32-year-old May. Benefiting from the rule change which allowed DPs (instead of Department Heads) to pick their own folks, Tommy got a shot at a major network show and took it.

In March of 1963, May received a rare opportunity to work with one of his cinematic heroes, director George Stevens, on *The Greatest Story Ever Told*. He's seen here next to Stevens (right) on a chilly morning in Death Valley while shooting Jesus' "40 days in the wilderness" sequence (courtesy Tommy May).

Shooting the series was fun, according to Tommy. Recalling a humorous episode starring Don Rickles, he described a scene where Smart (Don Adams) had been hurt and was being transported on a gurney. At take's end, with Adams still confined, Rickles jumped upon him and began to dog lick the face of the hysterically laughing actor. May said, "We had as much fun making that show as people had watching it."

The next year would be one of important change, both for May and the industry. Amid political strife at home, the American public and Hollywood in particular was desperately seeking a distraction in 1969. Paramount Pictures' answer was a western-comedy-musical starring two cowboys who shouldn't sing a note: Lee Marvin and Clint Eastwood in *Paint Your Wagon*.

The picture, lensed by cinematographer Bill Fraker, earned May his moniker. Striving for authenticity, the producers built the main sets on location in Baker, Oregon, utilizing interlocked logs arranged frontier-style. On the first day of shooting, Fraker required an

Get Smart came May's way in 1966. Referred to director of photography Robert Wyckoff by key grip Larry Milton, May leaped at the chance to do the secret agent send-up. Pictured here are, from left to right, actor Don Adams, Wyckoff, May standing by camera, gaffer Jim Hunter below him, camera assistant Dunny Willis and operator Harlo Stengel. Working as a key at only 32, Tommy was half the age of the other crew members in this photograph. Filled with its share of challenges for May, from coverage of stunts and pratfalls, to insert shots of the secret agent gadgets, *Get Smart* taught him a lot about low-budget action comedy in a short period of time (courtesy Tommy May).

additional few feet to place his camera for a scene in Elizabeth's (Jean Seberg) tiny bedroom. Turning to Tommy, the DP said, "The camera goes here," pointing to the wall. May (with a background in roof construction before gripping) had a trick up his sleeve: a McCulloch chain saw. Retrieving it from his kit, he yanked the gas-powered machine alive, and then proceeded to slice a four-foot opening in the log cabin wall. After the cloud of acrid blue smoke and swirling sawdust cleared, Fraker sarcastically said, "Thanks, Chainsaw," thus giving Tom his nickname, which stuck throughout the film and became Hollywood history.

Also on *Paint Your Wagon*, May met associate producer–second unit director Tom Shaw, who would change Tommy's career for good. Originally hiring him (through reputation and Bill Fraker), Shaw would eventually employ May on nearly all the features he did.

May was signed by new cinematographer David Walsh to key an old-school western. Directed by the young shooter's mentor, William Fraker (of *Rosemary's Baby* and *Bullitt* fame), *Monte Walsh* was a graphic, yet beautiful portrait of an old cowboy (Lee Marvin)

Cooling his feet on a warm June day in 1968 outside of Baker, Oregon (while operating crane on the western musical comedy *Paint Your Wagon*), a shirtless Tommy May awaits orders for his next move. The 26,000-pound Chapman Titan Crane required a combination of feather-light touch driven by brute strength to start and stop the extension platform while swinging through its 31-foot arc of motion (courtesy Tommy May).

coming to grips with the end of an era and his way of life. Referring to a scene where Monte rides a bucking horse into a saloon, "Chainsaw" explained the difficulty of the shot: "In order to get the camera mounted on the horse [for Marvin's P.O.V.], we rigged a saddle pack with an Arriflex camera attached. The result was perfect. Watching it in dailies made everyone dizzy."

Challenging the Titan Crane's limitations during the shooting of *Paint Your Wagon* (1968), grip Tommy May (bottom center) controls the counterweighted end of the arm before action is called. While the Titan's maximum payload is supposed to be 2,500 pounds including camera, men and the platform supporting them, for this rig a double set of grip scaffoldings was attached to the arm. Engineered with lumber and heavy bolts to hold the 16-foot riser in place, a series of rope lines were also employed to keep the whole thing steady (courtesy Tommy May).

Another interesting western was *Valdez Is Coming*. The Elmore Leonard picture starred Burt Lancaster portraying the title character, an honor-bound Mexican sheriff who dealt hard payback against bad guys and their racist boss. Filmed during the 102 degree temperatures of late summer Spain, the project taxed not only the actors but the crews' physical reserves as well. Not wanting to be outdone by the local hires from Madrid's Roma Studios playing soccer at lunch, Tommy and director Edwin Sherin threw an American football in

Top: Shot in the summer of 1970 in Tucson's "Old Town," *Monte Walsh* was the sad story of a panicky cowboy facing the end of his way of life. Hired by cinematographer Dave Walsh while Bill Fraker was enjoying his directorial debut, Tommy May (at right in white pants) required a moving lighting and camera platform for a walk-and-talk scene with Lee Marvin. He attached a frame to the top of a western dolly, then built sides and laid sleeper track for it to roll on (courtesy Tommy May). *Bottom:* This sleeper track through Old Tucson was nearly 200 feet long and made from high-grade 2 × 12s with timbers beneath for support. It was level in all directions and took a crew of grips three hours to build. A line of electricians can be seen to the track's left, preparing to pull cable as their 10K provides full light once the action gets to track's end. Having the technicians move along with the light, rather than let the cable run on the ground, avoided snags on the lumber, which could have resulted in a ruined take (courtesy Tommy May).

the sweltering midday heat: "They saw us running for long passes and thought we were nuts!"

Things became busy for "Chainsaw" and his crew in 1973 when they were hired by UPM Tom Shaw to do *Scarecrow*. The Warner Bros. release, featuring Gene Hackman as a slick ex-con and Al Pacino as a not-so-innocent drifter, possessed a down-and-out realism that was carefully crafted. One story circulating on set was that Hackman and Pacino had gone out panhandling disguised before shooting began, to better understand their characters. It was shot by cinematographer Vilmos Zsigmond (of *Deliverance* and *Deer Hunter*). May's job was to keep the famously picky DP contented by staying one step ahead of his needs.

In April of 1973 May key-gripped Warner Bros.' *Cleopatra Jones*. Directed by Jack Starrett, the movie spotlighted six-foot-two newcomer Tamara Dobson kung-fu fighting her way across the screen. The picture, May said, featured a troublesome silver Corvette Stingray with a custom T-top roof. He described the malfunctioning glass panel that was supposed to automatically slide out of the way as the statuesque Jones (topped with a five-inch Afro) descended into the driver's seat: "Her hair got crunched a few times, until we manually operated the top out of frame."

Also in 1973, May toiled on another motion picture which he wouldn't soon forget, Robert Blake's *Electra Glide in Blue*, directed by James Guercio. Engaged by mainstay Tom Shaw (who served the feature as assistant director), the picture was shot by Conrad Hall, who lensed the popular Robert Boris book with a combination of extreme close-ups and slow zoom-ins, utilizing broad panoramas of nature backdropping his actors. For one scene, May was challenged to rig a special driver's side hostess mount, with a camera operator's seat attached. The concept was for the cameraman to be able to ride aside the automobile, enabling the shot to follow the motor-cop (Blake) as he pulled a car over, dismounted his bike, then walked up to the vehicle—all in one move. Hall's ability to pan and pull focus from the special rig made the multi-tiered coverage possible.

Deprived of the Chevrolet convertible originally intended for the film (due to a blown engine the morning of principal photography), UPM Shaw was faced with a problem. Thinking on his feet, he spied a new red Triumph sports car just across the street from location. Approaching the young driver, he made a deal on the spot to use the Brit two-seater for the entire film. "The Triumph was a great save," May recalled, "but the car was low and with Connie being over six feet tall, I had to use speedrail outriggers to support the operator's seat so his feet wouldn't hit the ground."

A second Vilmos Zsigmond picture came to Tommy at the end of 1973, *Cinderella Liberty*. Directed and produced by Mark Rydell, the bittersweet drama starred James Caan in the lead role of John Baggs as a sailor awaiting orders and Marsha Mason as the hustler he falls for. Imbued with a paint-peeled real-life look (especially the apartment set), *Cinderella Liberty* was tough to photograph because of what they didn't have—a crane. One shot that sorely magnified its need came as DP Zsigmond insisted upon coverage outside the window for a scene looking into Mason's fifth floor apartment. Unfortunately he had not really scouted the building. Without a fire escape on that side to shoot from, "Chainsaw" and company were called upon to construct a five-story scaffolding to make the shot through the window.

While filming a montage of James Caan wandering the streets of Seattle's red light district, an actual panhandler approached him (somehow not noticing the camera and lights) and asked for money. Undaunted, the actor continued in character and gave the guy ten bucks. Ironically, the cash was Caan's lucky ten and the take wound up in the picture.

An important break came for May in 1974 when employed by Shaw to key *Bank Shot*. On that picture, he was reintroduced to cinematographer Harry Stradling Jr. (whom he met on *The Untouchables* a dozen years prior). May's can-do style of gripping was the perfect match for the laid-back DP. Beginning a relationship that would span fifteen features together, Tommy was Stradling's key grip until the great shooter's retirement.

May's next noteworthy film was a difficult-to-photograph action-drama directed by Richard Brooks, *Bite the Bullet*. The story of a 700-mile endurance horse race which took place in the 1890s (as a PR event sponsored by *The Denver Post*), the picture starred Gene Hackman, Candice Bergen and James Coburn and it was lensed in 1975 amid rugged locations such as Carson National Forest and the Cumbres-Toltec Railway in New Mexico. May focused from the start on finding ways to give Stradling the coverage he required. To capture the action, he stabilized the high-speed cameras (used for the slow-motion effects of the struggling horses and riders) as well as incorporating a platform for the dolly shots that put the camera level at the tops of the mounts, instead of shooting up all the time. That placement of lens (via the key grip's know-how) helped to make good shots, great ones! Reciting a story involving director Richard Brooks, who had drafted his stout key grip

Always on the cutting edge of camera placement, key grip Tommy May tests his "over the shoulder" rig while shooting *Damnation Alley* during July 1976 in California's Mojave Desert. Employing a speed rail frame mated to the bike which locked a small body Panavision camera into position, the set-up utilized a mounting plate with a grip arm connected to the magazine for help steadying the image while riding over rough terrain (courtesy Tommy May).

With Jan-Michael Vincent (on the motorcycle), May goes over the fine points of remaining balanced with the added weight of the camera rig while driving at high speed across the Mojave's sandy ground. Directed by Jack Smight and lensed by Harry Stradling Jr., ***Damnation Alley*** was plagued by triple digit temperatures, and the feature's star, a $300,000 military transport dubbed The Landmaster, had to be repaired so often that it was pulled by cable in some sequences (courtesy Tommy May).

to be thrown into a tent as part of a prisoner mistreatment scene, May recalled accidentally knocking down the supporting pup-tent poles, causing the shelter to collapse, resulting in laughter from the crew. Brooks, who had served as a Marine in the Pacific during World War II, said, 'This is no joke. Roughing up a prisoner isn't funny. Now let's do it again without taking out the tent!" After several takes (and reinforcing the tent poles), Chainsaw was done with his acting job and Brooks had his shot.

May also crewed on producer Hal Wallis' last round-up, *Rooster Cogburn*, in 1975. It was described as *The African Queen* meets a western (minus Bogart); among the picture's true strengths were its gorgeous locations and first-rate stunts (laid out by coordinator Mickey Gilbert) and performed by Wayne double Chuck Roberson. Filmed mostly in Deschutes National Forest and in Grants Pass, Oregon (along the Rogue River), the raft sequences in particular had their risks. At sixty-eight years of age, using oxygen because he had just one lung, Wayne's safety was the responsibility of May. Engineering practical methods of danger reduction for the aging star, he rigged special gantries to get the Duke on and off the raft safely, as well as standing rests the big actor could discreetly lean against once on shore.

In 1976, May keyed one of the largest projects of his career, Jack Smight's *Midway*. The Walter Mirisch film was shot mostly aboard the USS *Lexington* by Stradling and boasted a who's who cast. From Heston to Toshiro Mifune, there was much to watch on deck. Nevertheless, what impressed the former naval air guru most were two F-4 Wildcat fighter planes used on the film. May recalled they needed a shot of the aircraft warming up to take off. Unable to start the engines (due to a fuel cut-off switch in the wrong position), Tommy saved the day by knowing how to operate it.

Interestingly, *Midway* was the first release to have Sensurround in select venues that

Key grip Tommy May (left, in hooded rain suit), waits out a downpour while shooting director Frank Capra, Jr.'s ***Born Again*** in Baltimore in 1978. Dean Jones (center, with umbrella) stars as Watergate conspirator Charles Colson; cinematographer Harry Stradling Jr. (in plaid cap) walks by to the right (courtesy Tommy May).

Working a sandwiching stunt for Sam Peckinpah's *Convoy* (1978), May brought his DP's camera within twenty feet of the live-action gag. Shooting from the back of a chase vehicle doing 40 mph while on a closed stretch of highway in Needles, California, DP Harry Stradling Jr. didn't miss a moment of action (courtesy Tommy May).

year. The four huge (low frequency) speakers worked so well during the bombing scenes that loud explosions in the picture caused plaster to crack in many theaters.

A second Smight-Stradling project followed for Tommy, *Damnation Alley* (1977). The post-apocalyptic sci-fi featured an overblown RV dubbed "The Landmaster," which according to May broke down more often than it ran on the film. Next came *Go Tell the Spartans* with cinematographer Stradling. Their following collaboration required all of May's camera-rigging savvy to pull off: Sam Peckinpah's *Convoy*. Shot all over New Mexico, the picture starred Kris Kristofferson as CB-wielding trucker Martin "Rubber Duck" Penwald, playing off Ernest Borgnine as the evil sheriff. Along with its soundtrack (featuring the Paul Brandt radio hit "Convoy"), the motion picture was responsible for launching the civilian boom in CB use nationwide.

Peckinpah was known for his stylistic use of slow motion photography to accentuate his portrayal of violence (as he demonstrated on *The Wild Bunch*, *The Getaway*, and *Killer Elite*) and he trusted his key grip to get some demanding shots. One scene where timing and execution were critical was during the stunt finale: a sandwich crash of two semi trucks with a police car in the middle. It involved the use of gliders (big rig trucks towed by a cable, minus the engines); May described the shot as extremely dangerous. To film it,

6. Tommy May, Key Grip 131

Wielding a chainsaw, key grip Tommy May works in the desert on location during the filming of Blake Edwards' farce *S.O.B.* (1981). May's nickname—"Chainsaw"—was earned early in his career by his use of portable power cutting tools to quickly remove obstacles for rapid camera placement (courtesy Tommy May).

he was pressed to build a special oversized camera car platform. Converting an old school bus by removing its shell and seats, he used the drive-train and engine (with a plywood platform built on top) to complete the large yet maneuverable shooting vehicle. A little-known footnote on *Convoy*: actor James Coburn's participation as an assistant director. Earning his D.G.A. card, he filled in for pal Peckinpah on second unit shots.

Nineteen-eighty was a very busy time for the movie business in Hollywood and in May's career. Keying his twelfth feature in seven years with Stradling, he began to make connections with producers and directors as well. His first directorial marriage was to Blake Edwards, whom he met when keying *S.O.B.* in 1981.

Coming into his own at about this time, Tom switched from servicing one director of photography (Stradling) to an A-list of Hollywood's elite lensmen. Ultimately keying for DPs like Conrad Hall and Haskell Wexler, he also did gigs with Dean Cundey, Dante Spinotti, Michael Ballhaus, Joseph Biroc, Stephen Burum, and Nick McLean. During the 1980s and throughout the '90s, "Chainsaw" was the guy everyone wanted to helm their shows; he often went from one project to the next without a break. In one ten-year period, he worked over 21 features and yet still found time to do quality television like an Emmy Award–winning episode of *The Twilight Zone*, shot by his nephew Brad May. When pressed how he survived the grueling schedule, Tommy winked and responded that sleep was optional.

The second of his four features in 1981 was *Southern Comfort*. Despite the title, May and the crew found the picture anything but hospitable, as the Walter Hill version of "the National Guard meets *Deliverance*" was photographed in the leech-infested bayous around Caddo Lake, Louisiana. Uncomfortable water temperatures prompted the grip divers to wear wet suits; the leech problem was so serious that they had to rotate from the water every other hour to have the blood-sucking creatures removed.

His next 1981 movie was the action thriller *The Pursuit of DB Cooper*. Although minus the leeches, the film was equally wet and hazardous when it came to shooting the scenes in the rapids along the Snake River near Jackson Hole, Wyoming. Still, it was the scene where Cooper (Treat Williams) parachutes from a commercial jet that almost didn't happen. Refused an aircraft for the dangerous stunt by all leasing outlets (including the major airlines), May, through his past military connections, was able to help producer Michael Taylor swing a deal to rent a Boeing 727 from an undisclosed government agency.

Tommy's final feature of 1981 was Billy Wilder's *Buddy, Buddy*, starring Walter Matthau and Jack Lemmon. Wilder, director of such perfect cinema as *Sunset Blvd.* and *Stalag 17*, was in rare form on the picture, pulling his usual practical jokes on crew and actors alike. One gag involved a sloppy propman whom he had taken a dislike toward. While shooting Lemmon's bathroom scene where he's considering self-immolation, the lazy propman had been dumping lighter fluid after each take into the mock commode that Lemmon had been sitting on. After the last take cut, Lemmon stood up as Wilder crossed the set, lit stogie in mouth. Flicking a live cigar ash into the prop john, the director set off the flammable liquid, causing a momentary voluminous whoosh of flames that singed the curtains and charred the toilet seat black. "By the time we finished laughing," May said, "the prop guy was hiding in his truck."

Beginning in 1983 on the movie *The Star Chamber*, Tommy began another directorial marriage with triple threat Peter Hyams (producer, director and cinematographer on the flick). Always the innovator, Hyams' imaginative use of camera challenged his key grip from the start. On *2010*, May achieved a first that was as brilliant as it was boldly out of the box. Asked to place a camera down inside the horizontal body of the space craft, "Chainsaw" attached a Louma Crane off of a larger Titan to achieve the desired effect. Literally like a double-jointed elbow, the Luma arm was angled parallel to freely cover the interior of the oblong set.

When asked if his job was made easier or more difficult with a "three-hatter" like Hyams, May found it wonderful as you received answers to your questions at once from the three department heads who shape the entire look of the picture. "If he wanted it," Tom laughed, "Hyams got it as he was a consensus all by himself!" "Chainsaw" crewed five films over a 14-year span with Hyams, including *The Presidio* and *The Relic*, their last in 1999.

May worked his way through the mid–1980s on house payment fare such as Robert Blake's *Hell Town* as well as answering the call for Hyams on *Running Scared* and Blake Edwards' *Blind Date*. By 1987 he was on a professional glide path that allowed him to pick and choose his own projects. One that he looked back on fondly is *Blind Date*, which he did with Stradling. The Blake Edwards dark comedy showcased a new film star in town, brought up from the minor league of television, Bruce Willis. Tommy laughed when recalling the novice actor enlisting him and other grips to give him face slaps (just before takes) to help him get into the character.

6. *Tommy May, Key Grip* 133

Following the Edwards work, May was back with Hyams when he keyed *The Presidio* in 1988. Discussing its challenges, he mentioned the dynamic foot chase which utilized fast ATVs as camera platforms. Amazingly, "Chainsaw" visually judged framing for the shots by feathering throttle and brake to keep the action in frame. Looking over his shoulder to gauge distance to the actors, he engaged motorcycle master Jay Robert to steer the rig through the pedestrian stunt players along the sidewalk. For some of the scene's transitions,

Petulant look in place, May sits in his speed rail–rigged ATV between takes while filming Peter Hyam's *The Presidio* (1988). On Jackson Street in San Francisco's Chinatown, May drove for Steadicam operator Randy Nolan (behind him wearing a watch cap), providing coverage of Mark Harmon's violent foot chase through the crowded sidewalks. Visually judging the frame size of Nolan's 100mm lens behind him, May employed a combination of throttle and clutch to gauge and maintain his speed, while stunt pro Jay Robert rode along to steer the ATV around obstructions (courtesy Tommy May).

Tommy piloted the rig with Steadicam operator Randy Nolan filming off the tail. When necessary, Nolan could seamlessly dismount during a move by going on foot without breaking the flow of the action.

By decade's end, May ranked among Hollywood's finest key grips. Continuing to take calls from Tom Shaw, he helmed *Tequila Sunrise* (shot by Conrad Hall) in 1986. From *The Fourth War* to *Postcards from the Edge* to *Switch*, Tommy thrived. "You're there to do a job," the ex-linebacker said when asked for the key to his success. "Do what they ask you to do. After all, it's their movie!"

The '90s were Tom May's final decade of gripping in Hollywood, yet he never slowed down. In addition to keying the TV series *Hunter*, he also continued to test himself on big features such as *Batman Returns* and *The Last of the Mohicans*. On *Batman*, May cinched an ASC lifetime achievement award for his flying dolly. It spanned the length of the Gotham City set; his idea worked by using a dolly on track, hard-mounted down from the perms, just above the rooftops. Controlled by an attached wire cable wound around a take-up drum (for both slow and rapid moves), the rig was smooth as ice and able to perform where "no dolly had gone before." Another *Batman* problem solved by May was linear tracking issues while filming the Batmobile's tight turns. By attaching a shooting platform to the vehicle (braced with speedrail struts bolted through the car frame), jumpy shots were eliminated and the results were slot car–like, as director Tim Burton had requested.

Among May's final pictures, *Mulholland Falls* is one of his favorites. Shooting the crash-landing scene of a C-47 with DP Haskell Wexler, he utilized his superior knowledge of aircraft when rigging two Arriflex cameras beneath the nacelles under the plane's wing. When the pilot bellylanded the twin-engine in the Victorville desert that morning, May's Arris stayed put, nailing the shot.

A first-rate mechanic who's wrenched everything from go-carts to helicopters, the retired naval air reserve crew chief, at 77, continues to restore and fly vintage aircraft today. At interview's end, I asked Tommy May what drove him throughout his 60-plus feature career. With the chuckle of a man who knows something that you don't, "Chainsaw" quietly responded, "My wife, Jody. Without her letting me do what I loved, none of it would have been possible." Spoken like a true legend.

7

George Barris, Motion Picture Automotive Designer

In late 1940s America, a transition occurred from the Saturday morning matinees to the new concept of drive-in theatres. Abandoning bicycles for jalopies (with plentiful cheap gas to run them), the masses of teenage movie-goers were swapping Westerns for hot rod flicks, and enjoying the privacy of the venue. The fresh stuff was all about cars and the guy in "the driver's seat" was an automotive icon-to-be, George Barris.

Born in Chicago in 1925, George and older brother Sam lived with relatives in Roseville, California, after the untimely death of their parents. George exhibited a fine hand at crafting balsa wood airplanes; his childhood interest eventually led to car models. He received recognition in local competitions for his advanced designs and building skills.

When George was 16, the boys were given the family's restaurant delivery vehicle, a beat-up 1925 Buick. They mended its dents while refreshing the aging touring car with a custom orange paint job complete with blue pinstripes. Cleaned up, the Buick quickly sold at a profit, facilitating the purchase of a newer 1929 Model A Ford. Interest in the car-swapping biz increased throughout their teen years and the Barris brothers began to work on other people's automobiles.

His brother was mostly self-taught; George's first real automotive education came from a Sacramento body shop, Brown and Bertolucci's, where "old men" (guys in their thirties) showed the kids some basics of the trade. The tools of the craft back then (oxyacetylene torch, leather sand bag, and wooden mallet) required a hands-on touch to mend the steel cars.

Graduating from high school in 1942, George mastered the basics of body work by the time he and Sam enjoyed their first commercial success, fixing a beat-up Ford convertible. As war demand resulted in a shortage of new vehicles, people made do with existing models and the business of sprucing up old cars became a viable one. With many enlisting to fight, teens like George were left to fill the employment void. Now capable of driving to better paying jobs, the kids created an automotive economy for themselves, which fueled the rise of even better cars to come. Sudden wealth in hand, American youth found new ways to entertain themselves and hobbies like car clubs began popping up from New Jersey to Los Angeles.

The Barris boys' growing clique of "hot-rodders" joined what George called the Kustoms car club. Spelling custom with a K to differentiate it from other auto groups, he was ahead of the trend when it came to branding his moniker. It was more about "the shop" than a social order; the brothers utilized Sam's body work skills and George's paint craft (and PR chops) to keep a steadily growing business in the black. They expanded from a tiny place George had leased alone in 1943 (his brother was then in the Navy); at war's end the two reunited with a new garage in Compton. Capitalizing on America's hunger for new cars (fed by returning G.I.s with back pay as well as others with disposable income), the Barrises were in the right place at the perfect time.

Along with the specialized skills to service such "hot" machines as P.T. boats and fighter planes during World War II, a new era of automotive technology came home with its soldiers, showing up in the form of high performance automobiles. From turbochargers to sway bars, this advance in engineering produced a whole new by-product of car culture, with its grass-roots origins planted firmly in Southern California. Fueled by the motorhead types who labored in the States' renowned aircraft factories such as Lockheed, Boeing, and McDonnell Douglas during the Second World War and Korea, the resulting mixture of technical ability, marketing, and timing produced an automotive explosion heard around the world.

Supported by massive freeway construction projects and big oil, the automotive juggernaut was well underway when Barris received an invitation from publisher Robert Petersen, who cashed in on the nationwide auto craze when founding *Hot Rod* magazine. The forward-thinking publisher sponsored product shows for Detroit, as well as hawking his own car rag. George was booked to display his custom '41 Buick during the first auto show at the L.A. Armory in 1948; sporting a Cadillac grill, French headlamps, fade-away tail lights, and a chopped roof, it attracted a lot of attention. Barris' stuff was not only cooler looking, but performance functional as well. Taking advantage of the buzz regarding his cars, George promoted his brand by providing how-to articles and hot rod before-and-after photo spreads for Petersen's magazine.

Coming from a teenage background of drag-racing dares made at L.A.'s Piccadilly drive-in (off Sepulveda), George and his pals pulled midnight antics like high-speed runs along the Pacific Coast Highway amid the oil fields of Compton (in excess of 120 miles an hour), with the cops often in pursuit.

"In the morning," he said with an adolescent grin, "I would occasionally find bullet holes in my trunk. We liked cars and racing, and only had two rules to hang out: no booze and no drugs — just fast cars and girls."

Barris improved his driving skills by competing in weekend "dust-offs" at Saugus Speedway; his track experience would come in handy later when shooting racing movies. With PR from the auto shows and magazine layouts continuing to build his custom car biz, George moved to a larger shop in Linwood, until finally relocating to his current digs off Riverside drive in North Hollywood. Before the garages, however, Barris lived every hot rodder's dream in 1950s L.A.: hanging out and working on cars by day, then cruising and racing all night. As the real-life escapades of kids like George made the local papers, movie producers such as Roger Corman, Sam Arkoff, and William Castle cashed in on the buzz, courting Barris and his merry band of cohorts to help bring authenticity (and exciting car gags) to the big screen.

Implementing this new realism with George as technical advisor and or "car guy" on automotive fare such as *Rebel Without a Cause, Hot Car Girl, High School Confidential!* and *Speed Crazy*, the producers and their hired writers were now tapping into original source material for their stories. Adding texture to the screenplays extracted from his own history, Barris brought the real mechanics of the hot rod scene to bear with accurate dialogue about everything automotive, from carburetors to wipe-outs.

By the late '50s, car pictures had become the new Westerns. Instead of horse falls and six-shooters, these new action flicks were about rolling Fords, running from the cops, and getting the girl by picture's end. Trading ponies for horsepower had a profound effect on the United States and on motion pictures. Sitting in the catbird seat of a new social phenomenon, George realized the value of his unique perspective and proceeded full-bore with his movie projects, while continuing to customize automobiles for a living.

"We were the basis," Barris said, "of where the entire car thing originated. Most of what we did in those 'B' pictures was real, often at speeds in excess of 100 miles per hour along the Pacific Coast Highway through Manhattan Beach, where we shot all the time." One example of real not being possible was a car-roll gag in Jack Arnold's *High School Confidential!* Due to the low center of gravity of the '55 Chevy chop-top used for the stunt, DP Harold Marzorati enlisted Barris to fake the dangerous maneuver by employing stop-action photography combined with a crane to flip the vehicle over.

Always close to the action on these early pictures, Barris worked out the chicken-run sequences for director Nicholas Ray in *Rebel Without a Cause*. He not only staged a safe cut-away method to shooting the potentially deadly stunt, but also coached background actors as to the look, lingo, and attitude of authentic hot rodders. George was already acquainted with the film's star James Dean from weekend racing at Indian Wells; he recalled the actor's transition from a Triumph to the infamous Porsche Spyder, which he was driving when killed en route to a racing competition in Salinas, California. "Jimmy was a skilled and totally fearless driver behind the wheel," Barris said sadly. "If anyone could have pulled off staying alive that day, it was him."

George continued to land calls for automotive movie assignments through decade's end (as well as his continued success with the body shop). He was hired to rig a car crash for Hitchcock's *North by Northwest*: The scene (with stuntman Chuck Lawford driving a police car) culminated with the rear end impact of a vintage Mercedes holding Cary Grant. Utilizing a lead bolt and aluminum fittings set-up to allow the bumper to fall off on impact without damaging the pricey vehicle, Barris was shocked when the following silence was broken by a comically loud "bewang" sound. Leaving his director's chair as though kicked, Alfred Hitchcock said to George with a puzzled grin on his face, "How on Earth did you manage that?" Realizing it as complete luck, Barris cleverly answered, "All in a day's work, sir. Just don't expect another take." Considering that less than five seconds (eight feet of film) were cut from the final print, one can appreciate the perfect timing of the happy accident. The delay between impact and the chrome body molding popping off, added a comedic punchline to the scene that even the famed director had not imagined.

By the spring of 1960, George had become enough of a known player in the picture-car biz that he was able to land producer credit for another teen hot rod flick, *Juke Box Racket*. Furnishing the feature's automobiles, the newbie money-man learned valuable budgeting concepts such as vehicle depreciation and expendable pay-outs like gas and tire purchases that would serve him well for the remainder of his career.

Furthering his reputation as a studio car maker, Barris was next brought in by Paramount and Jerry Lewis to build a vehicle for *Cinderfella*. "The Golden Sahara" (as the car was dubbed due to its extravagance and color scheme) was based on a 1953 Lincoln Capri. Rigging the doors to "magically" open on cue (live-action on camera), George was years ahead of the field with his engineering of electronically controlled solenoids, wirelessly activated by a modified Zenith television channel changer receiver, adapted to remote use. With a mix of director Frank Tashlin's comedic sensibilities (as well as the art direction of Henry Bumstead), Barris blended the Sahara with a perfect "fairy tale" look it richly deserved. It was comic book cool wrapped in a 24-karat plated design; only Sy Devore's wardrobe for Jerry Lewis was a better fit for character on the movie.

Along with his feature work and thriving custom shop, George was also the king of self-promotion, both for the automobiles he transformed into works of art and his reputation as a trend-setter on the motor-vehicle scene. He paid his dues with early hot rod shows put together by renting gas station parking lots and advertising in local newspapers and high schools; within a few years George had the good fortune of being noticed by Lee Iacocca, who ultimately hired him to construct a prototype to be featured in Ford's International Caravan of Cars. Working only from designers' sketches supplied by the manufacturer (as no sculpted model existed), he transformed a 1962 Mercury sedan into "The Marauder" in just five weeks. Featuring such far-out design cues as pistol grip steering wheel, floating head rests, working hood scoops, and wrap-around windshields, the Merc was a study in modern streamlining. When the build was complete, Iacocca and the Ford folks met at Barris' shop to check out the goods. Fearful that he had killed the golden goose by overcharging the major auto maker for the car, George was relieved when the Ford boss looked up from the $155,000 invoice and said sternly, "You just saved us a million dollars, George, and the sedan is beautiful." Had Ford done the mock-up in its usual fashion, it would have required six months, a dozen engineers and a squadron of mechanics and body-men. George Barris did it with a team of six in less than forty days.

In step with Ford's incidental promotion of George's product (and subsequent PR from his movie work in the early sixties), Barris found himself in the spotlight of international acclaim as the subject of an essay written by avant-garde journalist Tom Wolfe. His observational reportage of the 1963 New York Automotive Show first titled "There Goes (Varoom! Varoom!), that Kandy Kolored Tangerine-Flake Streamline Baby (Rahghhh!), Around the Bend (Brummmmmmmmmmmmmmm)," included 18 pages of history on George that would soon make him a household name. Spurring the public's interest in what Wolfe described as the "Dionysian-streamline" style of automotive art, his writings touted the radically chopped and lowered painted creations of such design luminaries as Big Daddy Ed Roth, Barris, and Darryl Starbird. Frustrated by writer's block, Wolfe submitted his raw story notes to *Esquire* boss Bryan Dobell; the savvy editor ran the piece verbatim as an essay. Wolfe's focus on Barris (from his Bohemic artist lifestyle to his bootlegger moves behind the wheel) launched them each into the hip mainstream of Baby Boomer automotive history. Wolfe wrote of exhaust pipes through rear bumper treatments, elongated tail fins, twin head lights, radiused fender openings, and chopped roofs (including the bullet-bumpers on the 1958 Cadillac) as concepts that Detroit, and ultimately everyday car design, would adopt from this man.

Along with the increased public awareness from shows and magazine articles (as well as word of mouth in Movieland), Barris continued to receive car assignments. In the summer of 1962, he was hired by producer Paul Henning to create a backwoods pickup truck for the pilot of *The Beverly Hillbillies*. Possibly the world's first cross-over utility vehicle, it was constructed from a 1922 Oldsmobile touring car which had a flatbed connected to its rear for delivery use. George discovered it gathering dust behind a feed store while driving off Interstate 10 through San Bernardino, then towed it back to Los Angeles after showing Henning a snapshot of his find.

Using his body work knowledge to pull molds off fenders, hoods, and doors from an already restored '22 Olds, Barris eventually assembled five *Hillbilly* vehicles for the series. The show's classic opening image of Granny Clampett (Irene Dunn) perched in her rocking chair on the truck's flatbed was a direct result of Barris' shop building a special riser to stage her there. Another Barris variant fashioned for Jethro (Max Baer) was a metal-flake red 1921 Olds Roadster conversion featuring chrome supercharger relief pipes protruding from the engine, fat Firestone racing tires and special dual exhaust connected to an Oldsmobile 442 motor; the design was perfect for Baer's over-the-top character. Illustrating the popularity of the Barris autos (and the diversification he manifested for his wheeled creations outside of Tinseltown), Jethro's hot rod was marketed through M.P.C. models, earning George cash from plastic kit sales for years after the show was wrapped.

After getting the *Hillbillies* set throughout its second season, Barris and his boys did Norman Taurog's *Palm Springs Weekend*. *Weekend* was so intrinsically "early-'60s" that much of the cast (including Robert Conrad, Connie Stevens, and Dawn Wells) would soon have iconic television series of their own. Incorporating lots of high-speed driving stunts, set against the area's beautiful desert backgrounds, the picture was coordinated by Barris, who also supplied the cars, including a '63 convertible Corvette and Thunderbird and Mercury ragtop coupes. Many Angelinos flocked to the resort after the film's release; local motels were booked for months.

Staying on the "youth track," George's next cinematic effort, 1964's *For Those Who Think Young*, became another automotive notch on his career belt. Brought in by helmer Leslie Martinson, Barris customized a '63 Buick Riviera with a radical cantilevered roof, and swapped the vehicle's original candy-apple red paint job with 30 coats of lacquer pearl white. Dubbed the Villa Riviera, the rolling work of art also showcased early car phone technology.

Returning for a second Jerry Lewis project in the latter part of 1964, George provided a special futuristic automobile for character Stanley Belt in *The Patsy*. Bringing in an ultra-modern 1955 Mercury D-528 test-prototype (with exterior design by Gil Spear of FOMO engineering company), Barris did a massive solenoid and receiver modification (like he did with the Golden Sahara) to operate its doors, trunk, and hood as part of a comedic on-camera sequence.

Also in 1964, Barris was tapped for another Filmways Production: locate a one-of-a-kind automobile for producer Nat Perrin's *The Addams Family* based on the Charles Addams cartoon. Barris perfectly matched the program's campy yet richly manifested trappings with a stoic 1933 Packard V-12 touring car (with its separate driving compartment for Ted Cassidy's Lurch). Due to Cassidy's 6'7" frame, George had to lower the chauffeur's seat so that Cassidy's head wasn't completely above the windshield when driving.

On a roll with automotive television and feature gigs, George next built another car for the short-lived Jerry Van Dyke comedy series *My Mother the Car*. Transforming a '27 Model T Ford into a 1928 "Porter," he upgraded the old car's performance with a tuned 327 cubic inch Chevrolet V-8 engine mated to an automatic transmission. He built two vehicles for the pilot; the version used for stunts had beefed-up modern suspension and removable body components such as running boards and windshield while the "hero-car" (an Alberta) was rigged with a hidden driver's compartment with angled mirrors that allowed the operator to see to steer. Instilling "Mother" (as the auto was dubbed) with a personality not unlike the later *Knight Rider*'s Kitt, Barris constructed the vehicle's dashboard with a series of blinking lights that pulsated in synch to actress Ann Sothern's voice. "Like Kitt years later," the car-man recalled, "the talking dash gave Mother a human touch of whimsy, that audiences really liked. After all, everybody who's ever had a favorite car, talks to it occasionally when driving and would love a response!"

Along with Barris' non-stop contribution to studio projects into the 1960s (as well as the show car work for Detroit), the PR master continued to cultivate a growing celebrity clientele hungry to have him customize their wheeled toys. From old-school movie stars like Clark Gable and his stable of Jaguar XK-150s to Elvis Presley's lily-gilded Cadillac limo conversion, the wealthy folk of Movieland all desired something unique in which to be seen. Happily obliging, Barris turned out some stunning redoes of Detroit steel that looked like the future. His beautifully linear take on a Cadillac Eldorado station wagon built for Rat Packer Dean Martin inventively combined retro and futuristic syling elements.

George's next landmark assignment came from television producers Bob Mosher and Joe Connelly: He was asked to do a special auto for a kooky new series called *The Munsters*. Fans for years, they engaged Barris' hot rod view of the universe, to cut loose and create the type of fantasy drag race cars that he loved to build. Upon meeting with the producers who wanted him to utilize an old Cadillac hearse (purchased cheap), the designer said, "Your show's concept is so different, original, and inspirational, you gotta let me match the right car to the idea of a lovable Frankenstein, and build you something from scratch." Scratch, in this case, meant beginning with three Model T Fords spliced into a six-door stretched-frame platform. Focused on improving the huge auto's handling, Barris next installed split radius shocks with t-springs, all mounted into a dropped axle front end. He chose a Ford 289 Cobra engine (bored-out to 425 cubic inches), as well as ten chromed Stromberg carburetors, Isky cams, and Bobby Barr racing headers to take care of performance matters. George's 21-day build on the 18-foot-long dragster culminated with its custom paint job and polishing of the rolled steel scroll work and the engine's chromed motor parts. The manic energy required of Barris to see a project of this magnitude through was equal to any painter or sculptor in the fine arts field of his time. Laboring 16-hour days (often napping in the shop instead of going home between shifts), George and his crew brought symmetry to the construction of the automobile. An instant hit with viewers, the Munster Coach received more fan mail than Fred Gwynne's Herman, and was soon issued in scale by model car maker AMT. Recalling the network's blatant dismissal of his toy line idea for the series, Barris chuckled as he spoke of his hefty profits from the licensing deal for the models: "That was the last time that a network didn't want a piece of toy sales. Now, it's where negotiations begin." As *The Munsters'* ratings soared, fan interest in Grandpa (Al Lewis) rose to a point of giving the character his own set of wheels: Dragula. The name was a play on Grandpa's proclivity for all things vampirish. The casket-car was introduced in the "Hot Rod Herman" episode for a drag race gag at the track. Barris coached stunt driver Jerry Summers in the fine art of lifting a car's nose off the ground (doing a wheelie). Having mastered the "off the line show-boat" move in his street racing days, he showed Summers the "how-to" essentials: apply the brakes (both regular and emergency) while revving the engine with the gas pressed to the floor. "Put the car in gear," Barris continued, "then release the brakes as you simultaneously engage the clutch. This produces a surge of torque and power that lifts rear-end driven stuff right into the air."

Convincing the producers that waiting to fix expensive and sometimes finicky show cars was a waste of time and money, George was tasked with the construction of four additional Dragulas. In addition to reducing production's down-time with the multiple vehicles concept, it also allowed for the program's clever national marketing by displaying these television-character autos at everything from mall openings and car dealerships to regional raceways and toy stores.

George provided a custom automobile for the Frank and Nancy Sinatra comedy *Marriage on the Rocks* (1965) at the suggestion of Dean Martin, who co-starred in the flick. He came up with a wild-looking Ford mustang coupe with design cues such as an open T-top roof, ten-inch extended nose, and faux zebra hides applied to the side panels, trunk lid, and seat surfaces. It also included cool interior touches like a built-in working television and cup-holders (a first anywhere!). Barris and project engineer Richard Korkes were years ahead with their ideas. Taken with the modified Mustang, Sinatra purchased the car as a birthday present for his daughter Nancy, and presented it to her at the picture's wrap party. George said, "Working with those guys [the Rat Pack] was exciting as they had the money and clout to get great cars created."

Shot in November of 1965, Universal Pictures' *Out of Sight* tapped into Barris' inner mad doctor: He was hired to build ZZR, a double-motored dragster. Plying the vehicle with enough power to pull a house, the tandem 340 cubic-inch Buick engines (complete

Leaning against the custom Zebra Mustang he made for the film **Marriage on the Rocks** (1965), George Barris (right) is all smiles while delivering the car to good friend Frank Sinatra, who bought it as a surprise birthday present for his daughter Nancy. Once the vehicle was wrapped from shooting, it was sold to Frank for a sum exceeding $10,000. According to Barris, the automobile turned heads at every intersection and was fast as a Ferrari when floored (courtesy George Barris).

with Hilborn injectors and Ansen Posi-shift Power Glide transmission) was every inch a chrome-plated Barris Kustom. Carrying more make-believe weapons than a battleship, the ZZR included a telescopic machine gun, dual hydraulic ramming spikes, skid-juice rig, flame-thrower bumpers and more. While *Out of Sight* may have been just another comedic rock'n'roll secret agent film shot at Zuma Beach (with a bomb plot tossed in), it cameoed some pretty good Universal contract bands like Gary Lewis and the Playboys, The Turtles, and Freddie and the Dreamers.

Barris' next television tune-up would turn out to be his (and Movieland's) most iconic four-wheeled creations to date: the Batmobile. Like the Lone Ranger's horse Silver, the Batmobile became virtually a supporting character. Requiring three weeks' labor at a cost of nearly $30,000, the modification of the existing 1955 Lincoln Futura prototype (originally created by William Schmidt at the Lincoln styling department) was accomplished by a Barris-assembled group including design draftsman Herb Grasse and motorheads Bill Cushenberry, Gale Black, Richard Korkes, Les Tompkins, and Roy Johnson, with 20th Century–Fox's Eddie Graves also providing input. The Batmobile was the first television car undertaken with major studio backing. Capitalizing on the Lincoln's radical lines and dual bubble cockpit layout, Barris accentuated its futuristic aesthetic by elongating the car's existing fins to run from mid-door to tail and creating radiused wheel openings, a flared hood-scoop, and dual side-by-side cabin glass. It was rendered in a deep black paint scheme (rimmed with fluorescent cerise striping). The inclusion of the Futura's U-shaped aircraft-style steering wheel infused the machine with the menacing look of a World War II P-61 Night Fighter.

Staying with the flight motif (or at least the impression of it), George further tricked out the Batmobile with Cummings & Sanders safety restraints, a power T-handle accelerator, two ten-foot wide parachutes (for braking) and a fake exhaust turbine assembly constructed from a five-gallon black plastic bucket. The car was built to be performance-functional as well. The producers wisely chose stuntman Frank Hoary for the driving chores; the 429 Ford racing engine (spinning ten-inch-wide Rader Competition wheels shod with fat Firestone pro-racer tires) proved a handful for amateurs to manage. The Batmobile was also equipped with crimefighter musts such as mobile telephone, radar, built-in hydraulic cable cutter, and foam fire-suppression system. "I was thinking comic-book stuff during production meetings," Barris recalled, "so seeing storyboards with bullets flying off the cockpit immediately made me think of a shatter-proof glass sequence using the *Zing* caption."

Ultimately building five Batmobiles by series' end in 1968, Barris wisely secured the rights to show or otherwise advertise the car for his own uses, so long as they didn't conflict with 20th Century–Fox. He retained ownership of one of the Batmobiles until putting it up for auction in 2012.

Barris was next brought in to do a tongue-in-cheek take on the Bond craze for Dean Martin's *The Silencers*. Called by pal Martin, George converted a 1965 Mercury Colony Park station wagon into a combination shag shack and spy-car. Turning the bland interior from naugahyde-quirky to cool, he implemented white leather upholstered sofa benches (with a built-in bar on one side and a hidden gun locker on the other) to set the tone of the secret agent "bachelor pad on wheels." Rigged with blinds, silk curtains, a tailgate step-down entry, and a real television, the Sexwagon (as it was dubbed by grips on the set) was the perfect punchline for Matt Helm's persona. Building several variations for the

7. *George Barris, Motion Picture Automotive Designer*   143

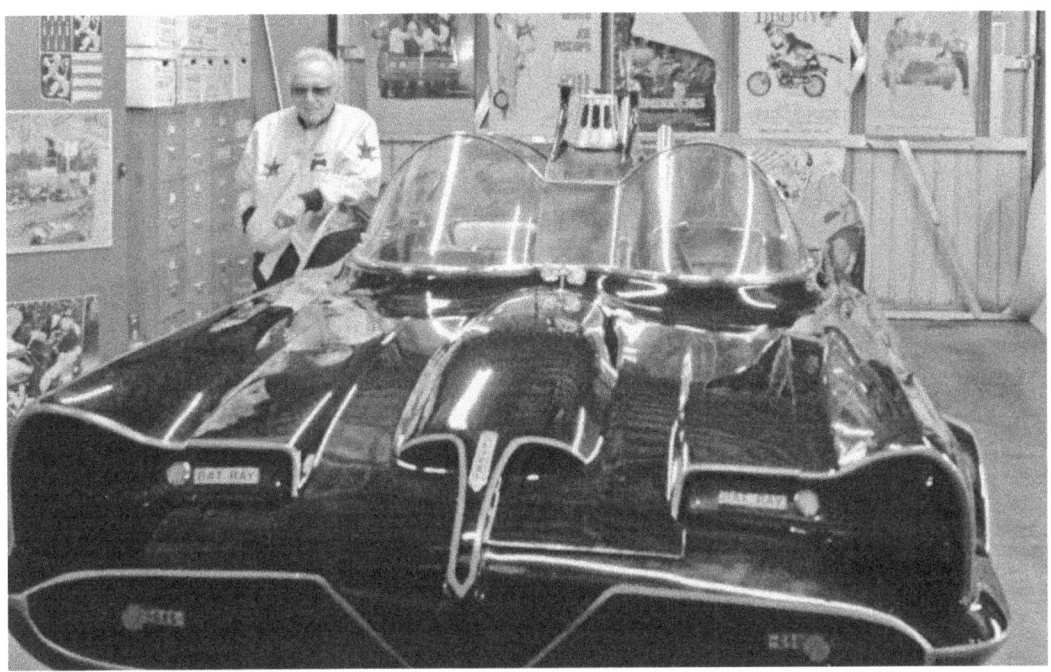

Photographed during the summer of 2011 in his North Hollywood shop, George Barris poses next to his most famous vehicle, the Batmobile. Constructed from a 1955 Lincoln Futura prototype, it was assembled by a who's who of automotive icons including Bill Cushenberry, Gale Black, Les Thompkins, and Roy Johnson. The Batmobile was as fast as it looked owing to the team's use of a bored-out 429 racing motor, competition wheel set-ups and advanced suspension. It was driven primarily by stunt legend Frank Khoury for the series (courtesy George Barris).

picture, Barris constructed a stunt version of the Mercury implementing performance and handling upgrades such as racing transmission, reinforced chassis, heavy duty shocks and suspension, as well as competition tires with Cragar wheels. The final variant was done as a cut-away process vehicle (mounted on a wheeled frame with rear projection often shown behind), utilizing removable sections including the roof, windshield, and entire front-end, allowing for unobstructed driving shots in studio. Recalling a camping-out scene filmed on stage, George laughed while describing the Mercury magically turning into an inflatable "Motel-Six" (complete with instant-up room and working campfire) and Martin shoving co-star Stella Stevens head-first into the set's bog-like fake pond. Covered in a pudding-like mix of muddy water, Stevens was fished out of the crud saying, "Dean, you son of a bitch, I'm gonna kill you when I get my hands on you!"

Nineteen sixty-six was a banner year for Barris. Challenged next on AIP's *Fireball 500*, George conjured up a hot new modification for an existing production car that not only looked futuristically cool, but also possessed advanced performance mechanics that gave it professional speed and handling characteristics. It was based on a stock Plymouth Barracuda; George planted a 426 Hemi-engine with Isky racing cams, Holly carburetors, Jahns pistons, dual Dupree electronic fuel pumps, and four-speed Ansen Posi-shift gear box, to make it big-track fast, with a quarter-mile run clocked at 140 miles per hour. Other Barris touches like enclosed rear cockpit cowlings, split windshield, flush drag-reducing door handles,

Putting the final touches on the Sexwagon, built for Columbia Pictures' *The Silencers* (1966), George Barris (right) supervises the installation of the rear cabin's tufted leather couch. Other Matt Helm amenities included a fold-out cocktail bar, armory lockers, texting taillights and silk curtains all around. One of three 1965 Mercury Colony Park station wagons converted for movie use, the performance version employed for stunts was given a racing transmission complete with reinforced chassis and heavy duty shocks. Barris also modified the picture car with low back swiveling front seats, allowing camera placement inside the vehicle for reaction shots between driver and passenger while moving. The third vehicle was little more than a shell on wheels with removable sections providing camera access; everything from the windshield to the doors and roof could be unbolted for all sorts of effect shots (courtesy George Barris).

square headlight assemblages, and Ram-thrust inlet tubes (protruding through openings in the hood) gave the red-hot racer a very streamlined look.

George teamed with technical advisor Charlie Murray and stunt drivers Ronnie Dayton and Bobby Brack to bring *Fireball 500*'s racing's dangerous reality to screen. When asked the advantages of collaborative working, Barris professed grandly, "I was always a team guy. Group creativity is what I'm all about with movies and building cars for them! I want to hear from everyone, including the DP, art director, and editor...if it makes a better car or a better way to shoot one." Placing cameras on the front and rear of the automobile, cinematographer Floyd Crosby was able to provide helmer William Asher with a bin-full of great action footage. Recalling his input, George said, "They respected me because of my experience on how to make things work for camera."

Producers William Dozier and Charles Fitzsimons took advantage of the *Batman* TV show's increasing popularity and decided to make *Batman* the movie. Released in October of '66, the film was directed by television skipper Leslie Martinson, and starred the same cast including Adam West, Burt Ward, and the talented bunch of bad guys. It was the first motion picture to use direct product placement with a superhero; Fox had a standing agreement with boat manufacturer Gladstone to make and supply the Bat-boat for the film.

With Barris' chores on the movie confined to Batmobile maintenance (as it was already built for the television series), much of his labors were second-unit efforts with DP Jack Marta and aerials flown by Nelson Tyler. George never missed a cue or a chance to have fun with the Batmobile on the open road. "We had to be very cautious where we filmed," he recalled. "Just the slightest glimpse of the car was enough to make 'looky-loos' pull over, hoping to see more of the strange vehicle. I remember kids with their noses pressed to the window-glass driving by, with eyes wide for a glimpse of the masked crusader from TV."

Returning to the racing scene for a second feature with American International, Barris worked on *Thunder Alley* in 1967. The movie revolved around the big-time stock-car racing world in Florida. Filmed at the fabled Daytona Beach Speedway in the off season (using actual race footage), the gritty picture was one of several that George and Sam Arkoff did together over the years. When questioned about what "clicked" between him and the B-flick producer, Barris revealed, "Sam always gave me room to do something different by providing the time and money on his projects for the creation of outstanding cars." Speaking of special autos, Barris' manifestation of the movie's Thunder Charger didn't disappoint theatergoing car fans. He endowed it with a monster 426 Plymouth Hemi motor with extruded side-pipes and chrome Ram-thrust air-scoops for increased power. Other modifications to the standard Charger such as a cantilevered open roof, rear fender channel wings and air-scoops, fast-back air spoiler, radiused wheel wells, and a custom grill up-front, gave the Plymouth the build of a stock-car on steroids.

Shifting back to television, Barris' shop next worked for Bruce Geller to create a signature auto for the Mike Connors private eye series *Mannix*. Chopping the roofs off two new Oldsmobile Toronado coupes, George (now minus brother Sam, who had passed away) outfitted one version for stunts, while the second was left pristine for standard driving shots. He upgraded the performance Toronado with his usual package of tricks like a souped-up 442 Olds engine, heavy-duty suspension, and better brakes and tires. The car was well-suited for the abuse it got from stunt drivers Lee Faulkner, Charlie Picerni and Hal Needham. The series' car stunts were better than those seen in theaters at the time.

Producing a new set of wheels for *Mannix* in the 1968 season, Barris went low-key cool with his rendition of a GTS-340 Dodge Dart convertible, complete with functional hood-scoops, off-set by blacked-out nose grill and tail light panels. Outfitted with a working Motorola car-phone, the Dart's British racing green color was chosen by producer Geller, who thought its original red paint would make it hard to buy as a private eye's ride. "Imagine," Barris smirked, "following someone in a candy-apple–colored convertible. It had to be dark to be at all believable."

In the winter of 1968, George was tapped by Walt Disney to create a character car for his new action-comedy *The Love Bug*. It was originally conceived as an Opel GT by George (who had a great connection at GM for the overseas market cars). Producer Bill Walsh and director Robert Stevenson chose another German-made icon as their star, the Volkswagen

Beetle. Instilled with an everyman's quality reflected through its over-sized headlights and its silly "bumper-grin," the vehicle had a comedic quality to it, perfect for the role.

Manufacturing the necessary stunt and picture-car versions of Herbie (as the gutsy little VW was named), Barris built the racing prototype with competition carburetors and beefed-up Koni shocks. He tweaked the motor's timing ratios, producing more low-end torque and speed for stunt work. Although a later version was assembled using a Porsche 356 engine and drive-train, the penny-savers at Disney preferred the simpler VW engine, as they were cheaper to maintain and build than the speedster variant. Some of the auto stunts in the picture included driving on two wheels while traversing around obstacles and through narrow alleyways. Barris constantly aided drivers Bill Hickman, Ronnie Rondell, Jack Perkins, and Bud Eakins with his innovative use of everything from counter-weights in the car, to jacking up the leaf-springs on one side of the vehicle to effect gravity-defying sequences. Other "tricks of the trade," such as hidden balance wheels and inverted camera positions, were employed for the staged high-speed near-misses and upside down runs; all photographed at angles to add believability to the wild action.

Featuring Dean Jones and Buddy Hackett (as well as a cameo by racing legend Andy Granatelli), *The Love Bug* was filmed around San Francisco's Lombard Street with most of the track action lensed at Riverside International Raceway. The titles *Beetlebug, Car, Boy, Girl,* and *Thunderbug* were considered before the *Love Bug* moniker stuck after cast and crew gave the VW its cute name.

In late 1967, Barris stayed busy with more television and civilian custom work at his shop. Juicing-up a Firebird 400 convertible for the show *I Dream of Jeannie*, George turned nice into magnificent. Adding a handmade Fiberglas twin-scooped hood, steel side-quarter panels and a dazzling green metal-flake paint-job with racing stripes, he was the only customizer to ever modify a Pontiac promotional car for a television series.

Along with the financial gain of a solid two-year run of business at the North Hollywood body, other notable automotive offerings to the small screen came in 1972 by way of Universal's private eye series *Banacek*, starring George Peppard. Barris provided the series' signature 1972 Cadillac Fleetwood limousine, play-driven by character actor Ralph Manza as Jay. Barris souped-up the second season opening episode ("Project Phoenix") with an ultra-mod conversion of a '69 AMX-400 with a 390 cubic-inch V-8 power plant (producing over 300 horsepower). George not only chopped the roof nearly five inches to its front eye-line, but also incorporated a body-contouring louver-grill and window treatment (both fore and aft) that gave the AMX an aggressive, rakish look. He finished with a lowered body, 15-inch extended nose, and chromed side exhaust pipes with Cragar wheels. The vehicle was a true Barris creation, perfect for the slickly written program.

In 1973, two historic films were serviced by Barris and the boys. The first was George Lucas' *American Graffiti*. Because it was based on the very stuff that Barris grew up doing around cars (including the rear axle being ripped out of a cop car via a steel cable), he added story credibility to the theme of cruising for chicks and racing for pink-slips all summer long. Not only did he help to obtain accurate-looking vehicles for the 300 required in the feature, but he also provided key staging and logistics help for the climactic two-lane blacktop race. The movie was photographed on location around various spots in Petaluma, California (except for the Mel's Diner scenes, grabbed in San Francisco). Its 29-night shooting schedule reminded George of his youth, spent raising hell in the San Fernando Valley of the 1950s. "Except for the lights and camera crew," he fondly recalled, "racing around in all those hot cars in the dark reminded me of being a kid again."

In the second half of 1973, Woody Allen's *Sleeper* took George forward in time to create auto-trams from the track up. Barris wisely used a vacuum-formed process to construct the egg-like shells, while engineering a VW chassis, motor, and drivetrain invisibly beneath, selling the illusion of silent, non-wheeled movement. "As Woody wanted Saab spaceships, and the budget allowed only the couple of Pods we got, it was amazing what we ended up with, for what little was spent," George said.

By 1974 Barris and his customs had become an industry. Despite the oil embargo of '73, the body shop's success (as well as his additional incomes derived from model car contracts, show appearances, and design work) allowed him the resources to come to the aid of old friend H.B. "Toby" Halicki. Writing, directing, and starring in his own fantastic car picture *Gone in 60 Seconds*, the vehicular virtuoso hired George to help with the staging of its hairier chase sequences. One take that spun out of control was a glancing but serious impact of Eleanor (the hero's '73 orange Mustang fastback) against a telephone pole. Hitting the wooden upright at over 60 miles an hour, Halicki was banged around and subsequently knocked unconscious, yet found still clutching the driver's wheel when the car came to a stop. In the ambulance on the way to the emergency room H.B. asked Barris through a swollen jaw, "Did we get it?" As it was the only available take that night (and was terrific), it wound up in the final picture. Filmed on the run, guerrilla-style, with no real script (other than some basic dialogue), the action in *Gone in 60 Seconds* was basically made up by cast and crew at the time of shooting. The exception proved to be an expensive one as director Halicki insisted on pulling out all the stops for the feature's final stunt. Having convinced a friend to allow the use of his Cadillac dealership on Hawthorne Blvd. H.B. accidentally crashed his orange Mustang through the showroom's plate glass windows at 80 miles per hour, taking out three cars in one impact and an additional two Caddies in another. He was forced to purchase all five damaged automobiles. Placing himself at risk during the 93 car wrecks in the flick, Halicki eventually ran out of luck when Eleanor flew 40 yards at 30 feet of height and crash-landed, seriously damaging his spine on impact.

The late 1970s was a lucrative period for Barris, although not so much in the car-picture biz. In pace with oil-money factors that continued to hamper the country's economic growth, Cinema City was also feeling a fiscal pinch. Suddenly, cheap was in and the films George worked were no exception. Always looking for trends, he found his next payday on the 1977 feature *The Van*. The aptly titled film, produced by Paul Lewis in the midst of the boxy truck's heyday, was a sparse excuse for drama yet spared no efforts with its coverage of the multitude of different accessories available in the market then. It was plied with Barris built-ins like a waterbed, mirrored ceilings, multiple televisions, a mini-kitchen, and eight-track tape system. With cameos of various van-tastic Barris vehicles such as the Sex-den (with its round bed and silk blinds) as well as other vannish sin-bins, the picture enjoyed enough drive-in success that producer Lee Jones drafted George for an even more ambitious version of the youth-van genre.

Brilliantly titled *Super-Van*, the "cinematic masterpiece" was little more than an excuse to put on a parade of Barris-modified Detroit "work-boxes." Even amid the rising gas prices of the late 1970s, the movie hit its mark with the kids as van sales were robust despite the vehicle's poor mileage. Vandora (one of Barris' more forward-thinking creations in the project) featured early solar-electric panel technology built into the Polaroid-tinted glass roof. It started as a standard Dodge Sportsman; George beefed up the van's performance package with aggressive motor timing, Bilstien shocks and a set of G-40 Formula racing tires over ten-inch wide, wire mag-wheels. Body aesthetics included a Mercedes-inspired gullwing passenger side door, "K.C." square headlamps, and hand-rendered sheet steel aerodynamic spoiler to effect "down-force" and improve traction to the van's rear end, as well as look cool. The cool factor continued inside as Super-Van was decorated like a mini-disco including a six-foot-long U-shaped sofa bed wrapped in faux-leather, twin Panasonic televisions, colored lights flanking a built-in musical cocktail bar, padded soundproof walls, Motorola phone and intercom system, hinge-mounted Cole snack-trays, Craig quad-stereo, and mounted mirror-ball. The thing was practically Studio 54 on wheels. One footnote of bar-fly fame was a walk-on by artist Charles Bukowski, playing a wet T-shirt contest judge in the film. Tied in to the movie's concept of teenage titillation to sell the shag shacks as sex magnets, the conversion-van era flourished until the mid-eighties, when eclipsed by the sport utility market.

Despite the downturn in Barris' automotive projects toward the end of the seventies, one of his more enduring efforts from that time was the conversion of a Lincoln Continental for a movie called *The Car*, directed by Elliott Silverstein. George retooled the 1971 Lincoln Continental Mark III with his signature chopped roof, half-lid custom headlights, lowered body and large tires tucked into radiused wheel openings, then wrapped the whole package in black, giving the vehicle a menacing look. Emulated 25 years later with the introduction of the Chrysler 300, the concept proved timeless. "We purposely designed the Car," Barris said, "to look evil and beautiful at the same time!"

Requiring a crew of a half-dozen mechanics and body men (led by Dennis Baird), the six-week build cost $84,000, with several versions manufactured, including three hollow props destroyed during the cliff sequences. The hero car (built like a tank to withstand the rigors of stunt filming) was fortified with flush-mounted 18-gauge steel bumpers, full body roll-bars, heavy duty suspension and wheels package, as well as a massive 460 cubic-inch V-8 motor powering a 4:11 rear-end differential, to execute rear-wheel spinning without burning out the transmission. As the Car was the main character in the flick, it had constant physical action to perform. One version of the Lincoln had a roll-over rig built into its frame. Initiated by an explosive charge that drove a telephone pole-plug through a thick steel flange under the automobile down into the road, the resulting roll-overs were done so effectively that director of photography Gerald Hirschfeld was able to capture the destruction of two police cruisers in one take, without any injury to the Car. Stuntman Everett Creach performed an extraordinary 360-degree backwards-spin maneuver for the rolling collision, then the edited footage was reversed to complete the illusion of multiple impacts with the Car driving away undamaged. George said, "These shots were a must to sell the Lincoln's indestructibility as a character." Only one all-steel version of the Car survived the picture, as one was destroyed during the final roll-over sequences and the other was totaled when crashing through a house.

George again paired with old pal Toby H.B. Halicki on the director's bio-feature *The Junkman*, shot in 1982. He acted and helped H.B. coordinate driving action when the helmer was behind the wheel; Barris (like in the old days) was able to use his automotive experience to bring excitement to the coverage. During a chase between an Eldorado convertible (driven by Halicki) and an airplane attempting an ultra-low fly-by, the pilot (Tony Ostermier) was killed when his landing gear accidentally smashed through the Cadillac's windshield. Covered in broken glass and blood from facial cuts, Halicki freed himself from the wreckage as Barris and U.P.M. Jack Vacek rushed up to the crash scene. With the destroyed aircraft in a heap just 30 yards away, Halicki (unaware of the fatality) glanced back at the damaged plane while shaking rubble from his hair and said, "Let's get another windshield in the Caddy ... and find us another fly-boy with a plane who wants to be in the movie business."

Barris' next creation was a variation on an existing show car, *Knight Rider*'s Kitt. Working on the series' later incarnation of "the character-car" in hyper-flight (super-speed or jumping mode), the old pro brought his years of experience to solve every problem production threw his way. The show began as a comedic pitch about a handsome leading man (with poor acting skills) who only speaks ten words an episode. Creator Glen Larson (and the network boys) came up with the idea of a talking car for a sidekick providing they could cast a perfect straight-man like David Hasselhoff, and write his character to take advantage of his minimal acting skill. The plan worked as producers enlisted veteran character actor William Daniels (with his nasal-blueblood New England delivery) to voice the part of Kitt; the balance produced good ratings for much of the series' run.

One image that often repeated itself on *Knight Rider* was the jumping, flying, and crashing of Kitt as he fought crime side by side with partner Michael Knight. To make the automotive flight a reality, stunt coordinators Jack and Andy Gill constructed a convection ramp to propel the cars airborne, then land them safely, 60 feet later, on four wheels. Losing vehicles on a daily basis due to the jumps and landings, Barris came up with the idea of creating rubber-nose sections for the Trans-Am, which spared the front end-heavy vehicles from smashing ground-first upon impact. Ultimately creating a batch of lighter, Fiberglas Trans-Am shells (minus the engine and transmission for the ramp work), George and the effects boys on latter seasons of *Knight Rider* were pulling off more with less to save producers' money. They often photographed the wrecks in ⅛ scale miniature engineered by Jack and John Sessums. One stunt (not possible with scale effects trickery) had Kitt flying through the air, while perilously close to landing on a fleeing bad guy's auto. Performing the dangerous scene himself, Jack Gill (unable to see through the roof of the Z-28 car he was driving) steered his auto by positioning the side-view mirrors skyward to track the above driver, while simultaneously feathering his brakes to avoid being crushed by the falling car. "Glen Larson was terrific to work with as he allowed creative ideas and suggestions regarding Kitt's endeavors for each episode." George said. "That new stuff was challenging and exciting to do every week. We were constantly trying to top what we had done before."

Hitting a 40-year career mark during the summer of 1993, Barris was enlisted by big-time Hollyrock helmer Steven Spielberg to build the tracked cars for *Jurassic Park*. Using a '93 Ford Explorer XLT for the basic vehicle (modified with full ceiling glass panels), the individual trams which appeared automated were actually operated by a hidden driver using two tiny cameras mounted on the front bumper and dashboard to visually control it by monitor and remote driving linkage. Further outfitting the film's characters for scooting around the island (both day and night), Barris provided all-terrain Jeep Wrangler Saharas, modified with red wheels mated to huge off-road tires, rooftop emergency light bars, and product placement JURASSIC decals pasted to their side. Rather dated, the equipment looked more "Hot Wheels" than scary dinosaur movie.

Along with the new age of CGI technology overtaking Hollywood in the mid-nineties, a return to cartoon content from yesteryear being made into feature films was the new *it* idea embraced by the studios. This directly affected live-action crafts (like those of motion picture automobile builders); the constant stream of jobs for Barris and other folks was drying up. Aside from the trend towards period pictures and the occasional call for a rare auto for a music video, the market for the "old-school" stuff was on hold.

Until the remakes of car lore classics like *The Fast and Furious* and *Gone in Sixty Seconds* in the new millennium, George made do with custom work and car shows to keep his PR machine going. Luckily, one of the cartoons turned motion picture reconnected Barris with producers Hanna-Barbera and Steven Spielberg: He was asked to provide the foot-powered cars on *The Flintstones* in 1994. Requiring practical vehicles in the Bedrock style of wood, granite, and leather, George's Stone Age interpretation of transportation for the live-filmed cartoon series utilized foam-molds taken from actual logs, combined with wood-reinforced Fiberglas bodies over square-tubing steel frames for support. Beginning production with the newly completed but rather heavy Flintstone mobile, actor John Goodman was expected to move the 200-pound car barefoot, just as animated Fred had. Overhearing John joke about wearing down his feet to nubs by picture's end (due to the crate's heft), Barris installed a silent golf cart motor and drive train to the contraption over the weekend, without telling the film star. The following Monday morning as Goodman was preparing to climb into the "log-car" (and playfully griping about it), George came up and showed the actor the hidden go-button for the engine. While acclimating himself to the controls to better "sell" the motion for camera (as well as practicing his foot-timing to keep the man-powered look in synch), Goodman was so appreciative of Barris' effort that he gave him a bearhug and said, "Thanks for saving my tootsies, George!" The vehicle was finished with Bedrock must-haves such as Saber-tooth tiger skin upholstery, rock slab dashboard, carved stone cylinder wheels, and wild animal hide canopy with monogram seat covers. Even though the Flintstone-mobile came from the minds of artists at Hanna-Barbera in the old days, George Barris still made it uniquely his own.

One of George's last contributions to the world of film-cars were his five character-autos for the kid flick *Turbo* (1997). Based on the original *Power Rangers* television series, the feature was little more than a toy-selling endeavor, pandering to the show's young fan-base. Building vehicles that represented the movie's main characters Red Lightning and Desert Thunder, the Barris team transformed a Pontiac Fiero, Chevy Astro Van, Suzuki "Jimmy" SUV, Ford X-150 4×4, and a Honda CRX into cool wheeled sculptures that children wanted to watch *and* play with at home. Once again tapping into the model and collectable toy vehicle residuals market, Barris' ever constant eye toward diversification paid off in spades, making *Turbo* another winning project for him and the name brand.

With the inevitable end of one era came the new millennium for Barris Kustoms, and at over 80 years of age, George was able to pick and choose projects. He remains the king of Hollywood customizers to this day.

Much of Barris' end-game strategy revolves around attending shows of his cars, as well as some licensed copies of other's automobiles he is contracted to own and exhibit. World-renowned vehicles like Dean Jeffries' GTO Monkee Mobile and Green Hornet car, as well as knock-offs of Rich Septons' General Lee (from *The Dukes of Hazzard*), were all after-market remakes either purchased from others, or built under license by Barris' shop, and used for everything from museum display and car shows to auto racing events and occasional commercial photo shoots. Taking advantage of the strong retro markets in the last decade, George also cashed in on private collectors (both domestic and foreign) who want to buy a piece of Tinseltown automotive history, even if it's just an expensive reproduction. Having dealt "photo-double" renditions of the Gran Torino from the *Starsky and Hutch* series to collectors, he has witnessed the rise in popularity and value of all things attached to that era regarding storied cars. Often mistakenly identified as the original source of others' proprietary "TV autos" (due mostly to sloppy reporting and bad information on the Internet), Barris' only wish is to continue filling museum floors with the cars he's had a hand in.

Lamenting the lack of originality among custom car builders in Hollywood, Barris referred to the latest feature for which he was passed over, *Speed Racer*. The producer's decision to construct only one live-action vehicle for the cartoon offering (and to have that carved from a block of foam by computer program without an actual engine or drive-train to run it) was enough to give George sleepless nights. Photographed totally in CGI in front of a green screen, the CAD-rendered "prop" was nothing more than a slickly painted piece of Styrofoam, with some wheels stuck on for good measure. Concerns over handling, speed, and survivability of usage while shooting became a moot point; Barris expressed a real fear that Cinema City's car biz may never be the same. "In the direction it's going," he said sadly, "we're bypassing a lot of the real craft of hands-on automotive construction skills. It's all computers and motion scanner technology now. When the age of two fast cars photographed drag racing can be replaced by a plastic kiddie cart made of foam like *Speed Racer*, the art is in trouble."

Whether it was shooting the chicken sequences in *Rebel Without a Cause,* or the spot-on rendering of the Flintstone-mobile, car-maker George Barris has always prescribed to the concept of functional believability: "For fantasy to work in film, it must be connected to a good amount of realism, otherwise the make-believe is never viable."

When asked what the future holds for the next wave of car builders to service Hollywood, Barris offered, "By not using more creativity and authentic stuff, we're losing the craft-base for the next generation of picture-vehicle artisans." The recipient of such automotive "uniform decoration" as the Robert E. Petersen Lifetime Achievement Award and Grand National Roadster Show award for America's Most Beautiful Roadster, N.H.R.A. Motor Sports Museum inductee, and State Assembly guest speaker offers the following mantras for his, and any newcomer's, success in the business: "If there's a will, you *gotta* make a way. And," he said with a youthful sparkle in his eyes, "there's no such word as can't!" That's for sure, if you're George Barris.

8

Albert Brenner, Production Designer

With nearly twenty crafts required to manufacture a motion picture, one discipline of "celluloid artistry" which stands alone in its artistic impact is that of production designer. Usually hired in tandem with the director, they are responsible for the entire look of a movie, encompassing everything from set design to locations and more. In addition to providing choices for the physical aspect of the story, their job is to create the reality of all that is photographed. Whether it's buildings (and the cars in front of them), or anything from carpet to the kitchen sink, it's the designer's imagination that fleshes out the movies we see. One such artist whose skills graced many films is five-time Oscar-nominated production designer Albert Brenner.

Like many others from his generation, his path to Hollywood began with the G.I. Bill and desire. Growing up in Brooklyn during the 1930s, young Albert longed for the open spaces and action depicted in his favorite Saturday matinee Westerns. His teenage interest in theater and his love of motion pictures (like Hopalong Cassidy and John Ford's *Stagecoach*) led to his first "art-job" as a window dresser for Staples-Smith in New York City: "The dresser job was wonderful training for films as you were telling a little story with mannequins and props, using the window as your stage!"

From the middle of World War II, nineteen-year-old Albert served a hitch in the Fifth Air Force aboard B-24s until the conflict's end in 1945. Returning to the Big Apple in pursuit of his old job at Staples, the twenty-something was refused his prior position. Turning to the G.I. Bill on the advice of a school counselor, Albert was able to parlay his display work portfolio to gain entrance to the prestigious Yale School of Theatre in 1947. Graduating three years later with a degree in Theater Design, he briefly attended the teacher's school at the University of Missouri before returning to Manhattan to seek his fortune designing for the stage.

Armed with a sheepskin covering the skills of drafting, character-sketching, costumes, furniture, color theory, fabrics and construction methods, Brenner ultimately landed a job doing scenic work in the New Jersey summer stock league. It was there he connected with his first real career influence, Samuel Levee. Hired as an assistant, the rookie learned the ropes of theatrical set design while toiling on plays like *Senior Chicago*. Beginning with scenic artist duties (detailing doors and walls by way of aging or other processes), Albert quickly advanced under Levee's mentorship and gained entrance into the Scenic Artists Guild, Local 829.

Once in the union, Albert continued cutting his art department teeth under designer Levee on such 1950s TV classics as *The Phil Silvers Show, Car 54, Captain Kangaroo,* and *Playhouse 90*. On *Phil Silvers,* he earned $250 a week on the show (a princely sum in 1958) while learning his first lesson in the pecking order of production politics: Given the task of obtaining a harmonica needed as a prop in one of the skits, Brenner was chewed out by head comedy writer Nat Hiken for selecting one that was ridiculously elaborate. "Just get me a regular harmonica," Hiken scolded. "Remember, no funny stuff. I do the jokes around here."

When Levee returned to strictly Broadway theater, Brenner made the leap from television to features thanks to an introduction to the Sylbert brothers, Richard and Paul. Identical twins (often standing in for each other on set), the Sylberts were first-rate art men whose touch would ultimately create two of New York's finest films from the 1960s, *The Manchurian Candidate* and *Rosemary's Baby*. Brought on as assistant to Dick Sylbert, Brenner was "his guy" whenever the art director was shooting in Manhattan.

Albert's first outing with Richard Sylbert was in 1960 on Elia Kazan's *Splendor in the Grass,* starring Natalie Wood and Warren Beatty, shot by director of photography Boris Leven (of *On the Waterfront* and *Twelve Angry Men* fame). More Sylbert pictures followed, such as the Jack Lemmon comedic masterpiece *How to Murder Your Wife* and Sidney Lumet's *The Fugitive Kind,* showcasing Marlon Brando in a Tennessee Williams-scribed melodrama.

While continuing to hone his talents on the Sylbert features, Brenner's depth of artistic knowledge paid dividends when he was able to gain employment with another major art department player from that generation, Harry Horner. Hired for his ability to read construction drawings, Brenner remembers two lessons learned from the iconic production designer of flicks like *Stage Door Canteen* and *The Hustler*. First — the only thing important to art direction is what the camera sees. Second — the greatest storytelling tool in moving pictures is the cut. When asked how it felt to be on the set of Robert Rossen's *The Hustler* (working with Horner) among biggies Jackie Gleason, Paul Newman, and George C. Scott, Albert talked about the actors' work styles: "Gleason was laid back, cracking jokes between takes, whereas Scott and Newman manifested an intense vibe that was riveting to observe. I was in awe, just to watch those guys act." Referring to the impact of Horner's carefully manifested sets, Albert remembers dressing out the pool hall locations in lower Manhattan: "It was a matter of details, from the old 'strung wire' ball-counting rigs to the light fixtures chosen for the pool tables. The joint was purposely rundown and funky, further underlining the desperate energy of the film."

Just after *The Hustler* wrapped, Albert resumed assisting Sylbert on a strange heroin-cult flick aptly called *The Connection*. He was handed an opportunity to lead the art direction for the first time (as Sylbert agreed to take the feature knowing that he was already booked on *The St. Valentine's Day Massacre*). Brenner laughed when recalling his moment of rapid advancement: When they left the production meeting (after signing with the producers to do the movie), Dick turned to him in the elevator and said, "Okay, Al, the movie's all yours. See ya around, kid!" Based on an off–Broadway play, *The Connection* was a gritty immersion into the drug and jazz culture of New York's Lower East Side in the early sixties. It was meticulously researched by Brenner, who went to shooting galleries and dive bars to ensure the picture's aesthetic accuracy; the singularly themed one-room set was staged as a loft to allow director Shirley Clark as many filming options as possible. After his success with *The

Connection, Brenner's final Sylbert gigs such as *All the Way Home* and Frank Perry's nuclear what-if *Ladybug, Ladybug* followed. Dealing with the concept of atomic annihilation, the feature was a precursor to another doomsday story which Brenner helped bring to theaters, *Fail-Safe* (1964). Before that, however, came another Sidney Lumet film, *The Pawnbroker*.

Perhaps the most artistically significant of his Dick Sylbert collaborations, *The Pawnbroker* was (like *All the Way Home*) lensed by DP Boris Kaufman. It utilized Brenner's ability to find the perfect locations to transform into sets, then convince the director of their worth. One accidental instance of art manifesting function occurred when the practical location for the pawn broker's shop (which Brenner had window-dressed with expensive-looking costume jewelry) was robbed overnight. The glass was replaced and security hardware added; the bars created an unforgettable image when their shadows played like black stripes across Rod Steiger's face during the Holocaust flash-back scenes.

After a Robert Shaw picture, *The Luck of Ginger Coffey*, Brenner next art directed Sidney Lumet's *Fail-Safe* (1964). The opposite to *Dr. Strangelove* (both films were owned by Columbia Pictures), *Fail-Safe* was a surgically accurate rendition of America's Cold War nuclear policy just after the Bay of Pigs. Brenner designed the war room set from his imagination (with its 360-degree unobstructed views of huge electronic wall maps and control room screens); his concept was so accurate that the government questioned him as to the source of his drawings. It mirrored the real thing (including individual console desks with computer-like Teletype machines linked together by thick black communications wire). Albert also incorporated oversized metal telephones (which were actually "blasting headsets" from the demolition trade) to sell the futuristic, military styling. Limited by the lack of a

Among Albert Brenner's most realistic designs, his vision for *Fail Safe* (1964) stood above his other works. Upon seeing dailies, the Justice Department noticed the similarity to the layout of the real-life secret war room and demanded that Brenner reveal his inside sources. Satisfied only after studying the designer's sketches, the government backed off and okayed the sets (photograph by Muky, courtesy Albert Brenner).

New York stage large enough to shoot the war room scenes in full depth, Brenner utilized front projection techniques to create the map-wall depiction of the battlefield. In order to pull off this effect, an almost dust-free environment was required; the stage was vacuumed and sealed (with the exception of the air conditioning) to make the projected scenes work.

Crewed as art director on the George Balanchine–choreographed *A Midsummer Night's Dream* (1967), Brenner used his theater training which incorporated stage elements such as colored light and sequined set pieces to better sell the Shakespeare fantasy. Shot as a feature on side by side stages at Fox Studios in New York City, dancer-turned-director Balanchine was a perfectionist which took its toll on the dancers so desperately trying to please him.

Building on the momentum from *Fail-Safe* and *Midsummer Night's Dream*, Brenner continued working as art director out of New York, landing good commercial accounts like Yardley soap and Pontiac cars. Receiving a call in 1967 from an old Yale pal, director Elliot Silverstein, Albert took a movie shot on location in Florida, *The Happening*. The campy but cool flick was the story of a past-his-prime Mafia big shot (played straight by Anthony Quinn) who is kidnapped by a band of hippies, then helps them rip off his old bosses when they refuse to pay his ransom. Once again finding the right location from the start, Brenner came up with the perfect run-down house used in the airport caper. And when no beat-up beach bungalow was available, he built the swamp shack on a stage at Columbia Pictures for the night sequences and climactic fire.

After a chance meeting with helmer Clive Donner, Albert agreed to production-design the director's next motion picture, *L.U.V.* Filmed in Los Angeles, it was Brenner's first West Coast IA gig. He was able to work by way of the reciprocal trade agreement, obtaining his art director's card in Local 827. Albert not only found Hollywood's weather agreeable, but its work climate as well.

Now living in L.A., Brenner was fortunate to meet avant-garde helmer John Boorman, who was in the States visiting his good friend Lee Marvin. Touting a new crime caper called *Point Blank* (in which Marvin starred as a hit man who gains a conscience while losing a girl), Boorman immediately hired Brenner as he liked his East Coast edge and understanding of how to portray danger and violence on the screen. Taking a page from his Horner experience on Robert Rossen's *The Hustler*, Albert utilized subtle set-cues to spotlight his actors. On this film, rooftop plaster busts of Janus (looking in two directions, forward and past, like Marvin's character) were devised to gain sympathy from the audience as the conflicted killer passed between them, gun in hand. Brenner incorporated a palate of gray tonal ranges supported by a clean, sharp-edged focus (contrasting the "white-hot" Marvin). The movie was an understated masterpiece of the "crime is cool" genre.

Now on a roll with crime flicks, Brenner was next crewed on a motion picture shooting out of San Francisco that would change the face of cop movies forever: Peter Yates' *Bullitt*. Hired because of his previous associations with other English directors (Clive Donner and John Boorman), he was selected by British director Yates, based on Boorman's rave reviews of the designer's talent for portraying reality in his sets. Applying that skill to *Bullitt*'s look, Albert sought to subdue the primary colors of the picture to sell its urban textures and funk, contrasting the suave Steve McQueen, in the title role. Shifting hues from red to washed-out brown or blues (with the exception of traffic lights in the chase scene and blood during the motel hit), Brenner's concept manifested a focus on the flesh tones and blue eyes of McQueen that drew viewers to the character. By reducing brightly colored background objects (like Coke machines, stop signs, and billboards), the foregrounds and actors pop off the screen by comparison. Reinforcing reality through texture, Brenner utilized his specialty of producing distressed inner city interiors, in the motel room layout where mob informant Johnny Ross (Pat Renella) is being "stashed" by police. Aside from rendering his "mainstay"' look of exposed electrical conduits, broken plaster, water-stained ceilings and aging fixtures on the set, Brenner also incorporated a phony wall (behind the bed) for the shotgun blast gag, yanking the stuntman backward upon impact. Referring to the cut when the motel door is kicked open, Brenner said he staged the flimsy door-lock to build suspense as the camera sees the barely adequate device as present, but not latched.

Next came "rent-payers" like director Garson Kanin's *Some Kind of Nut* (starring Dick Van Dyke) and *Where It's At*. The "rent jobs" provided not only a paycheck, but often taught him ways to obtain results with limited time or money. "You learn something on every movie," Brenner said. "If not, then you're asleep at the creative wheel."

While his mastery of the essential motion picture skills flourished, Brenner's reputation also grew. Serving his directors by translating their "physical" vision of the film, Brenner was in prime form for his next art direction project, John Frankenheimer's *I Walk the Line*, (1970). Lensed by William Fraker protégé David Walsh, the steamy melodrama starred Gregory Peck as a small town sheriff caught up in the consequences of a mid-life affair with a younger woman (Tuesday Weld).

Shot in Gainesboro, Tennessee, the feature owed much of its authentic "Southern look" to the expert location scouting done by Brenner. In those days, art directors were often first to hit the beach (search a new town for locations), as the studio provided no advance team to perform this chore. Today's film crews on location wouldn't make a move without first scouting (days or weeks in advance), to find what they require. "The only set we built," Albert recalled, "was the sheriff's office in Gainesboro, which we couldn't get permission to shoot in as it was also the town's jail and a busy place." The great DP James Wong Howe was originally slated to shoot the movie. Falling ill, however, he was replaced before principal photography began when Brenner suggested a good young camera operator he knew from *Bullitt*, David Walsh. Objecting to the unknown shooter, U.P.M. Howard Pine lamented, "Okay, he's in. But if he fucks up the movie, it's on your head!" Threats aside, Albert said the picture taught him an interesting lesson in Hollywood politics: "Don't be afraid of bullies. Just believe in what you know."

Albert's career was now in full flight, telling stories via the natural look of his designs. One feature where his vision was totally fulfilled was William Fraker's *Monte Walsh*, the story of a cowhand realizing he's at era's end. The work was an uncluttered visit to the real west of the late 1800s. Starring Lee Marvin (in the title role), Jack Palance, Richard Farnsworth, and Bo Hopkins, the superbly shot picture was real-look–fashioned from Brenner's extensive research, then agreed to by cowboy buff Fraker. One bit of historical accuracy brought to filming was the saloon set. Incorporating an oblong bar front, flanked by small parlors separated with etched glass for privacy, the single-floored layout allowed patrons (and the camera) to see the gambling tables while being "served" in their compartments. "The brothel was usually a tiny hovel in the back, or outside, if they had one at all," Brenner explained. "No upstairs rooms existed back then. The falsehood was a common misconception invented by Hollywood for stunt-staging purposes of falls over the stair rails and gun fights on the landings."

On location in Gainesboro, Tennessee, during the winter of 1969, Brenner (right) confers with director John Frankenheimer on the set of *I Walk the Line*. Brenner took advantage of Gainesboro's authentic rural charm, carefully selecting locations weeks before shooting (courtesy Albert Brenner).

What Brenner liked about working with cinematographer turned helmer Fraker, was having a director who possessed an artist's visual acuity, someone who compositionally understood what the lens would see before shooting. The advantage, according to Brenner, allowed a frankness in their collaboration which made Fraker more amendable to changes than other "skippers" might have been.

Remembering their playful relationship, Brenner said Fraker (always a sharp dresser) came to him on set one morning and undid the top buttons of his (Brenner's) shirt, saying, "You're too tight, Albert, loosen up, baby." Further illustrating the trust between these men, Brenner (after showing Fraker rough sketches of his *Monte Walsh* sets including cowboys in period garb) engaged costume designer Pat Norris to bring the drawings to life, as the director was so inspired by Albert's authentic concepts. Whether it was storyboards of a western town, or coming up with the clothes for the people in it, designer Brenner would cross any boundary to completely tell a story.

Following his return to a couple of rent jobs after the Fraker work (*Brother John*, starring Sidney Poitier, and *T.R. Baskin*, directed by Herb Ross), Brenner would next be challenged by "skipper" Robert Mulligan on *Summer of '42*. Providing much of the production design from his own childhood memories of Brooklyn during that time, Albert manifested the malt shop sets in short order. Sketching out the soda fountains with their ornate elephant head spigots, the swiveling high chairs, hanging-orb lighting fixtures, and quilted aluminum kitchen walls, Brenner lent to the film a sense of self that he seldom enjoyed on other productions.

Commenting on what gelled between him and Mulligan on the project, Albert admit-

Bill Fraker (left) worked with Brenner (right) for Fraker's directorial debut, *Monte Walsh* (1970). An ingenious solution to a scenic issue was posited by Brenner. Needing a barbwire fence along hundreds of feet of background in Old Tucson — a potentially expensive and time-consuming endeavor — the designer cleverly had his artists paint the distant fence on the dirt. Fraker doubted the technique would work, but was amazed by the final effect, which appeared to be a standing fence when viewed through the finder. Saving a day's work and the hassle of installation, Brenner's painted posts and barbwire was a hit as all it took to remove at day's end were several loads of soil and laborers with rakes to cover over the painted dirt (courtesy Albert Brenner).

ted, "We're both quiet but sure of our ideas on set. A great deal of being a production designer is solving the problems of staging and script, when they impede the ability to shoot. Simply put, art directors are troubleshooters of production. Whatever the problem, we paint, hide, or construct a solution to fix the issue at hand."

To better understand the difference between art director and production designer, one need only look three decades earlier to *Gone with the Wind*. First slated as art director, William Cameron Menzies was ultimately given the uber-classification of production designer on the movie, supporting his total control of all elements of the motion picture. From costumes to lighting and locations to hair, Menzies coordinated everything. It was his belief that directors should manage the words and staging of actors, but that designers created the who and what of a movie's reality; with art directors responsible for the physical transformation of a set. Throughout the years, art directors (taking on more responsibilities) became the answer guy for aesthetic issues, while production designers were ultimately elevated to the lofty position next to the director. Though a bit confusing (credit-wise), it explains why some films have one person with either title designing, and/or implementing the artwork.

8. *Albert Brenner, Production Designer*

Standing in front of the building being used as the apartment set on *T.R. Baskin* (1971), Brenner (left) confers with director Herbert Ross (fur coat). The feature was a natural for Brenner owing to its cluttered interiors and numerous urban settings all over Chicago (courtesy Albert Brenner).

Another Robert Mulligan motion picture, Fox's 1972 horror offering *The Other*, was their second outing together. "I liked Mulligan," Albert said, "You knew what the man was going to say no to beforehand, which saved a lot of wear and tear on both of us. Plus, Mulligan knew what he wanted but still had the openness to look at optional ideas when stuck for a solution."

After production-designing the 1973 Pacino-Hackman road flick *Scarecrow* (lensed by cinematographer Vilmos Zsigmond), Brenner stayed busy on such fare as *Bank Shot* and *Peeper* into the next year. For *Bank Shot*, Brenner recalls director Gower Champion coming to him in a panic to locate the right sort of trailer for the bank heist scene. He found one that could be modified by the effects folks to allow its back-end to pull completely off. The "money shot" went off without a hitch as the connected cables opened the "temporary bank" like a can of sardines.

On *Peeper* Brenner began a relationship with director Peter Hyams that spanned six features over a dozen years. Having met Hyams years before doing a television piece called *Rolling Man*, Albert enjoyed working on the 1940s period drama starring Michael Caine and Natalie Wood. "Caine was great with props and things," Brenner remembered. "Watching him move on set was a pleasure as he made it all seem so natural that it looked as though my designs were developed just for his character."

One strange flick that Brenner crewed in mid–1975 was Frank Laughlin's *The Master Gunfighter*, a train wreck of a feature based on a 1960s samurai film. Albert received much

In the fall of 1970, Brenner embarked on one of his favorite film endeavors, *Summer of '42*. Able to conjure up texture of set and location from his own East Coast memories, the World War II domestic historical drama allowed him the freedom to farm his fondest recollections from the period. Pictured here in Mendocino County (doubling as Nantucket where the story took place), director Robert Mulligan (right) and Brenner (left) ponder lens position (courtesy Albert Brenner).

of his pre-production direction via storyboards in Japanese made for the original motion picture. When queried as to his goal when taking a movie like this, his response was comic: "The object of a production designer on a film that bad…is to get off as soon as possible, as fully paid as legal!"

For the feature *The Sunshine Boys,* Brenner was hired by director Herbert Ross (whom Albert met on *T.R. Baskin* in 1971): The picture was Oscar-nominated for Best Art and Set Decoration that year. When asked what it felt like to be up for the award, Brenner said it was unreal at first, until the Motion Picture Academy called about his table assignment. Talking about its production design, he proudly described the multi-sided co-joining rooms which allowed for free-flowing camera movement (and conversation between actors), no matter the coverage required in the scene. The stage was dissected into a six-set circle (ranging from bathroom to kitchen and bedrooms to hallway and foyers); his door-through-door access between them allowed for artistic options seldom seen off Broadway. Brenner said he retained one trademark from the film which he would incorporate into all of his future designs: bathrooms with two doors, to facilitate conversational possibilities and the camera set-ups to cover them, in an otherwise one-dimensional location. Speaking of his fondness for the production, he recalled George Burns singing each morning as he arrived on set, always in good cheer. "Between the pleasure of working on a Neil

Simon script and listening to Burns tell stories all day, I didn't want to go home at night," Albert said.

Returning to westerns (his favorite genre), Brenner's next job was *The Missouri Breaks* (1976). Relying upon research and meticulous scouting to give director Arthur Penn the geographic locations he needed, the kid from Brooklyn not only came up with remote finds such as Red Lodge, Montana, but procured a giant teepee back in the woods for Marlon Brando to inhabit prior to filming, to get into character.

A less than stellar outing was Mel Brooks' *Silent Movie*. Brenner spoke of not being able to effectively communicate with Brooks "the director": "He's so funny and 'on' all the time. You're never sure how he'll react to new ideas. Often, it was the Nat Hiken rule: 'I'm doing the jokes around here, and you're not.'"

The second of what would eventually be five features with Herbert Ross was the Baryshnikov-driven dance picture *The Turning Point* (1977). With Ross demanding full use of the ballet virtuoso's dance skills, Brenner was tasked with creating a special, padded, smooth dance floor, to show off the choreography without injuring the artists. Constructed of seamless linoleum over a cork base, the floor was supple enough to give on the hard ballet landings, yet polished like ice to allow for jazz-like sliding for the dancers.

The Neil Simon–penned romantic comedy *The Goodbye Girl* was the first film in its category to gross over 100 million dollars. On the picture, Albert met his future wife Susan, and got to dictate the timing of a scene. Susan was working as an assistant to director Herbert Ross when she walked into the super-realistic Manhattan set on the picture and blurted out, "Who did the New York job on this apartment?" Regarding the timing, Brenner and DP David Walsh sought to give Ross the best of his production design wisdom, when staging the scene where Marsha Mason bursts into Richard Dreyfuss' room to make him stop playing guitar, only to find him sitting on his bed naked. To build the suspense of the joke (as she approached, losing her temper), Brenner lengthened the hallway to allow the actress to finish her lines just as she reached his closed door. The flow of her anger (versus shock at his nudity) better supported her surprise.

In the spring of 1978, Brenner did one of his more frightening flicks: Michael Crichton's medical sci-fi *Coma*. Staying true to the Robin Cook novel and subsequent Leon Harris illustrations, Albert's designs were both beautifully rendered and scientifically forward-thinking. Recalling one of the most memorable images from the picture, he revealed that the suspended bodies scenes (consisting of 20 dummies and six actual actors) were rigged from wires connected above and below, to give that guitar string linear look. "Before bluescreen and CGI," Brenner explained about the hanging-gag shots, "photographic effects were manifested physically, either with matte technology or clever live-action staging. On *Coma*, it was all really there!"

Another standalone sci-fi picture that Brenner was charged with was Peter Hyams' "what if" *Capricorn One*. The movie starred Elliott Gould, James Brolin, Sam Waterston, Karen Black and O.J. Simpson. With little chance to differentiate the characters visually (their costumes consisted of white spacesuits, military uniforms, and NASA gear), Brenner instead created environments for the actors to react within, to set the personalities apart. With design perspectives based on actual photos of Mars, the company built sets on stage utilizing perspective-cheating techniques, like incorporating large rocks in the foreground and smaller ones to the rear to sell the delineation of shapes as they recede into the distance.

Albert Brenner's continuity storyboards for Michael Crichton's 1978 sci-fi thriller *Coma* depict the "floating" animation lab suggested by the Robin Cook novel. His production design incorporated 20 dummies hanging from wires with a half dozen live actors interspersed in the foreground on tables (courtesy Albert Brenner).

Returning to Ross for Neil Simon's episodic comedy feature *California Suite*, Brenner was once again Oscar-nominated for Best Art Direction. Engaged by Ross to design the hotel set to allow no cuts when dollying from the lobby to the street, Brenner's solution was to construct the foyer through the large open stage doors, then transform the outside studio roadway into a working concierge lane, with cars and people coming and going. As on *The Sunshine Boys,* he again produced a time and place for his cast that was perfectly suited to tell the story.

Following more "rent films" like *Strangers* (a television heart-tugger starring Bette Davis at career's end) and *Hero at Large* (a spoof so warm and cuddly it's used as a suicide prevention film for state inmates), Brenner next experienced a spate of employment options that would see him through retirement, nearly thirty years later. Beginning with pal William Fraker's *Legend of the Lone Ranger*, the entire decade for Albert Brenner would be non-stop. Providing his signature New York apartments for two of Neil Simon's scripts, *Only When I Laugh*, starring Marsha Mason, and *I Ought to Be in Pictures*, directed by mainstay Herbert Ross, the in-demand production designer relied upon two concepts to keep his staging ideas fresh. First, always begin the design with a workable ground plan. Second, relentlessly search for new angles and action that brings actors a natural experience on set. "The key," Brenner said, regarding his famous apartment sets, "is to give the DP enough room to do his job. That way, you provide the director and crew physical access to the little boxes (which sets are) to tell the story. Plus, the more thought I gave to laying out a set, the better it looked photographed; and that's good for everyone!"

Continuing with Neil Simon stuff, Brenner did another feature with cinematographer David Walsh and skipper Ross, the Jason Robards vehicle *Max Duggan Returns* (1983). The picture was an exercise for Brenner in the theory that more is good, when it comes to blowing

Brenner pulled out all the creative stops for the design of Peter Hyams' *2010* (1984). Configuring the ship's interiors with cavernous oblong spaces, he sought to offset the vertical human form within, while selling the structure's immensity at the same time. Employing his own Syd Mead type of cockpit embellishment (including recessed monitors and flush mounted control stations), Brenner furthered the sci-fi upgrade with linear stretching of all wall surfaces and entries. This gave the interior a deep-space feeling of proportion and weight which most space mock-ups lack (courtesy Albert Brenner).

life into Simon's family stories. Decent budgets allowed for adequate sets to be built, and then lovingly dressed with the connective tissue of background history; everything from wall clocks to bathtubs on the Simon work came from Albert Brenner's heart.

Following rent jobs on *Two of a Kind* (featuring John Travolta and Olivia Newton-John at their most boring) and *Unfaithfully Yours* (with favorite lensman Walsh), Albert designed a film that would use all of his motion picture art skills to pull off: Arthur C. Clarke's *2010*. Like the initial brush-stroke of a painting, discussion of the spacecraft in the feature had to be realized first for Brenner, as director-writer Peter Hyams felt that the design shouldn't be too far into the future, as the mission was only nine years later than its prequel, *2001*. Brenner saw the new ship as obviously based on the original, only much more imperfect as though there was a rush to get it built. Hyams and Brenner's desire was for the craft to be a space-going, heavy duty industrial "tugboat," leaking oil and belching smoke like some off-shore derrick. Totally at home with the interiors of the ship, Brenner did his usual static layering with the presence of cobbled-together surfaces containing circuit boxes, gauges, wires, vents, pipes, hoses and bolt heads showing. Employing his signature "center of a circle" concept to set design, he drew the interiors to accommodate shooting angles into all of the bays, as well as the control room, sleeping quarters, and dining areas. Purposely designing the structures stretched out (to elongate the craft's entire appearance),

2010 (1984) was the type of project designer Brenner could really sink his teeth into. He incorporated everything from matte paintings to miniatures; his interpretation of the out-of-Earth near-future experience in the film was proven spot-on by the time of Skylab and the International Space Station some twenty years later. Pictured here with white hair, Brenner checks out the work on the entertainment effects group Discovery model while Hyams (to Brenner's left, hand on shoulder strap) joins in on the discussion (courtesy Albert Brenner).

he also established gravitational forces in space by use of the rotating main chamber. Much like the idea of centrifugal force holding water to the base of a bucket when swung overhead in an arch, the circular running track was Brenner's device to show artificial gravity aboard the spacecraft. Demonstrating weightlessness was comparatively simple for the designer, who employed invisible wire harnesses for the bay-pod wall-walking scenes.

Further contributing to the film's scientific accuracy, visual futurist Syd Mead (of Ford T-Bird and Phillips light-bulb fame) came up with the idea of having Vector-motors on the Pod-ship to control rolling, just like the ones used by NASA. But the movie version was nothing more than a dressed-up fire extinguisher photographed on a cold stage. Always striving for reality, Brenner brought Mead in for the consultation.

Following his design work on 1985's *Sweet Dreams* (the Patsy Cline story featuring Jessica Lange and Ed Harris), Albert again teamed with director Peter Hyams for the cop-buddy shoot-'em-up *Running Scared*. It was lensed by Hyams himself on location during a frigid Chicago winter. Much of Brenner's input into the Gregory Hines–Billy Crystal vehicle was finding suitable locations to shoot the tenement scenes. With a foot of snow on the ground and more falling, temperatures were just above freezing; Brenner recalled that finding a place that looked right (with proper heating) was his biggest hurdle. Ultimately propane space warmers were utilized to warm a South Side building that was chosen for its look and layout.

In 1986 Albert returned to *Fail-Safe* maestro Sidney Lumet for his newest film, *The Morning After*, starring Jeff Bridges and Jane Fonda. The suspense-thriller had a scene where Bridges leaves the dinner table after Jane Fonda passes out while on the phone. As Bridges (the suspect) tidies up the room, the camera is able to follow him unobstructed throughout the entire set. The design, purposely done in this open style by Brenner, gave 360-degree camera coverage of the scene, adding to the intrigue while the viewer is able to see both suspect and perceived prey in one frame.

Brenner was back with Hyams for his next project, the action-packed whodunit *The Presidio* (1988). Starring Sean Connery and Mark Harmon as unwilling allies, the picture was filmed around San Francisco's Presidio Army base and outlying areas. Tasked with establishing an identity for Connery's Lt. Colonel Alan Caldwell, he employed subtle but telling touches in the military man's private living quarters, such as mementos from his deceased wife displayed over the fireplace mantle, and a unit flag hung in the corner from some long-ago assignment. For the restaurant fight scene between Connery and real-life tough guy Rick Zumwalt, Albert built the bar with a large angled recess to it. Constructed in a U shape (with its edges rounded to decrease injury), the set allowed the actors to go at it realistically without any harm from being bounced off the bar.

Slated to work with his final "multi-feature helmer" (Garry Marshall), Brenner once again proved his proficiency on his first outing with *Beaches* (1988). *Pretty Woman* followed in 1990 and became the biggest box office hit of their seven-picture collaboration. It was designed in the vein of the Cary Grant movies of the 1950s. Brenner staged the Ambassador Hotel's lobby on lot, building mock-ups of the ornate elevators and connecting foyers. Cracking the hotel room color code of neutral beiges and buff tans, Brenner said, "All hotel rooms are decorated in bland colors designed not to excite. Our concept was the opposite, so we took liberty with the color schemes as the film goes on."

Connecting with the final new director of his career, Brenner was tasked with production design on one of the most ambitious motion pictures of its genre, the Ron Howard–captained *Backdraft*. Produced by master-showman Dino De Laurentiis, it featured a ton of pyrotechnics and live action effects that required more than just your average art director to pull off. Incorporating actual fires in a controlled atmosphere, the dress factory burn (for example) proved tricky as Brenner utilized actual rolls of fabric for the shot. Setting the whole factory to go with supposedly catchy fuels (rayon and other synthetic fabrics), Albert learned that those materials didn't burn so well and switched to a highly flammable cotton, cutting the long cardboard bolts in half, then standing them on end to assist the burning process. The second take was so successful, it only took twelve minutes to reduce the entire structure to the ground.

Another design issue on *Backdraft* was a scene that required an elevator shaft to fill rapidly with water and trap the firefighters. The problem was solved with the use of a studio pool set up to *sink* the three-sided elevator mock-up (while keeping the actors safe on a submerged platform). The rising water sequence was photographed from a stage up point of view, to better sell the urgency of the action.

Illuminating the dangers of doing stunt-filled features, Brenner said that communication between departments is of the utmost importance in getting any gag to work safely. In a *Backdraft* scene that nearly went astray, Brenner and crew didn't realize that a cinder block wall in a Westinghouse warehouse had no rebar reinforcement. An ensuing explosion ripped a twenty-foot gap in the structure that more than sold the shot. Prior to shooting, he insisted that a chain-link fence be installed as a safety device to control flying debris, and probably prevented a real-life catastrophe.

Brenner's phone continued to ring, netting him the James Caan thriller *The Program* and a Steven Segal smackdown, *Under Siege 2*. Now looking to work less but have more fun, he drafted his son David to labor as construction coordinator on the latter. "It was marvelous to work with your 'own' as David knew exactly what I wanted, often correctly anticipating my special construction needs as production designer." Originally taking the Geoff Murphy–helmed action flick for the fun of it, Brenner was soon mired down with the danger and difficulty of working around moving trains, combined with lots of martial arts stunts and action: "The problem was the amount of time required to move whole trains and finding room to shoot master and coverage shots."

Finishing a half-century of motion picture design and art direction, Brenner would work his final three films with Garry Marshall. The first, *Dear God* (1996), was a comedic look at a con man who goes straight by answering letters (prayers) to God. The lavishly designed *The Princess Diaries 2* (2004), coming after an eight year layoff for Albert due to health reasons, starred the original film's Julie Andrews and Anne Hathaway. Via Universal's back lot Little Europe and train station locations, the fictitious country of Genovia was further embellished by Brenner's use of rich tapestries, chandeliers, and furnishings for his royalty look in the queen's surroundings. Albert again employed his son David as construction coordinator on the huge palace set (built on Stage 27 at Universal).

Brenner's final Garry Marshall project (and the last of his career) was *Georgia Rule* in 2007. It was the first time that Brenner would see his sets manipulated by computer enhancement rather than a scenic artist with a paintbrush: from mountains added to the background of Harlan's fishing lake location, as well as puffy trees to the barren hills in the picnic sequences. He was not thrilled to have such a vital piece of filmmaking removed from his control as production designer. One instance where the maestro's old school art director logic still prevailed was when tasked with removing an offending structure across the street from Georgia's house. Utilizing the magician's trick of blocking, Albert rented a large boat on a trailer and parked it within frame, totally obscuring the unwanted building from camera's view. Another solution where know-how trumped technology was his decision to photograph the car-leaving shot (after the fight between Felicity Huffman and Cary Elwes resulted in a smashed windshield) from the reverse. "Without replacement glass available," Albert said, "the most efficient way to shoot the exit was from the back of the car. That way, the windshield was not seen."

When queried as to what prompted the production designer to call it quits at the finish of *Georgia Rule*, he chuckled and said, "It's tough to get hired when all of your directors are retired or deceased. Without my directors, I had to go on interviews for jobs with producers half my age who didn't know my work." For a man of Brenner's skill and experience, this became an untenable situation.

Brenner also spoke about the changes he's seen in the industry over the years. "Now the job of production design is more about replicating 'tear-sheet' rooms from fancy magazines and product inducement, than creating a set or atmosphere that supports an actor or story." Brenner reminds art newcomers to study all phases of the craft, from knowledge of furniture to construction, as well as color theory, costumes, drafting and photography; the lifelong education in these areas is a must.

Amid air scented with the perfume of turpentine, and surrounded by the canvases of works past, Brenner sat on a high-backed stool in his studio while being interviewed, with the smile of an all-knowing teacher. Now 81 years old, Albert stays in touch with his artistic side through daily painting in a hideaway behind his West Los Angeles home. No longer immersed in the "Hollywood two-step" of motion picture production, he now spends his days applying oil paint to canvas amid the books, sketches and storyboards of his extraordinary life making films. When queried as to the challenges of retirement for an art director of his experience, Brenner looked serious for an instant, then said with a glint in his eye, "The painting of hands has always been tough for me; now that I have the time, I can finally get it right!"

9

Richard Kline, Cinematographer

Counted among the cinematographers from Hollywood's heyday of independents, Richard Kline is one practitioner of lens craft who possessed a near-surgical perfection with his camera. Born to the biz by way of his father Benjamin (who started at Universal as a cameraman, then jumped ship to Columbia), Kline's Tinseltown pedigree also included his mom, who labored as personal secretary to Universal's Carl Laemmle. With Dad a charter member of the International Guild and the American Society of Photographers, young Richard didn't see much of his folks, as studio work back then was a six-days-a-week commitment. Much on his own, he was nurtured by matinees at the local movie theater sitting through double-billed Westerns, broken up by the usual newsreels and cartoons. Graduating high school in the middle of the Second World War put the kid on a fast track to the studios that would not be derailed. The high school senior was urged by his father to take a job in Columbia's camera department, to be able to qualify for a less dangerous photo unit assignment if he entered the service. The war's demand for personnel created studio job openings and 16-year-old Richard was assigned to his first picture, William Castle's *Klondike Kate*, in 1943. Crewed as a slate-boy under DP John Stumar, his responsibilities included clapping "the sticks" for each take. His first brush with camera-craft came with shooting a lily before each scene. Basically a triangulated card containing focus lines on one side with a gray-scale surrounded by primary colors on the other, a lily was used to rate film emulsion and check lens sharpness.

After another Stumar picture, *The Return of the Vampire* starring Bela Lugosi, Kline continued at his slate-boy position on Andre De Toth's war morals piece *None Shall Escape* in mid–1943. Rapidly learning the ropes thanks to his inquisitive nature, he was next chosen to work on his first big tent-pole at Columbia, *Cover Girl*. Starring Gene Kelly and Rita Hayworth, the Charles Vidor–helmed musical was the most popular picture among G.I.s during the war. It contained eight dance routines featuring Rita's legs and Kelly's footwork (including the masterful ghost sequence choreographed by the king of Hollywood musicals, Stanley Donen of *Singin' in the Rain*). It was here that Kline gained an appreciation for shooting complex numbers. Teaching him the photographic basics of music coverage, the twins gag was accomplished with Gene Kelly as the first dancer filmed; then mirrored off that image incorporating additional takes against a black backing, to produce a clean separation for the double-exposed footage. Impressed with Kelly's moves, he was even more amazed by the grace and speed of Donen (a large man who looked more bodyguard than hoofer) as he demonstrated the choreography to the actors.

Working under Rudolph Maté (who came from the German UFA discipline of 1920s film makers such as Karl Freund of *The Good Earth* fame), Kline stayed on the Columbia picture four months while taking advantage of its location on Stages 8 and 9 next to the camera department. Cramming practice sessions in between set-ups with Mitchell standards and BNCs to advance his camera craft, he received early mentoring by operator Burnett Guffey, who took interest in the slate-boy, constantly testing his progress. "Aside from being close to Rita," Kline joked, "making movies like that was very exciting, and it gave me the hunger for more." Kline's memory of the feature was everyone's kindness and support for his rookie efforts. "It was like family," he said of *Cover Girl*. "From the start, I felt very much at home."

"The rookie" moved up to assistant camera for William Cameron Menzies' *Address Unknown*, an anti–Nazi propaganda piece. Richard recalled, "With his calm manner and German accent, Maté was a kind man who demonstrated that civility on set was the only way to make a movie." Continuing at Columbia after assisting on the Chopin bio *A Song to Remember*, he was assigned a motion picture with cinematographer George Meehan, the wartime adventure–love story *Rough and Ready* (1944). Director Del Lord had worked with Kline's father on some Three Stooges shorts. Having lost his only son early in the war, the cinematographer embraced Kline as a surrogate child, and with a father's patience taught him all he could photographically.

In October of 1944 Kline enlisted in the Navy. Originally assigned to a film services lab near Washington D.C., he volunteered for duty in the Asian Pacific theater, where he served a photo intelligence role around Hong Kong until his discharge in August of 1946.

Returning to Los Angeles with his G.I. bill in hand, Kline decided to pursue law and was preparing to enroll at U.C.L.A. when he got a call from Columbia Pictures' camera department. Informed he was owed a year's employment based on leaving for military service, he was offered camera assistant work on *The Lady from Shanghai*. The only catch was he had to be on a plane to Acapulco the next morning. Starring Orson Welles (who also directed) and his wife, Rita Hayworth, the picture was filmed by Kline's mentor Rudolph Maté aboard Errol Flynn's yacht, *The Zacca*. Serving as skipper and entertainment director for his friends (but not really in the picture, except for some incidental background stuff), Flynn used the opportunity for a nonstop procession of women, liquor, and fishing while allowing Welles the use of his boat to make a film. After three months of locations in Southern Mexico, they returned to the Bay area for the magic-mirror shootout (filmed at Whitney's Playland in San Francisco). The picture finished with six weeks work at Columbia where the technical part of the mirror maze was recreated on stage complete with trick glass, reflection shots, and the destruction of the multiple mirrors at movie's end. Being around the likes of Welles and Flynn at such an impressionable age, Kline said it was interesting to find both movie stars to be just regular guys who lucked out and loved the life they lived.

More Columbia work came Kline's way when assigned to Burnett Guffey for the 1947 classic *To the Ends of the Earth*, starring Dick Powell. The strong bond established with Guffey resulted in five or more pictures in a six-year period. Having worked with a good cross-section of folks by that time, Kline said he began to categorize all his cinematographers by the way they dressed. Comparing lighting styles to choices in clothes, Guffey liked deep contrasts with vivid patterns for his master shots while his dressing tastes equated to fitted houndstooth jackets over gabardine gray slacks and black Italian shoes.

Looking in control of his camera assistant duties while measuring the distance between actor and lens (with help from Cornel Wilde) for *It Had to Be You* (1947), 21-year-old Richard Kline sits on the famous sweeping staircase previously used in *Holiday* (1938). After helmer Don Hartman failed to thrill boss Harry Cohn with his coverage of Ginger Rogers' legs, he was quickly replaced by team player Rudolph Maté (courtesy Richard Kline).

Laboring as an assistant cameraman throughout 1947 (and frustrated at being stuck there), Kline left the U.S. to study Fine Arts Appreciation at the Sorbonne. Then the G.I. bill lapsed. Returning to Los Angeles in 1950 to marry, he learned of the Taft-Hartley Act. Seeing his chances of making operator improving, he decided to give the movie business another shot. Working at Columbia as a number one card (giving him the pick of assistant jobs while waiting his chance to move up), Kline's first assignment back was in 1950 on a western called *Cow Town*. Directed by John English and featuring singing cowboy Gene Autry and his horse Champion, the picture was reminiscent of Richard's childhood matinees. Following work on a Bob Cummings musical comedy, *The Petty Girl*, under cinematographer William Snyder, Kline next took advantage of the television break-out and joined Karl

"Pappy" Freund on two of his gigs, *The Burns and Allen Show* (with DP Philip Tannura) and *I Love Lucy,* shot by Freund himself. After learning the broader style of TV lighting and camera coverage from the old master, he took an offer from Freund protégée Tannura to go on the road for a basketball film, *The Harlem Globetrotters* (1951). During the journey between Scranton, Pennsylvania, and Chicago, there were problems. Jim Crow laws affected service in restaurants, there were black-only motels, and they were pulled over by suspicious sheriffs. Kline the idealist (who would later marry an African-American woman) was greatly impressed by the players' resolve to get through it all. Kline was listed with the union as an assistant but allowed to operate camera as needed. His new teacher Tannura broke Richard in with long lens coverage from "sticks" and then moved him to crab dolly for linear movement to cover the back court game. In addition to incorporating coverage on spontaneous actions like trick shots or audience gags, the picture was also ahead of its time for camera placement over the backboard providing a view of the entire court.

Still pushing for an operator's card, Kline pestered his assignment boss at Columbia, Emil Oster, to help him move up. Turning him down, the Erich von Stroheim act-alike (complete with Prussian accent, balding head, and riding crop) told him he should just be glad to be working. Fed up, Richard decided to press the issue with the head of production Jack Fier, barging into his office and demanding a chance. Fier, a big guy with a gruff voice and a tough reputation, laughed and told Kline that he was impressed with his guts and promised to try and help. Seeing the production head around the lot nearly every day, he would ask the same question: "When?"

Finally in 1951, a series of Sam Katzman pictures slated for Columbia needed hustling young operators to handle the heavy load of camerawork. Quietly fixing it from above, Fier had Kline assigned to *The Magic Carpet* as an operator. Katzman, the king of the B-movies, had his own unit and was able to produce films so fast that the fads and headliners he based the flicks on were still hot when the feature hit the theaters. Wisely drafting talent and crew on their way up (or down), the producer always had a professional mixture working his pictures, capable of getting the job done with style. Since much of *The Magic Carpet* was built around a flying rug, Kline found himself learning new techniques for rendering the effects invisible. He was shown old-school tricks by DP Ellis Carter (keeping direct light off the carpet's support lines by flagging with solid fingers and dulling down the cables by application of lamp black) and the end result was fairly believable.

Staying with Katzman's unit over a five-year period (1951–56), Kline operated on over 100 features, each taking just six to twelve days to shoot. Working around such characters as William Castle and Fred Sears (plus cinematographer Henry Freulich), he received a master's course in shooting under budget and equipment limitations that would serve him well for the remainder of his career: "Learning under those guys was a great immersion into the business as I ran a lot of film through my camera covering every genre and shooting style possible."

Among the Katzman "classics" done by Kline were the Johnny Weissmueller *Jungle Jim* series, *King of the Congo* starring Buster Crabbe, and the John Derek howler *Prince of Pirates*. He was also assigned to a spate of George Montgomery films. Kline was shooting features at a dizzying pace and getting an amazing education in the process. Richard was behind the camera for the beginning of the 1950s crime, music, and sci-fi scene, working on titles like *Chicago Syndicate, Teen-Age Crime Wave, Inside Detroit, Rock Around the Clock,* and *The*

Lost Planet, to name a few. "He really knew where the money should be spent," Kline said of Katzman. "He didn't interfere, only helped." Toward the end of his Katzman run, Kline did *It Came from Beneath the Sea,* which is still viewed for its miniature effects and stop-action photography by Ray Harryhausen. Once again at Freulich's side, Kline operated on the sequences of the giant octopus (as well as locations at San Francisco's naval shipyard) without seeing so much as a daily owing to the compartmented nature of the work: "I would shoot inserts of the tentacles grabbing boats while director Robert Gordon and Harryhausen would cut in falling bodies for completion of a scene."

Kline's career arc continued on the up-swing when assigned by Columbia to work for cinematographer Burnett Guffey on the drama *Count Three and Pray*. Returning to operate for his past mentor (despite being categorized as an assistant in the credits), Kline recalled some humor used by Joanne Woodward when flubbing a line in her feature debut. Muttering "shitty," "fuck," and "screw" out-loud to purge the error, she endeared herself to director George Sherman and crew, who cracked up each time she said it.

At the request of Burnett Guffey, Kline labored on Richard Murphy's *Three Stripes in the Sun*. Starring Aldo Ray as an American G.I. in postwar Japan, the film was small enough that the DP was able to give up-and-coming operator Kline much of his teaching attention. "I liked Guffey," Kline responded when asked what he learned from the winner of Oscars for *From Here to Eternity* and *Bonnie and Clyde*. "He taught crisp imaging and composition, which are both things he's famous for. I like to think that some of that rubbed off on me!"

Further Columbia assignments for Kline included Jane Russell's *Hot Blood*, shot in late '55 by cinematographer Ray June, and another of the Burnett Guffey film noir pieces, *The Harder They Fall*, done in early 1956. Directed by Mark Robson, the crooked fight flick starred Humphrey Bogart (in his final film) and included Rod Steiger and boxing great Max Baer. Shooting the fight sequences with a parallax view camera used in sports coverage of the day, Kline had to adjust what he saw through the finder by looking over the lens through a wire target frame instead of what the glass was showing. Filming ex-heavyweight champ Baer one morning, Kline chatted with the pro in between setups about the violent realities of prizefighting. Max joked that he had been struck below the belt so many times that his testicles were cauliflowered. "It was a special picture to be on," Kline admitted. "Watching Bogart play backgammon in between shots with his makeup man Bob Schiffer, I sensed he wasn't well; but he was so cool, I just minded my own business and did the job."

More assignments with Guffey meant a steady flow of interesting work for Richard Kline including camera assistant on the story of a librarian accused of being a communist in the Red scare propaganda platform *Storm Center* (1956) starring Bette Davis as the suspected. Now a competent operator taking all job opportunities as they came, Kline (like almost everyone else in Hollywood) found work on *Around the World in 80 Days*. Originally contracted as one of a dozen operators, he was quickly grabbed by producer Mike Todd to shoot behind-the-scenes B-roll of him making the movie. Implementing a system of signals with his undercover shooter for camera direction, Todd used subtle hand gestures for orders to follow (e.g., go in for coverage, or cut) depending upon the shot he wanted.

Back with Guffey for perhaps his finest film noir effort, 1957's *Nightfall* (directed by Jacques Tourneur), Kline got a first-class lesson in using flashbacks and composite photography from a master. Appreciating the DP's use of menacing close-ups and high contrast lighting to slow dolly moves as the picture's signature look, Kline felt that the superb acting of Aldo Ray and Anne Bancroft sealed the film's fate to become a classic.

Parting from Guffey after being assigned by the Columbia camera department to a series of formula pictures beginning with Ronald Reagan's *Hellcats of the Navy* and director George Sidney's *Jeanne Eagles* featuring Kim Novak and Jeff Chandler, Richard began branching out with an ever-increasing client base for work. Grabbing *Escape from San Quentin* next with old pals Katzman and Fred Sears, Kline recalled the hustle of returning to the grueling 60 set-ups a day.

Another eventual classic on which Richard operated camera was *Pal Joey*, starring Frank Sinatra in the title role flanked by old friends Rita Hayworth and Kim Novak caught in a lover's triangle. Although it was helmed by George Sidney, Kline remembers Sinatra as king on set, regardless of who was directing. On the musical numbers with him singing and Hayworth doing everything else, Kline recalled it was the famous crooner who called the shots, not cinematographer Harold Lipstein (who patiently did his best to give Frank what he needed). "The music on set was fabulous," Richard recalled. "As a big Sinatra fan, I was speechless."

Hired by James Wong Howe for tank work on Warner Brothers' *The Old Man and the Sea*, Kline had to shoot for days in a kneeling position. Stationed on a floating platform to simulate low-angle shots from the water (as Spencer Tracy struggles with the fish), Kline also did a reverse set-up for the marlin's view of the boat. Long hours of extensive lighting set-ups were required to film the massive backings used for the in-studio ocean effects. Working from the unstable rafts in rough water conditions made it physically draining for everyone. "At the end of a twelve-hour day," he mused, "it felt like you had been tossed around like a doll."

Kline was assigned to another Spencer Tracy film at Columbia that year: John Ford's *The Last Hurrah*. It was lensed by cinematographer Charles Lawton Jr. whom Richard ranked by his "clothing-equation" as richly colored with a defined use of contrast. Ford was so interesting to talk with that most voluntarily stayed on set between lighting breaks, rather than miss his stories. Also appreciated by Kline was the director's ability to stage actors within the frame of a given lens for their optimal positioning. Kline operated on a pan shot of Tracy walking away from camera; rather than using a dolly to follow him out, Ford's lesson of utilizing the lens for sizing was one Kline would never forget. Recalling the stoic director's set as a hard-working but happy one, he said Ford hired an accordion player to play lively numbers while the crew was doing lighting set-ups. The mood music began in the morning when the helmer arrived on set with a robust version of "Anchors Aweigh," continued during lunch, then began again at afternoon tea time when delicate Irish classics were the fare.

Another bit of learning acquired by Kline was Ford's economical control of film. Using clever cuts in the camera to transition between scenes, he shot the entire picture with 40,000 feet of stock. Kline said, "Ford was also able to reduce takes by maintaining control and calm while working. No matter the content of a sequence, he would sit behind camera and start the action by calmly saying, 'Okay, we're rolling.'" Kline adopted this when he became a DP. The lesson of keeping talent calm served Richard well: shooting less, yet getting more from actors.

Requested by James Wong Howe for the 1958 Columbia feature *Bell, Book and Candle* (starring James Stewart and Kim Novak), Kline was gaining a reputation as an operator who could get any shot. After another camera assignment on Columbia's *The Battle of the Coral Sea* starring Cliff Robertson, he returned to Burnett Guffey's team for the pre–World War II drama *The Mountain Road*. The story of Theodore White's observations in China before the Japanese invasion, the picture featured Jimmy Stewart and placed actor and crew alike in some fairly tough situations while shooting on location in the brutal summer heat of Nogales, Arizona. With temperatures soaring above 120 degrees one afternoon, Kline held a camera position very close to a large explosion of a wooden bridge on the picture's Temple set. Due to the warm air and too much powder, the blast sent shards of debris and flaming lumber over Kline's head, narrowly missing. Additionally shooting large battle scenes at Columbia's Burbank Ranch, his responsibility levels were growing along with his overall filmmaking abilities thanks to the tutoring of his DPs.

While operating camera on director Richard Brooks' *Elmer Gantry* in early 1960, Kline found the tough-talking ex–Marine to be the total opposite of John Ford, yet every bit as effective with actors. Also written by Brooks, the film had a disclaimer describing it as an open discussion on Christianity, in order to avoid offending moviegoers. Remembering the scenes where Gantry (beautifully played by Burt Lancaster) first takes up the calling, Kline said the actor was so superb that the crew broke into applause after many takes.

Bouncing back and forth with Guffey as an operator, Kline was assigned by Columbia to the Billie Holiday–like picture *Let No Man Write My Epitaph* just after *Elmer Gantry* wrapped. With Ella Fitzgerald singing the iconic balladeer standards like "One for My Baby" and "I Can't Give You Anything But Love," the feature was memorable for Kline, who was a big Ella fan: "Standing there behind camera, listening to her sing gave me the chills."

Back with Charles Lawton, Jr. for the summer shooting of *The Wackiest Ship in the Army*, Richard was in familiar territory on a water picture and was subsequently called upon to make a shot from atop a sixty-foot-high crow's nest for an overhead of the 80-foot antique schooner while underway. Finishing the film unscathed despite its risks, he recalled the Richard Murphy show as being among his most fun as cameraman.

Another Lawton feature of importance for Kline (both socially and professionally) was Columbia's taboo-busting *A Raisin in the Sun*. Sensitive to the issue of racial prejudice due not only to his Jewish upbringing, but later exposure to Japanese classmates interned during the war and racial experiences on the Globetrotters' trip, Richard found Ruby Dee's performance to be truly moving and felt proud to be working on that picture.

Kline's last phase as an operator began with camerawork from his final mentor, cinematographer Phil Lathrop. Embraced by Oscar-winning DP Russell Metty, Lathrop (who operated on the famous crane shot in the opening of *Touch of Evil*) was the perfect finishing instruction for Kline. His daring concepts of filmmaking would rub off on the still maturing shooter.

Blake Edwards' *Experiment in Terror* (starring Glenn Ford, Lee Remick, and Ross Martin as the sunglasses-clad psychopath Red Lynch) was done in August of '61; the first of the Lathrop-Kline collaborations, it was filmed in a high contrast black and white. The feature's eerie look was further augmented by the cinematographer's bold decision to implement helicopters for the movie's chase sequences. With Kline in the chopper to operate a hand-held, Arriflex camera, the pre–Tyler-mount system put him to the test: flying 24 hours straight during the flick's exciting nighttime finale staged over San Francisco's Candlestick Park, Kline earned an impressive $600 for the shift: his airborne experience would not go unnoticed in the film community.

Undaunted by the hundreds of dives and passes done by pilot Bob Dempsey during the filming (absorbing multiple G's tethered merely by the waist), Kline would soon be called upon to do it all again for his next Lathrop gig, *Lonely Are the Brave*, in March of 1962. He operated on some of the movie's more difficult sequences (including the aerial pursuit through the mountains with Kirk Douglas leading his horse up a trail so steep the animal could barely make it). Kline recalled the coverage as a combination of helicopter work and tripods perched high on rock faces. It was lensed in the rugged mountains of Tijeras Canyon outside of Albuquerque, New Mexico; Richard said the final set-up in the rain (with the horse being hit by a truck) was his most challenging of the picture. He pulled focus while panning through traffic in the near-zero visibility of the prolific downpour. Kline's multi-tasking abilities nailed the shot on the first take.

Called by Burnett Guffey to help take over the camerawork on John Frankenheimer's *Birdman of Alcatraz* (after creative differences between Lancaster and the first shooter), Kline recollected his boss' genius of designing jail sets with removable sections for coverage within the cells. His favorite shot in the sequence was done while operating camera over the cell

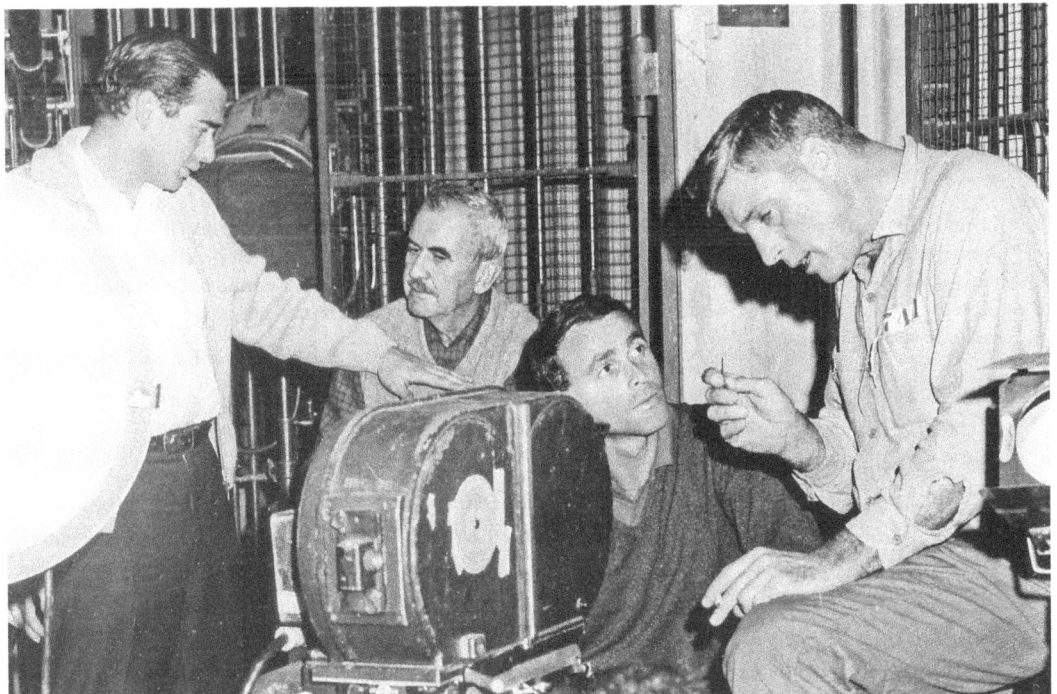

John Frankenheimer's *Birdman of Alcatraz* (1962) was shot mostly at Columbia Pictures, including the prison interior pictured here. Discussing the merits of employing a dolly in the action, producer-star Burt Lancaster (right) and operator Richard Kline (behind camera) agreed that, with so much of the jail bolted down, any movement of its coverage would be a good thing. Seated behind Kline, cinematographer Burnett Guffey confers with director Frankenheimer, left (courtesy Richard Kline).

Enjoying a light moment during a break from shooting *Days of Wine and Roses* (1962), cast and crew politely smile on what was otherwise a very heavy Warner Bros. set. Seen here left to right are cinematographer Phil Lathrop and operator Kline by camera; while Jack Lemmon, Lee Remick, and director Blake Edwards are seated. Standing behind Edwards with a pained expression on his bespectacled face is gaffer Lee Wilson (courtesy Richard Kline).

bars, looking down rows of bird cages, riding slowly on a western dolly. He said the imagery of the empty cages languishing in the silent cell struck him deeply, representing prison itself and those who perish there.

Kline was back with Blake Edwards and Lathrop for his last outings as an operator: *Days of Wine and Roses* and *The Pink Panther*. Shot in 1963, the films presented two widely different types of stories, but were each handled by Kline in his own professional fashion. *Wine and Roses* was shot in black and white as a straightforward drama with no photo magic (its depiction of a couple's booze-inflicted sorrow needed little window-dressing). *Pink Panther*, on the other hand, was a lively comedic series of stunt gags built around Peter Sellers' Clouseau character. Serving as Lathrop's first operator, Kline was responsible for much of the picture's camerawork including the interpretation of the DP's desires, while in the midst of Sellers' impromptu creative chaos. Learning the nuances of character and style of the actor's movements, he was able to anticipate the comedian's improvisational strays from the shooting script and adjust for them while keeping everything in focus. With two weeks left of filming on *The Pink Panther*, Kline received an urgent telegram from John

Frankenheimer asking if he wanted to move up to DP for *Seven Days in May*, stating, "Want you as my cinematographer. Repeat. Want you! Contact me at Goldwyn right away!" He shared his exciting news with Edwards and Lathrop; both were elated and told Kline to take the job. Agreeing to come in and hash out the details, he was shocked a few weeks later when rebuffed by studio honchos who stated that Kirk Douglas (the film's star) wanted a more experienced guy to do the show. Angry at the turn of events, he withdrew into a funk for a few days until he got a phone call from the head of MGM's camera department, Ray Johnson, saying that producer Bill Froug had requested a meeting. Seeing him the following week, Kline was asked to view a television pilot shot by Fred Koenekamp, *Mr. Novak*, and then give a verbal report on it. With no idea what Froug was after, he watched and gave his honest opinion that the look was great and that he liked it. Suddenly asked if *he* could shoot the series in that same style, Kline (still smarting from the *Seven Days in May* snub) bluntly asked Froug if he had the power to offer such a position without checking first. Assured he could, Kline took the job after being told by the producer he was chosen because of his mastery of black and white lighting and a poll taken among three associates (Richard Donner, Boris Sagal, and Lamont Johnson) regarding whom *they* would move up to DP from the operators they knew.

Envisioning *Mr. Novak* with a realism that matched the acting persona of James Franciscus' fluid energy and movement, Kline imbued those qualities within the show's look. Manifesting his idea subtly by way of stage design, he implemented the use of classroom sets with sliding walls built on quiet rails, dollying between when moved. Allowing for multiple levels of action to play out in the same scene, the concept gave continuous shots long before the advent of steadicam or technocranes. Another original concept Kline found for the series was the inspired use of film noir lighting through windows with slatted blinds to act as diffusion, producing dramatic shadows across the actors' faces and classroom walls in the background. Called a dirty look back in the '50s for its simple and harsh effect, the style resurfaced years later as *Miami Vice* cool, when borrowed by creator Michael Mann for the show's South Florida drug persona.

Taking other television pilots after *Mr. Novak*'s two-year run, Kline shot *The Mouse That Roared*, *Iron Horse*, *T.H.E. Cat*, and some episodes of *Honey West* before *The Monkees* in 1966: "When we shot *The Monkees* pilot, it was so 'out there' we were sure the industry had gone out of control. Upon seeing the dailies, the UPM and I looked at each other and said, 'If this shit sells, we're all in trouble.' As with all the BBS stuff, it sold."

For the pilot of a fright series titled *House of Wax* in mid–66, Richard was brought in by director-producer Hy Averback. After it failed to sell, he was asked to shoot additional blood and gore sequences to transform it into a releasable B-movie renamed *Chamber of Horrors*. At the Warner Brothers lab one afternoon, director Josh Logan (prepping for *Camelot*) accidentally saw some of Kline's horror footage containing medieval castle doors with a carriage drawn by a team of gray horses rolling through a bricked courtyard; all were swathed in the muted colors and mist of the heavy wood and stone structures around it. He was intrigued by what he saw, and an interview with Richard followed. During an hour-long meeting at the director's home, Kline expressed a desire to make a picture authentically textured instead of the shiny armored look previously embraced by Hollywood. Logan hired him on the spot with a binding handshake that would forever change his career. Finally getting a shot at a feature of his own, with *Camelot* Kline knew he was ready for the big time.

Taken under the wing of Jack Warner as the new "It" kid, Kline was allowed a year of pre-production on the picture to do tests with everything from film stock to costumes — even scouting trips to Spain to find the right castles. Working with designer Eddie Cardera and wardrobe genius John Truscott, Kline was involved with every decision from rocks to farmhouses and swords to saddles. Thoroughly researching all they put on screen, he stayed with his concept of historical accuracy by utilizing natural materials like rough-hewn wood, stone, and period clothes made from leather and wool, which blended perfectly with his design of muted flesh tones and washed-out color so liked by Logan from the *Chamber of Horrors* dailies. Shipping his stock back to stateside labs for processing while shooting at the Alcazar and Coca Castles in Spain, the cinematographer included detailed descriptions of the scenes to provide a better understanding of mood and intent for studio use. Jack Warner sent his "wonder boy" telegrams of congratulations for the great-looking shots." Suddenly all went to hell as executives got wind that Kline was "damaging" the original negative by using a dangerous process called pre-fogging. Kline assured Warner that his flashing technique was a harmless method to mute color and contrast; the mogul laughed and told him to keep up the good work. Quick to give technical credit for the pre-fogging to camera operator Frank Stanley, Kline said his cautious re-exposure of the film (loading it with frame-perforations lining up in the magazine for its secondary exposure) made him the unsung hero of the day.

The movie was filmed on location in Spain and in an elaborate medieval city built on the Warner back lot (dubbed *Camelot* Castle). Kline was shooting in a dense forest outside of Leon with an intricate balance of smoke and sun streaming through the thick trees for a dramatic image of Richard Harris (King Arthur) before a battle. Slowly turning, he realized the opposite direction was even more dramatic and swung the camera around to make his shot from there instead. "Sometimes, being observant is the key to good things happening." He shot a 200-foot magazine on the happy accident; the sequence was used for closing credits footage. Kline was nominated for a Best Photography Oscar on his first feature as a cinematographer; he lost to Burnett Guffey (*Bonnie and Clyde*). Following

At the Academy lunch for Oscar nominees, Richard Kline wears a look of sheer delight as the proceedings pay tribute to his first major motion picture in Hollywood as a cinematographer, *Camelot* (1967). He competed with Robert Surtees for *The Graduate* and *Doctor Dolittle* as well as Conrad Hall for *In Cold Blood*; all lost out to Burnett Guffey's *Bonnie and Clyde* (courtesy Richard Kline).

the nomination buzz, his stock in Tinseltown was on the rise and multiple offers began pouring in.

Approached by director Ted Post to shoot *Hang 'Em High*, Richard recommended his protégé Lenny South instead, then departed for London to do a George Cukor picture. After a falling-out between parties, and the cancellation of the Cukor deal, Kline regained the gritty Western's reins. Picking up the picture's already established look, he stuck with hard-edged illumination and rich shadows while photographing Clint Eastwood's Marshall Cooper character, utilizing existing light for exteriors to produce a cooler color palette to offset the dark tones of the town. It became one of Kline's favorite films; he referred to the lynching sequence in the beginning as being very unsettling to shoot. Watching the grips prepare the rope rig around the branch, the DP said he decided to portray the act as grotesque, and filmed it with a realistic accuracy to convey that. Using intercuts between the horse moving under the victim, the rope straining as it bites into his neck, and the hanging party's faces reflecting sheer madness and fear as Ed Begley urges them on, the shooter built a tension into the scene that made it unforgettable.

In Kline's early operating career, his most important on-set connection had been with the cinematographer. Once a DP, however, his crucial relationship became that with the director. His responsibilities now extended into areas of talent performance and script interpretation; he was suddenly given a say in everything, versus just being told what to shoot. More than ever, relationships with directors and the scripts dictated his creative choices. Luckily for Kline, his first new boss (Richard Fleischer) was a kindred spirit. Their partnership would be long-lasting and based on trust. While the director allowed his DP's daring reputation to dictate photographic choices on their first picture together, Kline rewarded that trust on *The Boston Strangler* by constantly challenging his operators with new lens ideas. One such concept was a dynamic series of integrated panels that began with Fleischer seeing them used at the Canadian World's Fair in 1964, then later hiring production designer Fred Harpman to bring them to life by use of storyboarding prior to shooting. The process, requiring mattes in the finder to isolate the composition within the frame (eliminating or masking out the unused portion of the background including walls, equipment, and ceiling pieces surrounding the primary object of focus) literally infused the remaining image with a pop-out quality that drew the viewers eye directly to it. It's simple to do with today's technology; the trick in those days was considerable as Kline had as many as five elements in montage blocked-out within his frame to make it all work. Starting with one panel, then two or more until reducing as another pops up, he also used off-setting sizes, enlargements, and moving frames to keep the viewer's attention on the screen. The use of this technique can be seen when Tony Curtis as Albert DeSalvo first appears parking his car, approaching a building and ringing the buzzer of his intended victim. The sequence contained contrasting panels showing the unsuspecting young actress in her apartment carefully ironing — then being murdered after letting him in. Equating the "moving boxes" to having the ability to control where the audience looks, Kline felt the forced shifting of people's eyes at strategic moments added a subconscious feeling of fear to the picture by causing viewers to automatically want to see what happens next. This method not only built suspense before the act but served to lead moviegoers on a voyeuristic peep at the anatomy of something only 13 victims ever saw — their own brutal death at DeSalvo's hands. The rape and murder of character Dianne Cluny (perfectly played by Sally Kellerman) is the movie's most violent scene because there were no shooting cuts while she's being hurt, versus the suggested violence of others which broke off before showing prolonged suffering.

Shifting from the animated style of Fleischer to the professional calmness of director Norman Jewison, Kline was hired by producer Hal Ashby to do the Ben Hecht turn-of-the-century bio *Gaily, Gaily* in 1969. Required to come up with an aged look for the film, he relied upon unbleached muslin for diffusion (bringing out tans and browns in skin tone as well as ambient light when used as an overhead); he often incorporated as much of the period set decoration and background scenic work as possible, adding historic depth to his composition. With more than just aging the props to worry about, he recalled Melina Mercouri coming to him during rehearsal concerned that she didn't look old enough for the part and asking the DP to light her older. Kline utilized a small handheld feather light for her eyes that added a flat glow to age her slightly. It boosted her self-confidence and she stole the scene.

With studios still dictating the *who* and *what* of motion pictures throughout the sixties, the look of the product was also theirs regarding film stock, lighting and camera movement. Kline's last picture of the decade *Dream of Kings* was no different. Circumstances forced the shooter to be daring when choosing prolific dolly work, despite the freezing street-side locations in Chicago's late fall. He built layer upon layer of experience with these various features; every film in the can brought the prolific lensmen closer to perfection with his camera.

Not long after *Dream of Kings*, Kline met a director he considered one of the most complete and talented filmmakers in Hollywood history: Robert Wise. Shooting *The Andromeda Strain* for him, Kline was again tasked with the photographic interpretation of production designer Boris Leven's work, complete with architectural layouts that included specs for space interiors with flying bridges, work stations, and crew quarters. He employed split-diopters in order to record both scientific space environment and the actors within them for over 80 percent of the feature. Kline explained the optical device held both grounds (fore and aft) in perfect focus, while still keeping people walking through sharp. Striving to capture the future space look of an antiseptic "clean room" (depicted in Leven's sketches), he worked with the artist and employed such tricks as having bulkheads and panel boxes painted with varying shades of gray and off-white to make surfaces appear larger or more defined in the background. In addition to removable ceiling pieces used for the shooting of overheads, Kline also incorporated a prodigious amount of white diffusion and bounce cards, to keep the light-needy set at the stop he required.

Another interesting feature from the early '70s was director Peter Ustinov's *Hammersmith Is Out*, starring Elizabeth Taylor and Richard Burton during their second marriage's honeymoon phase. Their unwillingness to rehearse was anticipated during the southern Mexico production, where the two were actually vacationing. With limited time around the actors, Kline and Ustinov blocked out intricate sequences using local stand-ins only to have Liz and Dick arrive on set without rehearsal, yet hit every mark perfectly. It was shot between 10 A.M. and 3 P.M. without stopping for lunch; the modified hours allowed the filmmakers to get the most from both actors. It was literally a photographic exercise of capturing the couple's love of craft and infinite control of their abilities; Kline's end result was like watching two dear friends enjoying each other's company. Shooting the piece more like a play than a feature, he boldly opted to let the two act by filming off dollies without track while hand-holding a fill-light as the gaffer manned a key and grips floated flags as needed.

No matter where on set the scene worked, the camera operators (hand-held or rolling) were able to follow without breaking the action for reposition. By providing a platform of self-expression and movement for the actors to take full advantage, the results on screen were long takes reminiscent of *Who's Afraid of Virginia Woolf?*, with a comedic twist. "It was very liberating for them to work that way," Kline explained, "as it gave them the freedom to continue a good scene, or end a bad one, without missing any magic due to lighting or camera issues."

Michael Winner's *The Mechanic*, shot by Kline in mid–1972, was the first of three pictures the two did over a ten-year period. Winner was considered difficult by many in Tinseltown; Kline found the prickly Brit likable when he met with him to discuss the project. He had a reputation as a perfectionist known for spur-of-the-moment firings fueled by a hair-trigger temper; most of the people fired from Winner's pictures were glad to be on their way. Aware of his own rep, the helmer jokingly congratulated Kline for having accepted an assignment with the most feared director in Hollywood: "Depending how this all works out, you've either won or lost a terrific bet. Good luck, old boy."

The movie featured Charles Bronson as a master hit man. Kline's photographic choices in the film's opening painted a thorough portrait of the profession of planning, stalking, and killing a human as if it were a military exercise. Languid tones of Bach are interspersed with details of the assassin's trade not usually revealed in motion pictures. Kline's choice to

Director Michael Winner peers through a finder as he and cinematographer Richard Kline (standing just behind him) prepare to shoot a montage of deadly martial arts for *The Mechanic* (1972) at Takayuda Kubota's Dojo in Los Angeles. Winner did as many as 65 set-ups a day for the coverage; actors Jan-Michael Vincent (front row left) and Charles Bronson (front row center) were less than thrilled with the director's demand for so many takes (courtesy Richard Kline).

Challenged by Winner's desire to do every job on set (including his), cinematographer Kline (center, hands in pockets) watches as the Brit looks through a finder at Bronson, cocking a wooden sword. Trading notes with assistant director Peter Prince (second from right), Kline was sorry to see the sequence cut from the film; as a lifelong practitioner of karate, he put a lot into the coverage from his own knowledge (courtesy Richard Kline).

shoot the first 16 minutes of film without dialogue beautifully served to keep the attention on the visual. We voyeuristically observe the mark through the hit-man's point of view (then watch Bronson plant explosives in a book after prepping the burner to leak gas). The cinematographer's use of existing light and a long lens from across the street framed the apartment like a stage, giving the audience a front row seat to the action four stories up. Utilizing a derelict downtown L.A. hotel slated for demolition in the stunt, the powder-man rigged the blast with so much explosive that windows shattered on both sides of the street and created a black smoke cloud five stories high. Thinking his DP responsible for the colossal size of the blast, Winner declared he loved it and then excitedly asked Richard while the debris cleared if he got the shot.

Testing Kline's photographic reach on *The Mechanic*, the motorcycle chase at the heavily guarded Mansion required the cinematographer to employ Arriflex cameras mated to follow vehicles with operators shooting handheld or riding backwards. Kline was becoming the go-to guy for action features.

Crewed on the Jim Brown action vehicle *Black Gunn* in late 1972, Kline thoroughly enjoyed working with the former football great, calling him a gutsy and courageous actor who was sensitive as well. Employing a series of his patented cut-away shots for Brown

Once again sticking his eye into Kline's finder, Winner looks at a low shot for *The Mechanic's* (1972) final scenes. "I got used to him," Kline (squatting on right) revealed, "and by the time we did *Won Ton Ton* four years later," he added, "he was almost cured with pre-checking my shots" (courtesy Richard Kline).

whenever faced with danger, Kline used the ex-fullback's athleticism to its fullest in the film's opening rip-off scene. "No matter how physical the movie work," he recalled, "Jim never refused a request. He was in such tremendous condition, he was able to do multiple takes without tiring."

The following year, Kline returned to director Richard Fleischer for their second film, *Soylent Green*. Kline was excited to be back with his friend and intrigued by the picture's dark prediction of the world in the future. The photographic look was produced with a proprietary gas-rig mounted in a box surrounding the lens (using a small fan to circulate green-tinted atmospheric smoke). The effect was a grime-tinged mist that subtly lingered in frame. Applying the box on back lot locations at MGM during its final picture (amid the dilapidated skeletal remains of the once great studio), Kline took advantage of the existing conditions to save money and time. Integrating as much foreground detail as possible to reflect the texture of a fractured society inhabiting an over-populated Earth (hiding recognizable studio features too prominent to shoot around), the always resourceful cinematographer also conferred with EPA big-wig Frank Bowerman for specifics of what a mechanical and ecological breakdown of cities would look like. Shooting a fortnight of back lot exteriors as well as locations at L.A.'s Sports Arena and the El Segundo sewage plant, Kline portrayed a futuristic portrait of the world gone wrong that was graphic, yet still believable.

Gravely ill while shooting *Soylent Green*, Edward G. Robinson told no one but co-star

Charlton Heston that he was dying. Deeply moved during Roth's death scene (as the actor was truly weeping at the loss of a friend), the DP was profoundly saddened when the great actor passed a week later. With Robinson no longer able to hear dialogue, the two actors worked out visual cues to ensure a proper verbal exchange without anyone noticing. When the shooter needed to give stage direction, he would tell Heston what he wanted: Heston would then relate the change to Edward G. by low-key gestures. Appreciating the bittersweet reality of his condition while watching the performance of a lifetime, Richard Kline said it was an honor to shoot Robinson's final work.

In early 1973 Kline collaborated with director Ted Post on their second outing, *The Harrad Experiment*, a daring "coming of age," sexually scientific picture. Limited by ratings how far he could go photographically with the film's more provocative subject matter, Kline wisely shared the critical decisions with producer Dennis Stevens and production designer Fred Harpman; their collaboration imparted a tone of academia to the sex that kept it from being smutty. Employing imaginative in-camera cropping and strategic pans and tilts to give the viewer quick glimpses of body parts, Kline would then cut away before the action became graphic — showing details of intertwined fingers, perspiring faces, and a clinical afterglow from the experiments, sensual but still restrained. Recalling the project's young male lead Don Johnson (early in his career), Kline said the handsome star on the rise not only showed camera savvy by hitting all his marks but dealt well with the subject matter and being semi-nude for much of the film.

For Kline, *Battle for the Planet of the Apes* was "a rent-gig"; its high sequel number guaranteed it had no real budget or good writing. It was directed by J. Lee Thompson and featured Roddy McDowall as Ceasar (who was in all the films). Richard was photographically limited by Fox's recycling of old facial prosthetics and beat-up ape suits left over from the previous pictures. Forced to work with the rubber mask look and dilapidated fur pieces, he skipped close-ups of talking creatures (since the face rigs didn't allow for articulated jaw movement) and kept the monkey suits darkly lit to conceal their balding condition and age. Since this sequel offered nothing new in look or character depth (with the exception of John Huston playing the Law Giver), Kline shot the movie to match the other versions and utilized the Fox back lot and Ranch in Calabasas for all exteriors.

Kline gladly returned for a third feature with Fleischer, *The Don Is Dead*, starring Anthony Quinn. He leapt at the chance to do something reminiscent of his film noir days with Burnett Guffey. Following his old mentor's recipe of high contrast ¾ Rembrandt light coupled with slow dolly moves and menacing close-ups of bad guys, Richard's work was a pure reflection of the '50s gangster flicks of his early days. Photographing two great actors of totally different styles and appearance, he shot Al Lettieri as Vince, with the focus on his piercing eyes set into his expressive face. Quinn's Don Angelo was scripted to move about the set, which required a wider initial coverage, then transitioned to tighter shots for effect.

Michael Crichton's *The Terminal Man* presented the cinematographer with the task of rendering on film a world of elegant, scientific horror some time in the near future. Choosing to shoot the project in muted colors and controlled saturation to the point of rendering a blue sky gray and flesh tones a pale pink, Kline teamed once again with designer Fred Harpman to provide an underlying starkness to the sets. Costumes by Dino Novarse produced in shades of white, black and slate further focused the sameness of the computer-controlled future reality.

Using an antiseptic off-white look for the operating room scenes where the sounds of clanking surgical instruments are intertwined with the background music of Bach's Goldberg Variations, Kline implemented top-lit gradated diffusion to render a monochromatic tone to the medical procedures. To provide a memorable photographic flourish (and metaphor of hope) to the movie's ending, he lit and exposed for the garish pallet of flowers, which had them visually leap from the screen as the only Technicolor hues in the picture.

Reuniting with Richard Fleischer on their fourth and fifth features consecutively, Kline lensed *Mr. Majestyk* in '74 and *Mandingo* the following year. Once again photographing the rugged faces of Charles Bronson and Al Lettieri in a violent picture, he produced a tight, well-balanced look for *Majestyk* that came from reading the script and discussions with Fleischer rather than any pre-conceived concepts held over from previous films. Two scenes challenged the cinematographer's originality: one of watermelons being machine-gunned by thugs and the other involving stunt shots of the Ford truck being driven through fields by Bronson. Kline used multiple cameras and included high-speed to get slow motion effects of the produce exploding; the same was done for the driving gag with an additional camera mounted to the pickup bed. Both solutions were "pure Kline" in putting the viewer right in the action.

Moving on to *Mandingo*, Kline's chameleon-like ability to shoot any genre paid off on this richly realized Dino De Laurentiis production. Impressing the maestro with his sense of time and place filmmaking (while collaborating with production designer Boris Leven amid the textured Louisiana Plantations of Houmas House and Ashland used in the movie), the cinematographer was offered Dino's next picture, *King Kong*.

Approached by Richard Fleischer to do *Mandingo* while still shooting *Mr. Majestyk*, Kline was so turned off by Norman Wexler's screenplay of blatant racial cruelty he rejected the job outright; he only agreed to take the project if the director gave him full control over the depiction of violence. Allowed to reduce the amount of sensationalized atrocities in the script, the cinematographer substituted imagination for gore, taking the viewer right up to the point of horrific actions — then cutting away at the last moment. Between Ken Norton's performance and Kline's gorgeous photography, the picture was far better than it was given credit for.

In the winter of '76, Kline was drafted for another Winner project, *Won Ton Ton, the Dog That Saved Hollywood*. Starring Bruce Dern, Art Carney, and countless cameos of Tinseltown T-Rexes (Alice Faye, Milton Berle, and Victor Mature to name just a few), it had so many great stars for the DP to shoot, it never got boring. He was also tasked with filming the title dog doing all sorts of amazing things; the work occasionally became a laughing matter as the animal had some peculiar rehearsal habits. Worked on set by renowned trainer Carl Lewis Miller, the male German shepherd was taught by copying his master; he would get down on all fours to show the dog what to do. Scripted to play confused for a gag, the dog was supposed to crash into a plaster wall by accident, and then fall down as if out cold. Demonstrating the action for the animal by scampering full speed into a reinforced set wall, Lewis mistakenly knocked himself out upon impact. Later ordering the dog through its paces with the camera rolling, Kline and the crew were in stitches as the dog refused to plow into anything, no matter what Miller tried. They finally got the shot by substituting a break-away panel for the dog to go through. The four-legged performer lifted his leg on the set-piece, as a show of his contempt for the whole process, at day's end.

True to his word to hire Kline for his next big picture, Dino De Laurentiis' *King Kong* (in 1976) was a big picture from its first day of auditions to the big ape's finale on the ground. The casting process for the role of Dawn (ultimately going to newcomer Jessica Lange) gave every producer's girlfriend in town a chance to read; from Bo Derek to Britt Ekland, they came in droves. Kline and screen test director Bill Kronick watched Meryl Streep get cut-off in mid-sentence by De Laurentiis, joking in his native Italian, "She's the best actress so far but too ugly for anyone to buy as a movie star." Streep spoke multiple languages; the producer was floored as she responded in fluent Italian, "You're not so hot either."

Smitten with Lange the moment he saw her, Kline recalled that Dino had her undergo quick fixes for her teeth and breast enhancement within a week of being cast in the role. Still not satisfied with her perfection of form (when picked up in a shot by Jeff Bridges that exposed a boney rib cage), the producer spent a small fortune having it mended in post by optical retouching of the negative. After seeing the results of the added flesh, De Laurentiis declared in triumph to his cinematographer, "There, now she no longer looks like a scarecrow."

Technical aspects of the film included the use of pre–CGI animatronics designed and engineered by Carlo Rambaldi. A 40-foot-tall mechanical Kong was made from a three and one half ton aluminum skeletal frame, dressed with over 1000 pounds of horse-tail hair. Referring to Rambaldi as the core of De Laurentiis' studio art department back in Italy, Kline indentified his genius in primate physiology coupled with the designer's background in electrical engineering and hydraulics as the real hero of Kong's look. Incorporating both full scale and miniature elements (including an articulated, six-foot-across gorilla hand weighing 1600 pounds), much of the believability of the picture came down to Rambaldi's designs and Kline's ability to photograph them. While testing the big hand, the DP recalled that Dino watched as the operator configured it into giving him the finger. Laughter turned to anger, however, when the rig blew a hydraulic line which required a day to repair. Photographing Kong's various fur surfaces with the patience of a fashion shooter, Kline saturated the dense suit with massive quantities of controlled light while slightly under-exposing the face for a balanced look.

The picture's toughest set-up had Kline lens a straight down POV shot from the top of the 110-story World Trade Center. Thanks to a six-foot wooden platform constructed off the lip of the roof (via key grip extraordinaire Bob Sordal), he was able to safely walk out to the edge while tethered in a full body harness, operating a handheld Arriflex for the sequence. With no safety rails and 80 mile an hour winds blasting his torso, he said it took all his strength and skill to keep the camera steady. Visiting the set while the gag was in progress, tightrope artist Philippe Petit (having just spanned the structures two weeks prior) complimented the cinematographer for his daring style.

When coverage was needed of the Village Fortress (where the audience first sees Kong), Kline had envisioned a sixty-foot-high scaffolding (fifty yards in length) for an elevated move along the top of the wall. Saving the time and expense of the back lot over-build, he instead had a 90-foot construction crane rigged with a pivoting camera-mount and operator's chair, thus allowing him to use the boom arm's size to photographically span the massive walls. *King Kong* required an eight-month production schedule of 14-hour days, including coverage of the 40-foot-tall ape figure and weeks of rugged outdoor shooting on Hawaii's

Hoponpu Beach and in New York City. It was one of the most physically demanding jobs of Richard's career.

He combined a multitude of camera disciplines in capturing the story, while always keeping his stuff believable. Avoiding trick shots while focusing on the physical mechanics of the picture, his end result was a natural-looking King Kong, minus any cheesy effects, to keep viewers sold. Oscar-nominated for best photography, Kline lost out to Haskell Wexler's *Bound for Glory*.

Teaming up with director Brian De Palma in the winter of 1977, Kline shot the supernatural thriller *The Fury*, based on the C.I.A.'s clandestine use of people with telepathic powers. Kline appreciated De Palma for his intricate staging of actors and movement of camera on the Plymouth Hotel sequence (where Kirk Douglas evades the agents pursuing him). He and the director worked out a series of dodges and near misses with a timing that kept viewers on the edge of their seats. While the film's climax had John Cassavetes exploding from within, Kline's photo magic entailed shooting the actor standing on set amid convulsions and spasmodic bleeding from every orifice. Using a momentary flash of white light, he cut to a dummy full of black powder and the explosion of the lookalike was filmed at various angles.

Who'll Stop the Rain (starring Nick Nolte and Michael Moriarty as Vietnam vets caught up in a heroin-smuggling operation gone wrong) was an extremely challenging picture for Dick Kline. Working within the dense jungle locations of Toreon, Mexico, proved difficult with its tropical heat, humidity, and deluge of biting insects. Led by director Karl Reisz, the DP survived the picture by surrounding himself with the best Hollywood had to offer like camera operator Al Bettcher and key grip, Bob Sordal. Reflecting his boss's commitment to getting the job done, Sordal engineered the use of a decrepit, 60-foot construction boom (mounted with a camera platform that could pivot, pan and tilt 45 degrees in motion) to produce an unforgettable five-story-high point of view for the picture's rain-soaked finale along the railroad tracks of the car driving away. Contracting a near deadly strain of Guillain-Barré syndrome during the final location work, Kline's key grip was rendered so ill he was practically unable to walk for the last week of the feature, yet still verbally imparted to his grips the mechanical particulars for the transformation of the rusting dock boom into a usable motion picture crane. Recalling Sordal's worth, the shooter said, "Bob was an asset that I preferred not to go without."

In the summer of 1979 Kline was signed by Hollywood veteran Robert Wise to lens *Star Trek: The Motion Picture*. Wanting to shoot the picture with a theatrical look (rather than the flat light evoked for the TV show), they decided upon the massive use of colored gels and lighting as a means of both establishing the scene's mood as well as saving money on sets that didn't have to be built. However, like all directors' decisions, the gel plan was subject to change without written notice. After ordering seventy thousand dollars worth of color diffusion for the film (excluding Red #25 which Wise sought to avoid because of its heavy use in the series), Kline was suddenly scrambling for exactly *that* after talks with creative voice Gene Roddenberry convinced the director that straying too far from the original show might turn off the very Trekkies they needed to fill the theaters. A costly nationwide search turned up the needed rolls of red at a cost of three times the going rate.

Kline attributes the picture's successful look to film effect guru Richard Yuricich and second unit director Doug Trumbull, whose cutting edge visuals eclipsed the cheap tinfoil and plastic space trappings of the original Desilu show. Focusing on the new *Enterprise*'s exterior as the film's primary outdoor set, Kline kept his overall key light reduced to allow the lamps surrounding the craft to read more intensely than the ship behind it. Another design fix implemented by the cinematographer was the replacement of original glass panels in the belly of the spaceship (switched out to unbreakable plexi) as 90 percent were smashed by crew members walking on them during filming. He also called for the removal of interior set walls because the production design had inadvertently closed off an elevator corridor needed for major battle scenes on the main deck. With no room for adequate camera placement or to circulate the thirty background actors through the bridge for an increased look in their numbers, Kline had the grips open an off stage cut-through as a solution. What would be digitally enhanced today was about filling the gaps with the clever use of real people and saws to get the shot back then.

Following *Star Trek*, Kline did a series of smaller pictures such as the Canadian tearjerker *Touched by Love*, shot in Alberta during a miserable late fall that included freezing rain and brutal winds. One wet afternoon on location, a grip returned from outside lighting duty, soaked to the bone. Watching him trudge across set with a scowl on his face that said he was seconds away from quitting, Kline intercepted the guy with a kind word and ordered him to get a warm shower and change of clothes before doing anything rash. Returning to the set 20 minutes later looking like a new man, the grip not only stayed on the difficult show but persuaded others to hang in there while spelling them for warm-ups as well. Always concerned for his crews' treatment, Kline never hesitated to get involved if something unjust happened on his set.

Another "lesser" picture was the Richard Dreyfuss–Amy Irving piano love story *The Competition*, shot in the late summer of 1980. Creatively stifled by the amount of excess footage required by director Joel Oliansky for getting the competitive feeling on screen, Kline utilized scores of dolly moves to break up the otherwise static act of playing a piano in a seated position. Boldly allowing backgrounds to go dark while using his favorite feather light to accentuate the player's hands, he incorporated film noir principles of high-key lighting (through Hampshire-frost diffusion) to render a needed feel of nostalgia to the otherwise boringly modern picture.

In early '81, Kline accepted an invitation from Lawrence Kasdan to shoot the film *Body Heat*. After reading the director's script, he immediately thought to render the show's steaminess by the use of gradated diffusion in combination with old-school Hollywood tricks such as Shibe gel and Mitchell-filters for the lens. Theorizing that the camera's extreme sharpness detracted from the softer sensual feel that he was after, Kline also used everything from camera flare and atmospheric smoke to adding as much contrast as possible to bring in warmth and texture for the love scenes between Kathleen Turner and William Hurt. With the crew aware of the impending full nudity sex sequences, the actors called everyone into a side room where they both disrobed and stood silently naked for all to see. They desensitized everyone by calmly letting it all hang out; there were no giggles or uneasy moments on set when they filmed the scenes. "It worked," Kline said with a grin. "Although better for Kathy's fans than Will Hurt's — her body was much nicer to look at!" Shooting the two passionate encounters, he surgically produced selected frames filled with thighs, backs, hips, and the sides of breasts to avoid full images of nudity. He lit the bodies with solar spots and fluorescent tubes to accentuate the texture of the skin that was shown.

Switching to 1940s gangster-film style, Kline shot a riveting sequence of Ned Racine (Hurt) approaching a boathouse rigged with explosives. Using an insert shot through a window as Hurt walks by a trip fuse attached to the bomb (then racking focus to follow the line connected to the door knob), the cinematographer built Saturday matinee suspense for the story with the economical but effective camerawork learned during his early Katzman pictures.

Nighttime location work was difficult due to a Florida cold snap with gusting winds and temperatures in the mid 40s; Richard cleverly resorted to using giant shipping containers stacked as a two-story wind-break to shield the outdoor action for shooting. Along with the jogging shots of Ned Racine (who was freezing while being filmed from the rear of a golf cart handled by Dolly Grip O.T. Henderson), Kline also placed his camera on a Fischer for close-ups of Hurt smoking. "It was so cold," he said, "that cigarettes (or not) steam vapor was coming out of his mouth whenever he spoke."

Kline challenged the grip with his idea to push the dolly through the wreckage of Racine's destroyed room, amid the overturned chairs, broken glass, and shattered window during his outburst. Capturing the destruction through the front door, following without track across the wall-to-wall carpet over broken door panels and smashed lamps, the camera stayed on Hurt until he threw a chair through the window. It required two dozen takes with an operator aboard the 500-pound sled; O.T. was so exhausted by sequence's end that he immediately took a two-hour nap with the boss' blessing. "With the dolly grip rolling over the broken furniture until he was ready to drop," Kline said proudly, "the shot had an imperfect realism to it that emphasized the chaos of violence."

Providing a style all his own for the conclusion, Kline's moving shot of Racine over the bars in his jail cell (during the ah-hah moment of realization that Matty had double-crossed him) suddenly transitioned into a slow zoom and close-up ending tight on his face — telling the audience all that he was thinking. Extremely happy with the work of Kline's grips on the show, producer Fred Gallo spotted the dolly man and key to an all-expenses paid stay in Hawaii for two weeks after the production wrapped.

Post–*Body Heat*, the bulk of the pictures Kline took were rent payers and favor trade-offs for those who could afford his price. Exceptions like *Breathless* and the Richard Benjamin films *My Stepmother Is an Alien* and *Downtown* fed his creative appetite while keeping him connected with the community he adored. Returning to Michael Winner's side on the Bronson reboot, *Death Wish II*, Kline continued his good working relationships with both director and star. Sticking to the script's photographic essentials during the grueling 44-day shoot around downtown's Southern Hotel and East L.A.'s Crescent Heights area for much of the gun play, he wisely reined in Winner's usual propensity for overshooting by limiting the takes to as few as possible while still getting the required coverage. With the parameters of Paul Kersey's character previously established in substance and filming style, Kline treated the sequel as a new story and infused Bronson's stylized cool-as-cucumber violence with quick cuts and multiple camera angles that gave a *Pulp Fiction* quality to the vigilante's killings.

On *Breathless*, the cinematographer lovingly lensed director James McBride's screen adaptation of the François Truffaut story, which took the story of a French car thief and American girl and made it about Richard Gere's Jesse Lujack character (Lujack pursues an exchange student from Paris while on a Las Vegas to L.A. crime spree). It co-starred Valerie

Kaprisky in the Monica role (Gere discovered her in Paris while scouting for an unknown for the female lead). Kline utilized his trademark gradation of diffusion and feather light for their love scenes to show her innocent passion without being graphic. From the intimacy of the swimming pool sequence with Gere embracing Valerie while perched under the diving board, to him pulling up in a variety of stolen cars, the cinematographer engaged a combination of filters and overhead diffusion that produced a Prince Charming aura to Jesse's character and highlighted the amazing automobiles as well. "The '57 T-Bird in the sequence," Kline recalled with a laugh, "was mine and the postcard moment of the adorable bad-ass behind the wheel was something we were aiming for with the vignettes." Having loved Jean-Luc Godard's 1960 version of the picture, Kline focused on the charming rogue element of the Lujack character while building tension through his displays of desire whenever he and Kaprisky shared the frame. In addition to infusing the feature with a good quantity of early '80s pacing, he subtly blended a throwback texture to its look by using Venetian blind shadows and natural light for the interiors. It's one of Kline's most underappreciated works, still amazingly alive and watchable today.

Hired in the winter of 1985 to shoot Stan Dragoti's *The Man with One Red Shoe* starring Tom Hanks, Richard was taking little more than one main project a year. With films becoming increasingly complex and requiring more of a cinematographer's pre-production attention, overlapping projects became a problem of the past. Poor logistics and difficult locations remained an issue on *Red Shoe* when he attempted to shoot in downtown Washington, D.C. Chased off by Capitol police due to an omission in the shooting permits, the DP moved to a side street with a small crew, pulling a manhole cover from the road with the intention of placing a camera inside for a street level shot. It was filled with a foul-smelling torrent of city waste (as they had accidentally tapped into a sewer main); Kline changed his plan of sending operator Al Bettcher into the hole for the footage. The only crew member present with the stomach to attempt the job, grip Dave Barrow handled the impromptu camera assignment but was required to change his smelly clothes before boarding the bus back to the hotel at day's end. Another difficulty that challenged the shooter's sanity was the last-minute need for 140 sheets of plywood to be installed over a new floor at the LAX terminal where they were scheduled to shoot. The DP patiently waited over two hours while the necessary lumber was found and installed, then started his day's work: "That cost the company about 10,000 bucks worth of overtime which could have been better spent on the film's look or at least on decent catering."

Still enjoying the rewards of the motion picture business, Kline shot the love story wrapped in a hockey flick, *Touch and Go* (1986). It required a lot of photography on ice; the cinematographer wisely implemented a Fischer Dolly (converted with steel runners by Bob Sordal) rather than confine the action's coverage to track. Allowing for a free flow of movement in the hockey sequences with Michael Keaton and John Reilly, the Fischer sled was able to mimic a player's skating including radical cuts and rapid starts and stops on the ice. Dolly grips John Miller and Dave Barrow wore track spikes to gain footing while following the action. Kline recalled operating off the rig as quite a ride. Remaining on Fischer's rental inventory after the show wrapped, the Kline Sled (as it became known) worked on numerous commercials and films for years to come.

For Richard Benjamin's *My Stepmother Is an Alien* (1988), Kline was brought in because of his expertise with sci-fi looks; the DP immediately chose to avoid shooting Dan Aykroyd and Kim Basinger with overdone spooky effects. He preferred straight-up master shots which then cut into coverage of dialogue or action. The result was a realistic yet interesting style reminiscent of Kline's early days on pictures like *Bell, Book, and Candle* (1958). Following *Stepmother* with another Benjamin feature, *Downtown* (1990), the cinematographer said he really loved working with the actor turned director as he understood both sides of the camera and was able to comically lead each during his day's work.

As a lifelong student of the martial arts thanks to Ed Parker's Kempo Karate many years back, Kline was excited to be asked by producer Paul Michael Glaser and director Sheldon Lettich to shoot Jean-Claude Van Damme's action flick *Double Impact*. It was filmed on location from Hong Kong to Long Beach's S.S. *Liberty Lane*; Kline treated the story of good and evil twins like one of his Katzman projects. Using split screen mirror-finders on the cameras to produce the double image gags of the brothers' two shots, the cinematographer also incorporated doubles for the actor lensed at an angle while cheating the real Jean-Claude in frame. Relying upon the oldest of movie tricks in the book, Kline's subtle use of ramps, apple boxes, and shorter actors to give Van Damme a bigger appearance was a constant solution to the star's vertical limitations. Kline and Jean Claude (along with the DP's ten-year-old son who was just three inches shorter than the actor) were entering a Westwood premiere for the film when a female fan looked at the three of them with puzzlement. The fan suddenly blurted out to Van Damme, "You're very short, aren't you?" and the demure Belgian took the comment in stride while jokingly telling Kline's son she was talking about him.

Richard said the sequence where they pushed Mercedes sedans off a boat was his favorite. They were initially barred from shooting the gag by the local police until a deal was struck to give the salvaged Benzes to the department, expediting all the waterway clearances. Approaching the cartoon-like violence of the Van Damme actioner with an eye for the form of the fighting craft, Kline applied his karate knowledge to help bring the complicated stunt-action to the screen. Covering the big shootout at the causeway drug factory, he used every camera technique he knew (including slow-motion effects and multiple angles) to give Lettich a punch- and kick-driven picture that would please at the box office.

Kline's final film as a cinematographer was the Rodney Dangerfield comedic vehicle *Meet Wally Sparks* (1996). Wishing to step back from the lens and take up the director's role for the duration of his time spent in Tinseltown, he sought to learn as much as possible from helmer Peter Baldwin (and anyone else who could offer tips on the craft). Returning to film school at U.C.L.A. after hanging up his light meter, Kline studied screenwriting as part of his new Hollywood director's package while completing and marketing eight scripts in the process. Recalling his decision to make that his final shooting assignment, the cinematographer stated that originality was the key to a long career in the movie racket. Having done every conceivable type of picture, he had nothing fresh to add to the medium. He shot *Wally Sparks* as a classic comedy without any clownish lighting effects or camera magic for added laughs; Kline attributed his concept to Dangerfield himself. He found the entertainer warm, engaging and quick with a joke on set: "With Rodney bringing so much spontaneous humor to the script, keeping the photography naturalistic and unnoticed placed that much more focus on him." Remembering one occasion where Dangerfield rose to the challenge, Kline said they were talking on set when a large dog featured in the picture suddenly ran up to Rodney (who had a fear of animals) and jumped up on his back from behind.

The dog then began dry humping the comedian and licking his neck. Trainer Mike Boxer informed the star that the dog didn't have a mean bone in his body, as he was a lover, not a fighter. Turning to wrestle free from the mutt's sloppy overtures, Dangerfield quickly responded, "If he's a lover he must have at least one aggressive bone; in fact, I think he just tried to bury it in me!" Smiling at the memory of his brief time with the talented comic, Kline said it was great fun working with Dangerfield and considers himself lucky to have known him.

Continuing to pursue personal perfection after *Wally Sparks* with his focus on scriptwriting, Kline said he loved the process of being around fellow students and hearing their ideas as to what's "cool" in Hollywood these days. Learning the unpublished insider's rules to the creation of successful screenplays, he realized the writing skills necessary to produce a Hollywood blockbuster were the same for an independent DP to shoot one — originality. Commenting on what he sees as the biggest challenge for the new generation of filmmakers is the industry's increasing demand for perfection of form. Without possessing some variation of beauty compared to the whole when appreciated, Kline felt that if something looks and feels unreal that it must ultimately be artificial to the viewer, and thus rejected.

Still writing and bidding scripts with himself attached as director, Kline embodies the very essence of old-school smarts that are irreplaceable in Cinema city today: experience and mastery of craft from a lifetime in the business. Feeling that it's much easier for current shooters with faster film speeds, lighter equipment, and the sophistication of cameras (including Red Ones, motion control and the absence of studio heads dictating your picture's look), Kline sees recent advancements as game-changing in opening up the field to all comers. "Without years of assistant work or mastering the emulsions and lighting," he reasoned, "people can *easily* shoot a movie thanks to digital technology. It won't look as rich as film. But studios these days could care less."

When thrown one last question about the secret of his success in Tinseltown, the 86-year-old cinematographer looked at me with a glint in his eye and said with his smooth and ageless baritone voice, "Be daring, but just don't get caught at it!"

10

Gaylin Schultz, Key Grip

Gaylin Schultz (1923–2008) was a grip who couldn't say no to a challenge. From race cars to airplanes and boat rigs to rodeos, he was largely responsible for some of the best automotive racing and chase action footage (including aerials) ever put on film. While other key grips avoided difficult set-ups, Gaylin's thing became the ability to bridge the existing practices of camera mounting with intelligent, workable, often cutting-edge concepts that were safe and photographically superior to what came before.

Like many Hollywood grips during the 1940s, the locally born Schultz served his country during World War II, enlisting in the Navy and assigned to a Pearl Harbor submarine base for the duration of the war. Sworn to I.A.T.S.E.'s Local 80 two years after the conflict's end in 1947 (by introduction from his grip father, Walter E. Schultz, an original union member since its beginning ten years earlier), Gaylin labored on the gangs at Goldwyn Studios under the watchful eye of department head Bill Thomas. Recalled to duty for Korea in 1951, he was attached to the destroyer tender U.S.S. *Ajax*, where his orders involved the mobile equipping of combat ships in the South China Sea. He learned to master every crane-arm, winch, and diesel motor for moving cargo on and off the boat; by tour's end in 1952, Schultz was a natural candidate for grip work on motion pictures, based on his knowledge of rigging loads.

While operating a small gas station in Palmdale and learning his new trade on the occasional night-shift at Goldwyn Studios, Gaylin's first break came when tasked with tarping-in a working generator for a midnight call in the pouring rain. News of the chore's successful completion (rigging heavy canvas tarps over wooden frames without binding) rapidly made its way back to studio bosses who took notice that he had saved them money pushing the crew to continue, despite the foul weather. As a result of the clutch leadership exhibited that evening, Bill Thomas (who knew Schultz's dad from the old days) began mentoring "the kid" and seeing to it that he always had a job.

By Hollywood's big production breakout of '55, Gaylin was rising rapidly among the ranks, working as a company grip for MGM's best keys Carl Reed and Dick Boreland. Tutored in the use of everything from Movieola dollies to stage cranes, he showed a capacity for quick learning that placed the complicated camera platforms in his hands years ahead of his peers.

One of Schultz's earliest out-of-town features was John Ford's *The Searchers*, filmed on location in Utah's Monument Valley. The first challenge for the newbie grip was adjusting to the region's 110 degree temperatures. Hired by key grip Carl Reed to help the older studio mechanics lay heavy sleeper track for crane and dolly work, Gaylin was also manning five-foot-across "shinny-boards," providing fill light to reduce facial shadow. Sleeping in tent cities amid the Valley's ancient plateaus, crew accommodations (with the addition of wooden cots to lie on) weren't much different from the cowboys' lives depicted in the film, including meals. Morning consisted of everything from steak and eggs, to bacon, biscuits, and coffee; box lunches were served at noon break, and an equally robust supper included sides of pit-turned beef, whole roasted chickens, or simple cheese sandwiches if that was your thing.

Gaylin recalled John Wayne staying in character between set-ups. As Schultz was laying sleeper track for a crane move one afternoon, the actor observed the shirtless 29-year-old grip sweating profusely in the midst of his labor. "Pace yourself, Pilgrim," the Duke said in his laconic tone, "the desert hurries for no man."

Becoming a well-regarded rookie entrenched with Goldwyn's grip department, Gaylin was assigned to the Joseph Mankiewicz gangster musical *Guys and Dolls* in late '55. He was tasked with operating the stage crane's hot-seat (driver) on the myriad of musical numbers transitioning from the original stage play to the film. Covering such tunes as "Take Back Your Mink," "Luck Be a Lady" and "Sit Down You're Rocking the Boat" (among others), Schultz had to move in response to musical cues (and the director's) to hit his marks at the same moment the actors hit theirs. Controlled like a car with an accelerator, foot brake, and steering wheel, the rig's considerable size necessitated an anticipatory touch to its movement; in coordination with the actors, it became a fine dance of spatial judgment and timing to make it all work.

Landing additional crane-op bookings, Gaylin was assigned to William Self's *Schlitz Playhouse of the Stars* in 1956. Exposed to future A-list actors including Lee Marvin, Vincent Price, and John Ireland, he quickly learned to perform under pressure. "Working 'the arm' every week on the series," Schultz said, "taught me to adjust to each actor's timing in the moment, not just going by rehearsal."

Again moving up the Hollywood food chain, Gaylin was plucked from the ranks of company grips for his first best boy position. Brought in by key grip John Livesley for the Gregory Peck western drama *The Big Country* in 1957, he was now responsible for scheduling and hiring of crew, providing equipment and dealing with production. Always a stepping stone towards the key job, the number two slot was a coveted assignment. Directed by William Wyler and photographed by Franz Planer (of *The Caine Mutiny* and *The Mountain*), the picture was filmed in the Mojave Desert between July and August of 1957 during a record heat wave with temperatures in excess of 120 degrees. "After two weeks of exteriors in Red Rock Canyon," Schultz said with a grin, "my tan was so dark I could pass as a background Indian with no problem."

To continue building his production experience, Gaylin was sent to Manhattan for Clifford Odets' *Sweet Smell of Success*. Hired to operate a portable crab-dolly for world class cinematographer James Wong Howe around the city's cramped locations (such as the 21 Club and a bustling Times Square packed with people), the young grip was in awe of the caliber of acting before him. "Watching Burt Lancaster play J.J. Hunsecker from six feet away," Schultz sighed, "I suddenly realized how much I liked making movies."

Remembering Howe's kid glove treatment of grips (the charming cinematographer adored them for their problem-solving prowess), Gaylin recalled him often thanking the boys at day's end with an expensive cigar. Not a stogie man himself, he would accept the

10. Gaylin Schultz, Key Grip 195

In this whimsical photograph of cast and crew from 1959's *A Hole in the Head* (with gag arrows included), a young Gaylin Schultz can be seen on the back row (second from left) holding onto a ladder. In the second row are Thelma Ritter, Edward G. Robinson, Eleanor Parker, director Frank Capra, Carolyn Jones, and an unidentified man. Front row center, seated with legs crossed, is the film's star, Frank Sinatra, flanked by child actor Eddie Hodges and playwright-screenwriter Arnold Schulman. Leaning into frame (bottom left) is sound man extraordinaire Fred Lau, whose credits also included *Some Like It Hot*, *The Apartment*, and *West Side Story* (courtesy Gaylin Schultz).

gift to avoid insult, secretly giving the buck-apiece Cubans to the Teamsters, who loved them. "I built up so much good faith with those cigars," Schultz laughed, "that my dolly was always off the truck first, no matter if it was needed or not!"

Another directing legend Gaylin was exposed to was Frank Capra. He was crewed as best boy on the Frank Sinatra vehicle *A Hole in the Head*; the mostly shot-in-Miami melodrama had its share of rough going: equipment difficulties in the fine sand, and the star being unable to work in the mornings or with crowds of bystanders watching. Co-producers Capra and Sinatra decided to complete the project back in Hollywood. Ultimately dressing Santa Monica Beach with twenty-five tons of white playbox sand and imported Royal Palm trees to double as Miami, the production logistics improved but the picture still had issues that a location change couldn't fix.

Among the films that Schultz did before 1960, Lewis Milestone's *Pork Chop Hill* was one of the toughest. Featuring Gregory Peck, Rip Torn, George Peppard, and Martin Lan-

Positioned on a ladder while holding a 4×4 double on Frank Sinatra, star of *A Hole in the Head* (1959), Schultz (shirtless with sunglasses) recalled those location days as physically difficult. He was challenged by the beach's fine sand and constant sun; the simplest of tasks required multiple grips, as evidenced by the "support crew" aiding him with the large scrim (courtesy Gaylin Schultz).

dau in his first role, the experience proved beneficial as Schultz was so efficient at best boy that DP Edwin Dupar field-promoted him to second unit key grip during the first week of filming. Shot in the winter of 1958 on a forbidding half-mile-high rock-face in the Alabama Hills area of Lone Pine, California, the Korean War battle scenes required shooting off of a huge McAllister dolly to capture the motion shots on the fly. The 400-pound studio-beast was hauled from shot to shot; the labor intensive process (employing four grips and 2 × 12 planks) became untenable with the ruggedness of the terrain. Putting his past naval cargo expertise to use, Schultz rigged up a carry sling attached to a massive old Army tractor that allowed the McAllister to be quickly motored anywhere Milestone called for it. Saving time and the backs of his men, Gaylin was exhibiting the type of improvisational thinking which would ultimately become his trademark.

Schultz was assigned to the Gary Cooper Western *Man of the West* in December of 1958 (again tasked as best boy grip). One morning his set duties placed him next to Cooper trading dialogue with a youthful Jack Lord: "Lord was playing a no-good type who had a knife to Cooper's throat." Eviscerated by a prop blade that squirts blood (following several takes and being soaked with the sticky red syrup in the process), the actor turned to Gaylin (who was manning a reflector) and said, "If he cuts any deeper, mister, you grab my pistol and shoot him, ya hear?"

On *A Hole in the Head* (1959), helmer Frank Capra was less than happy with star Frank Sinatra's unenthusiastic commitment to the project. Production started in October 1958 in Miami Beach; so little was accomplished on location that the two producing Franks (Capra and Sinatra) decided to return to Hollywood. Beach work was finished by doubling Santa Monica for Florida with imported palms to match the previously established footage. Schultz (right) waits to set a 4 × 4 net while Capra and Sinatra (center) talk about how to film the next scene (courtesy Gaylin Schultz).

Cinematographer Sam Leavitt (center of frame, behind star Gregory Peck in costume, in long-sleeved shirt and fedora) works on lighting a midday sequence for director Lewis Milestone's *Pork Chop Hill* (1958). Filmed in the rugged Alabama Hills of Lone Pine, California, the picture proved a challenge for best boy Gaylin Schultz (in background, at the top of the photograph in white T-shirt and shorts) as just moving the dolly between shots became a major undertaking due to the location's steep grades. Hiring every tough grip he could find for the labor-intensive call, Schultz employed lifting legend Big John Livesley (to Peck's right in a ball cap and white shirt) to put his 6'7", 300-pound physique into the work. Note the pump-up dolly on the bottom right (courtesy Gaylin Schultz).

The best boy duties on *Man of the West* revolved around sleeper track and shiny boards (including men to operate them in rugged locations such as Red Rock Canyon State Park); Schultz was noticed by Walter Mirisch, who thought him the best grip on the crew for his hustle. Mirisch filed away Gaylin's card for future reference; Schultz was hired by the producer just three years later to key his own feature.

Among the pictures that Schultz manned during the '50s, Billy Wilder's comedic classic *Some Like It Hot* was perhaps the most iconic. Pushing dolly at the request of DP Charlie Lang, all were put to the test by Marilyn Monroe, who experienced trouble with her dialogue. She was unable to deliver the line, "Sugar, it's me!"; a forty-take attempt not only drove Wilder to cigar-chewing, but pushed Gaylin's physical boundaries with the repeated thirty-foot dolly move required for each take. "Finally," Schultz said, "the director had Monroe's lines placed on a big chalk board, written in ten-inch-high letters just out of frame."

As his reputation grew with success from each new project, Gaylin's career arc was on the rise. Introduced by Lang to cinematographer Leon Shamroy, who was then shooting *Porgy and Bess* at Goldwyn, Schultz was tapped on the spot for second unit crane work being filmed that week. Fondly remembering doing both pictures at one time, he said, "It was terrific. Everyone from Sammy Davis, Jr., to Pearl Bailey was visiting us on the Monroe film. Likewise, Tony Curtis and Jack Lemmon were walking around *Porgy and Bess* dressed in drag, when Otto Preminger caught them mugging in the background while Pearl Bailey was doing a number. Cutting the take at song's end, Preminger said in his thick German accent, 'You two ugly broads, beat it. This is no comedy!'"

Talking about the challenges of operating crane on *Porgy and Bess*, Schultz revealed that during the complex dance routines (beautifully choreographed by Hermes Pan), he was using a combination of the music and the dancers' movements as a timing cue for positioning the arm: "Adding the playback gave me a feel for the shot that matched what I was hearing. As each take was slightly different, my adjustments could mirror that variation, and compensate for it as needed."

Returning to skills acquired in the Navy, Gaylin was hired by cameraman Lamar Boren as an underwater grip for the Ivan Tors–produced television series *Sea Hunt* in 1960. Operating everything from on-deck shiny boards to tying down underwater cameras (wearing only tanks and a swim suit), Schultz provided not just illumination for Lloyd Bridges' deepest dives, but additional safety for the actor as well. It was filmed everywhere from Marine Land of the Pacific (during the pilot) to the Bahamas later in the series and parts of Catalina Island (where Gaylin purchased a house during the show, then retired there some forty years later). His diving was yet another accomplishment that distinguished him among his peers.

Reaffirmed as one of Bill Thomas' favorites on the Goldwyn lot, Schultz was requested by producer Ed Small for best boy and second unit key grip duties on *Jack the Giant Killer*. The movie cashed in on the earlier box office bang of Ray Harryhausen's *The 7th Voyage of Sinbad*. With the work encompassing in-studio miniatures as well as rugged locations off the southern tip of Catalina Island, Schultz's second unit did everything from build scaffolding in the water to mounting cameras in the crow's nest to get the necessary live-action stuff. Recalling the rigors of the island's windward side while getting plate shots for the pterodactyl's sequence in the cliffs, Gaylin said that DP David Horsley became sea-sick when shooting on the water. "In between dashing to the bow to be ill," he laughed, "the poor guy would barely get a look through the eye-piece waiting for his shot, before quickly calling action, then losing his lunch again."

Hired by key grip Carl Reed for his third Billy Wilder movie, *The Apartment* (1960), Gaylin was once again responsible as best boy. Recalling a scene where Jack Lemmon gets decked by real-life tough guy Johnny Seven, he said the punch was supposed to miss the actor but accidentally connected with Lemmon, knocking him to the ground in a heap. Rising after rubbing his face for a few seconds, he turned to Schultz (who was first by the actor's side after the blow) and jokingly said, "Are you going to let him get away with that?" Looking over at the still glaring Seven, Schultz replied, "You bet I am," cracking everyone up.

Schultz's next crane job was one of his most challenging. Drafted to cover a few weeks of pick-up shots on *West Side Story* (while director Robert Wise filmed in downtown L.A. doubling for New York), he was again making crane moves to music. Remembering Wise calling for playback, then hearing the "Tonight" melody booming through loudspeakers all day long, Gaylin heard it so much that it continued to echo in his ears when lying down to sleep that night. On his last day on the feature (which ended with a stirring musical routine of "A Boy Like That"), the helmer came to Schultz with a stern look on his face. "I just wanted to tell you," he said, "that your crane work is marvelous and having you has been a pleasure. Thank you." This meant more to Gaylin than an Oscar; the eventual recipient of an SOC lifetime achievement award felt that receiving a personal gesture from Wise (in front of the crew) to be among the classiest highlights of his career.

In the summer of 1961, Schultz returned to rugged location work for the Rat Pack vehicle *Sergeants 3*; there, a connection was made with second unit director Jack Reddish that would last a decade. A hip rehash of *Gunga Din*, *Sergeants 3* featured Frank Sinatra, Dean Martin, Peter Lawford, Sammy Davis Jr. and Joey Bishop doing their thing on the big screen. Brought in as second unit key grip for DP Winton Hoak's filming of the exterior stunts (including the standard galloping horses and falls from roofs), Schultz was also challenged with rigging a camera to an out-of-control buckboard. Schultz and Reddish gave the sequences far more than scripted.

A challenging opportunity came for Schultz in 1962 on John Frankenheimer's political thriller *The Manchurian Candidate*. Crewed by key Dick Boreland to execute some cutting-edge shots designed by avant-garde cinematographer Lionel Lindon, many of the picture's flashbacks were done with a surrealistic twist that was often as much the work of Schultz's dolly as that of art director Richard Sylbert's pen.

While filming the hydrangeas lecture, for example, encompassing the sweet garden club ladies enjoying the speaker, Gaylin moved the camera with such a gentle flow that it momentarily put the viewer at ease. Transitioning into studies of the real audience as they existed, we are shown an assemblage of stone-faced political types and military brass from a consortium of communist countries including China, the Soviet Union, and North Korea. The resulting contrast between Schultz first moving at a creep, then crisply sliding his dolly to each face, added a voyeuristic dimension that set the whole scene. He was also tasked with figuring out an approach shot for Major Marco's flashback (where he remembers Shaw shoot two Americans during part of the enemy's brainwashing demonstration); Frankenheimer asked his dolly man for a compelling move to sell the scene's horror. Surrounding the actor with curved track, then executing a 360-degree dolly move, Schultz's answer acted as a visual punch in the stomach as we see the guy shot in the forehead, with a splatter of blood hitting the wall upon impact.

Regarding everyone's desire to contribute to the picture, Gaylin vouched for Frank Sinatra's commitment to craft after witnessing him smash his hand through a tabletop during a brutal fight sequence with Henry Silva playing the assassin, Chunjin. Cued by Lindon for a series of rapidly shifting dolly moves (to cover the scuffle's aggressive pacing), Schultz recalled hearing the bones break the moment Sinatra's fist hit the wood. Continuing to film the remainder of the set-ups, the star informed no one of his injuries: "Until they told everyone later that Frank had broken two fingers, the rest of the crew didn't have a clue."

Keeping his crane chops in tune, Schultz took work on the short-lived CBS series *The New Loretta Young Show* in September of 1962. Operating the arm during the half-hour episodes, Gaylin did 26 weeks on the variety program until its untimely demise in the winter of '63. Gaylin's crane was often Young's main camera. The *New Show* was filmed in front of a live studio audience, and Young used Schultz to feed her one-liners while entertaining the folks in between set-ups. He was fond of the series' star (and she of her crews); when the show folded in just six months, the gracious entertainer gave the company parting gifts of hundred dollar bonuses and a fifth of Scotch, with signed "Thank You" cards attached. "She was wonderful," Gaylin sighed with the look of an excited fan-boy on his face. "Doing the jokes with her was fun, 'cause she never made me the butt of the gag, I was just the next step to telling it."

Gaylin returned for John Frankenheimer's next film *Seven Days in May*, once again crewed as a dolly operator for Dick Boreland. Shot in 1963 on location in Washington, D.C., Lake Arrowhead and San Diego, California, the political thriller was another statement of warning from the dark helmer, sandwiched between *The Manchurian Candidate* and *The Train* during his thirty-feature career. Although President Kennedy was a Frankenheimer fan, intelligence types blocked the idea of Capitol Hill cooperation, denying all filming requests with the exception of the White House footage grabbed while JFK was in Hyannis Port. Due to the lack of official help, cinematographer Ellsworth Fredricks prompted Gaylin to engage in clandestine measures such as rigging a Panavision 70 camera in a blacked-out station wagon, to film sensitive DC locations including the FBI building and the Senate. Proven so effective at blending in, the set-up was used to shoot multiple sequences of Kirk Douglas in a Marine colonel's uniform on the steps of the Pentagon, even capturing high-ranking officers saluting when crossing the actor's path. None realized they were in a motion picture. "Had we been caught," Schultz laughed, "it might have been serious, as no one from Paramount knew what we were up to."

Requested for a fourth feature with the Wilder troupe in 1963, Schultz was assigned to operate crane on the Jack Lemmon comedy *Irma La Douce*, shooting at Goldwyn Studios. "Even though Joe LaShelle was the cinematographer," Gaylin recalled, "most of the crane direction came from Billy Wilder himself, because by this time I pretty much knew what he wanted." The Rue Casa Nova apartments were on three converging streets (connected by 48 building fronts on Goldwyn's back lot); the director used Gaylin's crane for coverage of the expansive sets. One scene which taxed talent and crew alike was a two-story move following Nestor (Lemmon) as he is brought down a stairway in manacles, then taken off to prison. It required exact timing between the actor's descent and the start of the crane move to follow. Schultz's anticipatory expertise of visualizing the arms placement before the shot saved Wilder a lot of time and effort by calculating his photographic options on the fly.

Gaining prowess in everything from crane operation to key grip since beginning in 1947, Gaylin was about to work again with the producer who would come to appreciate him as none other had to date — Walter Mirisch. The opportunity came his way in the fall of 1964 when he was hired by director John Sturges for his military sci-fi picture *The Satan Bug*. He was tapped to operate crab dolly (and second unit key grip for the stunts, including the Los Angeles evacuation sequences). Schultz's biggest challenge on the feature was rigging the camera for the helicopter fall climax. "Before such devices as Nelson Tyler's aerial mount became available," he explained, "locking-down a camera for flying shots was a major undertaking." He manufactured the threaded tie-down fittings in his own shop; they were used to screw the camera mount to the frame of the aircraft, which not only kept it rock solid but allowed for quick placement of the hardware anywhere on the chopper. During the Dodger Stadium panic scenes, there were aerial shots sixty feet above the crowd done at over 90 miles an hour without a single camera rig malfunction.

Schultz was being gradually brought along by Mirisch (who had taken a liking to him). It was only a matter of time before he would be keying entire productions on his own. Returning to the Sturges gang in late '64 for *The Hallelujah Trail*, photographed by Bob Surtees with Ultra Panavision-70, Gaylin was engaged by producer Bob Relyea for second unit key grip duties and first company best boy chores, shooting in such difficult locations as Ship Rock, New Mexico, and Alabama Hills in Lone Pine, California. Schultz remembered one action sequence in Lone Pine of a whiskey wagon crashing over a cliff, resulting in a tragic outcome. Stuntman Bill Williams and a partner were to leap from the buckboard at the last moment; he was accidentally hung up on the seat and was crushed upon impact. Gaylin said sadly, "There was just no helping Bill, while the other guy walked away."

On a lighter (and wetter) note, while bivouacking in tents on the high plains of Ship Rock, New Mexico, the company experienced the area's worst torrential rain in fifty years. It washed away roads, sets and shelters of all kinds. Gaylin and the guys were called upon during the downpour to try and save some of the canvas structures. The only things salvaged by night's end were some tent halves nailed to wooden pallet floors. The following morning, when meeting Sturges and the department heads amid two inches of standing water and tattered sets, costume designer Edith Head wore an ankle-length rain jacket replete with knee-high boots. Laying down walking planks so Miss Head wouldn't have to traverse the muck, Schultz and his grips leap-frogged ahead of her with the boards, creating a comical dance for the trio, as she remained spotless while the guys were covered up to their knees in mud.

One motion picture that proved to be an extraordinary opportunity for Gaylin Schultz was Melville Shavelson's *Cast a Giant Shadow*. Involved with many aspects of the project (including rounding-up suitable crews and equipment for the picture's international locations in Israel and Cinecita Studios in Rome), Gaylin was further tasked as key grip, paymaster, and multi-language location fixer. Devising a simple way for everyone from the Italian lighting crews and the American production personnel to communicate (including Israeli military types in charge of the locations), Schultz incorporated a combination of hands-on-parroting for the first few days; then repeated usage of words slowly bridged the language gap for all.

The big name cast included John Wayne, Kirk Douglas, Frank Sinatra, Yul Brynner, and Angie Dickinson, Gaylin recalled winding up with the chore of showing the dailies as well. Originally brought on the project by second unit director Jack Reddish (who sold the 39-year-old Schultz as a "key everything"), he would soon parlay the daunting feature's success into many more A-list jobs.

Opportunity came in 1965 on Walter Mirisch's next movie *The Fortune Cookie*, Schultz's fifth outing with director Billy Wilder. Gaylin was assigned to key the picture's second unit action scenes, including the football footage grabbed during the Cleveland Browns' 17-point loss to the Vikings at Municipal Stadium that year.

Laughing about a splinter-unit comprised of him and Jack Lemmon (shooting a nighttime driving montage of Hinkle frantically searching for Boom Boom), Schultz said, "It was Jack behind the wheel with me turning on the camera locked-off in a single on him from the back seat. In between takes, we talked about everything from the Dodgers to *Irma La Douce* and got so lost in the process we had to ask a cop for directions back to basecamp."

Earning his keep the next day, Schultz solved a safety problem incurred while Lemmon and his stunt double John Moio were shooting the film's bed-jumping sequences where Hinkle rips off his back-brace, performing acrobatic somersaults to the joy of Cliff Osmond (in the role of private eye Purkey). The bed frame jumped so dangerously that a real injury was imminent. Appealing for help, Reddish was amazed when Gaylin solved the problem with heavy sandbags laid inside the bed, then nailed the entire rig to the stage floor.

Schultz again worked with Jack Lemmon when assigned for interiors on MGM's *How to Murder Your Wife*. Contracted as best boy grip on the show, his job description grew to include security one morning when filming a racy scene between Lemmon and Virna Lisi. With Lemmon sitting undershirt-clad on the bed and Lisi nude beneath the sheets as scripted, a surprise visit from her real-life husband sent things spiraling out of control as the sight of his wife lying next to another guy (movie or not) sent him into a rage. He chased Lemmon off the stage and down the road; it took a gaggle of security guards to convince the 6'2" pro soccer player that this was "all in a day's work" in Tinseltown. Finding Jack hiding inside a trash closet behind the stage, they laughingly convinced him it was safe to return to work.

After best boying the 1966 Bob Hope bank spoof *Eight on the Lam*, Schultz was tapped to push dolly on Walter Mirisch's new feature *Fitzwilly*, moving the camera for DP Joe Biroc on the Delbert Mann–directed tongue-in-cheek caper.

Perhaps an ironic foreshadowing of his success to come (at least title-wise) was his work on the comedic musical *How to Succeed in Business Without Really Trying*. Assigned to the David Swift production based on his continuing relationship with Mirisch and his prowess with the dolly, Gaylin became cinematographer Burnett Guffys's "ace in the hole" when it came to shooting the difficult musical numbers. "Having done *Guys and Dolls* as well as *West Side Story*," Schultz explained, "I knew the importance of matching my dolly moves to the tempo of the number. Without that perfect timing, you can work all day and not get it."

Gaylin's biggest break occurred when called by Jack Reddish to take over key grip duties on *The Thomas Crown Affair*, after Morris Rosen (of *High Noon* and *Man with a Golden Arm* fame) suffered a fatal heart attack during the first week's filming. It was a case of one man's misfortune being another's "window of opportunity." Schultz was engaged at the suggestion of Mirisch, who fondly recalled his heroic action from *How to Murder Your Wife* a few years earlier.

His first day on the film was a challenge that would foreshadow much of his career success to come. He was tasked with staging a set of moving shots in an open field featuring a Schweizer SGS-1 sailplane for the picture's opening montage; the images required fly-by coverage of the sleek machine swooping low over the horizon, and then rapidly descending into a graceful landing, with Steve McQueen and Faye Dunaway exiting the craft at scene's end. Told to relax by Rosen's remaining grips (who resented the outsider taking over), Schultz was informed that the shot was already worked out by their boss. Patiently, he watched in horror as a Honda motorcycle (carrying an operator sitting backwards with a hand-held Arriflex camera) attempted to get the shot, but failed miserably with a dozen takes of unusable footage. Rapidly falling behind his shooting schedule with nothing in the can for his morning's work, cinematographer Haskell Wexler thought he had the solution when he got producer Norman Jewison to secure a Cadillac convertible for use as a camera-car. Again the results were poor as the heavy vehicle fishtailed worse than the Honda at half the speed. By lunchtime, there wasn't a single printable take; the mood in the chow line was less than festive. Instead of eating with the still glum grips, Schultz borrowed a heavy-duty 6 by 6 wheeled military work-truck from transportation; it was originally used for laying power cable in rough terrain locations. Removing the passenger seat first and mounting a camera in its place, Gaylin and the one grip who agreed to help, John Bearsdick, rigged two stout tow-arms from the rear of the truck's vertical A-frame, then attached the glider to them, keeping the support hardware out of the shot. Allowing for speeds in excess of 40 miles an hour before the towed glider would buck to become airborne, Schultz's cobbled together process trailer gave them the shot they wanted without the complications of multiple vehicles. Although it was ungainly in appearance, Wexler's initial skepticism was quickly replaced with thanks after seeing the set-up through a lens. "If it hadn't worked," Gaylin chuckled, "I think I would have been on the next plane back home. But as it happened, that one shot kind of made me; for the rest of the movie, I was walking on water, so to speak."

In addition to impressing producers Jewison and Mirisch with his ability to get the job done, Schultz also made an impression on Steve McQueen, who would ultimately be instrumental in hiring him for some of the most important films in his career. Recalling a moment of bonding between the two men (who both loved the mechanics of machinery and fast automobiles), Schultz said he was installing a camera mount on a Ferrari 275 GTS Spyder that Faye Dunaway drove in the picture, when the actor walked up and began observing him carefully padding all the straps and hardware which might come into contact with the pricey sport car's paint job. After watching Gaylin in silence for a few moments, McQueen said, "Christ, Schultz, you're an artist!" This was possibly the start of their friendship. Schultz said the talented actor trusted him implicitly from that day forward to do things right.

Following a six-week interlude on a dreadful Hal Barrett racing picture called *Changes*, he subsequently returned to the fold at Goldwyn Studios as a hammer on the television series *The Fugitive* for key grip Ray Rich. Starring David Janssen, the weekly episodic kept him busy with its wild plot twists and location-heavy shooting requiring extra grips; however, the level of expertise needed was hardly a challenge, compared to his motion picture work. In an ironic twist of fate, Schultz went from getting laid off his last television series to being hired for the most groundbreaking feature he would ever key: *Bullitt*.

One of his most photographically exciting pictures, *Bullitt* was produced by Philip D'Antoni, the same guy responsible for two other top-of-the-list car-action films, *The French Connection* and *The Seven Ups*. Schultz was brought in by Steve McQueen and his Solar Films production team (including Jack Reddish) following Gaylin's success on *The Thomas Crown Affair*. This time the inventive key grip cut loose in pursuit of a concept that McQueen had been waiting to do since his start in Hollywood: driving fast, and being well photographed while doing it. Not satisfied with the trailer shots or rear projection concepts in use by the studios for vehicular action up to that point, cinematographer Bill Fraker and Schultz came up with a whole new method to shoot, totally outside the box for its time: live-action, with cameras in and on the cars. To accomplish this, Gaylin incorporated a system of speed-rail pipe sections and starter-plates bolted to the frame of the vehicles; then dampened the structure with rubber gaskets to allow filming while driving at a high rate of speed, without the distracting vibrations normally produced. Schultz used the same erector set–type of hardware for the '68 Mustangs and the Dodge Charger; he recalled the rigs were so solid that even while doing camera tests in excess of 100 miles an hour, the car's odometer could be clearly read when shown in dailies. "The point was," Schultz explained, "to get close-ups of Steve [McQueen] behind the wheel at those speeds, and it worked great!"

Another Fraker-Schultz collaboration was the use of smaller Arriflex cameras which could be mounted inside the cars, for the action scenes. Unlike the Mitchell-BNC or Panavision rigs common during that time in Movieland, the Arris were used more for the hand-held guerrilla type of motion picture–making practiced in Europe where they are manufactured. With more than ten percent of the film's iconic chase scene involving close-ups of McQueen, placement of the lens *inside* the Mustang became of paramount importance. Utilizing speed-rail while bolting it through the car's floor, Schultz was able to stick the camera anywhere Fraker wanted it. In addition to camera placement, stunt coordinator Carey Loftin brought in world class drivers Loren Janes and Bud Eakins (McQueen's pal from *The Great Escape* who did the motorcycle into the barbed wire gag), to help with the dangerous stunts in the Mustang, including laying down a bike mid-chase. McQueen devised the idea of tipping back the rear view mirror in the car when the *other* guys were driving (obscuring their faces), versus always positioning the mirror down to see when he was behind the wheel.

One shot demonstrating this team effort (both the Mustang's performance in the actor's hands as well as Gaylin's proprietary camera mounts) was a section in the chase where McQueen over-ran his line of pursuit, failing to execute a sweeping right turn behind the Charger. With the Mustang beefed-up to a 390 cubic inch V-8 engine pumping out 325 horses and fitted with racing suspension and brakes by car builder Max Balchowsky, the actor came to a screeching halt and then shifted into reverse, smoking the back tires in the process of regaining traction. Then he lurched forward with enough G's to loosen bridgework when the clutch fully engaged. The inside shot of McQueen is still rock solid as though it was done on stage, rather than in a moving car on the street. "Loren Janes and Steve were putting that Mustang through hell," Schultz said, "but we never lost a camera or had to stop shooting because a mount came loose!"

Taking director Peter Yates a month to plan and three weeks to photograph, the *Bullitt* chase scene provided just nine minutes and 42 seconds of film. Cementing its place in cinematic history as one of the finest automotive pursuits of its time (or any for that matter), the vehicular action in *Bullitt* would pale in comparison to what was being discussed in hushed voices toward picture's end between Schultz and McQueen: the application of Gaylin's camera-mounting magic to making a movie of the fastest car race in motor sports: *Le Mans*. Gaylin had demonstrated to Reddish and McQueen with *Bullitt* that something like *Le Mans* was possible; the movie star told Gaylin that he was going to work on the idea, but first had to find funding, as he didn't want to use his own cash.

Schultz was hired to key Daniel Mann's *A Dream of Kings* during a frigid cold snap in Chicago with DP Richard Kline in November of '69. The job proved to be a test of climate versus grip fortitude for Gaylin Schultz. His second outing with Kline, the feature starred Anthony Quinn and Irene Papas and included many urban locations that would prove difficult to the Southern Cal native, in the midst of bouts of freezing rain. Recalling the need to lay track for an eighty-foot dolly move on top of the ice-impacted sidewalk, Gaylin went to set dressing and bartered a roll of carpet runner to make a dry path for his footing: "It cost me a bottle of good Scotch, but to keep my feet dry, it was worth every drop!"

Producer Walter Mirisch hired Gaylin to operate dolly on Blake Edwards' *The Party*. Lensed by old-school pro Lucien Ballard (who shot everything from Three Stooges shorts to *The Sons of Katie Elder*), *The Party* was the first collaboration between Edwards and Peter Sellers, and as such, a learning experience for talent and crew alike. Gaylin and the boys came to appreciate Sellers' quirky timing and embraced it with the best coverage they could, allowing him as many takes as Edwards wanted.

Schultz's next project of importance came in the summer of 1969 on director Sidney Furie's ode to motor-cross racing, *Big Fauss, Little Halsey*. Starring Robert Redford as Knox and Michael J. Pollard as his gullible sidekick, the picture's beautiful photography supplied by DP Ralph Woolsey incorporated state-of-the-art camera mount technology on everything from motorcycles to helicopters. Working with Nelson Tyler's gyro-stabilized control head to obtain stunning aerial footage of the riders racing through Arizona's Sonoran Desert, Gaylin came up with a few mechanical tricks of his own in the difficult shooting environment. He handled second unit key grip responsibilities, including camera mounts for the bikes that consisted of his usual aluminum pipe set-ups connected by tie-down hardware then bolted to a riser; Schultz's erector-set system proved to be the answer to the ground-bound shots in the film too. Incorporating special stabilizing gaskets to smooth the jolts of the trail, the mount worked so well that Woolsey utilized it for over-the-shoulder and reverse POVs of the riders in excess of 80 miles an hour, and it still looked railroad track–smooth. Producing a whole sequence of hare and hound shots of the motorcycles vying for position in the bush (brilliantly inter-cut by editor Argyle Nelson Jr.), Gaylin once again attributed much of his success to Arriflex cameras for their ability to be rigged anywhere.

Based upon positive work experience with Arris in the past (specifically on *Bullitt* and *Big Fauss, Little Halsey*), Schultz realized that for his next big picture on *Le Mans*, he would have to engineer more than just static car mounts to please his boss Steve McQueen. The effort encompassed everything from high-speed camera cars to electromagnetic jib-arms, to capture the racing action of the groundbreaking film. Approached by McQueen and Jack Reddish while shooting *Bullitt*, Gaylin was an early hire to the *tour de force* action picture,

10. Gaylin Schultz, Key Grip

with everything relying upon his hardware. The car-mount master went with what he knew when creating new rigs for the film at hand. Incorporating three Arriflex cameras on a Porsche 908 race car for one set-up, the vehicle (driven by team drivers Herbert Linge and Jonathan Williams) was actually entered by Solar Productions to compete in the race while filming. Completing 282 laps and placing ninth overall, the level of competition for the drivers was real, with the 908 coming in second for the P-3.0 class, despite the added weight of the cameras and batteries and blowing a starter near the race's finish. They substituted Lola T-70 cars disguised as the more expensive exotics for the film's crash sequences (recreated under racing circumstances at speed on the closed LeMans circuit); the edited footage from the cars flowed seamlessly, giving the viewer a voyeuristic look at a high speed race out of control.

To make it all happen, Gaylin took the extreme step of blending into the actual movie, giving him the ability to tend to the gear while in the film. Working as part of the pit crew (complete with white mechanic's coveralls), Schultz rotated six Arriflex cameras during the race, thanks to his custom-manufactured quick-release dove-tail camera mount, ingeniously

On *Le Mans* (1971) head grip Gaylin Schultz uses his hand to check for unwanted windshield reflections while a second, "low mode" camera is positioned for additional coverage on the Porsche 917. French director of photography Rene Guissart, Jr. (left) and producer/first assistant director/second unit director Jack Reddish (unzipped jacket next to Guissart) pay close attention to the work at hand. Notice the "forest" of aluminum CNC pipe struts (as well as the cantilevered rigging attached to pulleys) utilized to mount multiple Arriflex cameras for the shot. This proprietary hardware and its implementation was mostly Schultz's concept (courtesy Gaylin Schultz).

With its Arriflex camera framed on a close-up of the Porsche 917 racecar used in *Le Mans* (1971), one can see the elegant strength built into the rig, including the use of 1.5-inch aluminum pipe, steel struts, and machined couplers holding it all in place. Schultz's design included a circular mounting plate which allowed for vibration-free close-ups of the star, even while the car was going in excess of 130 mph (courtesy Gaylin Schultz).

held tight by two half-inch bolts removed in seconds with the blast of an air-wrench. Because he replaced an actual Porsche crew member to get his position, Gaylin not only had to change-out the spent Arris, but was responsible for the voided pit-gig as well: cleaning the windshield, mirrors, and gauge glass inside the race car each time it stopped.

As the cameras on the Porsche 908 picture-car had to be totally concealed (because of other units filming the race with long shots), Schultz incorporated lens placement inside of a hood scoop for the forward viewing unit, while the rear shooting Arriflexes were camouflaged among the exhaust manifold intakes, nestled amid the back suspension. They were activated via remote control trigger by the drivers; the images recorded had the real feel of competition owing to the timing of the racers' camera use, while vying to beat each other out on film. "With the whole package powered by a series of hidden camera batteries bolted down behind the driver's seat," Gaylin said, "all I had to focus on was popping out the Arriflex with its full magazine intact and then bolt another fresh one in its place." With no manufacturer of specialized clamps and camera plates in existence at that time, he had to fabricate all his own mounting hardware at John Weyer's Racing Garage in England, where they also converted a Ford GT-40 racer to an open cockpit camera car capable of keeping up with the Porsches and Ferraris in the long straightaways.

Gaylin was responsible for the safe operation of all gear he attached to the race cars

10. Gaylin Schultz, Key Grip

Having a conversation about the safe operating speed of his camera-laden 917 racecar used in *Le Mans*, star Steve McQueen (far left in tan jacket) and Schultz (obscured behind him) argue with a Porsche mechanic (in coveralls) as producer/first assistant director/second unit director Jack Reddish attempts to calm things down. Seen here with rear facing cameras mounted on a large frontal pipe set-up, one Arriflex was inches from the road just beyond the car's headlamp while the second was 30 inches higher and aimed at the driver. It was completely solid at driving speeds of over 100 mph in the straightaway, but its ungainly handling characteristics through curves concerned the Porsche folks, who thought it their obligation to warn McQueen about the dangers since he was the one driving the rig (courtesy Gaylin Schultz).

during *LeMans*; the picture marked the first (and only) time the French Racing Commission would approve such a stunt. Securing each bolt and bar with braided steel safety wires, Schultz enjoyed a zero percent failure rate on his mounts. With the vehicles going so fast, any mistake with his rigging (down to the smallest washer) could have been a catastrophic event.

Dealing with the pressure of getting it perfect each day, Gaylin recalled some sleepless nights, crafting new parts for the next morning's work. "For the high-speed stuff in the 908," he explained, "Steve wanted some vibration left in to better show the strain of driving 160 miles an hour." He used a firmer rubber gasket beneath the mounting plates (like he had on *Bullitt*); the rig provided a blurred-vision point of view that was exactly what McQueen and French DP Rene Gussart Jr. were after. "Even though director Lee Katzin was calling action, it was really McQueen's movie and everyone on the crew treated it as such."

While shooting the live-action sequences of the staged race, multiple cameras were attached to the Porsche 917 and driven at top speeds under competitive conditions. Utilizing a mounting system of half-inch diameter steel conduit struts (forming stabilizer arms bolting to the frame), the infinitely adjustable "tinker-toy" allowed for lens placement limited only by one's imagination. Incorporating a triangulated design for rigidity (capable of extending an Arriflex camera four feet out from the race car, just inches above the roadway), the groundbreaking POVs had never before been captured on film. In fact, Schultz often came up with his *own* shots based upon the geometric possibilities of his rigs. One idea was a camera arm above the rear quarter-panel of the Porsche; giving the audience a bird's eye view of the driver (over his shoulder), while looking forward at the road ahead.

Schultz (standing with his hand on the rig) supervises tweaks to a gate cam shot for *Le Mans*; Panavision pro Robert Goffshaw (in sweater) looks on. The "swinging arm" rig consists of a gate-like mechanism speed-controlled by a heavy-duty door piston (stolen from the offices at Solar Productions); its movement mimicked the drafting effect of one fast car overtaking another, while placing the lens just inches from the race track. Individually controlled via remote switch connected to an electromagnetic solenoid, real drivers triggered the camera and boom arm, which led to a far more accurate portrayal of the racing action from those behind the wheel. Note the CNC superstructure supporting a second Arriflex camera mounted to the cantilevered bridge, attached to the vehicle's front. Providing the necessary rigidity for its arcs into space, the "erector set" was pivotal in allowing the arm to sweep smoothly against the constant of gravity and centrifugal force, while traveling at speeds in excess of 100 mph (courtesy Gaylin Schultz).

Incorporated ostensibly to showcase McQueen behind the wheel in the long straightaway shots, the angle proved so useful it was also applied to other drivers in the race.

Another masterstroke of Schultz's camera placement engineering was his swing-gate design for a mobile crane arm, which provided a six-foot articulated sweeping move while traveling in excess of 120 miles an hour. Mimicking the appearance of one vehicle overtaking and sling-shotting past another, the magnetically released arm was speed-controlled by a heavy duty door-closing mechanism borrowed from the production offices at Solar Films. Able to move the camera through its arc like a miniature jib (which are common today), Gaylin's original contraption was the first of its kind ever seen. Testing each of his new mounts before turning them over to others, he routinely ran the rigs at high speeds without a single mishap. "At first," he said, "I had to gain the trust of the drivers. Adapting to the changes in balance and handling of a finely tuned machine with 300 extra pounds of gear attached it, took some getting used to!"

Wanting to find ways to further spotlight McQueen behind the wheel (versus the other drivers in the field wearing similar flame suits, scarves, and head protection with sunglasses enveloping their faces), Gaylin devised a close-up tray that attached a camera to the driver's door at a three-fourths angle to the star's face, leaving no doubt that he was really operating

Shown here in detail, *Le Mans'* rear facing Arriflex camera (from the tail of the Ferrari 512) had some unique anti-vibration modifications. Aside from a quarter-inch-thick piece of plate stock mounted with "isolation washers," it also had its aperture ring wired in place as well as a magazine clamp and oversized UV filter taped solid. It produced heart-racing scenes of vehicles coming up from behind (courtesy Gaylin Schultz).

the vehicle at speed. It was locked down like the others, and resulting images were rock steady even at over 140 miles an hour.

One of the cleverest mechanical set-ups Schultz developed for *LeMans* was an electromagnetic camera mount producing tight hold during racing action, then instantly removable with the flick of a switch for hand-held coverage. It was designed for a sequence where McQueen pulls off the track following a spirited lap, and then exits his car to walk across the pits. The continuous take was made possible by the camera's seamless transition from static to human, giving it an organic look that only both in balance could produce. "Steve loved those shots," Gaylin said proudly, "because once again, there was no mistaking that *he* was really driving."

Unlike Gaylin's previous automotive pictures where story motivated the action sequences, *Le Mans* was driven by function creating form, when it came to innovative car mounts. An example of this was a remote controlled articulated camera head that could be panned and tilted by an operator, sitting tandem in a small jump-seat in the GT-40 camera car. Incorporating a system of compressed nitrogen gas coupled with a crank-head, the device could rotate completely around, giving a fantastic rearward panning shot while driving at three digit speeds. Schultz recalled, "The force going through a banked corner was so great, despite the operator being unable to turn his face to follow the shot, the pneumatic tracking gear still functioned perfectly, capturing the image in excess of 120 miles an hour, pulling over 6 Gs in the process."

Le Mans received critical acclaim from *Cinematographer Magazine* at the time of its release, based on the proprietary sophistication of the camera rigs made for the movie. Its mediocre box office was ultimately eclipsed by racing fans the world over who made *Le Mans* a cult automotive favorite to this day. "The freedom McQueen gave me on a daily basis to build what I wanted," Gaylin Schultz said quietly, "had never happened to that extent before. From A to Z, I was in on every shot, and very much consider *Le Mans* my film."

Leaving behind the sophistication of France, Gaylin swapped mechanic's coveralls for a parka and snowshoes on Sydney Pollack's early west adventure piece *Jeremiah Johnson*. It starred Robert Redford in the title role and was lensed during the late fall of 1972 in Leeds, Utah (Snow Canyon State Park and the then unknown Sundance). Modifying three Snow-Cat tractors (for use as grip and lighting vehicles to make it through the six foot banks of early snow), Gaylin also mounted an eight-foot boom-arm to a Caterpillar for a mobile crane. Giving cinematographer Gene Callahan the ability to do sweeping shots while moving at the speed of a trotting horse, the rig was perfect for the Indian burial ground scenes when Johnson sees his wife's blue trinkets strewn on the ground, as the camera pans across the grave. Floating the arm unsteadily left then right while the focus remained on the objects below, Schultz gave the viewer a feeling of imbalance, as the rapidity of the cuts underlined the panic of the moment.

Other pivotal sequences were possible amid the difficult weather and terrain owing to the key grip's clever approach to production. Dealing with four foot snowdrifts while filming the Indian fighting montage, Gaylin employed ten-yard-long sections of sleeper track to span the glacial patches of white stuff. Allowing for quick repositioning when changing shooting angles, he and the crew (including director Pollack) would all pitch in to carry the track when it came time to move the shot. At times the conditions were so difficult that in order to film a sequence with pack mules in deep snow, boards and carpet were installed

10. Gaylin Schultz, Key Grip 213

While most of Schultz's camera rigs for *Le Mans* were sophisticated, this set-up mounted on a Ferrari 512 shell was little more than a few sticks of CNC tubing bolted to the car, then supported with a circular mounting head. This provided coverage of "staged crashes" while the pricey Porsche and Ferrari frames were swapped out for less costly Lola T-70s. Sitting patiently behind the wheel of his Ferrari 512, driver David Piper awaits the signal from helmer Lee Katzman before pulling away from his mark (courtesy Gaylin Schultz).

beneath to keep the animals from sinking in, and then covered to hide the platform from camera. Ultimately building a sled to pull the mules to and fro (after the construction method proved exhaustingly labor-intensive), Gaylin chuckled at the memory of him and four grips tugging on the ropes, while the burros seemed to enjoy the ride. "At one point, we were pulling the mules through a ravine to set up the shot where the wolves attack. Suddenly the leading grip, Bernie Schwartz, stepped into a sinkhole and disappeared up to his chin in snow. We all laughed so hard, the pack mules became agitated and we had to cover our mouths like school kids while pulling him from the drift."

One particular scene that captured the ferocity of Johnson's battle against the Crows (and Gaylin's uncanny ability to move the camera) began as a walking shot with Redford catching several braves relaxing in a wooded encampment. The visual element of the shift into a frenetic ballet of brutal killing was tricky to record. Illustrating the skirmish's rapid pacing, he designed a downhill dolly move that matched Redford's strides through the trees (closing in on his Crow adversary), then pulled the camera to a sudden halt for the savage collision. Four grips were needed to stop the rapidly moving dolly. The resulting action is one of the film's most compelling moments.

Shifting from the old west to the new, Gaylin's next gig was with Steve McQueen on the Sam Peckinpah–directed cowboy drama *Junior Bonner*, photographed by Lucien Ballard. Schultz was charged with putting cameras in difficult places. "Peckinpah loved the grips," Gaylin revealed, "and was always testing us with barbs and crazy camera rigs." Told to position a 40mm lens between the horns of Sunshine (a 900-pound bull McQueen ultimately pulls nine seconds on during the film's climax), he wisely acquired a stand-in for the dangerous animal and mounted a lightweight Eimo camera between its horns using clamps and a steel mounting plate. "The poor bull looked ridiculous," Gaylin admitted. "And when I showed it to Peckinpah, he said it was perfect, but didn't have time for it any longer. That was his idea of a joke."

Schultz's other contributions to the picture included a series of camera rigs that *did* get used in the picture such as a saddle mount engineered for a live action transition from a horseback POV to that of being thrown to the ground. It incorporated a quick release dove-tail mounting plate which allowed the camera to be released from the bucking animal then handheld through its impact with the turf. The resulting footage was some of the most bone-crunching in the movie.

In the summer of 1972, Gaylin again served cinematic master Lucien Ballard when drafted for Steve McQueen's sixth project between them, *The Getaway,* directed by Sam Peckinpah. He keyed the feature with his usual crew of grips including Clive Hart, Bernie Schwartz, and Kenny Adams. The ultra-violent road picture tested Schultz's rigging skills as well as his patience. Much of it revolved around automobiles (and actors having conversations in them), and Peckinpah felt auto glass a deterrent to the reality of his filmmaking after several days of overcast weather produced cloud reflections that obscured the shots. The windshield of the Ford station wagon carrying McQueen and Ali McGraw was removed as the two actors faced cameras and a row of lights across the hood, which became difficult to ignore during the heated exchange. After several failed takes, McQueen suggested working outside the car, where there was more space to move for the scripted slap. Rapidly stripping the wagon of its complicated set-up to shoot it clean, Schultz was tickled when the overcast sky cleared, allowing him to reinstall the glass for the last shot of the afternoon.

Underappreciated for its driving action (compared to *Bullitt* or *Le Mans*), the picture still possessed a vehicular reality that made it exciting to watch for its multiple escapes and pursuits.It presented plenty of mechanical challenges for Gaylin; one hands-on chore handled by the multi-tasking grip involved operating the controls of a trash truck with McQueen and McGraw trapped inside. As Peckinpah strived for as much reality as possible, he insisted upon shooting the scene live action. The hydraulic compacting ram moved half a ton of debris dangerously close to the entombed stars every take, with only Schultz to keep the talent from being crushed. Pushing the actors out the back with the press of a button, Gaylin was unable to see them directly during the shot. Relying upon a mark on the piston-rod to gauge his distance each take, Schultz said he was never so glad to be done with a gag in his life.

Called into Peckinpah's offices at Goldwyn Studios during the last week of filming, Gaylin was informed that the director had purchased a large boat with the intention of shooting an action adventure series on it. Hired on the spot to a lucrative long-term contract, Schultz began to design and manufacture custom mounting hardware for the deck that facilitated the rapid attachment of dolly track anywhere on board without pre-rigging. Following two months of tinkering, however, the whole deal died with Peckinpah, who passed away during the initial process.

Gaylin next got caught up in an 18-day quickie horror telemovie, *Gargoyles*, in mid–1972. From there he embarked on one of the most photographically individualistic features of his career, *Jonathan Livingston Seagull*. Hired by writer-producer-director Hall Bartlett as production supervisor in charge of all shooting units (including the additional crew on location in Hawaii), Schultz also served as right hand man for nature cinematographer Jack Couffer. With much of the movie depicting seagulls in flight the majority of the picture's labor proved to be the trapping, provision, filming, and releasing of wild birds. Getting to the first task at hand, Gaylin and his team were put in charge of capturing scores of seagulls. Working under the watchful eye of a fish and game warden whose department approved the use of live birds, Schultz and his boys approached the chore with a military precision and true desire not to injure a single creature in the process. Visiting landfills along the Monterey Peninsula, Gaylin and company (headed by apiary training expert Gary Gero) would have the crane operators gently stir up their trash heaps to draw in the hungry birds; then large rocket-propelled nets were triggered — launching attached nylon ropes 200 feet into the air, gently floating down to harmlessly trap the busily feeding gulls beneath. Once

Steve McQueen, celebrating his 42nd birthday, blows out the candles on his cake during a break from shooting *The Getaway* in the summer of 1972. Schultz (behind the tank top–clad woman, himself wearing sunglasses and a sports shirt) had a very close relationship with the actor, having previously done *Junior Bonner* (1972), *Le Mans* (1971), *Bullitt* (1968), *The Thomas Crown Affair* (1968), and *The Reivers* (1969) with him. Second assistant director Newt Arnold (left, with eye patch) did his best to keep order on the chaotic set while helmer Sam Peckinpah (next to McQueen with an open shirt and sunglasses) is jokingly congratulating his friend for living so long despite taking so many risks during filming (courtesy Gaylin Schultz).

the wild birds were caged comfortably and well fed, they became so docile that one could pick them up with bare hands without fear. In fact, the gulls were so content that while other wild birds flying up to the staging area wanted in, very few Hollywood-ized animals wanted out.

Tapped for his expertise with camera mounts for difficult shots, Schultz rigged Art Scholl's aerobatic plane and George Nolan's chopper on the feature. They were utilized as the two primary sources of aerial footage; many hours were logged with both, in an attempt to catch the seagulls in high flight. Lenses were placed under the wings of the agile aircraft and on the skids of the helicopter; the possibilities of coverage for the birds were limitless

Another of the challenging camera mounts Schultz (right) originated was the "under wing cage" for *Jonathan Livingston Seagull* (1973). Squatting next to him is legendary stunt pilot Art Scholl (in glasses). Employing Scholl's acrobatic skills with his de Havilland DHC-1B Super Chipmunk airplane, DP Jack Couffer (left) was able to come up with free-flight footage of the gulls that is still not surpassed to this day. Schultz bolted the cage directly into the aircraft's frame through strategically chosen access points. His welded steel tube box was capable of withstanding forces equal to five tons of pull without any failure. Consistently reaching seven to eight G's while performing midair stalls then going into dives behind the released birds, Scholl not only put tremendous strain on the airplane, but on Schultz's rig as well. Known as one of Hollywood's most gifted pilots, Scholl was killed in 1986 while doing an inverted flat spin over Santa Monica in his Pitts S-2 for the film *Top Gun* (courtesy Gaylin Schultz).

owing to the framing of a beautiful blue horizon above and the limitless expanse of pastoral earth tones beneath. To allow for the seagulls' safe disbursement in flight (avoiding props and exhaust turbines), specially designed drop-away cages were used, sparing the birds injury during release.

Filming the gull's eye view from various angles while in flight, DP Couffer recorded them as best he could, relying upon lots of takes and miles of footage to get flying action that could be cut to match the story. Since the tame birds flew away after each take, a constant trapping and training crew for the animals became necessary. They went through over 20 gulls an hour on some sequences; by the end of the movie handlers recognized previously released birds who had returned for the easy pickings of the motion picture business.

Gaylin was proud of the special care he and his folks showed the seagulls. He recalled a custom inclined chute that was built for herding the winged creatures into cages from the large holding pens. In order not to harm the ocean birds' delicate feet, the ramp was lined with padded outdoor carpet. "As soon as we wheeled out the soft ramp from the staging pen," Schultz said, "wild gulls would swoop down trying to get in on all the free food their pals were enjoying. Shooing away the wannabes became more difficult each day."

With lots of seagull conversations needed (two birds flying side by side for minutes at a time), much of the close-up "fly and talk" was only obtainable in the exotic weather patterns found in the highlands of Maui. Using the thermal updrafts that constantly blow along the Forbidden Ranch area of the tropical island's windward side, two model gliders with small cameras installed were flown to record the birds' point of view, while flying perilously close to the cliffs. They were forewarned by local priests to be respectful of the island's magic (and not to litter, smoke, swear, or speak in loud voices while filming). To Gaylin's horror, his unit lost one of the two expensive planes just before lunch, when the operator broke into a diatribe of curse words at the top of his lungs. Assuming it was stuck in some cliff face bushes or crashed on the rugged beach below, a search party looked for an hour and still failed to turn anything up. Concerned with the litter factor as much as the pricey camera inside, Gaylin hoped the plane would turn up, but had to get back to work. Continuing to use a remaining black glider into the afternoon, Schultz suddenly saw the missing white aircraft approach from the seaward side of the Island, lazily circle over and land gently in front of the truck from which it had been launched hours previously. While the models' batteries normally lasted just 40 minutes, all were mystified by how the aircraft had stayed aloft. They were told by the locals that the Island Spirits took the quiet-bird for a visit, then released it when satisfied with its intentions. The Park Rangers had an alternate explanation revolving around columns of thermal air known to rapidly carry weather balloons 10,000 feet in that very area. "Considering that it came down right in front of the van," Schultz said seriously, "I never bought the magic-act stuff."

Even though *Jonathan Livingston Seagull* was a popular book (and Couffer's stunning wildlife photography was Oscar nominated), the picture was poorly received. Critic Roger Ebert labeled it "the biggest pseudo-cultural would be metaphysical rip-off of the year." With viewers staying away in flocks, the picture barely made its money back for producer Hall Bartlett, who funded the feathered flick with his own birdseed.

After twenty years of working his way to the top of the independent key grips in Hollywood, Schultz next shifted gears to a simpler existence when he signed a contract with studio big shot Jack Foreman to run the grip department at MGM. His alma mater seemed like the perfect fit (he was engaged with motion picture administration versus the daily grind of filming movies personally), until he found himself missing the challenges of live shooting and decided to revisit production.

Director Sydney Pollack's heavy Japanese mob picture, *The Yakuza* (1973), was photographed mostly on location in Tokyo, Osaka, and Kyoto Studios in Japan. The Robert Mitchum gangster picture (penned by Paul Schrader) had a brooding look that was a throwback to the film noir pictures of 25 years earlier. In addition to the daily duties of key grip to cinematographer Kozo Okazaki, Schultz also took on the larger role of production coordinator on the difficult feature. He was tasked with preparing Hollywood-style production trucks for the picture, a ten-ton for both grip and electric's gear on the road. The Japanese method of location staging had equipment strewn in open flatbeds with departments mixed together (meaning you had to move the lumber to get to the lights, for example). Schultz procured separate vehicles for each, and an ancient delivery van for camera: "Those initial up-grades alone saved production two hours a day, normally wasted unloading equipment."

Working at studios that had dirt floors, no heat, and stages built on a four-foot riser (to allow coverage of such traditional Japanese acts as eating from low tables and squatting), production coordinator Gaylin solved each problem one at a time. First, he had his American crew install a proper floor. Bringing in central gas heating Schultz was able to make the place livable by Hollywood standards. They were forced to film off platforms with the camera on sticks to compensate for the riser issues (it would have been too expensive to rebuild the sets); many interiors were shot by moving from room to room due to space limitations, then cut together during editing.

Experienced with the problem of a language barrier, Gaylin communicated with the all–Japanese crews through interpreters and a smattering of the indigenous slang he picked up dealing with Okazaki and the locals at Koyoto Studios (where he became the go-to guy for getting things done), even if that meant paying a $5000 tribute in cash to a local mobster for his "technical assistance" on the film. For the picture's final scene where Mitchum severs his pinky by way of Yubitsume, then presents his "apology" across the table in a napkin to Japanese actor Kentara Kura, Schultz recalled nefarious gangster types (pals of the previously mentioned mobster) objecting to their sacred tradition being revealed in a Western movie and made their displeasure known around town. "We had a day or two of rumors, accompanied by the nerves of waiting for something to happen," Gaylin said of the implied threat. "But as that was our last week in Japan, we left the country right away, returning to Los Angeles without event or further shakedown."

In the spring of 1975 Gaylin was crewed on the Stanley Donen–skippered water-fest *Lucky Lady*. Brought on by cinematographer Geoffrey Unsworth after seeing early production notes about Schultz's special track rig for boats, he was also made responsible for coordinating all marine stunts, including the necessary water craft rigging and second unit key grip duties connected. He incorporated his deck cleats for shots all over the vessel.

Utilizing a 1930s racing cutter with a crew of eight to sail properly, the antique 65-foot yacht ran into more than its share of difficulties; the crew experienced problems with water leakage, blown engines, poor communications and Liza Minnelli's constant seasickness. By the time producer Michael Gruskoff had his movie in the can, the price tag was up to 22 million dollars, taking twenty weeks of production to get there. Gaylin laughed, "Between

Minnelli looking so green in the gills that her eyes were bulging, and the amount of unusable footage Unsworth shot every day, we were lucky to finish the film with our sanity, much less a watchable movie."

Arthur Penn's western cult classic *Missouri Breaks* was filmed on location in Billings, Red Lodge, and Virginia City, Montana, in the late summer of 1975. Schultz performed everything from fifty-yard dolly moves (staged off an elevated sleeper track to place the lens height even with a mounted rider), to constructing full gallop saddle rigs for "cowboy shot" POVs. Called upon to use multiple cameras while recording the frenetic pace of Penn's train robbery sequences, Gaylin employed a hand-pumped trolley car to gain movement in the shot, and a camera mounted to the train itself, just inches above the track beneath the freight car door.

As in most location-heavy westerns, the daily grind of filming horses and outdoor action on *Missouri Breaks* required a good dose of hand-held camera use by the second unit DP Rexford Metz. Gaylin was always there for his boss, with a furniture pad or special bit of help to make the operator's job more comfortable. He constructed a saddle extension which formed a back-brace while shooting from a running horse. The device worked so well that entire sequences were filmed using it, including walking dialogue between actors when the elevated "horseback" POV produced a crane-like look to the shot.

Although not a box office success, the Marlon Brando–Jack Nicholson picture was a memorable experience for Schultz: "Between Brando playing with the grasshoppers, and camping out in a huge teepee when not on set, it was a bizarre ten weeks."

Schultz was next engaged on director William Friedkin's jungle adventure *Sorcerer*. He was originally approached in late 1975 through Steve McQueen (who was attached to the project before Roy Scheider, but passed due to Friedkin's refusal to give the star's new wife Ali MacGraw a producer credit for little more than hanging out at the hotel); much of the Solar's crew stayed on the flick, including stunt coordinator and longtime pal Bud Eakins.

Interviewing with Paramount's executive production manager Lindsley Parsons Jr., Gaylin was hired and given the green light to start putting his package together for the picture's worldwide shooting (including Paris, New York, Mexico, Israel, and the Dominican Republic). Beginning his pre-production chores with the modification of a massive army surplus troop carrier parked in front of his La Canada home, Schultz was shocked a week later when handed a pink slip by two suit-wearing process servers.

As it turned out, Friedkin's visions for the film (grandly interpreted by David Lean's production designer John Box) involved the construction of an entire city in the jungle, including sewage, roads, electricity, air-conditioning and housing capable of supporting the hundreds of folks brought in to work the feature. Frightened by the scope and expense of the director's projected game plan, Universal boss Lew Wasserman abruptly cancelled production on the project, leaving Friedkin and his partner Bud Smith in need of a bigger piggy-bank. Shopping the movie to Warners to cover crew salaries while restructuring a deal with Gulf + Western's Charles Bluhdorn, the guys banked on two things known about Bluhdorn that would get the flick made. First, his dream of turning the Dominican Republic into one big tropical right-to-work state. Second were the director's connections at the studio (they were still impressed with the helmer's previous financial hits *The French Connection* and *The Exorcist*). Successfully pleading his case to Warners, Friedkin was in country during the first day's scouting when Schultz saw the director suddenly turn to impulsive behavior while in route to a distant location in an antiquated Sikorsky helicopter provided for the company by the Dominican Air Force. Gaylin said that, flying through a dense fogbank, Friedkin spotted a remote hilltop and instantly chose it as the perfect setting for his highland metropolis. He decided to build a scaled-down city in the forest (as the novel described); the location was so distant that it took several round trips to fly in the gear needed just for the blasting of roads required to sustain the construction crew. Lacking the funding for the grand jungle habitat that he had envisioned, work on the feature became brutal because they couldn't afford the bigger crews and machinery required to tame the harsh environment. Dealing with scorching temperatures and humidity throughout the days and plagued by insects, bad water and worse food the rest of the time, Schultz said the daily hassles of making *Sorcerer* tested the crew's reserve. However, once committed to Friedkin's vision, they all did their best to get the picture done.

In regard to his most innovative shot in the film as key grip, Schultz said, "It got really scary while we were filming the dynamite truck crossing over the suspension bridge." With the rain coming down in bucketfuls, the issue was the road planks under the water flowing over the partially submerged structure. Supplying a low-tech grip solution, he scored the treadles to channel the river away from the tires, gaining the necessary traction for the spinning wheels. "An hour's worth of cross-hatching," Gaylin said with a smile, "saved us $50,000 in time if we had to shoot it again."

After another location assignment in the jungles of Mexico (operating crane for key grip Bob Sordal on *Who'll Stop the Rain* in 1977), Schultz next signed on for a flick that was as foreign to him as the title implies, Cheech and Chong's *Up in Smoke*. Filmed entirely in Los Angeles (with the exception of the border sequences done in Yuma, Arizona), the movie was a welcome diversion for Gaylin who had been on one grueling feature after another for the past ten years. Caught up in the spirit of the picture's camp approach, he was talked into an acting gig by director Lou Adler, then cast as a police sergeant who answers the phone while the boys are being booked.

Returning for another Friedkin feature late in the summer of 1978, *The Brinks Job*, Gaylin was contracted with key grip responsibilities on the crime caper and served as neighborhood liaison to all of Boston's Prince Street locals, who were very much in charge of the North End area filming locations. It was shot at the old Brink's Headquarters where the real rip-off occurred. Gaylin and Producer Dino De Laurentiis handled everything from an extortion attempt of stolen film reels (which turned out to be worthless dailies and outtakes), to grossly inflated parking fees for production vehicles, and a hiring list of nephews and pals for the well-paid gofer jobs on-set. After telling the gangsters who snatched the film to "get a projector and enjoy it" (and other inside communication between Friedkin and the locals), the production was eventually left alone (once certain financial arrangements were made to insure cooperation). "I loved working in Boston," Schultz remarked. "But some of the extras in Doyle's Pub scared the heck out of me!"

By 1979, having labored as an independent key grip under some of Hollywood's most fabulous DPs (including Harry Stradling Jr., James Wong Howe, Charles Lang, William Clothier, Joseph LaShelle, Ellsworth Fredericks, Bob Surtees, Burnett Guffey, Haskell Wexler, William Fraker, Lucien Ballard, Duke Callahan, and Richard Kline), Schultz was a grip looking to settle down to just one guy. With the likes of Steve McQueen and Peckinpah long gone (and their shooters now spread to the four corners of Hollywood), Gaylin began a working relationship with cinematographer Victor Kemper that was unlike any that he had ever known before. "With Victor," Schultz explained, "I was an equal, whereas with some of the others I was definitely the help. Which is why we stayed together until my retirement fifteen years later."

They started with Norman Jewison's *And Justice for All*; Gaylin and Kemper's working relationship was built on trust from the very beginning. During a helicopter sequence filmed over the frigid winter waters of Maryland's Chesapeake Bay in the first week of shooting, Schultz said the DP was reluctant to be in the aging aircraft, since the script called for it to drop eight feet into the water simulating running out of gas for the shot. To eliminate the problem, Gaylin locked down the Panaflex camera with a series of clamps so that no one had to ride the rig into the drink except pilot Ross Reynolds, who simply turned the camera on before crashing.

Widely recognized as one of Hollywood's preeminent key grips, Schultz joined with gaffer Earl Gilbert and lensman Kemper to form a moviemaking trio that ultimately did more than 30 features together until their final opus, *Beethoven,* in 1991. First up for the threesome was Steve Martin's initial starring role, *The Jerk*. It was directed by comedic genius Carl Reiner from *The Dick Van Dyke Show*; the old pro knew how to get the most from the comic by strategically using Gaylin as his foil to prod the inexperienced actor to do things as rehearsed. Martin initially had trouble finding his marks without cheating an obvious downward glance to the floor; Gaylin came to the rookie's rescue with raised treads taped to the stage that Martin could feel through his shoes.

After work on *Xanadu, The Four Seasons* and *Chu Chu and the Philly Flash*, Gaylin Schultz crewed the Broadway hit turned feature film *Zoot Suit* in 1981. It was lensed in Prescott, Arizona, doubling as pre–World War II East Los Angeles. Gaylin and crew were last-minute replacements for key grip Harry Rez. With DP David Myers shooting the photographic transition from stage to screen, Schultz's chores on the flick included moving the camera for his temporary boss. Enlisting the help of crane-hand Rich Babin as well as dolly grip Mike Kinney to give the one-dimensional story a sense of movement, Gaylin also supplied director Louis Valdez with a neverending tapestry of driving car shots (thanks to his car mounts), which they plugged into the story as needed while showcasing the automotive and cultural styles of the era.

With the Chevy Chase road flick *National Lampoon's Vacation,* the 57-year-old workhorse had approximately 80 pictures under his belt. Crossing the country while working ten weeks on *Vacation* (including locations in Illinois, Missouri, Colorado and Arizona), Gaylin found himself in car mount heaven, as the picture showcased every automobile gag in the book. Flush with the satisfaction of tinkering with camera rigs like in the old days, he delivered a wide variety of coverage options, on what was otherwise a very limited photographic storyline. In addition to the vehicular challenges of *Vacation*, Schultz was also required by second unit DP Paul Vombrack to work out camera mounts for the rollercoaster segment at Wally World, shot at Six Flags Magic Mountain. He installed speed rail pipes with mounting plates clamped directly to the rigged cars; the set-up allowed for camera placement so dynamic that while watching dailies, actors Dana Baron and Chevy Chase became ill, just as they had the day before when actually filming.

Happily with Victor Kemper through 1983 for their eighth collaboration on the Michael Keaton dramady *Mr. Mom*, Schultz was now doing the kind of fare that was far less demanding. Without the car chases or the helicopters, his day at the office was over at 5:30 in the evening, instead of sunrise after an all-nighter. Next came two more Kemper pictures in '83, Arthur Hiller's *The Lonely Guy* starring Steve Martin and the Atari 5200 commercial disguised as a film, *Cloak and Dagger*. Without a car-mount or explosion on either picture, Schultz was finally free to sit back in his chair and delegate. Although word came out that he wasn't looking for big shows any more, a call from cinematographer Fred Schuler sparked his interest enough to accept key grip chores on the comedic action picture *Fletch* in 1984. Taking the Michael Ritchie gig while Kemper was on vacation, Gaylin was tapped for his world-class automotive rigging on a car chase in Long Beach. "Guy was a big fan of the car stuff in *Bullitt* and *The Getaway*," Schultz said, "and he wanted the action in *Fletch* to resemble that."

After another fill-in feature, *Violets Are Blue*, Gaylin's next project with Kemper was *Pee-wee's Big Adventure*. Gaylin considered Tim Burton a first-rate helmsman and a genius behind the lens; he said the artistically gifted guy voiced his appreciation of a camera mount rigged to Pee-wee's bike that was used in the big chase sequence through Warners' backlot. Borrowing hardware devised for *Big Fauss Little Halsey* 25 years earlier, he was amused to find the engineering still working so well. "Even though they had modern stuff like a monitor strapped to the bike so the operator could gauge his shot," Schultz laughed, "the rig from the sixties worked swell."

By 1985, Gaylin was on his 12th film with Victor, *Clue*. Describing Kemper as appreciative and easy to be around, Schultz likened his experience to a good marriage: "We had a lot of laughs, but did some serious stuff too."

Bill-paying in between Kemper jobs again, Schultz keyed a second Ralph Bode feature, Richard Pryor's *Critical Condition*. Filmed primarily in North Carolina's Regional Hospital in 1986, the picture is a sub-average flick. Back with "The Trio" for their 13th and 14th pictures (Michael Dinner's *Hot to Trot* and the Roy Scheider crime drama *Cohen and Tate*, both 1987), Gaylin was engaged in his favorite grip pursuit, camera rigging. Still preferring to do the wrench work himself, he did car interior camera mounts on the latter that incorporated everything from suction cup–assisted hostess trays to simple apple-box rigs off the floor allowing for easy camera positioning. "Over the course of time with so much driving stuff between Adam Baldwin, Roy Scheider, and [Harley Cross] the boxes saved us countless hours."

Requested to join director Michael Ritchie for the sequel *Fletch Lives* in 1988, Gaylin was up to his armpits in water when shooting the picture's Noah's Ark Ride sequences at Bible Land (doubled by Universal's Flash Flood ride). Combining the G-force of a roller coaster and the soaking wet splash of a watery ride, the master key grip toiled to make his set-up hold firm and devised a method to keep the camera clear when going through the violent spray. Turning to a trick discovered on *Le Mans* for blowing rain from the lens at high speed, Schultz attached a compressed air line to the bottom of the matte box in front of the filter, keeping the camera bone dry.

The last features with Kemper and Gilbert were Tony Brill's *Crazy People* in 1989 and the bark-fest *Beethoven* the following year. Schultz also did two last projects with DP Frank Tidy that carried him to career's end: *The Butcher's Wife* and *Under Siege* in 1992. On the latter, a Steven Seagal shoot-em-up, Gaylin rose to the occasion for one last large location film, lensed aboard the USS *Alabama*. Familiar with his Naval surroundings, he earned his keep by saving the producers a ton of money by coming up with the idea of using large backdrops behind the ship (moored in Mobile Harbor) for its schedule of night-time shooting. Utilizing his knowledge of boat material transference and sea docking to plan the setup, he employed multiple 100-foot rental barges (with 20-yard high blacks attached to their rigging) so that the coverage of the dark material behind the vessels adequately blocked out the surrounding city, giving the appearance of being far out at sea.

At the end of his nearly 100-feature career, Gaylin Schultz received a lifetime achievement award from the Society of Operating Cameramen on October 1, 2000. By the time Schultz was finished with the biz, many of his proprietary mounting gadgets had become available off the shelf, owned by simply paying money for them. In Gaylin's time, the ownership was earned through trial and error, with the sweat and blood of innovation. It was this spirit of individual invention for the end product (more than the immediate ego) that was the main difference between the mindset of the guys making movies "back in the day" versus some of the film school types doing it now. Not overly impressed with modern technology for its own sake in the motion picture business, Schultz preferred inventive common sense solutions instead of throwing money at problems or buying new toys.

Asked what made him so outstanding, and what the grips of today can do to follow in his path, Gaylin Schultz said, "First of all, follow no one. Make your own way but never say no. Our job as grips is to figure out safe, practical, and economic ways of getting the shots asked of us. Mostly, we're there to help, period. Anything less and you're a hindrance."

Glossary

A

Abby Singer— Slang for the next to the last shot of the day. It is jokingly named for an assistant director on the *Mary Tyler Moore Show* who would leave for the parking lot while the company was still on the final set-up.

aerial shot— High angle view of action or subjects on the ground; mostly captured by crane, stationary platform, helicopter or plane for filming the location below.

anamorphic lens— Specialized lens with a cylindrical surface that expands a wide angle view for more top and bottom coverage of a 35mm frame.

animatronics— The motion picture craft of articulated scale animals, creatures and people. Using pneumatic, electrical, and/or hydraulic engineering to control their movements, they are finished with lifelike over-skins made from latex, fur, plastic, rubber, neoprene or a dozen other materials that are highly realistic in their final appearances.

apple box— Wooden platform "box" constructed from high-grade plywood measuring 20 inches long by 10 inches wide and 8 inches deep. The backbone of any movie set, "apples" can be utilized for everything from temporary seating and construction to raising an actor for camera — thus the term "man-maker" in describing the use. Dating back to the silent era, the apple box was named because of its early modification from used wooden crates carrying L.A.'s local produce to market.

arc light— Carbon filament high-intensity lamp with its arc shaped between two electrodes and attached to a high electrical current providing a bright output motion picture light.

ASC (American Society of Cinematographers)— A Hollywood non-profit organization of cinematographers founded in 1918 to advance the art of motion picture photography through artistry and technological progress in an open exchange of ideas.

aspect ratio— The relation of width to height of a projected film.

assistant camera— Support camera tech responsible for everything from loading and unloading film magazines, writing lab reports, measuring distances from actors to camera (for the operator), as well as changing lenses.

assistant director (A.D.)— Assistant to the director, responsible for a myriad of tasks to make the director's job more streamlined.

B

"B" movie— A second-rate or otherwise less than quality film below the normal motion picture offering.

baby— Small motion picture light of 750 watts with a glass fresnel; also called inky or baby solar spot. Smaller than a junior.

backing— A staged textile positioned outside of a window, doorway or vista made from a transparency, painted canvas, black solid or any other designated material deemed useful in filling an otherwise empty or un-photographable area in a motion picture or television show set.

ball leveler— A type of camera mount focusing its brake and hardware on a single "ball" nut in its center for tightening the camera down to a specific shot on the working horizon. Quick to use and tight locking, the device is engineered to provide any frame angle possible with a single move.

barn doors— Flaps or doors attached to the front of lights for shadow and illumination control.

base camp— Temporary production headquarters comprised of all that is a mobile Hollywood City including power, craft service truck, catering, honey wagons, and provision vehicles for all departments including security and transportation to keep it all safe and running 24 hours a day.

batten— Piece of lumber stock (approximately 1" × 3") used by grips to temporarily secure items on set.

below-the-line— A reference to motion picture or television labor as opposed to that of more managerial or talent ranks in the business. Such crafts as special effects, grips, electricians and carpenters would all be below-the-line, while actors, producers, writers and directors are all "above."

best boy electrician— Ranked as No. 2 man below gaffer, the best boy electrician is also responsible for equipment, manpower, and time cards (payment) of all electricians.

best boy grip— Working as second man below key, the best boy is responsible for scouting locations, equipment, manpower and time cards of all grips. Meaning "top man" back in the nautical days of Shakespearean theatre work, the term referred to the high-rigging experts of their day.

Big Eye 10K— A 10,000-watt electrical lighting instrument with a focusing glass fresnel. Developed by Earl Gilbert for Charlie Lang on *The Greatest Story Ever Told*.

blue frost— Combination gel producing a blue hue while diffusing with a soft white touch.

blue screen— A deep blue colored backing that facilitates effects photography by its absolute absorption of light, enabling "key" outlines of actors for use with other backgrounds. A photographic process of filming action against a chroma-key color blue backing to achieve a clean separation for electronic or film edits, while inserting other backgrounds (photographic) in its place.

brute— Carbon arc light powered by 225 amps of electricity.

C

cameraman— The Director of Photography and/or first operator of camera. On a large crew, the first cameraman takes orders from the cinematographer (or DP), who may or may not operate their own camera on all shots. Also, operators of camera for a DP (either single or multiple cameras), are known as cameramen or camera operators.

catwalk— Narrow walkway engineered over stages made from lumber and steel fittings connecting the perms and green-beds for "high workers" engaged in getting from one point to the next over the sets for lighting and construction purposes.

CGI— Computer generated imagery.

CinemaScope— A wide-screen format for motion pictures using anamorphic lenses to expand the normal film format from 1.37:1 to 2.66:1. Based on French photographic inventor Henri Chretien's lens work in 1926, the concept was brought into the mainstream by 20th Century–Fox for the epic feature *The Robe* in 1954.

cinematographer— Director of photography on a feature or TV show; DP; shooter; person responsible for all photography of story. In charge of all camera operators.

cinemobile— A location vehicle constructed from a large mobile home with all production gear stored inside; suitable for shipping overseas on production work.

crab dolly— Compact camera platform on wheels capable of movement in all directions with the turn of a clutch gear and steering wheel.

cutaway shot—A single scene placed into a sequence that temporarily disrupts the story by way of introduction of new characters, impending action, or an explanation of past doings.

D

dailies— Exposed film shipped each day to the lab, and then reviewed by the director and cinematographer to ensure their quality before moving on to new scenes.

dart—Cigarette, smoke

dolly grip— Operator of wheeled camera platform who assists "the shooter" through articulation of the chassis and subsequent lens position via a mutually decided path for photographing an object or actor for a given set-up.

dramedy—A dramatic comedy on either film or television.

duvetyne— Soft black fabric used for light control by grips.

E

eye light— Small light on the face or eyes to accentuate the actor; also known as a catch or kicker light.

F

feather light–Lighting instrument mounted on or near camera as a slight fill-light for face, and details illumination.

fill light— Use of additional lamps to lighten dark areas or reduce overall contrast on an object.

five K (5K)— Focusable electric light with glass fresnel and steel or aluminum body producing 5,000 watts of light.

flag— Grip tool constructed of material (solid black flannel, silk, net or wood) mounted on a frame used to create shadows or control illumination output while lighting.

flag setting— The grip term for positioning lighting textiles such as solids, nets, and silks in order to enhance screen appearance for both actor and sets as light strikes them while being filmed.

fluid head— Camera head or mount engineered with hydraulics to allow for smooth movement of camera while filming from dollies, tripod or hi-hats.

follow shot— Moving with the subject by way of pan, zoom, or dolly from camera in the process of filming live action.

follow spot—Intense light with a focusing lens and swiveling mount that allows coverage of action with a characteristic "round" beam on the subject; often staged on balconies or in the back of theaters for live-action use.

forced dump tank— A vertical container holding thousands of gallons of liquid which can be released on cue to affect a tidal wave-like deluge of water for a flooding effect.

fresnel— Circular glass lens for lighting that allows a multitude of effects from broad illuminations to sharp focus, while softening the harsh beam from an otherwise bare lamp inside.

friction head— A camera mount whose construction is engineered for direct metal-to-metal contact without fluid lubrication by its own gear system.

fullers earth— Inert clay of a microfine composition used to provide backgrounds like dust; or laid on by hand to age costumes, sets or locations.

G

gaffer— Head of lighting department; responsible for placement, selection and amount of instruments used to illuminate a given scene for motion pictures or television. Also commanding crews to tasks at hand — the gaffer position is one of leadership while answering only to the DP and key grip.

gradated diffusion— Lighting material (made from gel, glass filter or linen) used in incremental grades or quantity to reduce direct light on a subject from one hue of brightness to dark by frame's end.

greensmen— Craft folk responsible for the dressing, maintenance and staging of all foliage, trees, bushes, plants and surface conditions (both artificial and real) pertaining to their use in a motion picture or television show.

grip— Studio mechanic responsible for all movement and mounting of camera as well as creating shadows and diffusion of lights in the making of a motion picture or television show. Other "on set" duties include safety, overhead rigging, cranes, dollies, ladders, lumber and tripods — as they may exist in filming. Originally so named based on the stout bags of tools they carried in the late 1930's.

H

hammers—see xtra hammers

HMI (Hydrargyrum Medium-Arc Iodide)— Electrical light powered by a ballast which ultimately replaced carbon arc instruments (through halogen gas enclosed within quartz technology) creating the close-to-sunlight color temperature of 5,600 degrees.

honey wagon— Portable trailers for all manner of uses from enclosed toilets to dressing rooms. They are generally used on back lots or while shooting on location away from the studio.

hostess / hood mount— A steel platform affixed to the driver's or passenger door with camera attached for driving and talking shots across the front seats. Hood mounts (rigged straddling the engine compartment of an automobile) are also used for driving while talking coverage (through the windshield), as well as forward p.o.v.'s of the road ahead.

hudson sprayer— Non-electrical mechanical pumping mechanism shaped like a fire extinguisher for spraying everything on set from scenic paint to greensmen colors.

I

inky— Small electrical lighting instrument rated at 500 watts with adjustable beam control.

insert car— Also known as a camera car, it is a flatbed truck with modifications for camera and lighting gear to allow filming of vehicles driving in traffic (or the open road), without disrupting normal movement and flow throughout the scene. Controlled by skilled drivers and manned by trained grip and camera personnel, the agile insert platforms allow for coverage of stunts and chases limited only by one's imagination.

insert shots— Set-up scenes for motion pictures and television stories that are to be used for detail (mostly without dialogue); thus segueing from one sequence to another while visually describing the action (i.e., a ringing phone or a car being started).

iron gang— Group of electrical workers on productions tasked with rigging all power and lights on stage and in perms before filming begins.

J

juicers— Slang for electricians, lamp operators.

juniors— Focusable electrical light of medium size with glass fresnel. Also known as junior spot and powered by a 1,000 or 2,000-watt lamp.

K

key grip — Person responsible for movement of camera and subsequent installation and use of diffusion, cranes, dollies, shooting platforms, lighting rigs and control of the grip crew within the process of motion picture or television production. Working directly alongside the cinematographer and gaffer with teams encompassing three to ten studio mechanics per show; the "first grip" or key, is not only well versed in all phases of production, but also handles on set safety as well, including designation of individual tasks to specific crew members with the appropriate skills.

key light — Main light source in a scene or shot; primary light; usually most powerful or focused.

M

maquillage — The craft of makeup as it is practiced in the production of a motion picture or television show; face fixing; powder man.

martini — Last shot of the day; final set-up; the martini, as in "the next shot's in a glass."

muslin, deswa — Fine cloth material used for intricate sewing tasks.

N

ND filters, gel or glass — Neutral density diffusion material (ND 3, 6, and 9) used to reduce bright sun or outdoor light for employment of wider apertures while filming. Manufactured in roll form for placement over lights or gradient glass inserts that fit in front of the lens; NDs are also used in conjunction with normal film stock under-exposed to achieve a nighttime look while actually filming during daylight — also known as "day for night."

nets — Part of a grip flag package consisting of semi-see-through knit-woven material attached to steel frame; designed to control light and create shadows. While a "single net" reduces light by 30 percent, a double would cut it by 60 percent and a triple net (three singles) would affect the light by 90 percent. A tool of gradation for shadows as well.

night sun — High output light mounted on helicopters with an intense beam for production night work and police use ranging from 5 to 40 million candle power.

nine lights — A lighting instrument manufactured to Earl Gilbert's specs by Color Tran; the unit had three stacks of diachronic heads mounted in a heavy steel frame (nine total, arranged tic-tac-toe style) with Fay-bulbs powering each lamp. In addition to having a very broad beam throw, the units could be individually aimed and could also be run on any electrical source.

O

opal — Translucent diffusion used to render a milky reflective high-light to its illumination while building contrast and detail in the shadows.

optical printer — Specialized film enlarger and printer which keeps the negative and subsequent print separate; allowing for special effects mats to be added, without damage to the original emulsion in the process.

over-cranking — A method to produce slow motion footage by speeding up the rate of the film through the camera, while projecting it at the normal rate of 24 frames per second when shown.

O-Zones — Open area of perms in studio ceiling superstructure left vacant for overhead rigging and shining lights through the set below. Often 10 feet across of open space, a fall from the four-inch wide beam walkways could be fatal, owing to the average stage height of 75 feet.

P

Panavision Ultra 70 (format)— Widescreen system that doubles ratio from ordinary 35 mm Panavision to much broader anamorphic images of 70 mm.

pee wee— Smaller, more compact dolly devised by Carl Manoogian and manufactured by Chapman.

perms—Steel and heavy lumber super structure suspended over stages in Hollywood for rigging greenbeds and catwalks where lights are hung and mounted to illuminate sets below. Ranging between 50 to 120 feet in height above the stage floor; work at these locations can be very hazardous due to the danger of falling.

phone-in— A movie or television project so rudimentary that one could stay home and tell others over the telephone all that the movie requires to properly film.

photo flood bulbs— Very stark, high-wattage bulbs used mostly in the days of black and white films for high key, high ratio lighting looks. It was also used between 1950 and 1960, until the common use of compact 1K zip lights replaced them.

pipe organ— Rolling rack of aluminum pipe (speed rail) cut to specific lengths; mostly used for car and other camera rigging.

poor man's process— The hands-on movement (shaking) of a picture car being photographed while stationary, to create a driving dynamic of a moving automobile. Other embellishments like sweeping head-light gags and rocking the vehicle with a two by four stud beneath the frame; were all 1950s era "grip-tricks" that served as solutions to otherwise static looking rear projection driving set-ups obviously done in the studio.

P.O.V.— Point of view; description to what the audience or camera sees on screen.

powder man— "Old school" Hollywood nickname for makeup person, implying the work of powdering an actor's face; also term for special effects technician skilled in explosions.

practical— Any light fixture on set that is used to add texture or fill illumination including lamps, wall sconces, overheads or floor lights.

production designer— Person responsible for the entire look of a film or television show. In charge of all art as seen on screen — the designer is usually hired in tandem with the director and is paramount to all that is shot.

pyrotechnics— A combination of electrical, liquid, gas, and or powder-based systems used in motion pictures and television to replicate an explosion or fire in a controlled fashion.

Q

quick cut— Fast, rapid editing of scenes in a motion picture or television show (interspersed with other vital action).

R

racking focus— Rapidly moving a lens through its focal range while keeping the subject sharp during the process of zooming in or out.

red gel #25— Color diffusion of deep red hue made in roll form and glass filter.

red one— State-of-the-art digital motion picture camera that uses capture software for its raw image rather than film or video tape.

ritter fan— Large wind machine utilizing a radial aircraft motor and propeller enclosed in a wire cage for special effects.

Roto-scope— Special effects animation technique originally devised for transfer of newsreels (or other film footage), to existing stock to allow for manipulation.

S

scenic artists— Technical artists responsible for all things rendered in the filming of a motion picture or television show incorporating painting and texturing of sets as well as anything else to be photographed; including floor coverings, doors, and window treatments seen in frame.

shiny board— A 4' × 4' reflective instrument used by grips to bounce sun for daylight fill on motion pictures and television. Generally constructed of silver foil or a painted wooden board and frame and often mounted on a stand, it bounces or reflects sunlight to fill a shot where electricity or lights are not possible.

shooter— DP; cinematographer

silk— Diffusion material used to control light as part of the grip flag package that increases contrast while softening skin tone; the overhead employment of silks 12' by 12' and greater are used to improve actor's looks on overcast days and reduce harsh sunlight on bright exteriors.

slate— Wooden framed slate board with hinged moving arm across the top that is painted with black & white stripes to I.D. each take before the action begins.

slate boy— Early camera department entry-level job involving snapping of slate-sticks to count takes and I.D. scenes.

sleeper track— Lumber constructed guideway for crane moves.

snoot— Attachment for lamp which narrows beam focus to a fine point.

speed rail— Fittings and aluminum pipe (from 1" to 1½" diameter cut to length) utilized to assemble camera, grip and lighting mounts in an erector-set like fashion with many different flanges, starters, couplers and parts as pieces with which to build. Originally part of high-technology construction trades, speed rail was also embraced by NASA for much of their safety guard and gantry needs due to its incredible strength and ease of use while building.

split diopter— Camera finder which allows for two separate planes of focus with a single lens; ultimately perfected by cinematographer Ralph Woolsey for director Richard Fleischer's *The New Centurions* in 1972.

squib— Electronically fired gun powder charge used in conjunction with blood packs to replicate bullet hits.

steadicam— Counter-balance arm and vest camera mount system invented by Garrett Brown that works off a combination of pneumatics and high tension springs to offset the weight and awkwardness of a hand-held camera. Capable of transverse movement both down and up steps, one master of the rig's offerings was Brown's test-dummy and best friend Ted Churchill (of *The Shining* fame), who became the new technique's most ardent and sought-after practitioner of his time.

sticks— Tripod, camera base, adjustable legs for camera mount (three) with a movable head attaching all beneath the camera.

T

Technicolor—A company driven color process for film (Technicolor Inc.) that saw its Hollywood use beginning in 1922 and lasting until the mid–1980s which provided a rich saturated look to skin tone and motion picture color not previously achieved.

techno crane— Automated camera crane with a 30-foot telescoping main boom arm connected to a remote control camera head; mounted to a center post riser capable of moving on or off track.

ten K (10K)— Large face lighting instrument with glass fresnel providing 10,000 watts of illumination each.

tent pole— Big budget studio motion picture that allows smaller films to utilize the larger movie's PR and pull the lesser offerings into the limelight as well; expected by studios to turn a profit in a short period of time.

Tinseltown— Hollywood, slang for 1930's Depression-era Los Angeles and the motion picture business of that time.

tulip crane— A riser mounted wheeled camera platform, with rotating boom arm 10 to 30 feet long. Engineered with a pivoting deck for two operators and camera, the rig is capable of using track, hard rubber, or pneumatic wheels for moves over almost any surface.

tungsten light— 3,200-degree color temperature instruments often used for television and motion picture lighting. Made in all sizes and styles, the lamp hue is of the bluer spectrum, while its white-end dynamic is quite good for accurate detail.

Tyler mount— Specialized gyroscopic camera mount originated and perfected by helicopter expert Nelson Tyler for airborne shots from choppers.

U

UFA— Universum Film-Aktien-Gesellshaft was a Berlin-based film studio during the silent era that made Europe's finest pictures. Established in 1917 to promote German culture, it ultimately launched the careers of Ernst Lubitch, Carl Freund, Rudolph Mate, and Fritz Lang, who did *Metropolis* in 1927. World War II resulted in the eventual emigration of many others who came to Hollywood such as Joe May, Robert Siodmak, Edgar G. Ulmer, and Billy Wilder (who left Germany just before the Nazis took over the studio for propaganda purposes). A product of the post–World War I Weimer Republic, UFA filmmakers' focus on expressionist movies containing crime and horror ultimately became the film noir offerings of 1950's America.

under crank— Operation of a camera at slower than normal speed resulting in a look of fast motion when projected at the normal 24 frames per second rate.

V

viewfinder— Camera's optical viewing device which shows the operator the area covered by his given lens and position from that distance before actually shooting or while exposing film.

X

xtra hammer— Grip; additional man to cover a hard day; temporary grip on a regular crew.

xenon lamp— Light with xenon gas trapped between tungsten electrodes producing a high intensity output similar to a carbon arc.

Index

Numbers in ***bold italics*** indicate pages with photographs.

Aardvark, Capt. (Charles Grodin) 100
A.A.U. Judo Nationals 44
Academy Award 10, 58, 66
Acevedo, Del 11, 13
Adams, Don ***122***
Adams, Kenny 214
Addams, Charles 139
Addams, Don 121
The Addams Family 139
Address Unknown 169
Adler, Lou 220
Adventures of Ozzie and Harriet 44, 70
An Affair to Remember 87
The African Queen 128
air ramp 59, 66
airbag 49, 60, 62, 63
Airplane 58
Airport '75 34, 35
Airport '77 35, 36
U.S.S. *Ajax* 193
U.S.S. *Alabama* 222
Alabama Hills, Lone Pine, California 94, 112
Alaina, Jack 44
Alberta, Canada 139, 188
Aldrich, Robert 47
Alfa Romeo Spider 120
Ali, Muhammad ***55***, 56, 58
alien attack sequences 66
All Night Long 40
All Quiet on the Western Front 5
All the Way Home 154
Allen, Irwin 48, 90
Allen, Seth 101
Allen, Woody 147
Aller, Herb 70
Alonzo, John 109, 110, 111, 112
Alpert, Herb 91
Altman, Robert 11, 89
Ambassador Hotel (Los Angeles) 96, 165
ambulance 62
American G.I. 172
American Gigolo 14
American Graffiti 146
American International Pictures 53

The American President 17
American Society of Cinematographers 168
A.M.T. (model company) 140
AMX-400 (1969) 146
"Anchors Aweigh" 173
And Justice for All 112, 221
Anderson, Dave 90
Andress, Ursula 47
Andrews, Julie 166
Andromeda Strain 180
Angelo, Don (Anthony Quinn) 184
animal trainer 58
animatronics 186
Annie 15
Another 48 Hours 63
Any Which Way You Can 59
The Apartment 200
Apollo 13 17
apology (Yubitsume) 218
apple box 191, 222, 225
approach, luminescent 111
Apted, Michael 14
Arbor system 114
arc lights 83, 101, 102, 104, 109, 116
Argentina 9
Arizona State University 25
Arkin, Alan 100, 102, 103
Arkoff, Sam 52, 53, 136
armistice signing 83
Arnett, James 63
Arnold, Newt ***215***
Around the World in 80 Days 5, 6
Arriflex cameras 75, 123, 134
Arthur, King (Richard Harris) 178
Arthur A. Middleton 69
Article 99 65
As Good as It Gets 67
Ascot Motor Speedway 28
Ashby, Hal 180
Asher, William 144
Ashland-Belle Helene Plantation 116
Asian Pacific theatre 169
Atari 5200 222
The Atlanta Child Murders 40, 106
ATV camera 62
audience gags 171
auto trams 147

automobile collisions 66
automotive economy 135
Autry, Gene 170
Avalon, Frankie 13
Averback, Hy 177
Aykroyd, Dan 14, 15, 190

B-movies 171
B-25 bomber 99, 102
Babin, Richard 221
Babocomari Ranch 82
Bach 181, 185
"bachelor pad on wheels" 142
back-lot exteriors 183
Backdraft 166
background lights 99, 102
Bacon, Kevin 15
Bad News Bears 110, 111
Baer, Max 172
Baggs, John (James Caan) 126
Bahamas 199
Bail, Charles 60
Bailey, Pearl 199
Baird, Dennis 148
Baker, Joe Don 52
Baker, Ox 58
Baker, Oregon 121
Balaban, Bob 102
Balanchine, George 155
Balchowsky, Max 205
bald cap 7
Baldwin, Alec 222
Baldwin, Peter 191
Baldwin Hills 93
Ballard, Lucien 23, 28, ***29***, ***30***, ***31***, 98, 103, 104, 107, 114
Ballhaus, Michael 131
Balsam, Martin 99
Baltimore 112, 116, 129
Banacek 146
Bancroft, Anne 35, 96
banister slide 66
Bank Shot 127, 159
Baretta 56
Barlett, Hal 204
Baron, Dana 221
Barris, George 135–151, ***141***, ***143***, ***144***

233

Barris, Sam 135
Barris Brothers 135
Barris Kustoms 139, 142, 150
Barrow, Dave 190
Bartlett, Hal 215
Bassinger, Kim 191
Bat Boat 145
Batman 50
Batman and Robin 67
Batman Returns 134
Batmobile 142, 143
Battle at Bloody Beach 90
Battle for the Planet of the Apes 184
The Battle of the Coral Sea 174
Bau, Gordon 7, 8
Baxley, Paul 54, 57
Bay of Pigs 154
BBS Productions 32, 177
Beaches 165
beam throw 97
bear attack 46, 47
Bearsdick, John 204
The Beast Master 60
Beaton, Alex 52
Beatty, Ned 108
Beatty, Warren 64, 69, **78**, **79**
Beaudine, William 47
bed-jumping sequences 203
Beddo, Philo 59
Bedig, Sass 55
Beethoven 221, 222
Beetle Bug 146
behind the scenes (B roll) 172
Bell, Book and Candle 173, 191
Belt, Stanley (Jerry Lewis) 139
Belushi, John 14, 15
Ben-Hur 35, 71, 91
Beneath the Planet of the Apes 12
Bengal tiger 60
Benjamin, Richard 102, 189, 191
Benny, Jack 7
Benyon, Jack "Warden" (Ben Johnson) 103
Berle, Milton 41, 185
Best Actor (Oscar) 12
Best Art (Oscar) 160, 162
Best Boy 194, 196, 200
Best Photography (Oscar) 178
Best Supporting Actress (Oscar) 12
Bettcher, Al 187, 190
The Betty Ford Story 40
The Beverly Hillbillies 138
Beverly Hills 113
Beyond the Valley of the Dolls 12
Big 15
The Big Brawl 58
The Big Country 194
Big Eye 10K light 93
Big Fauss, Little Halsey 206, 222
The Big Heat 71
Big Sky Ranch (Simi Valley) 119
"Big Tex" 91
The Big Valley 48
Bigelow, Kathryn 66
Billings, Montana 219
The Birdman of Alcatraz 175
Biroc, Joseph 131, 203
Birth of a Nation 59

Bishop, Joey 200
Bisset, Jacqueline 73
Bite the Bullet 127
Black, Gayle 142
Black and Blue crew 59
Black Gun 182
Black Sunday 56
Black Widow 85
Black Widows 57
The Blackbird 35
Blackula 52
Blake, Robert 56, 126, 132
Blankfield, Mark 40
Blaxploitation 53
Blind Date 132
Blocker, Dan 46
blood, fake 6, 7, 8, 11, 13, 18, 43, 101, 197, 201, 231
Blood in the Sun 43
Bloodsport 52
Blown Away 66
"Blue Dogs" 83
Blue Hawaii 50
Bluhdorn, Charles 219
BNC 169
Bobby Barr racing headers 140
Bode, Ralph 116, 222
Bodekker Gang 62
Bodine, Jethro (Max Baer) 139
Body Heat 188
bodyguards 14, 43
Bogart, Humphrey 128, 172
Bogdanovich, Peter 34
Bole, Terry 62
Bologna, Joseph 14
Bon-Ami soap flakes 85
Bonanza 22, 46
Bonaventure Hotel 66
Bondo 66
Bonfire of the Vanities 17
Bonnie and Clyde 172
boom arm 212
Boorman, John 155
Boreland, Richard 118, 119
Boren, Lamar 199
Borgnine, Ernest 130
Boris, Robert 126
Born Again 129
Bosom Buddies 15
Boston 106, 107
Boston Garden 107
The Boston Strangler 11, 179
Bottom of the Bottle 86
bounce lighting technique 86
Bound for Glory 187
Bowerman, Frank 183
Box, John 219
Boxer, Mike (trainer) 192
boxing 68
A Boy Like That 200
Boy on a Dolphin 87, 90
Boyle, Peter 35, 107
Boyle Heights 105
Brack, Bobby 144
Bradley, Dan 66
Brahma bull 60
Brando, Marlon 9, 71, 81, 87, 88
Brant, Paul (Convoy) 130

Brazil, Bo-Bo 44
breakaway plate 52
breast enhancement 186
Breathless 189
Brennan, Eileen 115
Brenner, Albert 152–167, **157**, **158**, **159**, **160**, **164**
Bridges, Jeff 66, 81, 156, 186
Bridges, Lloyd 199
Brill, Tony 222
Brink's headquarters 220
The Brinks Job 220
broadswords 60
Brolin, James 161
Bronson, Charles 8, 35, 47, 52, **181**, **182**
Brookley Air Force Base, Mobile, Alabama 111
Brooklyn, New York 152
Brooks, James 67
Brooks, Mel 121
Brooks, Richard 71, 72, **78**, 127, 128
Brother John 157
Brown, Jim 53, 182
Brown and Bertolucci's body shop 135
Brubaker, Tony 53
Bruce Almighty 68
Bryce Canyon National Park (Utah) 119
Brynner, Yul 8, 86
Bubba (Mykelti Williamson) 17
Buchholtz, Horst 8
Buckskin 30
Buddy Buddy 132
Buick 135, 136, 139, 141
building-to-building jump 59
Bukowski, Charles 148
Bullitt 72, 74, 76, 121
Bumstead, Henry 138
The Burbs 16
Burgess, Don 20
Burnett, Steven 54
Burns, George 36
The Burns and Allen Show 171
Burnside, Louisiana 116
Burton, Billy 64
Burton, Richard 85
Burton, Tim 66, 115, 134, 222
Burum, Stephen 131
Bus Stop 86, 89
Bustin' Loose 40
Butch Cassidy and the Sundance Kid 11, 18
The Butcher's Wife 117, 222
Butler, Bill 34, 77
Butler, Michael 111
Butterfield 8 96
butterfly bandages 47
Buttermaker, Morris (Walter Matthau) 110
Butterworth, Eddie 7

C-47 134
Caan, James 6, 28, 53, 55, 72, 126
Caddo Lake, Louisiana 132
Cadillac 138, 140, 146, 147, 204
Caesar (Roddy McDowall) 184

Caesar, Sid 13
Cagney, James 43
Cain, Kwai Ghang 52
Cain, William 52
Caine, Michael 159
The Caine Mutiny 194
Calabasas 51
Caldwell, Col. Alan (Sean Connery) 165
California Angels 22
California Military Academy 42
California Suite 162
Caligula 84
Callahan, Gene 110, 212
Cambridge, Godfrey 32
Camelot 177
Camelot castle 178
camera angles: multiple 189, 191; 360 degree coverage 165
camera flare 188
camera mount: electromagnetic 212; pivoting 186; quick release (dove tail) 207; *see also* hood mount
camera movement 69, 71, 160, 180
camera risers 41
camera, underwater 199
Can Can 7, 89
Canadian black bear 44
Canadian World's Fair 179
Candlestick Park (San Francisco) 175
canoe-sinking gag 60
Canutt, Joe 35, 51, 54
Canutt, Yakima 8, 35, 51
Cape Lookout, North Carolina 117
Capra, Frank 23, **195**, **197**
Capricorn One 161
Captain Kangaroo 153
Captains Courageous 36, 37
The Car 148
Car-Boy-Girl 146
car chases 37–38, 54, 59, 61, 62, 64, 66, 67, 74–75, 76, **130**, 147, 148–149, 174–175, 182, 193, 205, 206, 222, 228
car clubs 135
car crashes 56, 59, 137
Car 54 153
car jumps 57
car models 135
car mounts 28, 38, 41, 120, 206, 207, 212, 221, 222
car phone technology 139
car-roll gag 137
carbon rods 94
Cardera, Eddie 178
Cardiff, John 62
Cardinale, Claudia 72
Carlett, Lloyd 66
Carlsbad Caverns 89
Carney, Art 185
Carr, Charmian 9
Carradine, David 52
Carrera, Barbara 13
Carrey, Jim 68
Carson National Forest 127
Carter, Ellis 171
Cascarilla, Don 60

casket car 140
Cassavetes, John 73, 107, 108
Cassidy, Hopalong 152
Cassidy, Ted (Lurch) 139
Cast a Giant Shadow 202
Cast Away 16, 18
Castle, William 136, 171
Castlecomb Village (England) 95
Cat 177
Cat on a Hot Tin Roof 12
"the catacombs" 86
Catalina Freighter 110
Catalina Island 199
Catch Me If You Can 20
Catch 22 99, 100, 101
catering 57, 190
Cedars Hospital 43
celebrity clientele 140
Cesar Pavilion 44
CGI digital capture 20, 68
Chainsaw (Tommy May) 118, 119, 123, 126, 128, 131, 132, 133, 134
Chakiris, George 9
Chamber of Horrors 177, 178
Chambers, John 7, 10, 12, 13
Champion, Gower 159, 170
Chan, Jackie 52, 58, 67
Chandler, Jeff 173
Changes 204
Chaplin, Charlie 61
Chapman, Ralph 22, 34
Chapman crane 95
Chapman pee-wee dolly 33
character car 145, 149
character sketching 152
Chargon, Loraine 47
Charlotte Motor Speedway 28
Chase, Chevy 60, 115, 116, 221
Chase, Duane 9
Chatsworth 84
Chee Lee's Laundry 98
Cheng, George 55
Chesapeake Bay, Maryland 113, 221
Chevy Astro Van 150
Chevy chop top 137
Chicago 171, 180, 206
Chicago syndicate 171
China 174
Chinatown 109, 110
Chong, Tommy 220
Christie, Julie 69, 79
Christie, Vic 48
Chu Chu and the Philly Flash 114, 221
Chun (Joel Grey) 61
Chunjin (Henry Silva) 201
Church, Thomas Haden 82
CIA 187
Cimino, Michael 13, 14
Cinderella Liberty 126
Cinderfella 137
Cinecita Studios (Rome) 202
Cinema City 147, 192
CinemaScope 84, 88, 90, 93
Cinematographer Magazine 212
Cinemobile (Fouad Said) 106
Civic Playhouse 5
Clampett, Granny (Irene Dunn) 139

Clark, John 5
Clark, Royden 52, 53, 54
Clark, Shirley 153
Clarke, Arthur C. 164
Cleese, John 15
Cleopatra 71
Cleopatra Jones 105, 106, 126
Cleveland Browns 203
Cleveland Indians 21, 116
Clift, Montgomery 81
Cline, Patsy 165
clip lights, magnetic 104
Clooney, George 66
Close Encounters of the Third Kind 81
close-ups: extreme 126; facial 104; menacing 172, 181
cloud mats 84
Clouseau, Inspector (Peter Sellers) 175
Clue 222
Cluny, Diane (Sally Kellerman) 179
Clyde 59
Coburn, James 39, 72, 127, 131
CoCa Castles (Spain) 178
Cogburn, Rooster 98, 128
Cohen, Mickey 43
Cohen and Tate 222
Cohen Brothers 20
Cold War 10
Cole, Jesse 29
Cole, Tommy 67
Coleman, Doug 66
color theory 167
Colorado light 98
Colotrans 97
Columbia Studios 69, 116
Columbia's Burbank Ranch 174
Coma 161
combat, aerial 99
Combres-Toltec Railway (New Mexico) 127
Combs, Gary 62
The Comic 30
The Competition 188
composite photography 172
compressed nitrogen gas 212
Compton 135
Compton oil fields 106
Conaway, Jeff 13
Concord 39
Coney Island 53
The Connection 153
Connelly, Joe 140
Connery, Sean 165
Connors, Chuck 22
Connors, Mike 145
Conrad, Robert 51, 139
construction boom, 60-foot 187
construction methods 152
Continental Divide 14
continuous shots 177
convection ramp 149
Convoy 130, 131
Cook, Robin 161
Cooper, Gary 119, 197
Cooper, Marshall (Clint Eastwood) 179

Cooperman, Jack 107
Coppola, Francis Ford 40
Corleone, Don (Marlon Brando) 81
Corman, Roger 136
Cortez, Stanley 109
Corvette 126, 139
costumes, wool 82
Cotten, Joseph 86
Couch, Bill 56
Couffer, Jack 215, *216*, 217
Coughram, Larry 43
Count Three and Pray 172
Cover Girl 168, 169
Cow Town 170
cowbell instruments 101
crab dolly 171, 202, 226; portable 194
Crabbe, Buster 171
Crabbe, James 112
Crager wheels 146
Crassus 8
Crazy People 117, 222
Creach, Everett 56, 148
Crescent Heights (Los Angeles) 189
Crichton, Michael 40, 161, 184
Crosby, Floyd 144
Cross, Harley 222
crow's nest 174
crucifixion 119
Crystal, Billy 165
Crystal River (Ocala, Florida) 120
Cubans 195
cues, visual 184
cuing devices 102
Cukor, George 179
Culp, Robert 48
Culver City Drive-in 115
Culver City Theatre 45, 67, 83
Culver Studios 91
Cummings, Bob 170
Cummings & Sanders safety restraints 142
Cundley, Dean 131
Curtis, Tony 8, 9, 11, 110, 112
Curtiz, Michael 84
Cushenberry, Bill 142
custom rectifiers 116
cut away process vehicle 143
cut away set 98
cut away shots 182
Cyborg 2087 95

dailies 99, 102, 106, 203
Daisy Kenyon 83
Dallas, Texas 62, 91
Dalton, Timothy 112
Dalton — Code of Vengeance 60
Dalzall, Dennis 40
Damnation Alley 130
Dancer, Buck 62
Daneeka, Doc (Jack Gilford) 102
Dangerfield, Rodney 66
Daniels, William 149
D'Antoni, Phillip 205
Darby, Kim 98
Darkman 64
dashboard instruments 104
David and Bathsheba 84
Davidau, David 111

The Da Vinci Code 20, 21
Davis, Bette 163, 172
Davis, Gary 55, 67
Davis, Sammy, Jr. 199, 200
Dawn (Jessica Lang) 186
Day of the Dolphin 76
The Day the Earth Stood Still 84, 85
Days of Wine and Roses 176
Dayton, Ronnie 144
Daytona Beach Speedway (Florida) 28, 145
Deadrick, Vince 66
Dean, James 137
Dear God 166
Death Valley, California 84
Death Wish II 189
de Bordeaux, Dogue 16
Dee, Ruby 174
Deep Space Nine 65
The Deer Hunter 13, 14, 15, 126
Dehavilland DHC-1B Super Chipmunk 216
DeLaurentiis, Dino 166, 185, 186, 220
Deliverance 126
Delux Color 90
Delux lamps 117
Demetrius 84
DeMille, Cecil B. 5, 6, 118
Dempsey, Bob 175
DeNiro, Robert 13, 15, 110
Dennehy, Brian 15
The Denver Post 127
DePalma, Brian 17, 187
Depoe Bay Harbor, Oregon 76
Derek, Bo 186
Derek, John 171
Dern, Bruce 16, 185
DeSalvo, Albert (Tony Curtis) 179
Deschutes National Forest (Grants Pass, Oregon) 129
Desi-Lu Show 188
Desi-Lu Studios 9
Detch, Howard 65
The Detective 73
DeToth, Andre 168
The Devil's Hairpin 22
DeVito, Danny **76**
Devore, Sy 25, 138
Dexter, Brad 8, 9
Diabolique 72
Dial, Peter 52
Diamond, Neil 14
DiCaprio, Leonardo 20
Dick Tracy 64
The Dick Van Dyke Show 221
Dickenson, Angie 203
Die Hard 2 63
diffusion: amber 109; gradated 185
digital morphing 68
Dimitri, Nick 59
Dinner, Michael 116, 222
Disney 47, 118
Disney, Walt 145–146
The Disorderly Orderly 27
dive bars 153
Dmytryk, Edward 87, 88

Dobbins, Benny 51, 54, 62
Dobell, Bryan 138
Dobson, Tamara 105, 106, 126
Doctor Detroit 15
Doctor Doolittle 95
Dr. Strangelove 154
Dodge Charger 76, 205
Dodge Dart 145
Dodger Stadium 202
dog attack sequence 65
dolly, downhill 213
dolly, flying 134
dolly, low mode 72
dolly moves 188, 200, 206, 219
Dominican Air Force 220
Dominican Republic 219
The Don Is Dead 184
Donen, Stanley 168, 218
Donner, Clive 155
Donner, Richard 59, 177
Donno, Eddie 56
double image gags 191
Double Impact 191
Doucette, John 52
Douglas, Kirk 8, 175, 177
Dourif, Brad **76**
Doyle, Chris 64
Doyle's Pub 220
Dozier, William 145
Dragnet 15
Dragoti, Stan 190
Dragula 140, 141
Drake, Tom 88
A Dream of Kings 180, 206
Dreedle, Brig. General (Orson Wells) 103
Dreyfuss, Richard 17, 161
Drive, He Said 34
drive-in theatres 135
The Driver 37
driver's compartment, hidden 139
driver's side hostess mount 126
driving sequences 57, 58, 66, 67, 74, 75, 97, 103, 104, 105, 107, 108, 137, 139142, 143, 145, 146, 148–149, 185, 203, 205, 212, 214, 221, 228, 230
driving techniques 75
drop away cages 217
The Dukes of Hazzard 57, 58
Dunaway, Faye 54, 109, 204
Dunn, Irene 139
Dupar, Edwin 196
Dupree electronic fuel pumps 143
Duvall, Robert 99

Earthquake 34, 35, 53
East Los Angeles 221
East New Jersey State Prison 63
East of Eden 71
Eastman, George 83
Eastwood, Clint 57, 76, 121
Eaton, Cal 42
Ebert, Roger 12
Ed Wood 66
Edwards, Bill 88
Edwards, Blake 61, 131, 132, 133, **176**
The Egyptian 84

Eight on a Lamb 203
Eimo (camera) 214
Eisenhower 7
Ekins, Bud 54, 75, 146, 205, 219
Ekland, Britt 186
El Pachuco 114
El Paso, Texas 103
El Segundo Sewage Plant 183
Elam, Jack 52
Eldorado convertible 91, 148
Electra Glide in Blue 126
electrocution 107
Elliott, Sam 82
Elmer Gantry 174
Elwes, Cary 167
Embryo 13
emergency personnel 62
Emmerich, Roland 66
End of Days 67
English, John 170
English grips 95
Enter the Dragon 51
Enterprise 188
Epper, Gary 56
The Errand Boy 24
Escape from San Quentin 173
European embassies 10
Evans, Robert 109
Everson, Les 88
Every Which Way But Loose 57
The Exorcist 81, 219
Experiment in Terror 174
exploding door gag 56

F4 Wildcat 129
Fabens, Texas 103
Fabian 89
The Fabulous Invalid 5
Fail Safe 154, 165
Fair Park 91
Falk, Peter 107, 108
The Fall Guy 59
fall safety apparatus 49
Family Matters 41
Far Horizons 22
Farewell My Lovely 110
farmhouse location 112
Farnsworth, Richard 156
Farrow, Mia 73
The Fast and Furious 150
Father Goose 71
Father Kovak 67
Faulkner, Lee 145
Faye, Alice 185
The F.B.I. 49
feather light 180, 188, 190
Fenton and Feinberg 59
Ferrari 275 (GTS) 204
Ferrari 512 *211*, *213*
Ferrer, Jose 91
Field, Sally 17
Fiennes, Sgt. Ranulph (SAS) 95
Fier, Jack 171
Fifth Air Force 152
50 ASA stock 96
fight choreographer 58
fight scenes 165; barroom brawl 50
Fiji 18

Filgli Estate 79
film emulsion 71
film loader 70
film noir 172, 218; lighting 177; principles 188
Film Services Lab 169
Filmways Productions 139
filters, 30-pound 95
The Final Countdown 85, 113
Fine, Gerald 107
Fine, Milton 48
A Fine Mess 61
fire effects 17, 35, 53–54, 55–56, 59, 62, 102, 106, 155, 166, 230
Fireball 500 143, 144
Firebird 400 146
fireworks 67
First National Pictures 69
Fischer (dolly) 189, 190
Fischer sled 190
Fisher, Carrie 16
Fitz Willy 203
Fitzgerald, Ella 174
Fitzgerald, F. Scott 110
Fitzsimons, Charles 145
5 ASA film 83
flame thrower bumpers 142
Fleischer, Richard 14, 95, 104
Fletch 60, 115, 222
Fletch Lives 116, 222
Flight from Ashiya 9
Flintstone-mobile 150
The Flintstones 150
floating the arm 212
Florida 189
Flowers, A.D. 54
fluorescents, small 115
Flynn, Errol 169
Flynn, John 64
foam padding 49
follow cart 115
follow spot 87, 101
Follow That Dream 8, 120
Folsey, George 91
Fonda, Henry 88
Fonda, Jane 34, 155
footage: aerial 206; aircraft to aircraft 100
Footloose 15
For Those Who Think Young 139
Forbidden Ranch 217
forced dump tank 54
forced framing 74
Ford, Glenn 174
Ford, John 24, 49
Ford: Cobra engine 140; Explorer XLT 149; GT40 racer 208, 212; LTD Country Squire 115; Model A 70, 135; Model T 140; Mustang 68, 74, 75, 76, 141, 147, 205; Thunderbird 139, 190; X150 150
Ford's International Caravan of Cars 139
Foreman, Jack 218
Foreman, Milos 77
Forever Amber 83
Forrest Gump 17
Fort Utah 30

The Fortune Cookie 203
Forty Acres Studios 92
40mm lens 214
Forty Pounds of Trouble 9
4 AWG cable 84
Four for Texas 47, 48
The Four Seasons 221
The Fourth War 134
The Fox 72
Fox, Billy 59
Fox, Michael J. 17
Fraker, Alva 69
Fraker, Bill *73*, *74*, *77*, *78*, *79*, *80*, *81*, *158*
Fraker, Charlie 69
Fraker, William 69–82
Fraker, William, Jr. 69
France 212
Francis, Anne 49
Franciscus, James 177
Frankenheimer, John 56, 156, *157*, *175*, 177, 200, 201
Frankenstein make-up 48
Frazier, Joe 58
Freddie and the Dreamers 142
Fredricks, Elsworth 201
Freeman, Leonard 98
Freeze, Mr. 67
The French Connection 75, 205, 219
The French Racing Commission 209
The Freshman 81
Freulich, Henry 171, 172
Freund, Karl "Pappy" 171
Frick, "Ratchet Head" 120
Friendly Persuasion 119
Friends of Eddie Coyle 106, 107
Frogmen 84
From Here to Eternity 172
front projection 155
Froug, Bill 177
The Fugitive 204
The Fugitive Kind 153
Furie, Sidney 206
The Fury 187

G-40 formula racing tires 148
Gable, Clark 23, 140
gaffer, underwater 90
Gaily Gaily 180
Gainesboro, Tennessee 156
Gallo, Fred 189
The Gambler 53
Games 72
Garbutt, Frank 42
Garfunkel, Art 102
Gargoyles 215
Garner, James 54
Garson, Greer 87
Gary Lewis and the Playboys 142
gaskets: rubber 75, 205; stabilizing 206
Gaunt, Bud 102
Geer, Will 52
Geller, Bruce 12
General Lee 150
General Services Studio 70
Gentleman's Agreement 83

Gentlemen Prefer Blondes 84
Georgia Rule 166
Gere, Richard 14, 189
German Shepherds 58
German submarine generators 102
Gero, Gary 215
Gersh Agency 77
Get Smart 121
The Getaway 29, 103, 104, 130
Getting Straight 32
G.I. Bill 70
Giant 5
Gilbert, Earl 83–117, **85**, **92**, **105**
Gilbert, Mickey 54, 59, 60, 68, 129
Gilbert, Ray 83
Gilbert, Velma 83
Gilda 69
Gilford, Jack 102
Gill, Andy 59, 149
Gill, Jack 9, 149
Gittes, Jake (Jack Nicholson) 109
Gladstone (boats) 145
Glaser, Paul Michael 62, 191
Gleason, Jackie 153
Glenn, Scott 15
gliders 130
Glover, Danny 15
Go Tell the Spartans 130
Goffshaw, Robert **210**
Gold Card 21
Goldbloom, Jeff 15
Golden Cherry (Auburn, Alabama) 112
"Golden Sahara" 137, 138
Goldie and the Boxer 58
Goldstein, Louie 6
Goldstone, James **39**
Gone in 60 Seconds 147, 150
Gone with the Wind 106, 108
The Good Earth 70, 169
The Good-bye Girl 161
Goodman, John 150
Gordon, Robert 172
Gordon, Ruth 73
government cooperation 201
grab-shot assignments 70
Grace, Carol 108
The Graduate 71, 96, 97, 119
Graham, Billy "The Superstar" 44
Gran Torino 35, 151
Granatelli, Andy 146
Grand Canyon 114
Grand National Roadster Show 151
Grandpa (Al Lewis) 140
Grant, Cary 71, 87, 137
Graves, Eddie 142
Graves, Peter 52
gray scale 168
Grease 13
The Greatest Show on Earth 118
The Greatest Story Ever Told 91, 119
Green, Marshall 8
The Green Hornet 51, 150
The Green Mile 18
Green River 93
Grey, Joel 61
Griffith, Frank 14

Griggs, Loyal 91, 119
grip, underwater 199
Grodin, Charles 15, 16, 100, 103
Grosso and Grosso 93
ground-to-air warning signals 101
Gruskoff, Michael 218
GTO Monkee mobile 150
Guercio, James 126
guerrilla filmmaking 112
Guffey, Burnett 169, 174, **175**, 184, 203
Guillain Barré syndrome 187
Guillerman, John 56
Gulf + Western 219
Gunfight at the OK Corral 22
Gunga Din 200
Gunsmoke 119
Gussart, Rene, Jr. 209
Guyamas, Mexico 100
Guys and Dolls 194
Gwynne, Fred 48, 140
gyro-stabilized control head 206
gyro-stabilized counter-weighted arm 81

Hackett, Buddy 146
Hackman, Gene 40, 126, 127
Haggerty, H.B. 59
Hagio, Tasuke 43
Halacki, Toby 147, 148, 149
Halfway House Café (Santa Clarita) 117
Hall, Conrad 20, 70, 71, 126, 131, 134
Hall, Freddie 84
The Hallelujah Trail 94, 119, 202
Halloran, John 43
Hamilton, George 112
Hamilton, Guy 61
Hammer Brothers 89
Hammersmith Is Out 180
Hammett 40
Hampshire frost diffusion 188
Hang 'Em High 179
hanging practicals 109, 112
"The Hangman" 44, 46
Hanks, Tom 15, **16**, 17, 18, **19**, 20, 190
Hanna-Barbera 150
Hannah, Daryl 117
Hanson, Curtis 67
The Happening 155
Happy, Cliff 66
Hard Times 35, 52
Hard to Kill 63
The Harder They Fall 172
hare and hound shots 206
The Harlem Globetrotters 171
Harmon, Mark 165
Harper, Jessica 15
Harpman, Fred 179, 184
The Harrad Experiment 184
Harrelson, Woody 18
Harris, Ed 165
Harris, Leon 161
Harris, Richard 178
Harryhausen, Ray 172, 199
Hart, Clive 214

Hartoonians Gas Station (Pasadena) 113
Harvey, Orwin 52
Hasselhoff, David 149
Hathaway, Anne 166
Hathaway, Henry 28, 86, 98
Hauser, Bob 89
Havana cigars 48, 49
Hawaii Five-0 97, 98, 119
The Hawaiians 32, 87, 94
Hawks, Howard 27, 84
Hayes, Gabby 46
Hayes, Ira 8
Hayworth, Rita 69, 168, 169, 173
Head, Edith 25, 202
head rest, floating 138
head shots 13, 20
Heaven Can Wait 69, 81
Hecht, Ben 180
Hecht, Harold 9
helicopter work 111, 113, 174–175, 202, 216, 220, 221, 225, 229, 232
Hell Cats of the Navy 173
Hell Up in Harlem 53
Hello Dolly 11
Helltown 132
Helms, Matt (Dean Martin) 142
Henderson, O.T. 189
Henning, Paul 138
Henry, Buck **79**, 121
Henry Mayo Hospital 58
Herbie 146
Here Comes Mr. Jordan 69
Here Comes the Nelsons 70
Herman the Great 48
Hernandez, Jesse 66
Hero at Large 163
Heston, Charlton 30, 35, 82, 129, 184
Hickman, Bill 146
Hicks, Chuck 52, 59, 60
high contrast ratios 96
high falls 48, 49, 52, 53, 54, 56, 59, 63, 67
High Noon 203
High School Confidential 136
high speed stunts 60, 139, 209
Hiken, Nat 153
Hilborn Injectors 142
Hill, Steven 10
Hill, Walter 35, 37, 132
Hiller, Arthur 222
Hines, Gregory 165
Hinkle (Jack Lemmon) 203
Hirschfield, Gerald 148
hit-and-fall gag 57
Hitchcock, Alfred 22, 137
Hitler 9
Hoak, Winton 200
Hoary, Frank 142
Hodges, Eddie **195**
Hoffman, Dustin 17, 18, 96, 120
Hogan, Hulk 62, 63
Holden, William 54
A Hole in the Head 195
Holiday, Doc 82
Holly carburetors 143
Hollywood 195

Hollywood Dojo 43
Hollywood (old school) tricks 188
Hollwood Park 116
Hollywood-ized animals 216
Holt, Larry 54, 57, 59, 60, 66
Honda CRX 150
Honda motorcycle 204
Honey West 49
Honeymoon in Vegas 81, 82
Hong Kong 51
hood mounts 75, 103, 120
Hope, Bob 203
Hopkins, Bo 156
Hopkins, Stephen 66
Hoponhu Beach (Hawaii) 187
Horner, Harry 153
Horsley, David 199
hostess mounts 75
hostess trays 41, 75
Hot Blood 172
Hot Car Girl 136
Hot-Rod 136
Hot Rod Herman 140
Hot to Trot 116, 222
Hotel 40
Houmas House Plantation 116
House of Wax 177
Houstous, Pat 75
How to Murder Your Wife 153, 203
How to Succeed in Business Without Really Trying 203
Howard, Rance 16
Howard, Ron 17, 166
Howard, Trevor 9
Howe, James Wong 156, 173, 194
Hud 30
Hudson sprayers 91
Huff, Tommy 56
Huffman, Felicity 167
Huggins, Roy 89
Hughes, Terry 117
Hughes, Whitey 55, 59
Hugo, Victor 117
human Christmas tree 81
human embryo 13
humidity 187
Hung, Sammo 51
Hungry Joe (Seth Allen) 101
Hunt, Linda 15
Hunt, O. L. 91, 114
Hunter, Jim **122**
Huntsville, Texas 103
Huntsville Correctional Facility 103
Hurt, William 188
The Hustler 153
Huston, Angelica 110
Huston, John 12, 23, 184
Hutton, Jim 94
Hyams, Peter 67, 132, 133, **164**
Hyannis Port 201
hydraulic compacting ram 214
hydraulic gymbal 56
hydraulic ramming spikes 142

I Can't Give You Anything but Love 174
I Dream of Jeannie 146
I Love Lucy 171

I Married a Monster from Outer Space 22
I Outta' Be in Pictures 163
I Spy 10, 48, 121
I Walk the Line 156
Iacocca, Lee 138
I.A.T.S.E. (Local 80) 193
Ibiza, Spain 87
Iida, Tadasu 43
Illinois 114
image motion 20
Imelda, Jeff 66
improvisation 170
In Harm's Way 94
in studio miniatures 199
Independence Day 66
Indian burial ground scenes 212
Ingalls, Don 49
initiation fees 70
inky (light) 104
Inoki, Antonio 55
insect shot 189
inside moves 59
Invitation to a Gunfighter 9
Ireland, John 194
Irma la Duce 201
iron chores 84
iron gang 83, 84, 87, 90, 91
Iron Horse 177
Irving, Amy 188
Isky racing cams 140
Island of Dr. Moreau 13
island spirits 217
Israel 219
Israeli Military 202
It Came from Beneath the Sea 172
"It Kid" 178
Italian lighting crews 202
Italy 95
It's a Wonderful Life 88
It's Only Money 24
Ivan Tors Productions 199
Iverson Ranch 84

The Jack Benny Show 46
The Jack Rourke Show 5
Jack the Giant Killer 199
Jaguar XK-150 140
Jahns pistons 143
jail sets 175
Janes, Loren 49, 52, 54, 59, 205
Janssen, David 204
Janus 155
Japan, Post-war 172
The Jazz Singer 14
Jeanne Eagles 173
Jeep Wrangler Sahara 149
Jeffries, Dean 150
Jekyll and Hyde Together Again 40
Jeremiah Johnson 212, 213
The Jerk 58, 113
Jerusalem 84
Jesus 119
Jethro (Max Baer) 139
Jewison, Norman 112, 113, 180, 221
Jim Crow 171
Jingle All the Way 66

J.J. Hunsecker (Burt Lancaster) 194
J.J. Starbuck 76
Joe Versus the Volcanoe 16
Johnny Dangerously 40
Johnson, Ben 103
Johnson, Don 184
Johnson, Fred 22, 23
Johnson, Lamont 177
Johnson, Navin (Steve Martin) 113
Johnson, Pat 58
Johnson, Ray 177
Johnson, Roy 142
Johnson, Tor 66
Johnson, Van 41, 86
The Joker (Ceasar Romero) 50
Jonathan Livingston Seagull 215, **216**, 217
Jones, Carolyn **195**
Jones, Dean **129**
Jones, James Earl 35
Jones, Lee 147
Jones, Newt 7
Jones, Ray 90
Jones, Tommy Lee 66
Jordan, John 100
Jordan, Richard 107
Jourdan, Louis 89
Journey to the Center of the Earth 89
Judo Gene 63, 68
Judo lessons 43, 46
Juke Box Racket 137
jumping mode 149
June, Ray 172
Jungle Jim (series) 171
Junior 91, 95, 98, 115
Junior Bonner 214
The Junkman 148
Jurassic Park 149
"just killed" look 117

Kaiser Steel 70
Kaminski, Janusz 18
Kansas arc lights 84, 94, 102
Kansas City, Missouri 65
Kaprisky, Valerie 190
The Karate Kid 52
Karath, Kim 9
Kasdan, Lawrence 15
Katzin, Lee 209
Katzman, Leonard 119
Katzman, Sam 171, 172, 173, 191
Kaufman, Boris 154
Kazan, Elia 84, 110
Keach, Stacey 104, 105
Keaton, Buster 61
Keaton, Michael 190, 221
Keith, Brian **30**
Kelly, Gene 11
Kelly, Wallace 23, 30, 32
Kemper, Victor 36, 53, 106, 107, 112, 113, 115, 117
Kempo Karate 191
Kennedy, Arthur 28
Kennedy, John F. 201
Kenny, Ken **76**
Kerr, Deborah 86
Kersey, Paul (Charles Bronson) 189
Khrushchev, Nikita 7, 89

Killer Elite 35, 55, 130
Kilmer, Val 82
The King and I 9, 86
King Cobra 12
King Kong 56, 185, 186
King of Marvin Gardens 34
King of the Congo 171
Kingi, Henry 56
Kinnear, Greg 67
Kinney, Mike 221
Kismet 5
Klein, Kevin 15
Kline, Benjamin 168
Kline, Richard 168–192, **170**, **176**, **178**, **181**, **182**, **183**, 206
Kline-sled 190
Klingon 14, 65
Klondike Kate 168
knife fight 29, 56
knife gag 109
Knight, Michael 149
Knight Rider 139
Knots Landing 60
Knox (Robert Redford) 206
Kodak 5254 film stock 72, 77
Koenekamp, Fred 13, 177
Kolchak the Night Stalker 54
Korean War 5, 44, 136
Korkes, Jon 99
Korkes, Richard 141
Koster, Henry 90
Kovacs, Laszlo 34, 81, 111
Kowalski, Bernie 12
Kramer, Joel 66
Krasner, Milton 85, 87, 90
Kristofferson, Kris 130
Kronick, Bill 186
Kryptonite, Mr. 44
Kubota, Take 55
Kubrick, Stanley 8
Kung Fu 52
Kura, Kentara 218
Kustoms Car Club 135
Kyoto Studios (Japan) 218

L.A. Armory 136
L.A. Confidential 66
L.A. Fairgrounds 115
L.A. Sports Arena 183
lacerations 57
Ladd, Alan 87
The Ladies Man 23, 24
Lady Bug, Lady Bug 154
The Lady from Shanghai 169
The Lady Killer 20
Laemmle, Carl 168
Lake Arrowhead, California 201
Lake Powell 114
Lake Pyramid 60
Lamb, John 90
LaMotta, Jake 59
Lancaster, Burt 13, 94, 124, **175**
Landau, Martin 10, 28, 52, 66, 195
"The Landmaster" 130
Landon, Michael 46
Lane, Lois 44
Lang, Charles 71, 91, 93
Lang, Walter 7, 86, 89

Lange, Jessica 165, 186
Lansbury, Angela 40
L.A.P.D. 43
Larson, Bob 116
Larson, Glen 59, 149
Las Vegas 189
LaShelle, Joe 201
Lassick, Sidney 76
Lassick, Sydney **76**
Lassie 46
The Last Hurrah 173
The Last of the Mohicans 134
The Last Picture Show 34
The Last Tycoon 110
Lathrop, Philip 34, 35, 38, 40
Lau, Fred **195**
Laughlin, Frank 159
LaVigne, Emile 8, 9
Law, Jude 18
The Law Giver 184
Lawford, Chuck 137
Lawford, Peter 200
Lawton, Charles, Jr. 173, 174
Lazzara, Louis 67
Le Mans 206, 208, 209, 210, 211, 212, 213
lead shield 13, 14
Leary, Dennis 18
Leavitt, Sam **198**
LeBell, Eileen 42, 43
LeBell, Gene 42–68, **45**, **47**, **50**, **55**, **64**, **65**
LeBell, Maurice 42
Lee, Bruce 51
Legacy of Terror 54
The Legend of the Lone Ranger 81, 163
Leigh, Janet **28**
Lemmon, Jack 35, 132, **176**
lens selection 71
Leo Cabrillo State Park 89
Leonard, Elmore 124
Leonard, Fred 60
Leonard, Sheldon 48
Leonard, Terry 52, 54, 59, 67
Lettich, Sheldon 191
Lettieri, Al 103
Levee, Samuel 152
Leven, Boris 115, 153, 180, 185
Levin, Ira 72
Lewis, Al 140
Lewis, Jerry **23**, **24**, **25**, **26**, **27**, **28**, **32**, **33**, 34, **37**, 49, 137, 138, 139
Lewis, Paul 147
U.S.S. *Lexington* 129
S.S. *Liberty Lane* 191
Lifetime Achievement Award (S.O.C.) 223
light: asphalt-blue 108; direct 109; directional 109; incidental 109; *see also* background lights
lighting grid, submersible 87
lightning machine, focusable 93
lightning strikes 98
Li'l Abner 26
Lilly 168
Lincoln 137, 142, 148
Lindon, Lionel 200

Linge, Herbert 207
Linn-Baker, Mark 15
Linwood 136
A Lion Walks Among Us 89
Lipstein, Harold 173
liquid proofing 84
Lisi, Virna 203
Lithgow, John 15
Little House on the Prairie 46
live studio audience 201
Livesley, Big John 9, **198**
Livingston, Montana 81
Lloyd, Christopher **76**, 115
Lloyd, Frank 43
Lloyd, Harold 61
Local 80 40, 118
Local 705 5, 6, 21
Local 728 83
Local 827 155
location fixer 202
locations, rugged 127, 199
Lock-Up 63
Lockheed Aviation 70, 136
Loftin, Carey 52, 53, 205
Logan, Josh 86, 87, 177
Lola T-70 207
Lombard Street (San Francisco) 146
London 21, 96, 179
The Lone Ranger 70
Lonely Are the Brave 175
The Lonely Guy 222
Long Beach (Queen Mary) 110
Long Beach Auditorium 66
Looking for Mr. Goodbar 81
Lord, Del 169
Lord, Jack 97, 98
Lord Light 93
Loren, Sophia 87
Los Angeles 42, 51, 138
Los Angeles Ambassador Hotel 96
Lost in Yonkers 17
The Lost Planet 171
Louisiana plantations (Houmas House and Ashland) 185
Louma Crane 79, 132
The Louvre 21
Love, Buddy 25
The Love Boat 41
The Love Bug 145, 146
Love on the Run 40
Loving Couples 39
Lucas, George 146
"Luck Be a Lady" 194
The Luck of Ginger Coffey 154
Lucky Lady 218
Lugosi, Bela 66, 168
Lujack, Jesse (Richard Gere) 189
Lumet, Sidney 153, 165
Lupton, Cecil 116
Lupus, Peter 52
L.U.V. 155
The Lux Video Theatre 7
Lynch, Red (Ross Martin) 174
Lyon, Earl 95

M-16 rifle 53
Macavee Brothers 52
MacGraw, Ali 104, 219

MacIver, Norma 73
MacLaine, Shirley 7, 39
MacMurray, Fred 85
Macy, William H. 18
Made in America 17
The Magic Carpet 171
magic mirror shootout 169
The Magic Sword 8
The Magnificent Seven 8, 71
Maine 37
Malaysia 87
Malden, Karl 28, ***31***
Malibu Creek State Park 95, 120
Mame 34
The Man from U.N.C.L.E. 10, 48, 121
Man of Steel 45
Man of the West 197, 199
The Man Who Shot Liberty Valance 24
Man with a Golden Arm 203
The Man with One Red Shoe 15, 190
The Manchurian Candidate 153, 200, 201
Mandingo 185
Manhattan 53, 194
Manhattan Beach, California 137
Mankiewicz, Joseph 194
Mann, Daniel 206
Mann, Delbert 203
Mann, Michael 177
Manners, Marlo (Mae West) 112
Mannis 59
Mannix 145
Manoogian, Carl 22–41, ***23***, ***24***, ***25***, ***26***, ***27***, ***28***, ***29***, ***30***, ***31***, ***32***, ***33***, ***36***, ***37***, ***38***, ***39***, 121
Manza, Ralph 146
Marin, Cheech 220
Marine Land (of the Pacific) 199
Marlowe, Phillip (Robert Mitchum) 110
Marriage on the Rocks 141
Mars 161
Marshall, Gary 165, 166
Marshall, William 52
Marta, Jack 145
martial arts 55
Martin, Dean 47, 87, 140, 141
Martin, Ross 174
Martin, Steve 14, 113, 221, 222
"the martini" 98, 229
Martinson, Leslie 139
Marvin, Lee 121, 122
M.A.S.H. 11, 12
Mason, Marsha 126
Master Gun Fighter 159
master light 11, 111, 112, 113, 114
master shots 96, 169, 191
Maté, Rudolph 169
Matheson, Tim 115
matte inserts 111
Matthau, Walter 110, 132
Mattie Ross (Kim Darby) 98
Mature, Victor 84, 110
Maui 217
Maverick 7
Max Duggan Returns 161
Max Factor makeup 14

Maxwell, Marilyn 89
May, Brad 131
May, Cecil Thomas 118
May, Elaine 107, 108
May, Tommy 118–134, ***120***, ***121***, ***122***, ***123***, ***124***, ***125***, ***127***, ***128***, ***129***, ***131***, ***133***
May, William 15
Mayo, Virginia 30
Mazatlan, Mexico 69
Mazurki, Mike 47, 48, 49
McAllister (dolly) 196, 197
McBride, Alan 101
McBride, James 189
McCord, Ted 71
McCoy, Carol (Ali MacGraw) 103
McCoy, Doc (Steve McQueen) 103
McCoy, Sherman (Tom Hanks) 17
McCulloch chainsaw 122
McDonald, Joe 88
McDonnell Douglas 135
McGavin, Darren 54
McGirk, Tarzan 48
McGuire, Al 106
McLean, Nick 131
McMann's Minstrels 5
McNall, Bruce 114
McPherson, John 117
McQueen, Steve 8, 28, ***29***, ***30***, 54, ***74***, 103, 104, ***215***
Mead, Syd 165
The Mechanic 181, 182
mechanical Kong 186
mechanical leg-bleeding gag 18
Meehan, George 169
Meet John Doe 70
Meet Wally Sparks 66, 191
Mellor, William 88, 90, 91, 119
Mel's Diner (San Francisco) 146
Mendez, Sam 18
Menzies, Heather 9
Menzies, William Cameron 158, 169
Mercedes 38, 137
Mercouri, Melinda 180
Mercury 138, 139, 142
Meredith, Burgess 50
Metro Goldwyn Mayer (MGM) 6, 12, 60, 94, 119
Metty, Russell 23
Mexico 219, 220
Meyers, David 221
Meyers, Ross 12
Miami 195
Michelin Man 49
Mickey and Nicky 107
midget 98, 104, 115
Midnight Run 15
A Midsummer Night's Dream 155
Midway 129
Mifume, Toshiro 129
Miles, Terry 7
Milestone, Lewis 195, 197
military exercise 181
military sci-fi 202
Miller, Carl Lewis 185
Miller, Earl 22
Miller, John 190

Miller, Capt. John 18
Miller, Tom 117
Million Dollar Mystery 61
Milton, Larry 121
Minnelli, Liza 218
Minor, Bob 53
Mirisch, Walter 129, 199, 202, 203, 204, 206
Mirisch Brothers 8
mirrors: angled 139; split screen 191
The Misfits 23
Misfits Flats 23
Mission Impossible 9, 10, 12, 52, 66, 121
Missouri 114
The Missouri Breaks 161, 219
Mr. Hobbs Takes a Vacation 90
"Mr. Looking for Trouble" 42
Mr. Majestyk 185
Mr. Mom 114, 221
Mr. Novak 177
Mitchell BNC camera 205
Mitchell DE-43 (destroyer) 83
Mitchell filter 188
Mitchell standards 169
Mitchum, Robert 107, 110
Moab, Utah 81, 93
mobile crane arm 211, 212
Mobile Harbor, Alabama 223
Mobley, Mary Ann 49
model gliders 217
Moio, John 54, 59, 203
Mojave Desert 194
Mole Richardson (company) 97
Moment by Moment 38
Mommy (Shelley Winters) 106
The Money Pit 15
Money Train 66
Mongoose Manor 97
The Monkees 177
monochromatic tone 185
Monroe, Marilyn 23, 84, 86, 87, 89
Monroe Studios 69
Monte Walsh 76, 122, 125
Monterey Peninsula 215
Montgomery, George 30, 171
Monument Valley, Utah 193
Moore, Demi 117
Moore, Dudley 117
Moran, Benny 118
Moriarty, Michael 187
Morituri 9, 71
The Morning After 165
Morris, Greg 10
Morse, Terry, Jr. 9
mortician's wax 13
Moser, Bob 140
Motel Six (inflatable) 143
Motion Picture Academy 160
motion picture cinematography 70
motion sickness 75
motorcycles 52, 53, 54, 57, 59, 62, ***128***, 133, 182, 204, 205, 206
The Mountain 194
The Mountain Road 174
The Mouse That Roared 177
movie theatres 45
Movieland 56, 205

Movieola dolly 193
Movietone News Agency 70
mule suit 46
Mulholland Falls 134
Mulligan, Robert 157, 159, **160**
Mulray, Evelyn (Faye Dunaway) 109
multi-strut technology 120
Munster, Herman (Fred Gwynne) 48, 140
Munster Coach 140
The Munsters 48, 140
Murder She Wrote 40
Murphy, Geoff 166
Murphy, K.O. 48
Murphy, Richard 172, 174
Murray, Charlie 144
Murray, Don 86
Murray, Johnny 97
Murren, Dennis 111
muscular dystrophy 27
Museum of Modern Art 41
musical 168, 194
musical cues 194
muslin 11, 85, 93, 98, 100, 106, 180
mustang roping scenes 23
My Blue Heaven 17
My Favorite Year 14
My Mother the Car 139
My Stepmother Is an Alien 189, 190
Myers, David 114

The Naked Jungle 22
N.A.S.A. 165
Nat Hiken Rule 161
National Broadcasting Company (NBC) 7
National Labor Relations Board 5
National Lampoon's Vacation 114, 221
Naval Air Station (Key West, Florida) 113
Naval Shipyard (San Francisco) 172
Navy 193
Neal, Patricia 31
Needham, Hal 53, 145
Negulesco, Jean 87
Neighbors 14
Neill, Noel (Lois Lane) 44, **45**
Nellie (Carol Grace) 108
Nelson, Argyle 119
Nelson, Ozzie 44
Nelson, Ricky 44
Nevada Smith 28
The New Centurions 104
New Jersey 135
The New Loretta Young Show 201
New Mexico 94, 130
New York Automotive Show 138
New York City 73, 152, 187
New York Harbor 61
Newman, Paul 18, 30, 54
Newton-John, Olivia 164
Nicholes, Michael 76, 96, 97, 99, 100, 102, 103
Nicholson, Jack 34, **76**, 109, 110
Nickerson, Jim 53, 55, 56, 59
Nicola, Dr. 61
Night After Night 112

night driving sequences 107
night exteriors 105
Night of the Sedgewick Curse 51
night sun 105
Nightfall 172
U.S.S. *Nimitz* 113, 114
9 Lite 93, 97
No Holds Barred 62
Noah's Ark ride (Bible Land) 222
Nogales, Arizona 174
Nolan, George 216
Nolan, Randy 134
Nolte, Nick 187
Nomad stunt specialist 61
Nordstedt, Russ 40
Norfolk, Virginia 113
Norma Rae 112
North by Northwest 12, 137
North Carolina 222
North End, Boston 220
Nossis, Pat 157
Novak, Kim 173, 174
Novarse, Dino 184
Nowhere to Run 60
nudity 188, 203
The Nutty Professor 24
Nye, Ben 10

Oakland 120
Oakland Bay Bridge 75
Oberon, Merle 87
Occidental College 22
The Octagon 52
Odets, Clifford 194
off-lot call 118
Oh God 35, 36
O'Hara, Maureen 90
Okazaki, Kozo 218
O'Kelly, Tim 97
Oklahoma 91
The Old Man and the Sea 31, 173
"Old #2" 23
Oldsmobile 138, 139, 145
Oliansky, Joel 188
Olivier, Laurence 8, 14
Olmos, Eddie 114
Olsen, Merlin 46
Olsen, Tim 54
Olympic Auditorium 42, 43, 44, 47, 56, 59
on-the-job mentoring 92
On the Waterfront 153
One Flew Over the Cuckoo's Nest 76, 77
One for My Baby 174
170 Freeway 120
1-Y filter 95
O'Neal, Ryan 37
Only When I Laugh 163
Opel GT 145
Opelika Manufacturing Company 112
open cockpit camera car 75, 208
orangutan 59
Orasatti, Frank 63
Osaka, Japan 218
Osaka Judo System 43
Oscars 12, 34, 69, 77, 172

Oshima, Captain 43
Osmond, Cliff 203
O'Steen, Sam 101
Oster, Emil 171
Ostermier, Tony 149
The Other 159
O'Toole, Peter 15
Ouray, Colorado 98
Out of Sight 141
The Outsider 8
overhead bounce 99
overtime 87, 90, 190
oxyacetylene torch 135

P-61 Black Widow Night Fighter 142
Pacific Campaign 70
Pacific Coast Highway 136, 137
Pacino, Al 64, 112, 113, 126
pack mules 212
Packard V-12 touring car 139
Page, Arizona 62
Paint Your Wagon 76, 121, 122, 124
Pal Joey 173
Palm Springs Weekend 139
Palmdale, California 193
Palmisano, Conrad 58
Pan, Hermes 199
Panaflex camera 221
Panavision cameras 94, 107, 113, 127, 201, 202, 205, 210
panels, integrated 179
Panzer 102
Pappas, Irene 206
par lamps 42
parabolic lens, 60-inch diameter 93
Paradise Hawaiian Style 50
parallax view camera 172
Paramount Pictures 6, 46, 56, 69, 73, 76, 106, 117, 121, 137
Paris, France 21, 219
Park Rangers 217
Parker, Ed 50, 191
Parker, Eleanor 9, **195**
Parker, Larry 97
Parker, Suzy 9
Parsons, Lindsley, Jr. 219
The Party 206
Pasadena 109, 113, 115
patch fixing 8
pathology labs (UCLA) 13
Patriot Games 65
The Patsy 27, 139
Patton 11
The Pawnbroker 154
paymaster 202
Payton High School 15
Pearl City 97
Pearl Harbor, Hawaii 193
Peck, Gregory 156, 194, 195, **198**
Peckinpah, Sam 35, 55, 103, 104, 130, 131, **215**
Pee Wee's Big Adventure 222
Pee Wee's Playhouse 115
peel-off-face gag 10
Peeper 159
Pendelton, Joe 69
The Penguin 50

Penn, Arthur 161, 219
Penn, Chris 15
Pentagon 201
Penwald, Martin "Rubber Duck" (Kris Kristofferson) 130
Peppard, George 146, 195
Pepper, Ned 99
Perfect Strangers 41
Perkins, Jack 146
permit worker 5
perms 22, 118
Perry, Frank 81
Petaluma, California 146
Peters, Bernadette 14
Peterson, Robert 136
Petit, Philippe 186
Phaedra (Sophia Loren) 87
The Phil Silvers Show 153
Philadelphia 107
Phillips, Fred 5
photo floods 112, 114
photo intelligence 169
Piccadilly Drive-In (Los Angeles) 136
Picerni, Charlie 52, 54, 56, 145
Pickens, Slim 52
Pidgeon, Walter 112
pier explosion 66
pig blood 11
Pima Indian make-up 8
Pine, Howard 156
Pinewood Studios (England) 95
The Pink Panther 176
The Pinkey Lee Show 7
pipe organ kits 121
Piper, David **213**
pistol grip steering wheel 138
pit crew 207
Planer, Franz 194
The Planet of the Apes 10, 12, 51
Planette, Homer 88, 89, 90, 91
plate-glass window gags 59, 62
Playhouse 90 7, 153
Plummer, Christopher 9
Plymouth Barracuda 143
Plymouth Hemi (426) motor 145
Plymouth Hotel 187
pneumonia 61
Pocketful of Miracles 23
Point Blank 155
point of view *see* P.O.V.
Poitier, Sidney 157
Polanski, Roman 72, **73**, 74, 76, 77, 109
The Polar Express 20
Polaroid-tinted glass roof 148
Police Academy Judo Instructor 54
Pollack, Sidney 212, 218
Pollard, Michael J. 206
Pontiac Fiero 150
pop-out quality 179
poppy field destruction 106
Porgy and Bess 199
Pork Chop Hill 195
Porsche: 356 engine 146; 908 (picture car) 208; 917 195, **207, 208**, 210; Spyder 137
Porter, Bobby 59
"Porter" 1928 139

The Poseidon Adventure 12
Post, Ted 12, 179, 184
Postcards from the Edge 134
Postner, Steve 111
Potrero Hill, San Francisco 114
P.O.V.: blurred vision 209; straight down 186
Powell, Dick 169
power pole climbing 106
Power Rangers 150
pratfalls 61
Pratt, James 72
pre-fogging 178
preferred hire list 84
Preminger, Otto 199
Prescott, Arizona 221
The President's Analyst 72
The Presidio 62, 132, 133
Presley, Elvis 8, **50**, 120, 140
The Pretty Girl 170
Pretty Woman 165
Price, Vincent 194
Prince, Peter **182**
Prince Charming 190
Prince of the Pirates 171
Prince Street locals 220
The Princess Bride 166
Prisoner of 2nd Avenue 33, 35
Private Eye Purkey (Cliff Osmond) 203
Problem Child 63
production trucks (Hollywood style) 218
The Professionals 71
The Program 166
Promises to Keep 40
prosthetic "mean nose" 18, 20
prosthetics 8
protective package 57
Pryor, Richard 40, 116, 222
PT boats 136
Puerto Vallarta 35
Pulp Fiction 189
The Pursuit of D.B. Cooper 132
Pusser, Buford T. (Sheriff) 52
pyro-technician 57

Quarry, Gerry 58
Queen Mary (Long Beach) 110
quick-fix mechanics 66
quiet rails 177
quilted aluminum kitchen walls 157
Quinn, Anthony 88

Racine, Ned (John Hurt) 189
Rader, George 119
Rafelson, Bob 32
Raft, George 112
Raging Bull 58, 59
The Rains of Ranchipur 85, 90
A Raisin in the Sun 174
Rambaldi, Carlo 186
Rami, Sam 64
Rancho Delux 77
Rat Pack 200
Rathbone, Basil 8
Ratner, Brett 67
Rawlings, Richard 98

Ray, Aldo 172
Ray, Nichols 137
Rayford, Judge (Jack Warden) 113
Reagan, Ronald 173
rear view mirror technique 104, 107, 205
Rear Window 22
Rebel Without a Cause 136, 137
reciprocal trade agreement 155
red #25 187
Red Line 7000 27
Red Lodge (Montana) 161, 219
Red Rock Canyon State Park 84
Red Scare propaganda platform 172
The Red Skelton Show 7
Reddish, Jack **195**, 200, 203, 205, 206, **207**
Redfield, William **76**
Redford, Robert 206, 213
Reed, Carl 193, 200
Reeves, George 44, **45**, 46
reflection shots 169
rehearsal habits 185
Rehoboth Beach, Delaware 116
Reilly, John 190
Reiner, Carl 113, 221
Reisz, Karl 187
The Relic 132
Relyea, Bob 202
Rembrandt (3/4 light) 184
Rembrandt fill 102
Remick, Lee 174, **176**
Remo Williams 61
remote control trigger 208
remote controlled (articulated) camera head 212
removable body components 139
Renella, Pat 156
Rennie, Michael 95
rent jobs 156
rent payers 156, 189
restaurant delivery vehicle 135
retouching, optical 186
The Return of the Vampire 168
Reubens, Paul 115
Reynolds, Ross 221
Rez, Harry 221
rhinoplasty 109
Rich, David Lowell 38
Rich, Raymond 204
Richards, Dick 110
Rickles, Don 121
rigging, underwater 84
riot sequences 59
rippling mirror technique 34
risers, six-foot 119
Ritchie, Michael 110, 115, 116, 222
Ritt, Martin 31
Ritter, Thelma **195**
ritter fan 85, 230
Ritz Hotel 21
Riverside Drive (North Hollywood) 136
Riverside International Raceway 28, 146
RKO Studios 9
Road to Perdition 18
Robards, Jason 163

The Robe 84
Roberson, Chuck 129
Robert, Jay 133
Robertson, Cliff 174
Robin (character) 50
Robinson, Dar 54, 59, 62
Robinson, Edward G. 183, 184, **195**
Robinson, Jay 84
Robinson, Mrs. 96
Robo Cop 62
Robson, Mark 53, 172
Rocco, Alex 107
Rock Around the Clock 171
rocket propelled nets 215
The Rockford Files 54
Rockwell, Norman 20, 90
Rocky 56
Roddenberry, Gene 187
Rogers, Ginger 85
Rogue River (Grants Pass, Oregon) 129
Roizman, Owen 75
roll bars, full body 148
Rollin Hand 52
Rolling Man 159
Roma Studios (Madrid) 124
Romero, Ceasar 50, 100
Rondell, Ronnie 46, 53
roof top tie-ins 106
Rose, Bobby 119
Rosemary's Baby 72, 73, 74, 76, 97, 109, 122
Rosen, Morris 203, 204
Rosen, Robert 153, 155
Roseville, California 135
Ross, Herbert 14, 157, **159**, 160, 161, 163
Ross, Johnny (Pat Renella) 156
Ross, Katharine 72, 96
Roth (Edward G. Robinson) 184
Roth, Ed (Big Daddy) 138
rotoscope 101
Rough and Ready 169
Rousey, Ronda 68
Rube Goldberg gag 72
Rue Casa Nova Apartments 201
Rule, Janice 9
Rumble in the Bronx 52
Runaway 40
Runaway Train 61
Running Man 62
Running Scared 132, 165
running shots 57, 60
Rush Hour 67
Russell, Jane 84, 172
Russian accent 48
Russian Hill 75
Russian roulette 13
Ruttenberg, Joe 96
Rydell, Mark 72, 126

Saab spaceships 147
Sacramento, California 135
saddle extensions 219
saddle mount 214, 219
safety margins 75
safety shades 57
SAG card 44

Sagal, Boris 177
Said, Fouad 106
St. Croix, Virgin Islands 13
St. Valentine's Day Massacre 153
Salinas, California 137
saloon set 156
Salton Sea 88
San Bernardino, California 137
San Carlos, Mexico 99
San Diego, California 201
San Fernando Valley 146
San Francisco, California 44, 74, 155, 165
San Pedro, California 90, 110
sand bag, leather 135
Sands, Max (Steve McQueen) 29
Santa Monica, California 115
Santos, Joe 107
Sargent, John Singer 11
Saronic Islands, Greece 87
The Satan Bug 94, 202
saturation, controlled 184
Saturday morning matinees 135
Saugus Speedway 136
Savage, Milo 48
Saving Private Ryan 18
Scarecrow 159
Scarecrow and Mrs. King 40, 126
Scenic Artists Guild (Local 829) 152
scenic work 152, 180
Schaffner, Franklin 51
Scheider, Roy 219, 222
Schell, Maximillian 87, 88
Schiavelli, Vincent **76**
Schiffer, Bob 172
Schlitz Playhouse of the Stars (1956) 194
Schmidt, William 142
Schneider, Bob 32
Scholl, Art **216**
Schoonmaker, Thelma 59
Schrader, Paul 218
Schuler, Fred 222
Schulman, Arnold **195**
Schultz, Gaylin 75, 113, 114, 115, 116, 117, 121, 193–223, **195**, **196**, **197**, **198**, **207**, **215**, **216**
Schultz, Walter E. 193
Schumacher, Joel 67
Schwartz, Bernie 213, 214
Schwarzenegger, Arnold 66, 67
Schweizer SGS-1 (sailplane) 204
sci-fi 95, 130, 161, 162, 163, 171, 190, 202
Scilli-static 13
Scorsese, Martin 58, 59
Scott, George C. 11, 104
Scranton, Pennsylvania 171
scrims 95, 99, 119, **196**
script interpretation 179
Sea Hunt 199
seagulls 215, 216, 217
The Searchers 193
Sears, Fred 171, 173
Seattle 126
Seaview 90
Seberg, Jean 122

2nd and 4th Marines 70
second story balcony fall 62
second unit (action scenes) 23, 60, 62, 63, 67, 90, 92, 94, 100, 122, 131, 145, 187, 196, 199, 200, 202, 203, 206, 218, 219, 221
Segal, George 9, 35
Segal, Steven 63, 64, 166
self-immolation 132
self promotion 138
Sellers, Peter 176, 206
Senate 201
Senior Chicago 152
Sensurround 129
Septon, Rich (General Lee) 150
Sergeants 3 119, 200
Sergil, Jack 43
Sermon on the Mount 93
Sessums, John 149
set decoration 148, 160, 165, 180
Seven, Johnny 200
Seven Days in May 177, 201
The Seven Faces of Dr. Lao 12
The Seven-Ups 205
7 Women 49
The 7th Voyage of Sinbad 199
70mm Todd A-O format 89
77 Sunset Strip 7
sex sequences 103, 108, 184, 188
"Sexwagon" 142, **144**
Sextette 112
shag shacks 148
Shamroy, Leon 71, 84, 86, 87, 199
Shanley, John Patrick 16
Shavelson, Melville 202
Shaw, Robert 35, 154
Shaw, Tom 23, 122, 126, 134
Sheen, Martin 17
sheers, luminescent 20
Sheik Al Fassi (mansion) 113
Sheik Ilderim 91
Sherin, Edwin 124
Sherman, George 172
Sherman Oaks Castle Park 68
Sherwood Golf Course 21
Shibe gel 188
Shick, Elliot 13
The Shining 81
shiny boards 97, 119, 194, 199
Ship Rock, New Mexico 202
shocks, split radius 140
shooting galleries 153
Shrader, Paul 14
Sidney, George 173
Signoret, Simone 72
Sikorsky helicopter 220
The Silencers 142
Silent Movie 161
Silva, Henry 201
Silverado 15, 142
Silverstein, Elliott 148, 155
Simon, Neil 35, 160
Simpson, O.J. 58
Sinatra, Frank 7, 47, 73, 89, **141**, **195**, **196**, **197**
Sinatra, Nancy 141
Singapore Lake 35
Singer, Lori 15

Singer, Marc 60
Singin' in the Rain 168
Sinise, Gary 17
sink hole 213
Sisterhood 41
"Sit Down You're Rockin' the Boat" 194
Six Flags Magic Mountain (Newhall, CA) 114, 221
"16 Going On 17" 9
skid juice rig 142
skidding moves 67
skipper 87, 145, 157, 163, 169, 218
slaps 64, 132, 214
slapstick 61, 66, 80, 116
slash lamps 107
slate boy 168, 169
Slaughter's Big Rip Off 53
Sleeper 146
sleeper track 95, 119, **125**, 194, 199, 212, 219
slide: controlled 62; corner 67
slide turn 62
slow motion 104, 127, 130, 185, 191
slow zoom 126, 189
Small, Ed 199
Small, Mews **76**
Smight, Jack 39
Smith, Bud 219
Smith, Dean 57
Smith, Dick 13
Smith, Vic 95
Smith, William 59
smoke, atmospheric 71, 188
Smokin' Joe Frazier 56
Snake River (Jackson Hole, Wyoming) 132
snow 165, 212, 213
Snow Canyon State Park (Utah) 212
snow-cat (tractor) 212
Snowden 99
Snyder, William 170
S.O.B. 131
Society of Operating Cameramen (S.O.C.) 223
socket adapters 112
solar electric panel technology 148
Solar Films 75, 205
solenoids, electronically controlled 137
Some Kind of Nut 156
Some Like It Hot 22, 71, 199
A Song to Remember 169
Sonoran Desert (Arizona) 206
The Sons of Katie Elder 206
"Sons of Members" provision 83
The Sorbonne 170
Sorcerer 219
Sordal, Bob 186, 187, 190, 220
Sorvino, Paul 53
Sothern, Ann 140
Souchak, Ernie (John Belushi) 14
The Sound of Music 9, 71
South, Lenny 179
South Central (Los Angeles) 106
South China Seas 193
South Pacific 87
Southern Comfort 132

Southern Hotel 189
Soylent Green 183
Spain 11, 87, 124
Sparrow, Nick 60
Spartacus 8
Spear, Gil (Fomo Engineering) 139
Speed Crazy 136
Speed Racer 151
speed rail **133**; fittings 75; frame **127**; out riggers 126; pipes 205, 221
Speilman, Edward 52
Spelling, Aaron 49
Spendatz Team 7
Spiegel, Sam 110
Spielberg, Steven 18, 20, **80**, 111
Spilsbury, Klinton 81
spin, 360 degree 67
Spinotti, Dante 131
Splash 15
Splendor in the Grass 153
The Split 53
Split-Diopter 105
spy car 142
squibs, explosive 13
Ssssss 12
Stack, Robert 119
Stage Coach 152
stage crane 193
Stage Door Canteen 153
Stagecoach, Nevada 23
Stahr, Monroe (Robert De Niro) 110
stair fall 54, 59, 61
Stalag 17 132
Stallone, Sylvester 56, 63, **64**
standards and practices 51
Stanley, Frank 178
The Star Chamber 132
Star Trek (film) 187
Starbird, Darryl 138
Starder, Paul 48, 57
Starr, Ringo 112
Starrett, Jack 106, 126
Starsky and Hutch 35, 54, 151
starter-plates 205
State Fair 91, 114
Statue of Liberty 61
Stay Cool 119
Steadicam 81, 134
Steelyard Blues 34
Steiger, Rod 67, 172
Step by Step 41
Stevens, Connie 139
Stevens, Dennis 184
Stevens, George 88, 91, 119, **121**
Stevenson, Robert 145
Stevenson, Robert Lewis 40
Stevsvold, Alan 95
Stewart, Jimmy 16, 91
stock car racing 145
Stoney Burke 71
storm center 172
Stradling, Harry, Jr. 11, 119, 127, **129**, 130, 131, 132
Strange Days 66
Strangers 163
Streep, Meryl 186
Streisand, Barbra 40
Striepeke, Dan 5–21, **16, 19**

Strode, Woody 8, 49
Stromberg carburetors 140
Strongbow, Jules 44
Studio Mechanics Local 37 118
Stumar, John 168
stunt choreography 49, 72, 75, 161, 168
Stunts Unlimited 53
Sturges, John 8, 94, 119
submission move 45, 63
suction cups 222
Sugar, It's Me 199
Sugarfoot 7
Suisun Bay 55
Sullivan, Michael (Tom Hanks) 18, 20
The Summer of '42 157
Summers, Jerry 140
Sun-arcs 92
Sundance, Utah 212
Sunset Blvd. 132
The Sunshine Boys 160, 163
Super Bowl 57
Super Van 147
Superman 45
Superman Road Show 44
Surtees, Bob 23, 34, 35, 71, 91, 94, 95, 98, 119
Susann, Jacqueline 12
Sutherland, Donald 34
Swafford, Ken 60
Swashbuckler 35
Sweet Dreams 165
Sweet Smell of Success 31, 194
Swenson, Jeep 67
Swift, David 203
swing gate design 211
swinging arm rig **210**
sword fights 60, 66, **182**
Sylbert, Paul 153
Sylbert, Richard (Dick) 96, 153, 200
Sylbert Brothers 153

"tackles and tickles" 54, 66
Taft-Hartley Act 170
Takayuda, Kubota 181
"Take Back Your Mink" 194
Tanaka, Toru (Professor) 62
Tango and Cash 63
tanks 36, 54, 61, 80, 96, 173
Tannura, Phillip 171
Taras Bulba 9
Tarzan's Greatest Adventures 22
Tashlin, Frank 24, 138
Taurog, Norman 139
Taylor, Don 113
Taylor, Elizabeth 96, 180
Taylor, Michael 132
Teacher's Pet 22
teamsters 195
Technicolor Lab 94, 99; Technicolor hues 185
Teen-Age Crime Wave 171
telescopic machine gun 142
television lighting 171
television work 7, 9, 12, 15, 40, 49, 51, 54, 58, 60, 61, 68, 70, 71, 76,

89, 97, 119, 121, 131, 139, 142, 145, 146, 147, 150, 153, 159163, 170–171, 177, 199, 204, 205
television stations 45
The Ten Commandments 5, 22, 91
Tennant, William 106
The Tennessee Ernie Ford Show 7
tent cities 194
Tequila Sunrise 134
The Terminal 20
The Terminal Man 34, 184
terrorist attack 57
textures, photographic 71
Thailand 13
Thalberg, Irving 110
That Thing You Do 17
T.H.E. 177
theatre design 152
thermal up drafts 217
Thomas, Bill 119
Thomas, Bob *77*
The Thomas Crown Affair 203, 205
Thompson, J. Lee 184
Thorin, Donald 63
Three on a Couch 28, 49
The Three Stooges 47
Three Stooges Shorts 169, 206
Three Stripes in the Sun 172
throwback Western 76
Thunder Alley 145
Thunder Charger 145
Tidy, Frank 117, 222
Tierney, Gene 85
Tiger-guy 13
Tijeras Canyon (Albuquerque, New Mexico) 175
Times Square 194
Timonian Islands, Malaysia 87
Tinseltown 181, 191; automotive history 151
Titan crane 24, 124, 132
To the Ends of the Earth 169
Tobak, James 53
Todd, Michael 172
Tokyo, Japan 218
Tombstone 82
Tompkins, Les 142
"Tonight" 200
Toreon, Mexico 187
Torn, Rip 195
Tornatore, Joe 56
Torso armor 60
Touch and Go 190
Touch of Evil 174
Touched by Love 188
Tourneur, Jacques 172
Tover, Leo 91
The Towering Inferno 53, 54, 56
T.R. Baskin 157
track spikes 190
Tracy, Spencer 173
The Train 201
trash truck sequence 103
Travolta, John 13, 164
The Treasure of the Sierra Madre 44, 71
Trekkies 187

trick glass 169
trick shots 171
Triumph (sports car) 126, 137
troop carrier 219
True Grit 29, 98
Truesdale, Tuffy 44
Truffaut, François 189
Trumball, Doug 111
Truscott, John 178
tubing, aluminum 75
Turman, Lawrence 96
Turner, Debbie 9
Turner, Kathleen 188
Turner, Lana 85
Turner and Hooch 16
The Turning Point 161
The Turtles 142
Tuttle, William 12
Twelve Angry Men 153
Twelve O'clock High 71
20th Century Fox 6, 7, 83, 114
20th Century Fox Ranch 95
25 ASA film 89, 90
21 Club (NYC) 194
Twenty Thousand Leagues Under the Sea 118
The Twilight Zone 131
250 AMP yoke 112
Two of a Kind 164
2001 165
2010 132, 165
tying-in 107, 108
Tyler, Nelson 120

UCLA 13
Ultimate Fighter 52
ultra Panavision (70) 201
Under Siege II 166
"under wing cage" 216
underwater sequence 97
Unfaithfully Yours 165
Union Hall 118
United States Coast Guard Reserves 44
Universal Pictures 7, 141
Universal Studios 113, 114; Flash Flood ride 222; Black Tower 34
University of Missouri 152
Unknown 71
Unsworth, Geoffrey 218, 219
The Untouchables 119, 127
Up in Smoke 220
urine bottle 101
Urquidez, Benny "The Jet" 68
U.S. Coast Guard 44, 70
U.S. Marshalls 67
U.S.C. Film School 70, 82
Ustinov, Peter 180
Utah 88, 119

Vacek, Jack 149
Valdez, Luis 114, 221
Valdez Is Coming 124
Valley of the Dolls 12
The Van 147
Van, Artie 107
Van Damme, Jean-Claude 191
Vandora 147

Van Dyke, Dick 156
Van Dyke, Jerry 139
Van Horn, Buddy 57, 59, 63
Van Rose's Fitness Supply 43
Vargas, Billy "The Count" 46, 48
Vasquez Rocks 30, 42
Vaughn, Robert 8
vehicle shots: riding backwards 182; shooting handheld 182
vehicle stunts: station wagon leap 115
Ventura, Jesse 62
Verhoeven, Paul 62
Victor (bear) 44, 47
Victor, Paul 50
Victorville 134
Vidal, Gore 12
Vidor, Charles 168
Vietnam 17, 56
Village Fortress 186
Vincent, Jan-Michael **128**, **181**
Violets Are Blue 116, 222
Virginia City, Montana 219
Viva Zapata! 84
Vogel, Virgil 51
Voight, Jon 99, 103
Volkswagen Beetle 146
von Stroheim, Erich 171
von Sydow, Max 93, 119
Vorkapich, Slavko 70
Voyage to the Bottom of the Sea 48, 90

Wackiest Ship in the Army 174
Wag the Dog 17
Wagon Train 46
Walken, Christopher 13, 14
Walker, Joe 69
Walker, Texas Ranger 76
walking-on-water gag 61
Walking Tall 52
Wallach, Eli 8
Waller, Don 62
Wallis, Hal B. 98, 128
walls, sliding 177
Wally World (Six Flags Magic Mountain) 114
Walsh, Bill 145
Walsh, David **74**, 106, 122
Walters, Chuck 60
Warden, Jack 113
Warlock 88
Warner, Jack 178
Warner Bros. 6, 7, 52, 69, 115, 126, 177
Warren, Lesley Ann 115
Washington, Richard 57
Washington, D.C. 169, 190, 201
Wasserman, Lew 219
water work 16, **31**, 35, 36, 54, 60, 67, 84–87, 90, 97, 101, 118, 132, 166, 173, 174, 191, 199–200, 202, 218–219, 222, 227
Watermelon Man 32
Waterston, Sam 81
Watkins, David 99, 100, 102
Watts 105
Wayne, Jesse 52
Wayne, John 98, 99, 119

weather: humidity and scorching temperatures 220; rain, torrential 202; record heat wave 194; tropical heat 187
Webb, Jack 15
Webner, Chuck 56
Weissmueller, Johnny 171
Weld, Tuesday 156
Wells, Dawn 139
Wells, Orson 103
Wenders, Wim 40
Wendkos, Paul 98
West, Mae 12, 87, 112
West Side Story 119, 200
Westinghouse generator 86
Westmore, Bud 7
Westmore, Perc 48
Westmore, Wally 6
Wexler, Haskell 77, 131, 134
Wexler, Norman 185
Weyer, John 208
wheels, hidden balance 146
Where It's At 156
Which Way to the Front 34
whiskers, hook-on 6
White, Theodore 174
White House 201
Whitlock, Albert 101
Whitney's Playland (San Francisco) 169
Who'll Stop the Rain 187, 220
Who's Afraid of Virginia Wolf? 181
Who's Minding the Store? 25
Widmark, Richard 9, 88
Wilber, George 52
The Wild Bunch 29

The Wild Seed 71
The Wild, Wild West 51, 119
Wilde, Cornel **170**
Wilder, Billy 199, 200, 201, 202, 203
Wilder, Glen 53, 58, 66
Will Penny 30
Williams, Bill 119, 202
Williams, Dunny **122**
Williams, Jonathan 207
Williams, Tennessee 153
Williams, Treat 132
Williamson, Fred 53
Williamson, Mykelti 17
Willis, Bruce 132
Willis, Gordon 14
Willy (Peter Lupus) 52
Wiltern Theatre 114
Winner, Michael 181, **182**, **183**, 185, 189
Winters, Shelley 12, 106
Wise, Robert 9
Wiseguy 76
Wolfe, Thomas 138
Wolheim, Louis 5
Wolsky, Albert 18, 20
wolves 213
Won Ton Ton, the Dog That Saved Hollywood 185
Wood, Natalie 153, 159
Woodward, Joanne 172
Woolsey, Ralph 105
working the arm 194
World Trade Center 186
World War II pp 10, 22, 69, 70, 71, 99, 102, 128, 136

Wyckoff, Robert 121
Wyler, William 194

Xanadu 221

yacht club sequences 91
The Yakuza 218
Yale School of Theatre 152
Yamada, Kenji 44
Yardley soap 155
Yates, Peter 74, 75, 107
The Yellow Submarine 99
Yerkes, Bob 54
Ying, Koop Lien 55
York, Jay 48
York, Michael 13
Yossarian (Alan Arkin) 100, 101, 103
Young, Burt 53
The Young Lions 87
Yubitsume 218
Yuma, Arizona 220
Yurich, Richard 187

The Zacca 169
Zanuck, Darryl F. 84, 86
Zebra Force 56
Zemeckis, Robert 20
Zig Zag (Vilmos Zsigmond) 112
Zoetrope 40
Zoot Suit 114
Zsigmond, Vilmos 111, 112, 126
Zuma Beach 142
Zumwalt, Rick 165
ZZR dragster 141

www.ingramcontent.com/pod-product-compliance
Ingram Content Group UK Ltd.
Pitfield, Milton Keynes, MK11 3LW, UK
UKHW050534150426
5217IPUK00026B/1938